Interconnections

Gender and Race in American History

Alison M. Parker, The College at Brockport, State University of New York
Carol Faulkner, Syracuse University

ISSN: 2152-6400

The Men and Women We Want
Gender, Race, and the Progressive Era Literacy Test Debate
Jeanne D. Petit

Manhood Enslaved: Bondmen in Eighteenth- and
Early Nineteenth-Century New Jersey
Kenneth E. Marshall

Interconnections: Gender and Race in American History
Edited by Carol Faulkner and Alison M. Parker

Interconnections

Gender and Race in American History

Edited by
Carol Faulkner and Alison M. Parker

UNIVERSI

First published 2012

University of Rochester Press
668 Mt. Hope Avenue, Rochester, NY 14620, USA
www.urpress.com
and Boydell & Brewer Limited
PO Box 9, Woodbridge, Suffolk IP12 3DF, UK
www.boydellandbrewer.com

ISBN-13: 978-1-58046-421-5
ISSN: 2152-6400

Library of Congress Cataloging-in-Publication Data

Interconnections: gender and race in American history / edited by Carol Faulkner and Alison M. Parker.
  p. cm. — (Gender and race in American history, ISSN 2152-6400 ; v. 3)
  "The chapters in this volume, collected for a conference held at the University of Rochester, see the interconnections between gender and race as fundamental to American identity and central to American history"—Introd.
  Includes bibliographical references and index.
  ISBN 978-1-58046-421-5 (hardcover : alk. paper) 1. African American women—History—Congresses. 2. African American women—Race identity—Congresses. 3. Gender identity—United States—History—Congresses. 4. Sex role—United States—History—Congresses. 5. United States—Race relations—History—Congresses. 6. Feminist theory—United States—Congresses. I. Faulkner, Carol. II. Parker, Alison M. (Alison Marie), 1965–
  E185.86.G427   2012
  305.48'896073—dc23

                                                              2012011963

A catalogue record for this title is available from the British Library.

This publication is printed on acid-free paper.
Printed and bound by CPI Group (UK) Ltd, Croydon, CR0 4YY.

Contents

Part 4: Sexuality, Class, and Morality

Introduction

Alison M. Parker and Carol Faulkner

The chapters in this volume, collected for a conference held at the University of Rochester, see the interconnections between gender and race as fundamental to American identity and central to American history. Organized by Carol Faulkner, Alison Parker, and Victoria Wolcott, the conference celebrated the launch of a new book series at the University of Rochester Press called Gender and Race in American History. Building on decades of interdisciplinary research by feminist scholars and historians of African American women and gender, these chapters bridge the gap between well-developed theories of race, gender, and power and the practice of historical research. They reveal the interdependent construction of racial and gender identity in individuals' lived experiences in specific historical contexts, such as westward expansion, civil rights movements, or economic depression, as well as national and transnational debates over marriage, citizenship, and sexual mores.[1] All of these chapters consider multiple aspects of identity, including sexuality, class, religion, and nationality, among others, but the volume emphasizes gender and race—the focus of our new book series—as principal bases of identity and locations of power and oppression in American history.

Previous historical scholarship on race, like the scholarship on gender, focused on the way American society has imbued perceived biological differences with social meaning, thus legitimating slavery, inequality, disfranchisement, and lynching. As historian Nell Irvin Painter plainly asserts, "Race is an idea, not a fact." Barbara Jeanne Fields suggests that race is not only an idea but an ideology with origins in the American Revolution, when it "supplied the means of explaining slavery to people whose terrain was a republic founded on radical doctrines of liberty and natural rights." In a parallel argument, Joan Scott argues that gender must be considered as a "primary way of signifying relationships of power" and a "constitutive element of social relationships based on perceived differences between the sexes." Inspired by Scott's insight, historians now understand gender as a dynamic concept that simultaneously constructs sexual difference and political power.[2]

Intersectionality, a term coined by critical race theorist Kimberlé Crenshaw, rejects the idea that race and gender are separate or competing categories of identity.[3] In 1989 Crenshaw published an article titled "Demarginalizing the Intersection of Race and Sex," in which she argued that scholars and activists must consider black women's "multidimensionality" rather than viewing their racial and gendered identities as in tension. She has subsequently elaborated on this concept, noting that "any discourse about identity has to acknowledge how our identities are constructed through the intersection of multiple dimensions," encouraging us to think carefully "about the way power has clustered around certain categories and is exercised against others."[4] Taking this theory to heart, the authors in this volume explore gender and race as necessarily linked categories that shape and reflect power relations and privilege in American history.

Intersectionality is not just an abstraction; Crenshaw initially developed it to understand and advocate for African American women's specific experience within the American criminal justice system. Deploying intersectionality to initiate substantive changes, activist-scholars have called attention to the fact that laws and punishments often categorize individuals by either race *or* gender; they do not recognize women of color as a class with distinct needs or priorities, who are subject to multiple types of oppression and power hierarchies based on a multitude of interacting factors such as race, gender, sexuality, and class. Neither the formal inclusion promised by a now ostensibly "color blind" legal system nor the wide acceptance of equal rights as an ideal means that inequalities no longer exist. Rather, inequalities are masked behind a "neutral" legal system that refrains from an explicitly racist language and operation but still creates these inequalities and does so systematically and consistently.[5] Moreover, theorists hope that intersectionality can build coalitions across barriers and categories to achieve substantive change in our society.[6]

This collection advances the literature on intersectionality as well as the uses of intersectional analysis for American history. Intersectionality is a vital tool for exploring the historical experiences of multiple groups. It allows us to understand gender and racial identity—and sexism and racism—as always interacting and not "exclusive or separable."[7] The authors in this volume respond to Leslie McCall's insistence that researchers must reveal "the range of diversity and difference *within*" as well as between social groups by complicating the category of "black woman." They do so in part by showing the intragroup diversity of perspectives and experiences, along with levels of privilege or oppression. The authors also explore the ways race and gender intersect in the lives of mixed-race, black, and white men, as well as white women. As a result, they illuminate, in Jennifer Nash's words, "privilege and oppression as complex, multi-valent, and simultaneous."[8]

This volume moves the concept of intersectionality from the realm of dominant—yet methodologically underdeveloped—interdisciplinary theory to empirical historical research. The authors' case studies pay careful attention to nuance to illuminate the construction of gender, race, and class differences as mutual and inseparable historical forces, even as they insist on the instability of these categories in American history. African American women's historians have demonstrated the importance of considering multiple forms of oppression and various categories of identity. For example, in her biography of activist Sojourner Truth, Painter writes that Truth became a symbol for the antislavery and women's rights movements, a status that disguised her real experiences as first an enslaved and later a free woman. As Painter points out, "at a time when most Americans thought of slavery as male and women as white, Truth embodied a fact that still bears repeating: Among the blacks are women; among the women, there are blacks."[9] To widen their field of inquiry, the authors in this volume explore the intersection of race, class, sexuality, and gender in nineteenth- and twentieth-century America in the lives of not only African American women but also black, white, and Native American men and women.[10]

Serious and sustained attention to intersectionality transforms major themes in American history. Moving across the broad expanse of the nineteenth and twentieth centuries, these chapters explore the raced and gendered conceptions of marriage, property, and citizenship articulated on the nation's urban and territorial frontiers; the way antebellum and postbellum movements for the abolition of slavery and racial equality simultaneously responded to and created racial and gender difference; how black Americans' claims to equal citizenship in the Jim Crow era often if unintentionally reinforced ideas of the citizen and African American as male; how African Americans' experiences of the Great Depression were shaped in part by national debates over sexual morality; and the ways some white and black women in the late twentieth century viewed marriage and motherhood as sites of power and coalition building rather than as sources of oppression. The chapters in this collection examine the intersectionality of power and identities and deliberately blur the artificial boundaries between the scholarship on race, gender, and American politics and between the fields of African American history, women's history, and mainstream American history.

Crenshaw and other contemporary black feminist theorists recognize that the concept of intersectionality has a long history, going back at least as far as antislavery lecturer Maria Stewart in the 1830s.[11] Collectively, the authors in this volume explore intersectionality's intellectual roots and employ the full theoretical framework it offers. The eight chapters are divided into four thematic sections: "Bridging History, Theory, and Practice," "Frontiers of Citizenship," "Civil Rights and the Law," and "Sexuality, Class, and Morality." Together, they consider the questions of voice and resistance so central to intersectional theory while illuminating the contested and shifting meanings of race and gender in individual lives and at significant historical moments. The first chapter argues that at the turn of the twentieth century, the educator Anna Julia Cooper wrote from the theoretical stance now identified as intersectionality, which, as Vivian M. May reminds the reader, is the "premise that both lived identities and structures of power and privilege should be understood as interwoven and not as additive factors or as separable dynamics." The other chapters continue this discussion, as they explore the intersections of race, gender, and power in mixed-race households, movements for racial and sexual equality, American Indian allotment policy, and the nation's courtrooms, railroads, and public spaces.

In this first section, Vivian M. May's chapter, "Historicizing Intersectionality as a Critical Lens: Returning to the Work of Anna Julia Cooper," argues that theory must be connected to the practice of empirical research and analysis. May begins with an intellectual genealogy for the concept of intersectionality, arguing that it has a long history within black feminist thought. In particular, May points to Cooper as an early theorist of intersectionality whose 1892 *A Voice from the South by a Black Woman of the South* and 1925 Sorbonne PhD dissertation, *France's Attitudes toward Slavery during the Revolution/L'attitude de la France à l'égard de l'esclavage pendant la Révolution,* directly critiqued systems of inequality and power by looking at, first, the American South and, later, France during the French Revolution from the perspective of an outsider. As scholar Kristin Waters points out, Maria Stewart and Anna Julia Cooper "both succeed in 'fracturing' the conceptions of race and gender while at the same time calling on the power of group identities, obliquely addressing concerns about essentializing that were not even to be raised officially until a century later."[12] By starting from this different perspective, Cooper exposed the myopic vision of white women's rights activists who spoke of equality and universal womanhood but excluded black women from their organizations or ignored the fact of white privilege or what she called "Anglo-Saxon power." Cooper also retold the story of the French Revolution as being influenced by and coming out of the Haitian Revolution. In Cooper's telling, the French Revolution began as an international and transatlantic story of slave resistance in Saint-Domingue; slaves, she claimed, initiated the essential dialogue that insisted on the incompatibility of slavery—of humans held as property—with the ideals of freedom and equality, the very rhetoric or principles that the French embraced in their own revolution. As May suggests, Cooper "used this comparative method to direct our attention to many suppressed aspects of the history of revolution" in ways that allowed her to tell a new history.

Though May demonstrates the relevance of intersectionality for historical research, she warns that such analyses continue to be constrained by the very marginality of those who engage in them. Thus, Anna Julia Cooper's groundbreaking comparative work on the Haitian and French Revolutions has been ignored even by recent scholars of black diaspora, black Atlantic and black European studies. Instead, scholars have focused on the works of black men such as C. L. R. James or W. E. B. Du Bois, who wrote about the Haitian Revolution from a more derivative perspective, whereby Haitians were "Black Jacobins" and Toussaint Louverture the "Black Napoleon." Cooper's challenging, oppositional historical interpretation remains silenced and ignored precisely because of her position on the margins, as a black woman in America.

The section "Frontiers of Citizenship" explores race, gender and citizenship in the expanding American nation. Rashauna Johnson's "'Laissez les bons temps rouler!' and Other Concealments: Households, Taverns, and Irregular Intimacies in Antebellum New Orleans" provides an urban case study "to reveal diversity, variation, and heterogeneity" in African American women's history.[13] She takes up "the challenge of telling the story of a marginalized community" and attempts to "show how different systems of oppression converge."[14] Johnson uncovers the fluidity of racial, social, and economic boundaries in an antebellum New Orleans neighborhood. In the process of uncovering the neglected history of women of African descent, Johnson reveals the instability of the identity category itself. In spite of the financial and social barriers to free women's home ownership, she finds a neighborhood with households owned by free women of color. Just as remarkable is the fact that these households included whites and people of mixed racial origins as well as those legally categorized as free, freed, and enslaved. Johnson uses court records, the census, and antebellum accounts of the neighborhood and of life in New Orleans to discover how social hierarchies played out in these ostensibly private domestic spaces.

Not only did neighborhoods on the urban frontier allow for property ownership by a wider range of individuals and autonomy for a greater range of inhabitants, but these "interzones" were also the site of a New Orleans nightlife characterized by taverns, interracial socializing, and illegal amusements. Rather than simply celebrating these neighborhood taverns as sites of egalitarianism and radical politics, Johnson emphasizes the "intersecting inequalities of race and gender" that characterized them, such as the exploitation of enslaved people, who were literally bought and sold in the taverns, and of free and enslaved women who sold their sexual services there in exchange for money or goods. Johnson's microlevel history of the taverns and the multiracial households of this neighborhood on the margins of antebellum New Orleans reveals the often obscured but pervasive power differentials and barriers that its occupants encountered and navigated each day.

"'There Are Two Great Oceans': The Slavery Metaphor in the Antebellum Women's Rights Discourse as Redescription of Race and Gender," by Hélène Quanquin, explores antebellum white women reformers' problematic use of slavery as a metaphor for understanding the subordinate status of white women in marriage and as citizens without full voting rights. Taking up Jennifer Nash's challenge that "feminism itself must better examine its history of exclusion," Quanquin argues that some white women reformers ignored the fundamental differences between the legal conditions of slavery versus freedom by pressing for a literal understanding of married women's "enslavement."[15] Although the slavery analogy was meant to increase the sympathy and reform activism

of white women for the abolitionist cause, it ignored the much more fundamental subordination of enslaved women. It also overlooked the privileges of
race and class status granted to white women, thereby "distorting the reality of
slavery." Other white women reformers recognized the fundamental incompatibility of the comparison and either rejected the slavery metaphor or used it,
Quanquin suggests, in a more qualified, nuanced way.

Quanquin's research into the use of the slavery metaphor reveals that white
women reformers were particularly interested in the relevance of the slavery metaphor at the moment when they considered the possibility of marrying. As part of their courtship, Abby Kelley and Stephen S. Foster debated,
for instance, if marriage was necessarily a form of slavery and subordination
or whether it could be compatible with personal autonomy. In contrast, Lucy
Stone wrote to Henry Blackwell that a "wife's position is capable of being made
horrible enough; but chattelism is a still 'lower depth' to which marriage, bad
as it may be made, should never be compared. And I have carefully refrained
from doing so." In these and other courtship letters, Quanquin finds white
abolitionist women grappling with their own concerns about personal equality but not always in ways that allowed them to keep the actual subordination
of slaves at the forefront of their thought. Overall, Quanquin concludes that
"while the analogy contributed to the idea that race and gender might be
considered comparatively, it did not ensure the effective integration of both
causes, often obscuring their specificities, as in the displacement of the experiences of African American women in favor of those of white women."

Kendra Taira Field's "'Grandpa Brown Didn't Have No Land': Race, Gender, and an Intruder of Color in Indian Territory" examines ideas of race and
gender in contested borderlands. Using the case study of Thomas Jefferson
Brown, Field explores the changing notions of what it meant to be black,
American, Indian, and an aspiring landowner from the 1870s through the
early 1900s in Indian Territory (what became the state of Oklahoma in 1907).
Field looks at this specific historical context to see how "multiple grounds of
identity" interplay and were constructed while accounting for privilege versus
various subordinations.[16]

A mixed-race man with an Irish mother and black father, Brown moved
from Arkansas into Indian Territory, where he married a Creek woman of
African descent. In this way, Brown joined white and some black Americans
in what Field pointedly calls "an American national project" of land acquisition and expansion into Indian Territory after the Civil War. This ambition for
land is quintessentially American and represents Brown's interest in claiming
and expanding his US citizenship rights. Field identifies Brown as a nonnative
"intruder" who, like white male settlers, gained access to land and citizenship
rights in the Creek nation through marriage to a Creek woman. In this matrilineal system of inheritance, his children gained land and Creek citizenship
rights through their Indian mother.

Yet Brown's story cannot simply be that of an American man fulfilling his capitalist dreams of land ownership and upward economic mobility through encroachment on Indian Territory. Complicating categories and simple understandings, Field convincingly demonstrates that Brown's status as an African American man might have initially helped him marry into and become a part of the Creek community. Indeed, Brown married an African Creek woman whose ancestors were slaves or freedpeople within the Creek nation who were formally given Creek citizenship in 1866. In contrast, by 1887, Brown's mixed race became a potential obstacle when the US Congress passed the Dawes General Allotment Act, which created a system of determining Indian citizenship by "blood quantum" in a way that excluded people of mixed ancestry, including African Creeks, and privileged "full bloods." Field argues that by the turn of the twentieth century race and racial purity became defining characteristics of Indian citizenship and of US citizenship in ways that excluded people of African descent from truly belonging in either nation. As "mixed bloods" lost their rights to land allotments and were dispossessed, they also faced a more hostile climate of Jim Crow segregation throughout the South, including in the new state of Oklahoma. This new racial order effectively excluded Thomas Jefferson Brown and other southern African Americans from full citizenship and inclusion in the expansionist "American national project," Field concludes, creating instead a landless and dispossessed people defined almost entirely by their race.

The section "Civil Rights and the Law" examines race, gender politics, and the law in the early twentieth-century civil rights movement. Michelle Kuhl's "Countable Bodies, Uncountable Crimes: Sexual Assault and the Antilynching Movement" demonstrates that in the 1890s reformers initially linked the lynchings of black men with sexual assaults on black women, seeing both as part of a problem with white Americans' characterizations of all blacks as oversexed. In this racist paradigm, black men were rapists who deserved to be lynched and black women were so sexually impure that they did not deserve the protection implied by a rape charge. As a result, Kuhl argues, activists saw black men's and women's vulnerabilities as problems that needed to be addressed and solved simultaneously. The antilynching movement began in the 1890s when reformers such as Ida B. Wells explicitly rejected the standard excuse that lynchings were somehow an understandable, if excessive, response to black men's unacceptable raping of white women. Collecting reports of lynchings from white newspapers, Wells proved that in most cases, the black male victims of "lynch law" were not even accused of rape and that this justification for lynching was clearly illegitimate. Just as antilynching activists tried to deconstruct the myth of the black male rapist, they highlighted a real problem of sexual assault and unequal power relations represented by white men's unpunished sexual assaults on black women. If whites could agree that rape of white women was a sin, how could they disagree that rape of black women was also a sin? Moreover, if all agreed that rape was wrong, then reformers could focus on ways to use the legal system (not extralegal mob violence) to protect women of any race from assaults. Tactically, this seemed like a good way to undermine justifications for lynching and violence against black men and women alike.

By the third decade of the twentieth century, two other tactics gained supremacy that, as Kuhl argues, "severed the link between antilynching activism and antisexual assault activism." In particular, careful statistics compiled by the Tuskegee Institute helped prove that black men were not being lynched for alleged rapes. The NAACP disseminated these statistics; by the 1930s spectacle lynchings became less socially acceptable among southern whites and began a long, slow decline. Second, beginning in the 1890s African American Christian ministers developed a masculinist martyrdom discourse around the suffering of lynched black males that equated their suffering to that of Christ on the cross. In the early twentieth century, black female rape victims were excluded from this rhetoric as well as from the statistics gathered by Tuskegee. The reasons behind this, Kuhl suggests, are complex but due in part to "the nature of sexual assault and how it differs from murder. In a lynching, no matter what disagreements there were over what first sparked the rage of the mob, at the end of the day there was a dead body that could be counted. There is no such certainty in sexual assault."

Meredith Clark-Wiltz's "Persecuting Black Men and Gendering Jury Service: The Interplay between Race and Gender in the NAACP Jury Service Cases of the 1930s" explores the NAACP's strategy for gaining black representation on juries. Seen as a fundamental obligation and right of citizenship, jury service was also understood to be a masculine prerogative. Indeed, even when black and white women won the right to vote in national elections in 1920, they did not automatically win the right to serve on juries. Clearly, advocates for the rights and obligations of citizenship for black women have had to "speak against internal exclusions and marginalizations" within the groupings of both race and sex.[17] Separate battles had to be organized in each state by groups such as the National Woman's Party; most states made it easy for women to decline jury service by making it voluntary for them, rather than required. Perhaps in part because all women's service on juries was so tenuous, the NAACP as a matter of strategy ignored the issue of black women's lack of representation on juries. Instead, its legal team chose to focus on gaining black men their rightful place—as men—in jury pools and on juries. Clark-Wiltz explores how the NAACP led a jury service litigation campaign in the 1930s that challenged the links among white males, citizenship, and jury service by arguing that black men deserved, as men, to have their manhood and their citizenship rights affirmed through their service on juries. Interestingly, as part of this strategy, NAACP lead attorney Charles H. Houston insisted on creating legal defense teams composed entirely of black male attorneys. NAACP defense teams used gendered arguments about manhood to claim that white and black men equally had the right to appear in all capacities beyond that of defendant—as prosecutors, defense attorneys, and jurors.

The NAACP's main objective was to gain black male defendants better possibilities for fair trials in what was undeniably a highly racist and hostile criminal justice system. If that meant perpetuating gender stereotypes and ignoring the plight of black women as second-class citizens, then so be it. As Clark-Wiltz explains, the organization perpetuated the notion that black and white women figured in legal proceedings only as the passive and silent victims of crime (especially of sexual violence) who had to rely on "the paternalistic legal system and male jury for protection." The NAACP, she concludes, willingly mobilized its own gender stereotypes about men, especially "gendered notions of jury service . . . as a patriarchal duty undertaken by male citizens in their need to protect the weak," even as it tried to break down racist stereotypes that assumed black men's criminality and guilt.

The final section, "Sexuality, Class, and Morality," features the conference's two keynote speeches and considers the way discourses of morality and ideas about sexuality and gender roles shape the possibilities and limitations of cross-class and interracial alliances. In "A 'Corrupting Influence': Idleness and Sexuality during the Great Depression," Michele Mitchell researches the hitherto underexamined experiences of unemployed and transient black women during the Depression. Faced with gaps and silences in the historical record, Mitchell examines a range of sources, including the writings of lawyer and activist Pauli Murray who, as a young woman, was a sometime transient; articles in the African American press; the work of a University of Minnesota researcher published under the title *Boy and Girl Tramps in America* (1934); and three Depression-era films. In part because of the dominant white society's willful ignoring of black women's experiences, Mitchell finds that in popular culture, discourses of idleness were clearly "moral and sexualized" but were not as explicitly racial. Mitchell's study helps us to see the interplay of gender, race, sexuality, and class in new ways; she does not assume, for instance, that black women faced no special hurdles on the road. Indeed, Mitchell suggests that they might have been more vulnerable to sexual assault. While cross-dressing as teenaged boys, as Pauli Murray and her female companions did, offered some protection from rape, they still faced other race-based dangers. But Pauli Murray was not simply trying to evade sexual assault on the road; as Mitchell explains, Murray had romantic relationships with women on the road and in the camp for unemployed women that she attended as part of a brief New Deal experiment extending the Civilian Conservation Corps experience to some young women. Arguing that transiency was widely feared as a morally corrosive and unnatural state of being, Mitchell shows how these fears within American popular culture intersected with fears about homosexuality and other "corrupting" influences. In particular, observers were concerned about what idle, unemployed women would do together in those few federally sponsored all-female camps that existed in the mid-1930s. As Mitchell demonstrates, many Americans strongly disapproved of these camps, seeing them as expensive havens for the idle, a fear that included the potential promiscuity of heterosexual women and lesbians. The fact that the women in the camps were meant to rest and relax—in other words, that they did not have the rigorous work projects associated with the all-male Civilian Conservation Corps—only compounded these negative perceptions. Mitchell finds that the discourse on corruption included condemnations of possible interracial sex between black men (nonresidents) and white women in the camps and the surveillance of relationships among women. In her larger work-in-progress, Mitchell hopes to explain more fully these findings across different racial and ethnic groups; in particular, she will show how "contemporaneous anxieties about idleness were infused with potent racialized, gendered, and sexualized meanings for young black women and other youths alike."

Deborah Gray White's "What Women Want: The Paradoxes of Postmodernity as Seen through Promise Keeper and Million Man March Women" takes on a different set of gendered and racial stereotypes to make sense of women who supported two ostensibly conservative, male-centered social movements of the 1990s. White begins her chapter by outlining feminist critiques of the Million Man March and the Promise Keepers by the National Organization for Women and by black feminist academics. In particular, they objected to the exclusion of women from the march and from Promise Keeper gatherings and expressed concerns over the rhetoric of both movements, which privileged men as patriarchs who could be the only true saviors of their families and communities. In the predominantly white Promise Keepers movement, the white evangelical and fundamentalist Christian wives accepted the view that wives must submit to their husbands. Promise Keepers justified women's submission by emphasizing that men's and women's physiological differences mandated gender-specific marriage roles sanctioned by God. But most Promise Keeper wives, White argues, "understood equality not in the sense of sameness but in the vein of equal complementary roles." Seeing the increasing divorce rates among Christian couples, these wives welcomed the revitalization of their marriages offered by men's participation in the movement.

White argues that most black women similarly accepted their exclusion from the 1995 Million Man March, agreeing that men needed to take more responsibility for their families and their lives. Although it might have appeared that they were accepting their own subordination, White points out that they were most concerned with empowering their own sons, brothers, fathers, and husbands who were statistically at higher risk of incarceration or murder than the rest of the American population. Black women welcomed any attempt by their men to help end the cycle of black men's imprisonment and of deaths and injuries due to gun violence in their communities. Patricia Hill Collins helps to explain these women's acceptance of patriarchy by noting that "In contrast [to race], gender is organized via inclusionary strategies where, via family, neighborhood, and religious groups, women live in close proximity to or belong to common social units with men. Women are encouraged to develop a commonality of interest with men, despite the gender hierarchy operating within this category of belonging."[18] Not only did both sets of women accept these male-centered, patriarchal movements, but, as White suggests, their condemnations of feminism were part of their clear antihomosexual agendas. For white Christian women, homosexuality was the ultimate taboo. After all, ministers insisted that homosexuality was a sin; they also linked the feminist movement to the promotion of a "gay lifestyle." To disassociate themselves from these causes even as they spoke in favor of equality as a form of complementary sex roles, Promise Keeper wives expressly condemned feminism and homosexuality. Similarly, for black women and men consistently caricatured by white Americans as highly sexed or prone to deviant sexualities, White points out that their denial of homosexuality was part of a political and rhetorical strategy for trying to overcome these racist stereotypes. While attacking homosexuality as a way of bolstering their own respectability from racist attack, black men committed themselves to important changes, such as taking charge of their families, improving their communities, and bolstering the patriarchal family structure. Struck by the similar agendas of women who supported both the Million Man March and the Promise Keepers in the 1990s, White points to the fact that "there were paradoxical similarities in the ways and means used by each group to address the realities that beset them in the 1990s."

The paradox of a possible cultural alliance or coalition between white and black women at the end of the twentieth century based on conservative models of patriarchy and gender relations suggests the way each of these chapters shows the value of intersectional approaches to alter the standard narratives in American history. They cover not only the rise of conservatism in the wake of the social ferment of the 1960s but also the national struggle over slavery and freedom, the formation of a black elite, public antipoverty programs, first- and second-wave feminism, and the long civil rights movement. By paying attention to the interconnection of gender and race, as well as class, sexuality, citizenship, and religion, and by listening to the voices of those not considered central to American history, such as Grandpa Brown, Pauli Murray, or the women of the Promise Keepers, these chapters allow us to tell a different American history.

This volume concludes with a brief epilogue written by Carol Moseley Braun, US senator from 1993 to 1999. She did not speak at the conference but graciously offered her essay on "Gender and Race as Cultural Barriers to Black Women in Politics"—a provocative statement that uses the personal to highlight the political. Moseley Braun's essay raises concluding questions about the intersectionality of race, gender, and class in America today. She notes that her 2003–4 run for US president was hampered by three linked questions of identity: her gender, race, and economic class. From her perspective, Moseley Braun takes the stand that "in America, gender is more of a cultural barrier than is race." To prove her point, Moseley Braun first highlights her experience as the US ambassador in New Zealand, where her race was a "nonissue," but her sex meant that she was prohibited from touching a "symbolic icon" during an indigenous installation ceremony. Discussing her campaign for the presidency, Moseley Braun details the gendered stereotypes that created extra barriers to voters' accepting her campaign as legitimate. The media offered negative commentary on her looks, clothes, and marital status, while ignoring these issues when reporting on the male candidates. Thinking about Barack Obama's successful run for the US presidency during the 2008 presidential campaign, Moseley Braun reiterates her conviction that "gender remains a more elusive touchstone in the march to liberate the human spirit than race." Denying that she is insensitive to the difficult discrimination against and suffering of black men throughout American history, Moseley Braun is convinced that any black female candidate in the United States would face bigger obstacles to public acceptance than a black man. As Deborah Gray White points out, black feminists are often suspected of being race traitors and are much maligned within the black community. In spite of these pressures, Moseley Braun proudly claims her identity as a black feminist, insisting "that women have every right to equality of opportunity and power in the public arena." Moseley Braun explores how those intersecting categories of race, class, and gender have shaped her political career, reminding readers of how the histories in this book persist in our times.

The editors would like to thank a variety of people and institutions who made it possible for us to produce this volume and the conference that preceded it. First, we'd like to thank the University of Rochester Press and its editorial director Suzanne Guiod for inviting us to launch the Gender and Race in American History book series and for working with us on the first few books so efficiently and capably. We'd also like to thank Victoria Wolcott and Jeffrey Tucker for facilitating the grant application process and logistics that made it possible for the conference to be held at the University of Rochester. A special thanks to the University of Rochester for awarding us a Humanities Project grant and for the financial and other support we received from the Frederick Douglass Institute and the Susan B. Anthony Institute. The directors of both institutes, Jeffrey Tucker and Honey Meconi, as well as Dean Tom Di Piero, President Joel Seligman, and Ghislaine Radegonde-Eison, were very helpful throughout. Graduate student Michelle Fin provided excellent graphics for the posters and took care of some of the planning details.

We are grateful for the careful commentaries provided by the anonymous reviewers of the manuscript. It was our privilege to work with such a talented group of authors, and we appreciate their high-quality work and intellectual commitment to the project.

Notes

1. For classics on gender and race, see Gloria T. Hull, Patricia Bell Scott, and Barbara Smith, eds., *All the Women Are White, All the Blacks Are Men, but Some of Us Are Brave: Black Women's Studies* (Old Westbury, NY: Feminist Press, 1982); Angela Y. Davis, *Women, Race, and Class* (New York: Vintage, 1981); bell hooks, *Feminist Theory from Margin to Center* (Cambridge, MA: South End Press, 1984); Evelyn Nakano Glenn, "Racial Ethnic Women's Labor: The Intersection of Race, Gender and Class Oppression," *Review of Radical Political Economics* 17, no. 3 (1985): 86–108; Cherrie Moraga and Gloria Anzaldúa, eds., *This Bridge Called My Back: Writings by Radical Women of Color*, 2nd ed. (New York: Kitchen Table, 1984); Patricia Hill Collins, *Black Feminist Thought: Knowledge, Consciousness, and the Politics of Empowerment* (New York: Routledge, 1991); Deborah Gray White, *Ar'n't I a Woman: Female Slaves in the Plantation South*, rev. ed. (New York: Norton, 1999); Hazel V. Carby, *Reconstructing Womanhood: The Emergence of the Afro-American Woman Novelist* (New York: Oxford University Press, 1989); Darlene Clark Hines, Wilma King, and Linda Reed, eds., *We Specialize in the Wholly Impossible: A Reader in Black Women's History* (Brooklyn, NY: Carlson, 1995); Glenda Gilmore, *Gender and Jim Crow: Women and the Politics of White Supremacy in North Carolina, 1896–1920* (Chapel Hill: University of North Carolina Press, 1996); Michele Mitchell, *Righteous Propagation: African Americans and the Politics of Racial Destiny after Reconstruction* (Chapel Hill: University of North Carolina Press, 2004).

2. Nell Irvin Painter, *The History of White People* (New York: Norton, 2010), xi; Barbara Jeanne Fields, "Slavery, Race, and Ideology in the United States of America," *New Left Review* 181 (May/June 1990): 114; Joan Scott, *Gender and the Politics of History* (New York: Columbia University Press, 1988), 42. The best overview of the impact of Joan Scott on American women's history is Joanne Meyerowitz, "A History of 'Gender,'" *American Historical Review* 113, no. 5 (December 2008): 1346–56. For a recent reconsideration of gender, see Jeanne Boydston, "Gender as a Question of Historical Analysis," *Gender and History* 20, no. 3 (2008): 558–83.

3. Kimberlé Crenshaw, "Demarginalizing the Intersection of Race and Sex: A Black Feminist Critique of Antidiscrimination Doctrine, Feminist Theory, and Antiracist Politics," *University of Chicago Legal Forum* (1989): 139–67.

4. Crenshaw, "Intersection of Race and Sex"; Kimberlé Crenshaw, "Mapping the Margins: Intersectionality, Identity Politics, and Violence against Women of Color," *Stanford Law Review* 43, no. 6 (July 1991): 1299, 1297.

5. Kimberlé Crenshaw, "Race, Reform, and Retrenchment: Transformation and Legitimation in Antidiscrimination Law," in *Theories of Race and Racism: A Reader*, ed. Les Back and John Solomos, 2nd ed. (New York: Routledge, 2009), 622–23.

6. See Patricia Hill Collins, "Some Group Matters: Intersectionality, Situated Standpoints, and Black Feminist Thought," in *Fighting Words: Black Women and the Search for Justice* (Minneapolis: University of Minnesota Press, 1998), 124–54; and

Collins, "Toward a New Vision: Race, Class, and Gender as Categories of Analysis and Connection," in *Oppression, Privilege, and Resistance: Theoretical Perspectives on Racism, Sexism, and Heterosexism*, ed. Lisa Heldke and Peg O'Connor (Boston: McGraw Hill, 2004), 529–43.

7. Crenshaw, "Mapping the Margins," 1242, 1244.

8. Leslie McCall, "The Complexity of Intersectionality," *Signs: Journal of Women in Culture and Society* 30, no. 3 (2005): 1782; Jennifer C. Nash, "Rethinking Intersectionality," *Feminist Review* 89 (2008): 12. See also Avtar Brah and Ann Phoenix, "Ain't I a Woman? Revisiting Intersectionality," *Journal of International Women's Studies* 5, no. 3 (2004): 75; and Julia S. Jordan-Zachery, "Am I a Black Woman or a Woman Who Is Black? A Few Thoughts on the Meaning of Intersectionality," *Politics and Gender* 3, no. 2 (2007): 254, 263. Brah and Phoenix argue, "we regard the concept of 'intersectionality' as signifying the complex, irreducible, varied, and variable effects which ensue when multiple axes of differentiation—economic, political, cultural, psychic, subjective and experiential—intersect in historically specific contexts."

9. Nell Irvin Painter, *Sojourner Truth, A Life, A Symbol* (New York: Norton, 1996), 4.

10. See Nash, "Rethinking Intersectionality," 1–15.

11. See, for instance, Collins, *Black Feminist Thought*, 1.

12. Kristin Waters, "Some Core Themes of Nineteenth-Century Black Feminism," in *Black Women's Intellectual Traditions: Speaking Their Minds*, ed. Kristin Waters and Carol B. Conaway (Burlington: University of Vermont Press, 2007), 382.

13. McCall, "Complexity of Intersectionality," 1782.

14. Jordan-Zachery, "Am I a Black Woman?," 257–58.

15. Nash "Rethinking Intersectionality," 11.

16. Crenshaw, "Mapping the Margins," 1245.

17. Ibid., 1299.

18. Collins, "Some Group Matters," 210.

Part 1

Bridging History, Theory, and Practice

Chapter I

Historicizing Intersectionality as a Critical Lens

Returning to the Work of Anna Julia Cooper

Vivian M. May

Scholars of intersectionality, historically and presently, start from the premise that both lived identities and structures of power and privilege should be understood as interwoven and not as additive factors or as separable dynamics. Intersectional approaches therefore entail a significant shift in epistemological, ontological, and methodological frames: fundamentally emphasizing simultaneity, scholars of intersectionality employ "tactics, strategies, and identities which historically have appeared to be mutually exclusive under modernist oppositional practices." Because this alternative mode of reasoning can readily lead to charges of illogic, as Kimberlé Crenshaw has discussed at length, those who employ intersectionality frequently confront being misread or misunderstood.[1]

For example, intersectional models of "both/and" thinking and simultaneity are frequently characterized as too complex or as impossible to engage in, and although intersectionality is widely acknowledged and even lauded as pivotal to feminist studies today, the degree to which the basic premises of intersectionality are understood and its intellectual contexts and history are engaged with and known are highly uneven: it is often interpreted reductively or used acontextually. As Stephanie Shields documents, for instance, "In conventional social and behavioral research, intersectionality frequently becomes redefined as a methodological challenge. . . . [Researchers] have typically responded to the question of intersectionality in one of three ways: excluding the question; deferring the question; limiting the question."[2] Thus, despite soaring rhetoric suggesting intersectionality is de rigueur in contemporary feminist research, it is too often instrumentalized—as a descriptive or demographic factor, for example, but not employed to develop research questions or to inform theoretical or empirical analyses.[3]

In addition, the rather common notion that intersectionality is a recent development in feminist thought relies on a truncated theoretical genealogy. While the late twentieth century certainly marks the emergence in the critical lexicon of the term *intersectionality* by Crenshaw, and while the 1970s and 1980s were shaped by wide-ranging discussions of the interplay among systems of race, gender, class, and sexuality, it is inaccurate to suggest that the past forty years constitute the only historical moment in which the examination of *intersections* among systems, identities, and politics has been pivotal in the history of feminist thought in general and within black feminist thought in particular.[4] To clarify, in arguing for a more adequate intellectual history of intersectionality, I am not suggesting that Crenshaw's coining of the term was insignificant. The metaphor has provided a concrete way to name and trace a mode of inquiry that has been long-standing in black feminist thought.

Crenshaw herself acknowledges this longer trajectory when delineating the concept in relation to the law and the limits of single-axis models of redress and rights: she suggests that a matrix worldview informed the work of earlier nineteenth-century black feminist theorists, including Anna Julia Cooper and Sojourner Truth, who laid the foundations for what we would now recognize as intersectional analyses and methods.[5] Presentist approaches to the concept therefore erroneously imply that theorizing by women of color constitutes a later theoretical development (to be tacked on to an extant and unrevised timeline of feminist thought); it can also reinforce the rather problematic (and widely critiqued) wave model of historicizing or periodizing feminism.[6]

Moreover, as Beverly Guy-Sheftall has amply demonstrated in *Words of Fire*, in which she documents two hundred years of black feminist thought, analyses starting at and asserting the need to examine the nexus of race-gender-class have long been offered forth as necessary to realizing more adequate models of personhood, politics, and liberation.[7] Intersectional theories and methods have been developed by black feminists as a means to foreground race as a central factor shaping gendered experience and gender's impact on raced experience; to emphasize that addressing racism is fundamental to feminism and vice versa; to contest the false universalization of gender or womanhood as monolithic, as with the false universalization of race and racialized experience; and to highlight and address gaps, erasures, and silences in the historical and political record resulting from such false universals.

Unfortunately, this longer history is too often unknown or ignored, even as intersectionality may be widely celebrated today. Paradoxically, these nineteenth-century origins and applications are more visible as prior instances of intersectionality (albeit without the terminology developed by Crenshaw) when the historical or theoretical research itself *starts from an intersectional lens*. Utilizing an intersectionality framework therefore aids in understanding more fully not only the relationship among systems of oppression in the present day but also how and why the concept itself (and the interconnectedness it seeks to name and examine) remains relatively invisible within prevailing analytic frameworks. In other words, an intersectional approach is pivotal to uncovering and understanding intersectionality's precursors as well as ongoing resistance to the insights an intersectional model of knowing has to offer.

Moreover, as a historiographic tool, intersectionality can be particularly useful as a metahistorical lens through which to lay bare issues of power and inequality and to question conventional historical terms, timelines, and values. In other words, it is invaluable for plumbing history's silences; for understanding oppression as having a history and as existing within a set of cultural, political, and social conditions; and for unearthing a vision of historical agency for those whose personhood and agency have been denied. As black feminist lawyer and activist Pauli Murray so aptly put it, "The lesson of history [is] that all human rights are indivisible and that the failure to adhere to this principle jeopardizes the rights of all."[8] For early black feminist scholar and educator Anna Julia Cooper, such an intersectional vision of history and approach to liberation informed her body of work (though no specific term such as *intersectionality* appears, per se, in her scholarship). Cooper's writings are therefore pivotal to tracing the genesis of intersectionality as a theory and method long before its late twentieth-century iterations.

Who Was Anna Julia Cooper?

Born into slavery in Raleigh, North Carolina, in 1858, and living to the age of 105, Cooper was an internationally known African American feminist educator, activist, and scholar.[9] Postemancipation, Cooper was one of two girls to enroll in the first class at St. Augustine's Normal School and Collegiate Institute (founded in 1867), which opened its doors in January 1868 in Raleigh. Cooper received a scholarship upon entry and, around age ten, began tutoring other students to help supplement her scholarship, thereby beginning her long career as an educator. She fought for entry to the "gentlemen's" courses (including Greek, Latin, and mathematics) and earned her high school diploma in 1877, also the year she married George A. C. Cooper, a St. Augustine's theology student from the Caribbean.

Cooper continued studying beyond her high school diploma and teaching at St. Augustine's until 1881, two years after George Cooper's untimely death in 1879. She then applied to Oberlin and was granted entry in the fall of 1881 with a scholarship and employment as a tutor: Mary Church (Terrell) and Ida Gibbs (Hunt) were also in her class. Cooper earned her bachelor's degree in mathematics in 1884 and became chair of Languages and Science at Wilberforce for a year before returning in 1885 to St. Augustine's as a professor of math, Latin, Greek, and German. Due to her college-level teaching experience, Oberlin awarded Cooper a master's degree in mathematics in

1887, the same year she was recruited to teach math and science at the Washington (Colored) Preparatory High School in Washington, DC (known as the M Street High School), where she would work for over thirty-five years of her teaching career.

While teaching at M Street, Cooper was engaged in community activism, publishing, and speaking on the lecture circuit (at home and abroad—she was one of two African American women to speak before the first Pan-African Congress in London in 1900).[10] For example, she wrote columns in the black press on issues from folklore to black women's unpaid labor in the home, helped to found many important organizations in the Washington, DC, area (such as the Phyllis Wheatley YWCA, the Colored Women's League, the Washington Negro Folklore Society, the Colored Settlement House, and the Bethel Literary Society), and wrote several books during her teaching career, including *A Voice from the South by a Black Woman of the South* (1892), which Mary Helen Washington characterizes as "the most precise, forceful, well-argued statement of black feminist thought to come out of the nineteenth century."[11]

In January 1901 Cooper was promoted to principal of M Street when Robert H. Terrell stepped down to take a judicial appointment, but her appointment was to be controversial and short-lived because Cooper's educational leadership was both rigorous and unwavering. She rejected the racist textbooks assigned by the board, ensured that M Street students scored well on district-wide tests (often better than white students), sought and earned accreditation for M Street diplomas for college-entrance equivalency, and refused to separate vocational and liberal arts curricula. Cooper believed all students deserved a well-rounded education: M Street offered full college preparatory as well as industrial and vocational curricula. Her battle with the board was made public, drawn out, and covered at length in the press: her ethics and professional skill were questioned, her pay denied, and her leadership challenged. Cooper eventually lost her employment by the fall of 1906 at M Street (whereupon her contract simply was not renewed) but won the curriculum fight: M Street's comprehensive curriculum remained intact. After working out west for a few years, Cooper was invited to return to M Street in 1910 and remained on the faculty for twenty more years.

Shortly after returning to work in DC, Cooper began traveling to France, studying French literature, history, and phonetics at the Guilde Internationale in Paris in the summers of 1911, 1912, and 1913, prior to applying for entry to Columbia University to pursue a doctorate in Romance Languages: she would engage in doctoral studies there during the summers of 1914 through 1917. However, Cooper could not fulfill Columbia's residency requirement due to the fact that she was working full-time as a teacher and could not give up her position, having taken in five nieces and nephews (and therefore also having bought a house in the Washington neighborhood of LeDroit Park near Howard). The advent of World War I also posed an impediment: Cooper got involved in war work summer camps and other activities. Determined to earn her PhD, after the war Cooper sought the aid of Abbé Félix Klein, a longtime friend in Paris, for help in transferring the Columbia credits to pursue a doctorate in history there.[12] Cooper was the first African American woman to earn a PhD at the Sorbonne and the fourth African American woman to earn one in the United States.

In addition to several short essays, pamphlets, and speeches published across her career, in 1925 Cooper would publish *Le pèlerinage de Charlemagne* (*The Pilgrimage of Charlemagne;* a translation of the epic poem from the medieval to the modern French, which was to have been her doctoral thesis at Columbia) as well as her Sorbonne dissertation *L'attitude de la France à l'égard de l'esclavage pendant la Révolution* (France's attitude toward slavery during the Revolution).[13] In 1930 she retired from M Street to become president of Frelinghuysen University, an alternative postsecondary educational institution for working adults who could not attend full-time at Howard, the only other postsecondary educational institution open to African Americans in Washington.[14] After stepping down from the presidency of Frelinghuysen but still working as its registrar, Cooper took up some other scholarly projects. Her two-volume set, *The Life and Writings of the Grimké Family* and *Personal Recollections of the Grimké Family*, was privately published in Washington, DC in 1951. During the 1950s Cooper also asked the historian Ray Allen Billington to edit Charlotte Forten Grimké's teaching journals and to help to get them published: they were published in New York by the Dryden Press in 1953 as *The Journal of Charlotte Forten: A Free Negro in the Slave Era.*[15]

Cooper and Intersectionality

As this brief biographical snapshot illustrates, Cooper was a committed educator, engaged activist, and talented scholar. She took up many different causes and interests throughout her long life, but central to much of her work was her multifaceted vision of justice and rights. In her scholarship, Cooper used critical tools that anticipate what we would currently describe as an intersectional approach to reveal how, for instance, both sexism and racism are systemic in nature (and interrelated) and to argue that these systems have a history that needs to be named and examined.[16] Moreover, she developed an interdisciplinary lens to highlight how historical actors are multiply situated and to underscore the significance of location on one's worldview. Simultaneously, Cooper named obstacles to telling a more inclusive history: bias and arrogance built into normative modes of recounting the past (and of analyzing the present) can mean that views from the margins are often devalued or simply missing altogether from the textual or historical record.

In her earlier work (1892–1913) Cooper emphasized the centrality of race to gender and vice versa, with issues of class, capital, geographic region, and nation taken up intermittently within her analyses of race-gender matrices. Cooper argued that this (unacknowledged but nonetheless formative) history of the interlocking structures of both racism and sexism continued to shape American cultural narratives and to impact the nation's operative assumptions about (and legal frameworks concerning) personhood, agency, and citizenship. In an attempt to highlight who has been ignored or forgotten, for instance, Cooper queried, "who shall recount the name and fame of the women?" and referenced women who were generally forgotten or dismissed, from Ruth to the Amazons, Sappho to Madame de Staël. Cooper also pointed to black women artists and activists who were her contemporaries yet were also often overlooked "sisters in the service" of humanity, among them Frances Watkins Harper, Sojourner Truth, Charlotte Grimké, and Hallie Quinn Brown.[17]

In her later work, especially in her Sorbonne dissertation, which she completed at age sixty-six while working full-time at the M Street High School, Cooper's focus became increasingly comparative and international and attended more deeply to questions of class and capital.[18] Here again she illustrated how an unacknowledged history and an epistemological absence can have an immense impact on world events, even as they may be willfully ignored or dismissed as irrelevant. Cooper exposed how France's notion of the citizen-subject during the revolutionary era remained so deeply tied to ideals of capitalist profit and to notions of white superiority that the French were in many ways incapable of truly achieving the full potential of their republican vision of democracy. Moreover, in tracing connections between capitalism, citizenship, and race in her Sorbonne thesis, Cooper took up questions of within-group differences (e.g., differences in terms of capital, class, and citizenship status) among blacks in Saint-Domingue; she refused both to homogenize blackness and to rely on reductive binaries of race (white/black) and of empire (metropole/colony) for her analysis.

Thus, in both of her major works, *A Voice from the South* and *L'attitude de la France*, Cooper confronted a key methodological and political problem: since the ways in which the historical meanings of personhood and citizenship are racialized, gendered, and classed are usually ignored, or denied altogether, a flexible and dynamic method was necessary to break open cultural silences, expose the systemic workings of power, and offer an alternative worldview. Cooper delved into absences, straddled disciplinary boundaries, refused harmful cognitive and epistemic norms, and spoke up from history's fissures. I want to underscore that Cooper was not alone—she worked in dialogue (though not always in full agreement) with many other men and women of her time (including W. E. B. Du Bois, Fannie Barrier Williams, Ida B. Wells, Charlotte Forten Grimké, Nannie Helen Burroughs, Walter White, Martin Delaney, Kelly Miller, and many more) who were likewise engaged in thinking through the politics of knowledge, reexamining the past, theorizing resistance, and envisioning liberation strategies.

Nevertheless, Cooper's work is especially central to tracing a more comprehensive history of intersectional thought and politics not only because her approach was highly innovative in terms of her inclusive and nonhierarchical notions of freedom and of personhood (i.e., of rights and of ontology or identity) but also because she combined this matrix model of race, gender, region, and class with a highly interdisciplinary methodology. Epistemologically, her work stands out for the ways in which she consistently sought to reshape norms of logic and rationality from the standpoint of black womanhood.[19]

To illustrate in more detail Cooper's contributions to the history of intersectional thought, I will discuss some examples from her 1892 *A Voice from the South*, the first book-length example of black feminist theory in the United States. I shall also draw from other short speeches and essays by Cooper from the period 1892–1913. In these earlier writings, Cooper broke open the all-too-common false universalization of race and womanhood at play in the wider body politic by starting from the analytic and political standpoint of black southern womanhood. Using simultaneity as her lens, Cooper insisted that the fullest sense of freedom, personhood, and autonomy could be arrived at collectively only by seeking to eradicate all forms of domination simultaneously. Exposing myriad ways in which marginalization (whether by race, gender, region, or class) is socially enforced and not an ontologically fixed state of being, Cooper developed a theory of resistance and a view of historical and cultural representation grounded in everyday experience.

Next, I examine Cooper's analysis of race, class, and capital in her 1925 Sorbonne dissertation, *L'attitude de la France*, as well as in her dissertation defense, or *soutenance*, papers.[20] In her thesis she highlighted the racialized workings of modernity, capital, and revolution. She pointed to the politics of historical understanding by exposing the limits of conventional approaches to the age of revolution and by identifying silences within extant historical studies and archival materials. Cooper also laid bare the reciprocal, transatlantic workings of history in the way she approached her subject in that she presented enslaved and free blacks as agents of history, not imitators of European Enlightenment.

In developing a framework of reciprocity rather than one of mimesis and by addressing race, class, nation, and citizenship as interdependent factors, Cooper highlighted how the revolutions in France and Saint-Domingue were interlaced. She also illustrated how notions about race and racial hierarchies shaped Enlightenment ideas about citizenship, agency, and personhood, while, simultaneously, ideas about property, capital economy, and social class impacted intraracial and interracial politics in both France and Saint-Domingue. Cooper suggested that without the uprising of the slaves and free blacks in Saint-Domingue, the French republic would have remained mired in an illogical attachment to hierarchy, exploitation, and dehumanizing oppression: she positioned black and

transatlantic history at the center of French history, shifting the epistemological contours and political boundaries of revolutionary history.

Having Her Say: *A Voice from the South* and Other Early Works

As the title *A Voice from the South* suggests, issues of voice (from the politics
of raising or lifting one's voice to the politics of being heard) and questions
of the meanings of location permeate her book. Not only does the motif of
voice shape the structure of the volume (e.g., the first part is titled "Soprano
Obligato" and the second "Tutti ad Libitum," such that the solo voice leads
to the collective voicing in coalition), but Cooper also modulated her writing voice and style throughout the text. In the preface, she paralleled black
women's collective voice to a "muffled chord," a "mute and voiceless note,"
and an "uncomprehended cadenza"—suggesting right off that questions of
voice entail more than a lack of speech or problem of silence at an individual
level, but also a lack of rhetorical space into which to speak and be understood
collectively (i).[21] As the text unfolds, readers are asked to attend to a more
nuanced politics of voice and reception and to think through the many obstacles to being heard. For instance, Cooper urged readers to acknowledge that
"rhetoric" alone cannot "annihilate" inequality since "the man who is dominated by the sentiment of race prejudice," she found, tends to be "impervious
to reason" (232).

Cooper's shifting rhetorical tone and her tactical uses of humor, sarcasm,
and irony amid theoretical and political analyses are important for thinking
about how she developed and utilized intersectionality in her work, for these
modulations mark the writing and analysis as embodied and located (rather
than detached or remote). Cooper emphasized that she spoke to and took up
universal issues and questions from a particular location as a black woman who
is also of the South: she contended that all knowledge, including her own, is
particular, contextual, and located within a time, place, body, and set of social
relations—her ideas have come, she argued, from her own "peculiar coigne of
vantage" (138).

Moreover, Cooper understood fully that men do not see the world from
women's standpoint, nor do black men, in their "busy objectivity," necessarily
view reality as black women do (122, ii). She wrote, just "as our Caucasian bar-
risters are not to blame if they cannot *quite* put themselves in the dark man's
place, neither should the dark man be wholly expected fully and adequately
to reproduce the exact Voice of the Black Woman" (iii). Cooper underscored
the centrality of social location and of lived experience to knowledge production. She therefore demanded that the "truth from *each* standpoint be
presented. . . . The 'other side' has not been represented by one who 'lives
there.' And not many can more sensibly realize and more accurately tell the

weight and the fret of the 'long dull pain' than the open-eyed but hitherto voiceless Black Woman of America" (ii). Though not usually consulted, black women, she contended, can better analyze and understand social structures because of their social location and lived history. Likewise, she suggested, those who have had access to more power and privilege may be *less reliable* knowers due to *their* social location: just as marginality can yield insight, access to power can skew perception.[22]

In addition to underscoring that black women have long been "open-eyed" knowers, throughout *A Voice from the South*, Cooper reminded readers that, due to their social location at the nexus of compounding structures of oppression, black women have had extensive experience confronting indifference, ignorance, and silence. She underscored that the "colored woman of to-day occupies . . . a unique position in this country. She is confronted by both a woman question and a race problem, and is as yet an unknown or an unacknowledged factor in both" (134). Cooper repeatedly affirmed that knowledge gained from marginalization is equal to if not more adequate than dominant modes of knowing. She often used humor to get at this idea, as in the following passage, in which Cooper positioned herself as a male patient awaiting his diagnosis: "the doctors while discussing their scientifically conclusive diagnosis of the disease, will perhaps not think it presumptuous in the patient if he dares to suggest where at least the pain is" (36).

Drawing on her own experience, Cooper also argued that what may appear to be intrinsic characteristics are often, in fact, socially constructed. Taking on biological determinists of her time by arguing that "there is nothing irretrievably wrong with the Black man's skull," Cooper further explained that "race, color, sex, condition, are . . . the accidents, not the substance of life" (125). By this she did not mean that race or gender have no meaning (i.e., that they are insubstantial); rather, their meanings take shape within sociocultural and historical contexts. Thus, Cooper derided the pseudoscientific notion that the "shape of the female cerebrum" is incompatible with higher education and showed instead how women's secondary social status has been both legally enforced, socially encouraged, and rationalized to seem natural (65).

She also argued that women themselves have been pushed to be a "mere toy," whose value in the world is ascertained by their capacity to please men: moreover, they have been wrongly "compelled to look to sexual love" as their only path to fulfillment, while being denied access to an education as well as the right to own property. As a black woman, Cooper remarked, she has had to "struggle" especially hard "to fight [my] way against positive discouragements to the higher education" (65, 68, 77). Recalling some of her more difficult moments at St. Augustine's, particularly her conflicts with the Reverend Dr. Smedes, who did not think it necessary for her to study the full curriculum (since he assumed she was there only to find a husband), Cooper wrote, "I constantly felt . . . a thumping within unanswered by any beckoning from without" (76).

In addition to emphasizing her own social location, Cooper deftly exposed how the partiality of those who speak or write from dominant locations is rarely pointed to, even when their bias and arrogance are glaring, as Cooper suggested was the case with William Dean Howells's plying of trite racist/sexist stereotypes in his various literary endeavors, particularly his 1891 novel, *An Imperial Duty*, "which he ha[d] no right or authority to hawk" (206). When it came to African American life, Cooper contended, "Mr. Howells [did] not know what he [was] talking about": his work, steeped in "vulgarity," was "superficial" regarding racial matters. Though Howells's point of view was "precisely that of a white man who saw colored people at long range or only in certain capacities," he would pay no price for his narrowness and would never be asked to account for it in any way (201, 203, 206).

In contrast, Cooper illustrated that she must dance around the presumption that her writing will be biased or overly emotional (and thereby less rational) on account of both her race and gender status. For example, in the midst of an argument about the central role black womanhood will play in the future of the race, both in theological and educational causes, Cooper paused, "may I not hope that the writer's oneness with her subject both in feeling and in being may palliate undue obtrusiveness of opinions here" (42). She also exposed how the biases and emotions of those in power are usually denied outright (though she aimed to make them visible, hence her recasting "Anglo-Saxons" as "Angry Saxons" in a later essay) or are obfuscated through powerful theoretical traditions, such as that of taking on a mantle of objectivity to mask fundamentally narrow-minded thinking.[23] For example, the philosophical movement known as positivism, for all its claims to pure objectivity, she suggested, is inherently biased against women, since within the theoretical framework, women can occupy only the position of the contemplated (or worshipped) object but cannot engage in contemplation itself (since they are the objects, not the subjects, of knowledge) (292).

Cooper's focus on the politics of location as it intertwines with the politics of knowledge and voice is especially significant in relation to understanding how her work presages what we would now characterize as intersectionality, because scholars of intersectionality demand recognition of how power asymmetries impact rhetorical space and thereby not only constrain public discourse but also hinder access to full recognition and rights as citizen-subjects. As with contemporary theorists of intersectionality, Cooper's focus on voice and location draws our attention to the margins as a site of knowledge and resistance and to lived experience as a criterion of meaning. As her insights illustrate, an intersectional approach considers marginalization both in terms of social structure and lived experience. This dual focus is a hallmark of black feminist theorizing and, as Patricia Hill Collins has argued, it entails analyzing resistance within the margins and redefining "marginality as a potential source of strength," not merely "one of tragedy."[24]

The epistemological shift at work in Cooper's analyses is important, because she debunked a "god's-eye" view, challenging the might and power of the eye of the iconic American eagle with the voice and song of the "starling," offering alternative views on social reality and historical circumstance that pushed readers to shift away from the prevailing viewpoint of the eagle.[25] For instance, Cooper revised the nation's origin story. Rather than the usual account of Pilgrims, Thanksgiving dinners, peaceful settlement, unjustly imposed tea taxes, and revolutionary uprising, she offered a different genealogy: "Uprooted from the sunny land of his forefathers by the white man's cupidity and selfishness, ruthlessly torn from all the ties of clan and tribe, dragged against his will over thousands of miles of unknown waters . . . the Negro was transplanted to this continent in order to produce chattels and beasts of burden for a nation 'conceived in liberty and dedicated to the proposition that all men are created equal.'"[26]

Cooper also made clear that the meanings of our positionality and even our embodiment are not fixed but variable and contextual. This is of course implied in her argument that race, gender, and class are better understood to be the "accidents" and not the "substance" of life. But she also illustrated this concept more completely when discussing her own travels abroad: she recalled what it felt like to be outside of the Jim Crow United States and spend time in Toronto (where she traveled in 1891 on a teacher exchange with friend and colleague Ella D. Barrier). Referencing herself in the third person as "the Black Woman of the South," Cooper remarked on "a hospitable, thawing-out atmosphere everywhere—in shops and waiting rooms, on cars and in the streets" that not only made her see her own "countrymen" in "unfavorable contrast" but also impacted her own internal sensibilities. Cooper became aware of the ways in which, in the Jim Crow South and in the nation's capital, she lived with a "whipped-cur feeling," but in Toronto she found she not only had to negotiate different attitudes in others but also had to confront a degree of internalized oppression within herself (88–89).

Thus far, I have focused more on epistemological questions and rhetorical approaches in *A Voice from the South* as a means of highlighting Cooper's uses and development of intersectionality. But she also applied an intersectional lens to debates about rights and freedoms, especially with regard to questions of black liberation and women's liberation at the turn of the last century.[27] As her remarks before an audience of white feminists at the 1893 Chicago World's Exposition illustrate, the black feminist worldview she drew on and fleshed out was collective and grounded in a vision of solidarity. Cooper stated, "We take our stand on the solidarity of humanity, the oneness of life. . . . The colored woman feels that woman's cause is one and universal . . . not the white woman's, nor the black woman's, nor the red woman's, but the cause of every man and of every woman who has writhed silently under a mighty wrong."[28] Hazel Carby contends that, as with other black feminists in her time, "Cooper . . . exposed the historical and ideological framework within which white women defended their own class and racial interests."[29]

By starting from the premise of the indivisibility of all aspects of the self, as well as from the insight that systems of oppression are interlocking, Cooper advocated a matric model of rights and activism, rather than what Crenshaw in the contemporary period has negatively characterized as a "single-axis" model.[30] Cooper offered an early example of the limits of single-axis thinking in her sharp critique of "Wimodaughsis (a woman's culture club whose name was created using the first few letters of *wi*ves, *mo*thers, *daugh*ters, and *sis*ters)." Too often, she wrote, it is as if "Pandora's box is opened in the ideal harmony of this modern Eden without an Adam when a colored lady, a teacher in one of our schools, applies for admission to its privileges and opportunities." Cooper astutely rechristened the Kentucky women's club "Whimodaughsis," both to reveal and to discredit the tacit whiteness at the heart of this club (80–81).

Cooper named other examples of white feminists' adherence to race supremacy on the path to "women's" liberation. She illustrated how "Mrs. Mary A. Livermore . . . was dwelling on the Anglo-Saxon genius for power" and not on a vision of liberation for all peoples when, in a speech, she seemed to make light of the fact that an "unoffending Chinaman" was beaten on the streets because he was perceived as effeminate and weak (53–54).[31] Cooper also challenged Anna Howard Shaw (who would later become president of the National American Women Suffrage Association from 1901 to 1915) for her exclusionary politics and myopic thinking. Shaw posed the problem of "women's" rights as that of "Woman versus the Indian" so that, according to Cooper's point of view, women thereby made themselves plaintiffs in a fictional lawsuit Cooper fittingly named "Eye vs. Foot" to highlight the absurd and racist logics of white feminist frameworks.[32] In response, Cooper queried, "Why should woman become plaintiff in a suit versus the Indian, or the Negro or any other race or class who have been crushed under the iron heel of Anglo-Saxon power and selfishness?" (123). Furthermore, she asserted, "It cannot seem less than a blunder, whenever the exponents of a great reform . . . allow themselves to seem distorted by a narrow view of their own aims and principles. All prejudices, whether of race, sect or sex, class pride and class distinctions are the belittling inheritance and badge of snobs and prigs" (118).

Cooper also refuted false equivalencies between blackness and masculinity. With reference to Martin R. Delaney, Cooper admonished, "no man can represent the race," even if he is a self-proclaimed "unadulterated black man" (30). Asserting that the "dark man [should not] be wholly expected fully and adequately to reproduce the exact Voice of the Black Woman," she insisted that black men—including Alexander Crummell (whose famous pamphlet she here referred to and responded to)—should not venture to speak for black women (iii).[33] She contended, "We might as well expect to grow trees from leaves as hope to build up a civilization or a manhood without taking into consideration our women" (78).

Cooper added that black women's needs and issues should be considered at the *center* of what constitutes race politics and liberation, rather than secondary or marginal, but she found that the fundamental enmeshment of race and gender politics was too often ignored by black men, leaving "the colored woman . . . hampered and shamed by a less liberal sentiment and a more conservative attitude on the part of those for whose opinion she cares most" (78, 135). She called black men to task for holding onto the patriarchal romantic notion "that women may stand on pedestals or live in doll houses, (if they happen to have them) but they must not furrow their brows with thought or attempt to help men tug at the great questions of the world" (75). Instead of asking black women to silence their voices and dull their intellects, she argued that black men should recognize that the black woman "finds herself in the presence of responsibilities which ramify through the profoundest and most varied interests of her country and race." Cooper concluded, "Such is the colored woman's office, she must stamp weal or woe on the coming history of this people" (142, 145).

In critiquing both white women and black men for foolishly emulating or seeking access to white patriarchy rather than dismantling interconnected systems of inequality, Cooper exposed how privilege and oppression are not mutually exclusive but simultaneous and relative. She therefore advocated a different model of thinking about the meaning of freedom and the notion of rights. In other words, connected to Cooper's view of the human subject as multiply situated was her advocacy of an alternative approach to difference as a starting point for a more adequate vision of the body politic. Cooper explained, "Caste and prejudice mean immobility. One race predominance means death. The community that closes its gates against foreign talent can never hope to advance beyond a certain point. Resolve to keep out foreigners and you keep out progress" (160).

Cooper argued that differences should not be opposed, nor should they be ignored or erased: they should be balanced in a state of "universal reciprocity" rather than placed in a hierarchical relationship (165, 168). The alternative, she suggested, would be a society that suppressed differences, entered "the passivity of death," became mired in "stagnation," and pursued tyrannical "unity without variety," resulting both in xenophobia and ethnocentrism (149–50, 152, 160). By beginning from the premise that "no one is or can be supreme. All interests must be consulted, all claims conciliated," Cooper could then insist that the "co-existence of . . . racially different elements" should be considered to be at the core of America's potential, not its so-called problem (164, 151). More than thirty years after first positing this notion of the meaning of democracy founded in multiplicity (and not false unity), Cooper embarked on a historical study of the French and Haitian Revolutions: in this work, she built on her earlier intersectional approaches, including her vision of differences as fundamental to meaningful freedom, but shifted her attention to a transatlantic lens and to questions of how class and capital intersect with race and citizenship.

Shifting Mindsets, Examining Attitudes: Cooper's Sorbonne Dissertation

If Cooper's dissertation is referenced at all in contemporary feminist scholarship, the question often is raised as to why Cooper appears to have "dropped" her gender analysis in this later major work, and whether, therefore, her dissertation should be considered to be feminist. The answers are quite complex, but in brief let me first emphasize that her archival materials had little if any documentation about women—free black, enslaved, white, or *gens de couleur* (people of color)—in Saint-Domingue (or in France for that matter). Using France's military archives and having few studies on hand focusing on women on either side of the Atlantic during the revolutionary era meant that Cooper's primary and secondary materials did not include gender content per se. It is therefore hard to imagine how she might have engaged in a project examining the politics of black womanhood in the age of revolution. Nevertheless, Cooper remained interested in challenging false universals, refuting simplistic binaries, shifting the analytic focus to the margins, and thinking through matrices of power, consistent with her earlier writings.

Moreover, in her dissertation Cooper continued to explore questions of liberation, to trace the origins of supremacist modes of thinking, and to address silences in the historical record. This is in keeping with her earlier analyses, though she attended to the nexus of race, class, and nation in the dissertation rather than her focus on race, gender, and, to varying degrees, class, region, and nation in *A Voice from the South* and other early works. In addition, times had changed. From the 1890s to the 1920s space for black feminists in the public sphere shrank intensely: a sharp rise in xenophobia, racial backlash, empire building, and lynching marked this period. On a personal level, Cooper's struggles with Oberlin College in the 1920s help to illustrate how institutions that formerly had been proudly inclusive became quite hostile in terms of race relations.[34] The suffrage movement had also further cemented a false divide between women's rights and racial equality, while at the same time, the masculinist focus of civil rights organizing (e.g., the Niagara Movement) intensified during this period. Finally, black feminists have long taken up issues that do not necessarily appear to be feminist from a conventional (and white-centered) view, but that are, in fact, central to women's liberation writ large (lynching; access to food, employment, and housing; welfare rights; poverty;

incarceration and the prison-industrial complex, to name a few). I suggest that Cooper's dissertation can be read within this larger frame (and in conversation with her larger body of work).

Thus, while most scholars have focused primarily on *A Voice from the South*, Cooper's 1925 Sorbonne dissertation, *France's Attitude toward Slavery during the Revolution*, deserves more attention than it has received to date.[35] In her thesis, Cooper analyzed the dialectical nature of the Haitian and French Revolutions and contended that these political moments arose out of a transatlantic consciousness, not merely out of French intellectual or political innovation. Writing during the United States' military occupation of Haiti (1914–35) and having at her disposal a definitively Eurocentric data set, Cooper spoke out against imperial expansion (past and present).[36] By recounting some of history's suppressed stories to offer a different reading of the revolutionary era, and of the French Revolution in particular, Cooper situated both black history and French history within an international, transatlantic framework.

To put it mildly, France's parliamentary and military archives (from which Cooper drew her materials) are imbalanced. As Frances Richardson Keller has documented, "of the thousands of published cahiers . . . only . . . eleven demand the eventual abolition of slavery. Twelve ask for improvement in the condition of the slaves, but are indefinite as to what should be done. One cahier expressed concern with the condition of free [Blacks]."[37] Is it any wonder that, much as she characterized the state of the black woman at the opening of *A Voice from the South*, in her dissertation Cooper described the suffering of the blacks in Saint-Domingue, and particularly of the slaves, as, likewise, "silent"?[38] Nevertheless, as in her earlier works, Cooper found ways to make this silence speak. Carefully sifting through these materials, she uncovered evidence to support her claims that slaves and gens de couleur in Saint-Domingue were agents of political consciousness who pushed the emerging French republic to take up a more comprehensive vision of democracy.

Unlike other works on the Haitian Revolution written by more widely recognized black male scholars (e.g., C. L. R. James's 1938 *The Black Jacobins* or W. E. B. Du Bois's 1938 *Haiti: A Drama of the Black Napoleon*), in her dissertation title (*L'attitude de la France à l'égard de l'esclavage pendant la Révolution*) Cooper did not frame the actions in Saint-Domingue as black versions of French politics or as imitations of French resistance, which both James and Du Bois implicitly did do, with their metaphors of the "Jacobins" and of "Napoleon," respectively.[39] In the title, as throughout the study, Cooper never limited the "Revolution" to denote the French Revolution alone; she left the referent open-ended, perhaps to allow her (potentially biased) readers at the Sorbonne (including her chief examiner, the renowned civilizationist sociologist Celestin Bouglé) to *presume* that Cooper was referencing the French Revolution alone, while at the same time, she created space in which to advance her argument that the Haitian Revolution was as much a part of the age of revolution as the political upheavals in the United States or in France.

Certainly Cooper was writing against the grain, in her own time and even by current measures. Prevailing approaches have tended to imply that the root source of liberation and political action in Haiti was European. Analogously, as Laurent Dubois has illustrated, the Enlightenment is often deemed to have occurred only within the bounds of Europe "proper," rather than in an Atlantic context of cross-fertilization.[40] In contrast, Cooper's intersectional method allowed her to highlight a wider array of forms of agency or resistance. While she acknowledged that the French Revolution offered a fruitful environment for the Haitian Revolution, she also clarified that it should not be characterized as its *source*: it was one cause, but not *the* cause.[41] The prime source of revolt in Saint-Domingue was, for Cooper, the "divine Spark," meaning agency and the desire for freedom are intrinsic and cannot simply be granted or taught by other, more "advanced" nations, as a paternal (or maternal) rescue narrative or as the concept of the "white man's burden" would suggest (both popular rationales for imperial and colonial expansion).[42]

Although the agency of the *noirs* (or blacks—free and enslaved) was generally disregarded in France and in Saint-Domingue, Cooper illustrated that they had played a pivotal role. Even as they had been absented from history, she argued they were an "active element of the insurrection" and documented how slaves and maroons had resisted in the century leading up to the revolution: prior to the uprisings of 1788–91 were those of 1679, 1691, 1703, and 1758. She also uncovered references to slaves using work stoppages to undermine the sugar trade and slave labor systems. Cooper carefully unpacked the archival materials to illustrate how, despite ample evidence of organized resistance, and even after François-Dominique Toussaint Louverture and his army of twenty thousand engaged in battle, the colonists and the French continued to erroneously describe both the enslaved and free blacks as submissive and obedient, even when the revolution in Saint-Domingue was well underway.[43]

Cooper's study also departs from conventional approaches to the French Revolution in that she opened her thesis by discussing Spanish and Portuguese conquest in the Americas, by highlighting unrestrained exploitation in the "Age of Discovery," and by decrying the heinous rise of racial slavery, after the genocide of Native populations, to satisfy voracious European empires.[44] Contending that the development of racial slavery in the Americas had as its only principle an "abuse of force" that was "without cause or excuse" other than "the imperative of the most powerful," Cooper shifted her focus to the margins and accentuated slaves' excessive mortality rates—nearly triple the birth rate—and documented how, for every slave brought to the colonies, four would die. By starting with a different timeline and geopolitical framework and by seeking out evidence that others had been unable or unwilling to appreciate, Cooper stressed ontological power asymmetries of race and class and highlighted the complex cartographies of power at work in the colony.[45] She used this comparative method to direct our attention to many suppressed aspects of the history of revolution. Starting from the basic facts of racial slavery and colonial domination (rather than ignoring or minimizing their historical significance), she pointed to the subsequent supremacist political, economic, and philosophical legacies of conquest and attended to the pivotal role of race politics in the French Revolution.

When writing about the situation in France, Cooper placed questions of slavery, property, and rights at the center of her inquiry, departing from standard approaches to the French Revolution and to the evolution of the French republic. By using a different origin story and by pivoting her angle of inquiry, Cooper highlighted Europe's economic reliance on human exploitation and critiqued the escalating gap between theories of universal reason and rights and the abusive practices of capitalist empires dependent on slave and colonial labor.[46] Focusing on what Michel Rolph-Trouillot has characterized as an ongoing "encounter between ontological discourse and colonial practice," Cooper highlighted how, as Enlightenment ideas of universal rights became more widely accepted, the slave trade and colonial sugar economy grew by leaps and bounds; in other words, the "gap between abstraction and practice grew."[47]

This "vast gulf," as Cooper described it, led to a dead-end political situation in France, wherein debates about human rights kept butting up against debates about property rights, with no end in sight.[48] In highlighting unremitting political debates that were never accompanied by any attempts at real action, Cooper illustrated that the predominant pattern of French political behavior was one of inaction, delay, and evasion.[49] She exposed the extent to which France sought to avoid questions of race and slavery, even when appearing to discuss them and even though, as she argued, they *had* to be addressed if the true principles of égalité were to be realized. To Cooper, France's protracted debates about race as an intellectual concept demonstrated a propensity to evade justice through rhetoric (i.e., theory for theory's sake, in contemporary parlance); abolition was thought about mostly as a theoretical conundrum or economic crisis, not as a human problem, structural issue, and moral quandary. As in *A Voice from the South*, here in her dissertation Cooper remained deeply suspicious of theories disconnected from the realities of inequity, consistent with an intersectional approach, which not only emphasizes located knowing, but seeks to connect theoretical analysis with social change or liberation politics.

As a countermeasure to such abstraction, she accentuated how enslaved blacks in Saint-Domingue were a flesh and blood "living negation of [France's] noble principles."[50] She insisted that ideals of liberation must always connect to the exigencies of lived experience and that injustice should be engaged with through action, not delay. Furthermore, she argued that without transforming the legal and economic structures of the colonial slave economy, no amount of conjecture about the meanings of liberty and autonomy could alter the reality of a racially divided, exploitative, profit-driven society. She therefore highlighted how the *structural* economic and political relationships in place directly undermined philosophical ideas about universalism and political goals of republicanism.

To drive this point home, Cooper used an intersectional analysis of race and gender as the basis for her argument that a key issue inadequately addressed by the philosophes and the politicians was that in the French Caribbean, as well as in France, systems of "work and profits" were organized around slavery.[51] In other words, capitalism's profits, which had helped to spur change in the class and political structures in the metropole, relied on conquest and slave labor in the colonies: France's emergent democracy depended on exploitation. She argued that this contradiction was willfully ignored because "the colonists, the rich merchants, had too much to gain from the shameful traffic in slaves to be willing even to consider the possibility of suppressing slavery"; trade with Saint-Domingue, in fact, represented almost two-thirds of France's total trade.[52] In addition, she underscored that most of Europe depended on the sugar produced by the two hundred thousand slaves working sugar plantations on Saint-Domingue alone. Astutely, Cooper also drew attention to the fact that the Caribbean was crucial to the geopolitical emergence of capitalism. In addition, she showed the colons' worldview to be informed by class pretensions and an outright refusal to face the reality in front of them.[53]

Repeatedly Cooper demonstrated that, contrary to Enlightenment ideals, what held sway was "that absolutely corrupt principle of forced labor . . . for a whole class of human beings, outrageously exploited." Cooper argued that it was the slaves' labor (not European intellect) that "made . . . fortunes," both in Saint-Domingue and France.[54] Her focus on the enslaved as an exploited class is noteworthy, because they were regarded as beasts of burden ("*bêtes de somme*") incapable of being exploited. Underscoring their extreme alienation and exploitation, she wrote that they were forced "into work that profited only others."[55] Although Cooper framed the political conflicts that arose (both in France and in Saint-Domingue) over race, property, and rights as a class struggle, she did not reduce race to class or vice versa. After all, many of the gens de couleur were propertied. As Joan Dayan documents, "By 1789, they owned one-third of the plantation property, one-quarter of the slaves, and one-quarter of the real estate property in Saint-Domingue."[56] They also made up "forty-seven percent of the colony's free inhabitants in 1788."[57]

By starting from the assumption that the politics and structures of class, citizenship, and race are intertwined, Cooper showed that the interests of the gens de couleur as plantation owners and slave owners shaped their struggle for equal rights as people of color: they initially sought equality with propertied whites, not universal rights for all. Highlighting how race and class operated as shifting and entangled factors, Cooper suggested that the networks of power in Saint-Domingue and in France could not be adequately understood if the clash over rights, the ensuing revolution, and the eventual Haitian independence were framed only as struggles of class or race in isolation. To add nuance to her comparative analysis of race and class dynamics, Cooper also attended to details about the French context that were usually overlooked or considered inconsequential. For instance, she emphasized how major French ports and maritime regions were economically dependent on and profited from slavery and the sugar trade. Rationalization of slave labor was widespread in France, not just in the colonies, and this lucrative financial system of "unbridled waste" and "oppression and excessive despotism" shaped politics and daily life as much in the metropole as in the colony.[58]

Conventionally, French influence on Saint-Domingue is underlined, but Cooper shifted gears to delineate how both labor productivity and political organizing by blacks, slaves, and gens de couleur in Saint-Domingue impacted debates in France about the nature of democracy, the implications of humanism, and the meaning of citizenship. In accentuating Saint-Domingue's influence, Cooper rejected what Charles W. Mills has, in his scholarship on the role of race in social contracts, described as the usual "*writing out* of the polity of certain spaces [and people] as conceptually and historically irrelevant to European . . . development."[59] Cooper illustrated that without the collective uprisings of gens de couleur, free blacks, and slaves in late eighteenth-century Saint-Domingue, slavery would not have been abolished (in France and in all French colonies) so early, nor would universal political rights without distinction of race or property have come to fruition. Moreover, a new juridical order uniting the colonies and the metropole as one polity with one set of laws would have been out of the question, since both the colons and *petits blancs* (literally, the "little whites," meaning poor whites in Saint-Domingue; *grand blancs* connoted the colons, or white colonial upper classes) preferred to sidestep the French constitution and be exempted from the "rights of man," an evasion Cooper was particularly critical of, given the egregious inequalities made legal in the United States under Jim Crow after *Plessy v. Ferguson* (1896).[60] Cooper had critiqued *Plessy* in an earlier speech: she found the decision and the "re-enslaving black codes" in the United States to be a direct result of the violent "resentment and rage" of the "master class."[61] Likewise, the increasingly hysterical colons advocated "special" laws for Saint-Domingue's "unique" local conditions, wherein it would "be necessary to modify the French constitution in favor of the colonies," since "laws incompatible with local customs . . . should not be imposed."[62] Basically, white French citizens on both sides of the Atlantic fought a unified jurisdiction between France and the colonies in the name of securing "order" (a code word for slavery).

But the colons and the Club Massaic were not the only groups with inflexible attitudes, for as free landowners, most gens de couleur were, likewise, interested only in limited modification to the law, not revolution.[63] As Cooper emphasized, many saw themselves primarily as "colonists of color," with little connection between their cause and the lives of free blacks or slaves.[64] Though later the gens de couleur and noirs would ally to overthrow the French state, for a long time the gens de couleur were uninterested in abolition or in altering the economy from which they profited. Cooper was especially critical of the well-known planter of color, Julien Raimond, who made his fortune in indigo and who "never ceased to urge his brothers to endure everything in order to preserve tranquility in the colony and to allow the whites all that they wished."[65] Later, Raimond's resolute proslavery attitude would prompt Toussaint Louverture to oust him from Saint-Domingue for a time. Louverture sent Raimond to France, she argued, because "he was guilty of . . . never having favored freeing the slaves, and of always having separated the question of slavery from that of political liberty of men of color." Cooper further castigated Raimond, emphasizing how he had "carried this separation to the point of . . . [bragging] that his fortune, that of his family, and that of all the colony as well, were based on slavery." Cooper also exposed General André Rigaud's prejudice, for example, in choosing to take his "'elite corps' of mulattoes . . . to Cuba rather than surrender to a black" (i.e., Louverture).[66]

By focusing on Raimond's and Rigaud's colonized imaginations, Cooper pointed to a more systemic problem. A supremacist way of thinking, going back to the Spanish-Portuguese conquests with which she opened her study, was so deeply entrenched in the colonies that it molded the perceptions of the colons, the petits blancs, and the gens de couleur: few could see beyond it. As she explained, "color prejudices . . . had grown so deep that they were even stronger than all the other social distinctions made between the free man and the slave since ancient times, to the point where a mulatto slave would have refused to obey a free Black, even if the latter had the audacity to buy him."[67]

In addition, Cooper pinpointed how, in France, the more politically radical Amis des Noirs, or Friends of the Blacks, advocated gradualist abolition but not full citizenship. For instance, their main goal was to ready public opinion for the *idea* of emancipation in the abstract: they had no concrete action in mind.[68] Here, Cooper identified an undercurrent of similarity between supposed political enemies. In different ways, both the elite, procolonialism, proslavery Club Massaic and the Amis des Noirs denied slaves' humanity, for even the Friends of the Blacks insisted on an essential distinction between "natural rights" and a guarantee of political rights, a division Cooper did not accept. Of course, as Laurent Dubois illustrates, many Enlightenment thinkers "were not particularly antiracist and certainly not anticolonial. Enlightenment critiques of slavery attacked the institution as [only] a violation of the natural rights that all human beings shared."[69] Since many of the Friends of the Blacks who supported eventual abolition still believed in a hierarchical scale of humanity, they divorced the protection of natural rights from any guaranty of (or capacity for) the full political rights of citizenship ("*droits de cité*").

Cooper undermined these troubling distinctions through her intersectional approach. She revealed that to comprehend the political forces at work, questions of class interests and racial domination could be neither collapsed nor fully separated. Otherwise, the class interests of the gens de couleur, in which they sought their own rights but wanted to maintain slavery and keep their plantations profitable, would be obscured. Additionally, France's "excessive and mistaken patriotism" equating profit with the democratic good, or collapsing whiteness with national identity, would fade into the background.[70] This willful ignorance and widespread acceptance of human exploitation that Cooper so meticulously documented would not be captured by an analysis focusing on one system of domination in isolation.

By shifting the genealogy of republican ideas and politics, Cooper illustrated that without an adequate history of slavery and colonialism, our understanding of the culture of citizenship developed during the age of revolution remains incomplete. She countered what Sybille Fischer has recently characterized as an entrenched "Eurocentric bias against considering issues of colonialism and slavery relevant to the high history of the metropolis."[71] Cooper's transatlantic repositioning and intersectional analysis exposed bias within ostensibly universal philosophical principles and broke open silences within normative historical frameworks. She thereby stretched the parameters of what counts as historically significant, rejected an internalist historical and political framework in favor of an Atlantic model of analysis, and advocated an intersectional approach to race and class exploitation.

Unfortunately, the fact, much less the content and meaning, of Cooper's Sorbonne dissertation is mostly forgotten. Like the many examples of agency and resistance Cooper uncovered in the military and parliamentary archives—historical fragments that were always there but were unseen or, if noted, discounted as irrelevant—Cooper's dissertation has been before us but remains generally unread. Even in the newly emergent area of black European studies, in the further development of black Atlantic studies, or in the resurgence of work on the Haitian Revolution, Cooper's thesis has barely been acknowledged. The same holds true in historical approaches to feminist thought and in current developments in women's studies, even as intersectionality and transnationalism increasingly shape the field.[72]

Paradoxically, then, questions of voice and of silence—of lifting one's voice and seeking a hearing, as well as the issue of not being heard, of having no rhetorical space into which to speak—are themes that not only shape Cooper's two major works but also continue to impact the reception, interpretation, and dissemination of her work. Today, too much of Cooper's work remains unknown or is read in bits and fragments out of context.[73] Without attending to her larger oeuvre and by focusing mostly on excerpts of her writings in isolation, we not only miss out on Cooper's larger vision but also stifle a longer history of intersectional, radical feminist thought. This is untenable, both intellectually

and politically: a longer and more complex genealogy of intersectional feminist thought and analysis must be delineated, documented, and analyzed.

The politics of voice, silence, and reception that Cooper navigated in her
time (and that continue to impact much of what is—or is not—known about
Cooper's work today) are of course not unique to Cooper. Even as intersectionality has been developed in part as a way to address what Carole Boyce
Davies has described as "that condition of 'unheardness' to which dominant
discourses . . . relegate a range of voices," theorists of intersectionality, past and
present, are too often themselves relegated to the margins or silenced.[74] The
issue of being silenced or repeatedly misunderstood remains an ongoing issue
for scholars of intersectionality.

Intersectionality's "Unheardness," Past and Present

Although black feminist theorists have repeatedly pointed to the longevity
of intersectional approaches to more adequately conceptualize the meaning
of identity and lived experience and to envision a wider view of liberation
politics, the question remains: have they been heard? This, of course, is the
question embedded within Audre Lorde's observation more than twenty-five
years ago, when she stated, "We find ourselves having to repeat and relearn
the same old lessons over and over. . . . For instance, how many times has this
all been said before?"[75] Unfortunately, the ability to engage with a longer
view of multiracial feminist theorizing and intellectual history is often stymied because our prevailing conceptual models of feminism and of theory
remain both constrained and inflexible. Paradoxically, intersectionality cir-
culates within a kind of intellectual and political vortex, and its impact is
often delimited or constrained by the very within-group power asymmetries
and multiple vectors of privilege and oppression it seeks to make visible and
address. I point to this contemporary conundrum regarding intersectionality's reception and application because Cooper negotiated similar vortexes
in her own time, and they impacted both the shape and the reception of her
work to a great extent.

Intersectionality's historical recursiveness should therefore not be seen
as *mere* repetition. Rather, the chronic need to reiterate ideas essential
to what would now be called *intersectionality* underscores how it entails a
major transformation in thinking—one that remains partial and ongoing.
Moreover, while useful for naming differences that have been subsumed
or ignored, it is not merely the descriptive for which intersectionality was
developed. Yet intersectionality is still often treated as if it were just a demographic instrument or descriptive tool, reducing it in scope and role by
instrumentalizing it.[76] Intersectionality is also made to seem as if it lies outside the terrain of theory "proper," though multiracial feminists have long

maintained its capacity to explain social reality, analyze data and social systems, and theorize change.[77]

At the risk of being read as perhaps presentist or even as hagiographic in my approach to the work of Anna Julia Cooper, and despite what incomplete mappings of feminist theorizing might suggest, I contend, like others before me, that Cooper's scholarship amply illustrates that intersectionality can be understood to be a long-standing mode of analysis: its genesis cannot be adequately understood if one attends only to theoretical and political debates from the late twentieth century. Cooper developed an intersectional framework as a means of writing against the erasure of gender, race, and capital in the cultural imaginary at large (e.g., in literature, philosophy, school curricula, theology, popular culture, and liberation politics) as well as in historical analyses (e.g., in accounts of major civil rights decisions, conventional approaches to the Haitian Revolution, and studies of the historical meanings of race, gender, and class). She exposed the workings of power within history and sought to shift the focus of our historical understandings and analyses toward the margins.

At the same time, she utilized intersectionality to point to circumstances and events that she and her contemporaries found to be beyond utterance, such as black women's lived experiences of sexual violence and physical trauma that could not be adequately represented or understood through language itself—or what Cooper characterized as the "Black Woman's . . . unnamable burden inside."[78] Cooper also identified other forms of the unsaid, including gaps in archival materials, bias and prejudice (e.g., racism or sexism) shaping the scholarly record, and the absence of black women in scholarly studies across a range of disciplines in any guise other than as ubiquitous stereotypes or as targets of remediation or cure.

The fact that the many contributions to intersectionality by earlier black feminist scholars such as Cooper remain comparatively invisible is troubling on its own, but it also points to a larger issue of undertheorization.[79] Certainly, excerpts of her work are occasionally referenced, yet the level of intellectual engagement with Cooper remains fairly nominal in nature. Paradoxically, the substance of her intellectual, activist, and educational contributions continues to be relatively overlooked, even as she was celebrated with a first-class US Black Heritage postage stamp in 2009 and even as a Cooper quotation about multifaceted justice and liberation now appears in the pages of the US passport. While I am certainly pleased to have Cooper's words and life celebrated publicly and memorialized in national documents, I remain wary, since a double tactic of honoring and commemoration on the one hand, and a narrow historical view of theory combined with subtle philosophical exclusion or marginalization on the other, constitutes a complex form of tokenism that should not be underestimated.[80]

In laying out how many of Cooper's methods remain relevant to contemporary feminist scholarship, I do not want to suggest that Cooper's theorizing should be embraced without question: there are indeed aspects of her work I find troubling (e.g., her reliance on a Christian theological framework and her ethnocentric references to Muslims or to women in China), but I do not think that these errors in judgment and analysis on her part totally undermine her analysis. Other facets of her work are, as expected, somewhat dated (e.g., much of the scientific data or theories she draws on or her nearly total silence on questions of embodiment, sexual agency, and more). In other words, I find such philosophical and political tensions in Cooper's work to be both natural (i.e., they are to be critiqued yet do not ruin her overall vision) and also fruitful, in part because they remind us in the contemporary period how much we are shaped by our times and our circumstances, even as we work to transform and radically modify the world in which we live and work.

Since intersectionality as theory and method invites us to "come to terms with the legacy of exclusions of multiply marginalized subjects from feminist and anti-racist work, and the impact of those absences on both theory and practice," attention to these legacies of exclusion must also focus on Anna Julia Cooper's larger body of work, including *A Voice from the South* and her dissertation.[81] In other words, even as we may find questionable some of Cooper's analyses, we must also work to acknowledge how Cooper employed and developed innovative methods and analyses as a means to explore the politics of the unimaginable, the invisible, and the silenced. No longer should her contributions to the theoretical and methodological innovations that intersectionality provides us today be dismissed or overlooked.

Notes

1. Chela Sandoval, "U.S. Third-World Feminism: The Theory and Method of Oppositional Consciousness in the Postmodern World," in *Feminist Postcolonial Theory: A Reader*, ed. Reina Lewis and Sara Mills (New York: Routledge, 2003), 88; Kimberlé Crenshaw, "Demarginalizing the Intersection of Race and Sex: A Black Feminist Critique of Antidiscrimination Doctrine, Feminist Theory, and Antiracist Politics," in *The Black Feminist Reader*, ed. Joy James and T. Denean Sharpley-Whiting (Malden, MA: Blackwell, 2000). In "Demarginalizing the Intersection" Crenshaw demonstrates how, because the US courts cannot engage with both/and logic when it comes to civil rights claims (e.g., 216), the notion that black women as litigants seeking recognition by the courts are *both* "unique" *and* "central"—that is, the same as *and* different from white women and black men when it comes to group claims, rights, and redress—lies outside the realm of the possible in the law's single-axis, either-or imagination (217). Reflecting on these constraints, Crenshaw writes, "Perhaps it appears to some that I have offered inconsistent criticisms of how Black women are treated in antidiscrimination law. . . . It seems that I have to say that Black women are the same [as white women or black men] and harmed by being treated differently or that they are different and harmed by being treated the same. But I cannot say both" (216). Yet she can and does say both—and asserts the logic

of her both/and analysis, but the question she raises repeatedly is, in many ways, this one: can her statements and those of other black women in the justice system be heard? Refusing the charge that her analysis lacks reason and merit, Crenshaw identifies the court's either-or "single-axis" logic as sorely lacking rather than her own (209). She concludes, "This apparent contradiction is but another manifestation of the conceptual limitations of the single-axis analysis that intersectionality challenges" (216).

2. Stephanie Shields, "Gender: An Intersectionality Perspective," *Sex Roles* 59, nos. 5–6 (2008): 305.

3. For instance, Kathy Davis asserts, "At this particular juncture in gender studies, any scholar who neglects difference runs the risk of having her work viewed as theoretically misguided, politically irrelevant, or simply fantastical." See "Intersectionality as Buzzword," *Feminist Theory* 9, no. 1 (2008): 68.

4. If space allowed, numerous important anthologies could be discussed in more detail, including Cherríe Moraga and Gloria Anzaldúa, eds., *This Bridge Called My Back* (New York: Kitchen Table, 1983); Chandra Talpade Mohanty, Ann Russo, and Lourdes Torres, *Third World Women and the Politics of Feminism* (Bloomington: Indiana University Press, 1991); Gloria Anzaldúa, ed., *Making Face, Making Soul / Haciendo caras* (San Francisco: Aunt Lute Books, 1990); Gloria Hull, Patricia Bell Scott, and Barbara Smith, eds., *All the Women Are White, All the Blacks Are Men, But Some of Us Are Brave: Black Women's Studies* (Old Westbury, NY: Feminist Press, 1982); and Toni Cade [Bambara], ed., *The Black Woman* (New York: Mentor, 1970).

5. Crenshaw, "Demarginalizing the Intersection," 220–24.

6. For more on the problem with the wave temporal framework to periodize US feminism, see, for example, Chela Sandoval, *Methodology of the Oppressed* (Minneapolis: University of Minnesota Press, 2000), 47–53; and Benita Roth, "Race, Class and the Emergence of Black Feminism in the 1960s and 1970s," *Womanist Theory and Research* 3, no. 1 (1999), http://www.uga.edu/womanist/roth3.1.htm.

7. Beverly Guy-Sheftall, *Words of Fire: An Anthology of African-American Feminist Thought* (New York: New Press, 1995).

8. Pauli Murray, "The Liberation of Black Women," in Guy-Sheftall, *Words of Fire*, 197.

9. For more information about Cooper's life work as an educator, intellectual, and activist and for a discussion of the potential limits of a biographical focus, see Vivian M. May, *Anna Julia Cooper, Visionary Black Feminist: A Critical Introduction* (New York: Routledge, 2007), esp. the intro. (1–12) and ch. 1 (13–43); and Louise Daniel Hutchinson, *Anna J. Cooper: A Voice from the South* (Washington, DC: Smithsonian, 1981).

10. The other speaker was Cooper's longtime friend, the black feminist activist and educator Anna H. Jones of Kansas City, Missouri. For more information on Cooper's talk at the Pan-African Congress, see Hutchinson, *Anna J. Cooper*, 110–11.

11. Mary Helen Washington, introduction to *A Voice from the South by a Black Woman of the South*, by Anna Julia Cooper (1892; repr., New York: Oxford University Press, 1988), xxvii.

12. Klein had first encountered Cooper on his 1903 tour of American and Canadian schools and religious institutions. Klein spontaneously visited the M Street School, where Cooper was serving as principal at the time, and observed her teaching Latin. Klein described Cooper as one of the most exemplary educators he

encountered in all his travels, a statement that did not help her in the public battle with the school board over curriculum. For more details, see Hutchinson, *Anna J. Cooper*, 58–60; May, *Visionary Black Feminist*, 26; and Karen Baker-Fletcher, 'A *Singing Something': Womanist Reflections on Anna Julia Cooper* (New York: Crossroads, 1994), 53–54.

13. The Sorbonne required an entirely new committee-approved research topic: the translation of *Le pèlerinage* counted toward general degree credits, not her thesis. Anna Julia Cooper, *Le pèlerinage de Charlemagne* (Paris: Lahure, 1925). Katherine Shilton documents that Cooper could not secure distribution for the volume in the United States, even from Oberlin College, her alma mater, due to increasing racist and sexist backlash in the 1920s. "'This Scholarly and Colored Alumna': Anna Julia Cooper's Troubled Relationship with Oberlin College," History 322, Spring 2003, Oberlin College, accessed February 1, 2012, http://www.oberlin.edu/external/EOG/History322/AnnaJuliaCooper/AnnaJuliaCooper.htm.

14. Frelinghuysen was akin to a community college today, with night classes and satellite classrooms—some eventually held in Cooper's own T Street home, also the location of the registrar's office and a small library for student use.

15. Cooper was close friends with Charlotte Forten Grimké and the Reverend Francis Grimké, who gave Cooper Charlotte's papers and journals after Charlotte had passed away. Sydney Kaplan, introduction to *From Slavery to the Sorbonne and Beyond: The Life and Writings of Anna J. Cooper*, by Leona C. Gabel (Northampton, MA: Smith College Department of History, 1982), xi–xii.

16. I would argue that intersectionality also informed Cooper's work as an educator, principal, and college president, as well as her community activism and service. But I shall limit my discussion here to some examples from her scholarship.

17. Anna Julia Cooper, *A Voice from the South by a Black Woman of the South* (1892; repr., New York: Oxford University Press, 1988), 129, 48–49, 140–42.

18. Cooper's earlier work was also transnational in nature, as illustrated by her advocacy work on the organizing committee for the Pan-African Congress (e.g., they petitioned Britain to divest of colonial rule). In addition, in *A Voice from the South*, Cooper references other cultural and theological practices vis à vis women as instances of both systematized sexism and misogyny (though these analyses can be quite ethnocentric). Thus Cooper's overall emphasis gradually shifts from thinking about inequality primarily within a national frame (and among or between women as a group) to a more comparative frame that can be seen as a precursor to a black Atlantic or black European studies framework.

19. For more about Cooper's philosophical contributions, see Vivian M. May, "Anna Julia Cooper's Philosophy of Resistance: 'What Is Needed, Perhaps, to Reverse the Picture of the Lordly Man Slaying the Lion, Is for the Lion to Turn Painter,'" *Philosophia Africana* 12, no. 1 (2009): 41–66. See also Vivian M. May, "Thinking from the Margins, Acting at the Intersections: Anna Julia Cooper's *A Voice from the South*," *Hypatia* 19, no. 2 (2004): 74–91.

20. Cooper's dissertation is important to bring into the conversation in that she builds on and uses intersectional frames and methods developed in her earlier work, though differently. Moreover, her approach to history in her Sorbonne thesis bridges a twentieth-century analysis of the revolutionary era, which anticipates works such as C. L. R. James's 1938 *The Black Jacobins: Toussaint L'Ouverture*

and the San Domingo Revolution (New York: Vintage, 1989) with what John Ernest has characterized as African American historians' earlier method of "liberation historiography" (blending liberation theology with a black liberation historiographical approach). See John Ernest, *Liberation Historiography: African American Writers and the Challenge of History, 1794–1861* (Chapel Hill: University of North Carolina Press, 2004).

21. Cooper, *Voice* (hereafter cited in text).

22. In many ways, therefore, Cooper's approach anticipates what would later be named standpoint theory or standpoint epistemology, which emphasizes that all knowers are located (and thus critiques a "god's-eye" notion of disembodied objectivity); examines the impact of power structures on knowledge practices; draws on lived experience as an analytic resource; underscores that marginalization and subjugation can offer important epistemic insights; and highlights how normative models of reasoning, including dominant practices of knowledge production and justification, systemically disadvantage, silence, and objectify marginalized groups. But many strands of standpoint theory often draw on *one* structure of identity or social location as primary when thinking through the politics of situated knowledge/located knowers (e.g., social class as primary for materialist or Marxist standpoint; gender as central to feminist standpoint; blackness or race as primary for developing an Afrocentric standpoint, etc.). This single-axis approach to standpoint falsely universalizes group identity to make knowledge claims and critiques. In contrast, Cooper employs a more matric approach to social location (drawing upon the *interacting* forces of race, gender, and region, for instance) to develop and build her analyses. For more background on standpoint theory, see Patricia Hill Collins, *Black Feminist Thought: Knowledge, Consciousness, and the Politics of Empowerment* (London: Unwin Hyman, 1990); Sandra Harding, *The Feminist Standpoint Theory Reader: Intellectual and Political Controversies* (London: Routledge, 2004); and Nancy Hartsock, *The Feminist Standpoint Revisited and Other Essays* (Boulder, CO: Westview, 1998).

23. See Anna Julia Cooper, "Angry Saxons and Negro Education," *Crisis*, May 1938, 148.

24. Patricia Hill Collins, *Fighting Words: Black Women and the Search for Justice* (Minneapolis: University of Minnesota Press, 1998), 128.

25. Anna Julia Cooper, "The Ethics of the Negro Question," in *The Voice of Anna Julia Cooper*, ed. Charles Lemert and Esme Bhan (Lanham, MD: Rowman and Littlefield, 1998), 214.

26. Ibid., 206–7. Note that Cooper references, with some irony, Lincoln's 1863 Gettysburg Address to make her point.

27. To clarify, I use the term "liberation" here and elsewhere because the late nineteenth-century and early twentieth-century women's rights and civil rights movements, as Cooper and other black women saw them, were too narrow—focused not only on false notions of race and of womanhood but also on separable notions of rights. The concept of liberation that is cross-cutting and not demarcated by one identity or one set of rights more fully captures the intersectional vision of freedom and rights that Cooper advocated.

28. Anna Julia Cooper, "The Intellectual Progress of the Colored Women in the United States since the Emancipation Proclamation: A Response to Fannie Barrier

Williams," Cooper's 1893 speech at the Chicago World's Fair, in Lemert and Bhan, *Voice*, 205.

29. Hazel V. Carby, *Reconstructing Womanhood: The Emergence of the Afro-American Woman Novelist* (Oxford: Oxford University Press, 1987), 102.

30. In "Demarginalizing the Intersection" Crenshaw explains how "dominant conceptions of discrimination condition us to think about subordination as disadvantage occurring along a single categorical axis": this "limit[s] inquiry to the experiences of otherwise-privileged members of the group" and "marginalizes those who are multiply-burdened and obscures claims that cannot be understood as resulting from discrete sources of discrimination" (208–9).

31. Livermore was an abolitionist, journalist, and leader in the suffrage and temperance movements.

32. In many ways, Cooper's "Eye vs. Foot" analysis anticipates later articulations of this same issue by Audre Lorde and Barbara Smith, for example. In *Sister Outsider: Essays and Speeches* (Freedom, CA: Crossing, 1984), Lorde queries, "Can any one here still afford to believe that the pursuit of liberation can be the sole and particular province of any one particular race, or sex, or age, or religion, or sexuality, or class?" (140). Likewise, in her introduction to *Home Girls: A Black Feminist Anthology*, ed. Barbara Smith (New York: Kitchen Table, 1983), Barbara Smith underscores a "multi-issue approach to politics . . . [and] institutionalized oppression" in her delineation of black feminist thought, which "has no use for ranking oppressions" (xxxii, xxviii).

33. See Alexander Crummell, "The Black Woman of the South: Her Neglects and Her Needs," in *Traps: African American Men on Gender and Sexuality*, ed. Rudolph P. Byrd and Beverly Guy-Sheftall (Bloomington: Indiana University Press, 2001), 46–57.

34. See Shilton, "Scholarly and Colored Alumna."

35. Frances Richardson Keller recently published a second edition of her translation into English of Cooper's thesis titled *Slavery and the French and Haitian Revolutionists* (Lanham, MD: Rowman and Littlefield, 2006). Note there are very few remaining copies of Cooper's doctoral thesis in French (Anna Julia Cooper, *L'attitude de la France à l'égard de l'esclavage pendant la Révolution* (Paris: Maretheux, 1925). When citing Cooper's thesis in French, I refer to it as "*L'attitude*"; when citing Keller's translation, I refer to it as "*Slavery*." When citing Cooper in English, the references to *Slavery* are Keller's translations, whereas the references to *L'attitude* in English are my own translations. I have previously and in more detail argued that her dissertation deserves more attention; see chapter 4 of May, *Visionary Black Feminist*, 107–39; and also my article, "'It Is Never a Question of the Slaves': Anna Julia Cooper's Challenge to History's Silences in Her 1925 Sorbonne Thesis," *Callaloo* 31, no. 1 (2008): 903–18.

36. The occupation was fueled by the US desire to control Haiti's customs house and banks and to alter the law (so whites and foreigners could own property there, which was outlawed in Haiti's 1804 constitution). For a contemporary of Cooper's view on the subject, see James Weldon Johnson's "Self-Determining Haiti: The American Occupation," *Nation*, August 28, 1920.

37. Keller, "The Perspective of a Black American on Slavery and the French Revolution: Anna Julia Cooper," in Keller, *Slavery*, 20.

38. Cooper, *L'attitude*, 23.

39. Du Bois's play is not available in print, but it was performed first in New York at the Lafayette Theatre, and then in Boston at the Copley Theatre in 1938 as part of the WPA Federal Theatre Project.

40. Laurent Dubois, *A Colony of Citizens: Revolution and Slave Emancipation in the French Caribbean, 1787–1804* (Chapel Hill, University of North Carolina Press, 2004), 6.

41. Cooper, *L'attitude*, 18.

42. Here, in Cooper's reference to the divine, we can see how she drew on an earlier mode of interpretive thought—a "liberation historiography" tradition in African American thought, as John Ernest defines it (though his study does not address Cooper's work given that his time frame is 1794–1861), even as she simultaneously spoke to contemporary sociological and historical literatures of the period. See Ernest, *Liberation Historiography*.

43. Cooper, *L'attitude*, 22–23 ("*ils n'allaient pas manquer d'être un élément actif d'insurrection*"), 104, 72, 82. Cooper also references successful revolts organized by maroon leader François Makandal ("Macaudal"), whom the French burned at the stake in 1758 (61n1).

44. For example, studies usually open with the more immediate time frame of the revolution and focus primarily on contexts within France. Thus, they begin with a discussion of public outcry in France against the king, the nobility, and the bourgeoisie; move to discussing the 1789 storming of the Bastille, the elimination of feudalism, and the rise of secularism; and then focus on the writing of a constitution, the fall of the monarchy, and the creation of an elected, national legislature. Cooper, *L'attitude* 8–9.

45. Ibid., 7 ("*sans prétexte comme sans excuse, et seulement au nom du droit du plus puissant*"), 9, 20–22, 25.

46. Cooper, *Slavery*, 70.

47. Michel-Rolph Trouillot, *Silencing the Past: Power and the Production of History* (Boston: Beacon), 78.

48. Cooper *L'attitude*, 60.

49. See, for example, Cooper, *Slavery*, 86.

50. Ibid., 35.

51. Cooper *L'attitude*, 14.

52. Cooper, *Slavery*, 37, 66.

53. Cooper, *L'attitude*, 19. The active role one plays in ignorance is emphasized more in the French with the reflexive verb *se refuser*: "*se refusaient à faire face aux réalités*" (23).

54. Cooper, *Slavery*, 57.

55. Cooper, *L'attitude*, 23 ("*au travail qui ne fructifiait que pour autrui*").

56. Joan Dayan, "Codes of Law and Bodies of Color," *New Literary History* 26, no. 2 (1995): 283–308, quote on 297.

57. John D. Garrigus, "Blue and Brown: Contraband Indigo and the Rise of a Free Colored Planter Class in French Saint-Domingue," *Americas* 50, no. 10 (1993): 233–63, quote on 233.

58. Cooper, *Slavery*, 91–92, 43.

59. Charles W. Mills, *The Racial Contract* (Ithaca, NY: Cornell University Press, 1997), 74, 122.

60. Dubois, *Colony of Citizens*, 172.

61. Cooper, "Ethics," 210.

62. Cooper, *Slavery*, 77, 80.

63. Founded in 1789 by white planters from Saint-Domingue in alliance with French politicians sympathetic to the colonists' rights (over universal rights), the proslavery group Club Massaic was formed while the French National Assembly was discussing the wording of the declaration of the rights of man. They feared that if propertied men of color were given the rights of citizenship and equality with whites, the property rights of slave owners would be eroded. In contrast, the Société des Amis des Noirs, founded the year prior, in 1788, advocated the (eventual) eradication of slavery in the colonies, as it was already outlawed in France. The Société published abolitionist literature and addressed the National Assembly about the need to end slavery. In her dissertation, however, Cooper pinpoints an underlying adherence to racial hierarchy within the Amis des Noirs's philosophical and political premises.

64. Cooper, *Slavery*, 79, 64.

65. Cooper, *L'attitude*, 106. Raimond, a free man of color and outspoken planter on Saint-Domingue, was part of a coalition of gens de couleur who addressed the French Assembly and sought the rights of citizenship for propertied men of color. He worked closely with the Friends of the Blacks and published many political pamphlets. Although abolition was not on his agenda at first, over time, he came to advocate gradualist abolition. Raimond later returned to Saint-Domingue and allied with Toussaint Louverture. Nevertheless, Cooper condemned his early short-sightedness.

66. Cooper, *Slavery*, 64, 105, 106.

67. Ibid., 114.

68. Ibid., 78, and Cooper, *L'attitude*, 113, 58.

69. Laurent Dubois, *Avengers of the New World: The Story of the Haitian Revolution* (Cambridge, MA: Harvard University Press, 2004), 58.

70. Cooper, *Slavery*, 35.

71. Sybille Fischer, *Modernity Disavowed: Haiti and the Cultures of Slavery in the Age of Revolution* (Durham, NC: Duke University Press, 2004), 215.

72. In addition to Keller's work on Cooper's dissertation, some examples of scholarship engaged with the dissertation include Errol Tsekani Browne, *Anna Julia Cooper and Black Women's Intellectual Tradition: Race, Gender and Nation in the Making of a Modern Race Woman, 1892–1925* (PhD diss., UCLA: 2008); Donna Hunter, "Historically Particular Uses of a Universal Subject," in *French Civilization and Its Discontents: Nationalism, Colonialism, Race*, ed. Tyler Edward Stovall and Georges Van den Abbeele (Lanham, MD: Lexington Books, 2003), 129–46; David W. H. Pellow, "Anna J. Cooper: The International Dimensions," in *Recovered Writers/Recovered Texts: Race, Class, and Gender in Black Women's Literature*, ed. Dolan Hubbard (Knoxville: University of Tennessee Press, 1997), 60–67; Stephanie Y. Evans, "African American Women Scholars and International Research: Dr. Anna Julia Cooper's Legacy of Study Abroad," *Frontiers* 18 (2009): 77–100. While he does not directly analyze her dissertation, Brent Hayes Edwards points to Cooper's influence on the Nardal sisters in Paris, especially Paulette, in his chapter, "Feminism and l'internationalisme noire: Paulette Nardal," in *The Practice of Diaspora: Literature, Translation, and the Rise of Black Internationalism* (Cambridge, MA: Harvard University Press, 2003), 119–86.

73. It is mostly chapters from *A Voice from the South* that are excerpted, taught, or referenced, particularly from the first half of the book; the later chapters focusing on ideologies of race and gender in the cultural imagination or on the structural ways in which inequality are reinforced are not referenced as often. Sadly, the layering of argument about the connections between race and gender, self and society, social location and structures of power—all of which emerge by reading *A Voice from the South* as a whole—gets lost. Cooper's later writings and speeches are usually ignored altogether—or referenced in passing but not meaningfully engaged.

74. Carole Boyce Davies, *Black Women, Writing, and Identity: Migrations of the Subject* (New York: Routledge, 1994), 108.

75. Lorde, *Sister Outsider*, 117.

76. Lisa Bowleg, "When Black + Lesbian + Woman ≠ Black Lesbian Woman: The Methodological Challenges of Qualitative and Quantitative Intersectionalty Research," *Sex Roles* 59 nos. 5–6 (2008): 316, 323; Catherine Harnois, "Different Paths to Different Feminisms? Bridging Multiracial Feminist Theory and Quantitative Sociological Gender Research," *Gender and Society* 19, no. 6 (2005): 813. See also Ange-Marie Hancock, "When Multiplication Doesn't Equal Quick Addition: Examining Intersectionality as a Research Paradigm," *Perspectives on Politics* 5 no. 1 (2007): 66; and Julia Jordan-Zachery, "Am I a Black Woman or a Woman Who Is Black? A Few Thoughts on the Meaning of Intersectionality," *Politics and Gender* 3, no. 2 (2007): 261.

77. Maxine Baca Zinn and Bonnie Thornton Dill, "Theorizing Difference from Multiracial Feminism," *Feminist Studies* 22, no. 2 (1996): 329.

78. Cooper, *Voice*, 90.

79. For more on the concept of undertheorization, see Barbara Christian, "The Race for Theory," in Anzaldúa, *Making Face*, 335–45. See also Linda Martín Alcoff's essay about the work of Gloria Anzaldúa, "The Unassimilated Theorist," *PMLA* 121, no. 1 (2006): 255–59.

80. For full disclosure, I served as an academic consultant to the United States Postal Service for the 2009 Anna Julia Cooper Black Heritage Stamp collectors materials and authored the brief bio that appears on the back of the stamp as well as the longer bio that appears in other materials and releases.

81. Jennifer Nash, "Re-Thinking Intersectionality," *Feminist Review* 89, no. 1 (2008): 3.

Part 2

Frontiers of Citizenship

Chapter 2

"Laissez les bons temps rouler!" and Other Concealments

Households, Taverns, and Irregular Intimacies in Antebellum New Orleans

Rashauna Johnson

This essay uses a deceptively discrete category—"women of African descent in antebellum New Orleans"—to highlight the instabilities within all social categories, even those premised on unities of time and space, gender and race. Unfortunately, sociocultural histories of the antebellum South devote precious little attention to women of African descent, let alone to the diverse, multidimensional modes of hierarchy that subdivided them. This essay writes into that silence by using one free woman of color's household and neigh-borhood as a microcosm in which frontier Louisiana's hierarchies of race and gender conspired with cleavages of class and status to produce vastly different life experiences for women of African descent. This microlevel analysis ultimately illustrates the workings of social hierarchy in daily life, the domesticity and intimacy of power, and the modalities of inequality within perceived "good times."[1]

Meet Melanie Drouet, free woman of color, unmarried mother of two, and owner of a colorful Faubourg Marigny household. This freewheeling former plantation took its name from Bernard Marigny, the neighborhood's one-time owner whose claim to fame, aside from his enormous fortune, was his equally sizable affinity for gambling. Though contemporaries thought the new neighborhood an atypical and open space on an urban frontier, it nonetheless operated on the bedrock of structural inequality, including—but not limited to—chattel slavery. Rather than view inequality within perceived permissiveness as a contradiction, this work centers the codependence between the selective flouting of some social and economic norms—taboos about visible interracial sex, disproportionate property ownership by free women of color, for example—within a scene defined by human bondage, the elevation of phenotype to juridical status, and the sexual availability of the relatively less privileged. Such sites of social promiscuity in antebellum New Orleans anticipated the twentieth-century "interzones" of Greenwich Village, Harlem, and Chicago, spaces that fostered interracial socializing while replicating the hazards of hierarchy and the privilege of dominant society.[2]

The power disparities underlying *les bons temps*—the good times—in antebellum New Orleans are most fascinating in the realms of domesticity and amusement, the Marigny's dual raisons d'etre. The Marigny's households, for example, were rarely nuclear, though some hewed to this convention. By and large, these domiciles were multiracial and crossed all manner of social borders, sheltering people of European descent, free men and women of color, freed men and women, and enslaved persons, all of varying social, national, and linguistic backgrounds. Heads of household came in all varieties, but free women of color owned a striking number of properties, the result of shrewd business acumen, concubinal *plaçage* partnerships with men of means, or some combination of the two. In this history of a single household that contained multiple color lines, we explore the gender, race, and status cleavages that defined not only a single household but also the neighborhood within which it existed.[3] This essay consists of two sections, the first of which enters Melanie Drouet's household and examines the melee that erupted there in 1822. That fracas revealed the opportunities and contradictions of gender, race, class, status, and family within a single household, the varying dreams that antebellum New Orleans made possible depending on race and gender, and finally the reaches and limits of juridical power in daily life. The second section moves from Drouet's household to the illegal amusements headquartered in nearby taverns and pubs. Despite the outcry over the heterogeneous crowds that illegally congregated in tippling houses to drink, gamble, and barter, people from all backgrounds nonetheless patronized these establishments and participated in the vibrant culture—even enslaved persons who were legally prohibited from joining the fun. In this doppelganger of dominant society, alternative communities became possible, yet privilege and risk defined every social interaction. This section explores the possibilities and risks of the servile and sexual labor that defined this realm, ultimately revealing the risks and relational requirements embedded in its hierarchies.[4]

The 1822 scuffle at Melanie Drouet's home occurred after a decade of great personal and financial transition. Sacramental records of Saint Louis Church document at least two sets of Drouets: the Euro-American Drouet-Senet-Chenault clan and free women of color, whose relationship to one another and the white Drouets remains unclear.[5] Though they had different national backgrounds, the free women of color with the surname Drouet had much in common, including so-called single motherhood. In 1810, the year Melanie Drouet gave birth to a son, Gustave Frederic Drouet, the federal census listed "Melanie Duret" as head of a household of four free persons of color in Faubourg Marigny (their names and ages are not listed, but they could quite possibly have been her other children). The following year she gave birth to another son, Joseph Harman Drouet.[6] Likewise, on October 17, 1809, free woman of color Rosa Drouet "of Jacqmel on the island of Santo Domingo" gave birth to a son, Santyago, in New Orleans. In 1800 Marie-Claire Drouet, another free woman of color and a native of Cap Républicain (Cap Français), migrated to Louisiana before having a child whose father is also unlisted.[7] Likewise, Clarissa Drouet bore twins, Maria Adelaida and Maria Julia Honorata. Their father's name is not listed, and there is no indication of Clarissa's national background.[8]

The ambiguousness of these children's paternity was no accident; instead, it resulted from the hierarchies of gender that made sexuality a fraught arena for women of African descent, whether slave or free, across the antebellum South. Harriet Jacobs mused on this asymmetry in describing an unfortunate bondwoman who suffered blows from her mistress for daring to articulate an enslaved baby's paternity: "She had forgotten that it was a crime for a slave to tell who the father of her child was."[9] *Partus sequitur ventrum*, the legal doctrine by which the status of the child followed from that of the mother, ensured that, among other things, all enslaved women gave birth to enslaved children. Likewise, many free women of color stood alone before the representatives of the church with their newborns. By contrast, prominent families, most of them of Euro-American ancestry, enjoyed the privilege of linear and documented genealogy. Napoleon Druilhet is one example of many. At his January 28, 1810, baptism at the Saint Louis Church, the priest recorded not only his parents' names (Hanrrietta Perenau Druilhet, of Jacmel, Haiti, and Jean Druilhet, St. Joseph Parish, Saint-Domingue) but also the names of his maternal and paternal grandparents. Even a hasty escape from the Haitian Revolution did not destroy this child's recorded genealogy. Not so for people of African descent. Chattel slavery and plaçage, prostitution and disfranchisement, ensured the erasure of their paternity.[10]

Melanie Drouet's status as head of household, then, was not at all unique in the Faubourg Marigny, a neighborhood where many unmarried free women of color raised their children and owned property, including houses and bondpersons. By 1812 Melanie owned both. In February of that year she purchased an enslaved woman, Charlotte, for four hundred dollars. A week later she bought several lots of land from another affluent free woman of color, Eulalie Foucher (alias Brion or Beyaron). In March 1812 she entered into an act of mortgage and six months later retired that debt, presumably by selling Charlotte to Pierre Feu for fewer than three hundred dollars.[11] Agnes Mathieu, another free woman of color and household head, was listed as a shopkeeper in the 1811 city directory and shared her Marigny home with Jacques Mathieu, a carpenter; Louis Mathieu, a blacksmith; ten other free persons of color; and three bondspersons.[12] Mathieu's neighbor on Moreau Street, Marie-Louise Herbert, headed a household composed of four free persons of color and three bondpersons. Other households consisted of what must have been white couples and their bondpersons. For example, the La Hueze household on Bagatelle Street consisted of one white male, one white female, one free person of color, and twelve enslaved persons.[13] By extension, some free women of color lived with what must have been their white partners and their biracial children. For example, on Rue des Champs Elysées (present-day Elysian Fields Avenue), the Renaud household consisted of one white male, three free persons of color, and one enslaved person; their neighbors, the Zuimpres, were one white male, three free persons of color, and five enslaved persons. Finally, Mathurin Pacaud's household consisted of one white male (Pacaud), seven free persons of color, and six bondspersons. A prominent citizen, Pacaud worked as a clerk for the Banque de la Louisiane and served as grand orator of the Grand Convention of Ancient York Masons, formed in 1812. In other words, Pacaud was a prominent citizen who lived with his partner, a free woman of color; his free, likely biracial children; and his bondservants.[14]

The demographic profiles of the Pacaud, Mathieu, and Drouet households reflected the makeup of the larger neighborhood. The 1810 federal census lists an estimated 1,943 residents of the Marigny: 578 white residents (320 males, 258 females), 854 free people of color, and 511 enslaved persons, a total that included Bernard Marigny's 75 bondpersons. Officials did not enumerate enslaved and free persons of color by gender or age as they did for the white population, but the numbers nonetheless provide a compelling demographic picture of the neighborhood. So while several monographs focus on the free persons of color in antebellum New Orleans, and rightly so, these statistics also reveal that enslaved persons represented about one quarter of the Marigny's population, a figure far too high to go unremarked.[15]

The Francophone free men and women of color in antebellum New Orleans justly receive a significant amount of scholarly and popular attention; their commercial acumen, intellectual and cultural achievements, political activism, and religious devotion made them one of the most fascinating and complex communities in the antebellum South. But to excise their histories from their surroundings is to miss the complex ways in which their political, economic, and social lives crossed the racial categories that "take a life of their own" in New Orleans historiography. To focus exclusively on the free people of color in Faubourg Marigny is to efface the hundreds of enslaved persons who worked for and alongside them and the Euro-Americans who lived with and near them. Melanie Drouet's story, for example, is incomplete without a consideration of her bondwoman Charlotte's life, since their divergent paths highlight the lifelong implications of racism, inequality, and, ultimately, power.[16]

Melanie Drouet was a free woman of mixed racial ancestry; Charlotte, an enslaved black woman, but these two categorizations alone reveal nothing more than presumed phenotype. The meanings imputed to that difference, however, held grave implications for their respective paths: Melanie was a property owner; Charlotte, owned property. And in antebellum New Orleans, physical appearance became conflated with juridical status, thanks to an 1810 case tried before the superior court of the Territory of Orleans. In *Adelle v. Beauregard*, the plaintiff, a young woman of mixed racial ancestry, was born in the Caribbean and later attended boarding school in New York. She sued her master, Beauregard, for her freedom upon reuniting with him, citing a Spanish law still in effect in territorial New Orleans that placed the burden of proof of a mixed-race person's slave status on the master (slaves who appeared to be black had to prove their own freedom). Based on Adelle's physical appearance as mulatto, the burden to prove her enslavement fell on Beauregard, who did not establish Adelle's enslavement. The court therefore upheld the Spanish law and granted Adelle her freedom. Her case set a momentous legal precedent in postcolonial Louisiana: Adelle's mulatto body fit the phenotype of freedom; had the court classed her as black, her legal battle would have proved infinitely more difficult.[17]

Adelle's victory became bondwoman Charlotte's constraint, because Adelle's case made the legal route to freedom in Louisiana all the more difficult for those who did not appear to be of mixed racial ancestry. For Charlotte, one such bondwoman who had what was generally recognized as a black phenotype, both her appearance and notarial records reinforced her status as a slave. She was the property of Melanie Drouet, and, as such, she lacked control of her body, her labor, and her movements; as a bondwoman, even her name was fungible. Her individual journey from Maryland to Louisiana was but part of the larger domestic slave trade, which forced many thousands of bondpersons from the Old South to the Deep South. At sixteen years old, this young woman involuntarily traveled from one port city to another. Perhaps she recognized some commonalities between Maryland and Louisiana, since Baltimore and New Orleans had intertwined histories of Francophone Saint-Dominguan refugees, Catholicism, and international connectivity through a major seaport. But if she hailed from the grand plantations of rural Maryland, then the Faubourg Marigny, a neighborhood where few masters owned more than five bondpersons, may have seemed completely foreign. If she spoke only English in such a polyglot neighborhood, she may have felt all the more isolated. It is impossible to recreate this enslaved woman's biography beyond imagining her experience of migration and settlement. Perhaps she participated in some of the neighborhood's amusements (which are explored in the second section of this chapter), or perhaps she never adjusted to urban slavery. Whatever the case, Charlotte did not have long to adjust to her new setting. Within ten months she was back on the auction block, this time becoming the property of

Pierre (or Pedro) Feu, a slave dealer party to at least twenty slave transactions between 1801 and 1819.[18]

Unlike Charlotte, whose life depended on the vagaries of the notorious New Orleans slave market, Melanie, a homeowner, could remain in the Marigny for as long as she could afford it. That was the burden and privilege of property ownership. Yet her privilege relative to Charlotte did not mean she was completely free of regulations, as she discovered in 1822. In June of that year, Joseph Mitchell, a man of European ancestry, swore to the following complaint before Mayor Louis Philippe de Roffignac:

> [Mitchell] has lodgings in the home of a free colored woman named Melanie Drouet, D'Amour Street, Suburb Marigny, one part of which house is occupied by a free negro woman named Victoire L'esperanza who appears to be a concealer of thieves and stolen things—and the Declarant says that last night at nine o'clock he saw the Negro Louis a slave of Mr. Stais entering the room occupied by Victoire L'esperanza—as he the Declarant has been informed that his Louis had robbed four hundred dollars from his master, he intended to caught the robber, for that purpose he entered the room and attempted to seize and arrest him, but he was prevented by a free negro woman named Esther, the mother of said Louis, who took hold of him the Declarant and so preserved the escape of her son Louis. The Declarant further says that in the bosom of the said Esther he described a big and heavy load like money wrapped in a kind of white linen.[19]

This curious account implicates at least six people in a drama at Melanie's now-crowded house, three of them residents, three of them interested parties: Victoire L'esperanza, a free or freed black woman who lived as a boarder in Melanie's home; Victoire's friend Esther, likely a freed black woman; Esther's enslaved son Louis; his master, Mathieu Charles Staes; Joseph Mitchell, another of Melanie's boarders; and homeowner Melanie Drouet. Each player's involvement and interests in this scene illuminate domestic life across socioeconomic lines in Faubourg Marigny and provide a rich segue into the subsequent discussion of multiracial and, at times, illicit fraternization in the neighborhood.

The tumult described in the complaint stemmed from a conflict between the diverse group of lodgers in Melanie's house. As an unmarried mother of at least two sons, Drouet earned income by leasing rooms to those who could pay, irrespective of race or gender. Mitchell described Victoire L'esperanza as a "free negro woman," indicating that she was not believed to have been of mixed racial ancestry. Both "Victoire" and "L'esperanza" were common names among the city's enslaved population, so she may have once been a bondperson. In addition, sacramental records from the period do not list the surname "L'esperanza," so she did not have recorded family ties the way many free people did. This woman likely secured her freedom, perhaps through *coartación*, the right to self-purchase granted bondpersons during Louisiana's Spanish period, which lasted from 1764 until 1803. Perhaps Victoire's friend Esther had a similar background, since her name was also common among bondpersons and her son Louis remained enslaved. Whatever their personal backgrounds, material imperatives brought them and others to Melanie Drouet's home.[20]

If Esther somehow secured her own freedom, her son Louis remained the property of Mathieu Charles Staes, a man of European descent whose ascent in the Louisiana Territory paralleled the arc of so many others on the frontier. The circumstances of Staes family's arrival in New Orleans are unclear, but as of 1810 Staes and his younger wife lived on Levée Street (present-day Decatur Street). The couple owned one bondwoman at that time, likely Maria, the twenty-three-year-old bondwoman Staes purchased in 1810 for 280 piastres. The following year the city directory listed Staes's occupation as "ironmonger and storekeeper." Between that year and 1817 Staes bought and sold several enslaved persons, but none of them appear to have been Esther's son Louis. It remains unclear when, if ever, Staes came into legal ownership of the young man. Yet Melanie's lodger Joseph Mitchell recognized Louis to be the property of Mathieu Staes, reflecting not only the juridical reaches of slavery but also the everyday governmentality of chattel slavery. In other words, the power differentials of bondage went beyond the master-slave relationship; the fact of his enslavement left Louis subject to all of free society. Even when his master was not present, others recognized him as the property of another, a recognition that prescribed his actions, movements, and possibilities.[21]

Joseph Mitchell, the final actor in the fracas, leveled a complaint before the mayor but is otherwise absent in documentary records. His name suggests an Anglo-American background and perhaps participation in the outward migration that sent settlers like Mathieu Staes westward following the Louisiana Purchase. His seeming lack of family ties and his living as a boarder suggest as much. Yet Mitchell risked his personal safety to apprehend Louis, an alleged thief and fugitive, perhaps in pursuit of a financial reward from Mathieu Staes or to get even with Esther or Victoire. The relationship between Mitchell and Melanie Drouet is unclear. It appears that he was a boarder, but this label could be a euphemism for another relationship, as plaçage and prostitution were both prevalent institutions in the Faubourg Marigny.

Whatever the relationships connecting the members of Melanie Drouet's Marigny household, Mitchell reported Victoire, Esther, and Louis to the mayor, and in his complaint he leveled an incendiary accusation. Mitchell accused Esther of harboring her fugitive son and concealing the four hundred dollars he stood accused of filching. Beyond whether or not this mother-son duo conspired to fleece Mathieu Staes, however, the import of this accusation lies in the insight it provides into family and household dynamics. Louis lived in what is today called the French Quarter, and Esther lived in a diverse Marigny household; Louis was enslaved and Esther free. Yet they maintained a bond—if illustrated through vice—that transcended the physical separation of different households and the social distance of different statuses. And while aiding and abetting the escape of a fugitive may not embody certain class-based conceptions of virtuous motherhood, this episode highlights another commonality between Melanie and Esther beyond gender and home address: a desire to ensure the material prosperity of their sons. Just as Melanie likely maintained a household in hopes that her sons would one day inherit it and its privileges, Esther also aimed to protect her son's property—and, likely, his body—from the consequences of his alleged crime. Whatever the case, Esther and Louis may have inserted themselves into the Marigny's culture of vice, and though it is impossible to know what became of them, this episode highlights the wildly contradictory and contested constraints and possibilities of people of African descent in one household, particularly in a neighborhood that defied most of the remembered conventions of the antebellum South.[22]

But just what did Louis and Esther plan to do with such a large sum of illegal cash, since the Bank of Louisiana was not a likely option? In the dynamic world of taverns, the enslaved and other less prominent members of society accessed bustling centers of commerce where the commodities denied them by law and custom—alcohol, sex, ill-begotten cash, chance, or even illegally imported Africans—could be exchanged or purchased for the right price. Much to lawmakers' chagrin, neighborhood taverns functioned as unregulated markets and cultural and commercial institutions, spaces where enslaved men and women, free people of color, and people of European descent of varying national and class backgrounds enjoyed profitable—if illegal—amusement. These tippling houses in the Marigny and across the city replicated the diverse (if stratified) demographics that defined their domestic arrangements. And, as in their households, the interracial intimacies beneath the tavern's roof seemed to destroy society's lines and hierarchies, admitting enslaved customers alongside their free fellow revelers. But social relationships across the slave-free line also involved significant risk for bondpersons who, as nonwhite noncitizens, were particularly vulnerable to maltreatment. Each time these men and women crossed the tavern threshold, they found the excitement of festival and the thrill of reward, but revelry quickly became danger, and, for enslaved persons, its consequences might prove irreparable. Despite the ongoing battle to keep the lower orders from indiscriminate socializing, a vibrant and, at times, violent social and market culture nonetheless emerged in neighborhood taverns.

In 1802 Pierre-Louis Berquin-Duvallon, a sugar planter from Saint-Domingue, observed the following about New Orleans:

> The city abounds with tippling houses. At every cross street of the town and suburbs, one sees those places of riot and intoxication crowded day and night. The low orders of every colour, white, yellow, and black, mix indiscriminately at these receptacles, finding a market for their pilferings, and

solacing their cares with tobacco and brandy. Gambling is practised to an incredible excess. To dancing there is no end. Such a motley crew, and incongruous scene!

Along with the Mississippi River and the auction block, taverns proved a constitutive part of the physical, economic, social, and cultural landscape of antebellum New Orleans. And much to the dismay of Berquin-Duvallon and many others, these "incongruous scenes" featured participants from all races and backgrounds, seemingly a direct affront to the racist segregation they believed necessary for social order. And this exiled planter from Saint-Domingue had immediate experience of the social upheaval that might result when persons from various backgrounds united around a common cause—freedom.[23]

Coffee houses, cafés, and taverns operated across the entire French Quarter, but their locations and clienteles sometimes reflected and sometimes subverted the fractures of the larger society. The establishments that catered to prominent men, for example, lined Royal and Chartres Streets. The Café des Améliorations, located on the edge of the old city at the corner of Rampart and Toulouse Streets, served primarily French Creoles, while the Cafés des Refugiés (or Café des Exiles) catered to Saint-Dominguan émigrés. Jean Lafitte's Blacksmith Shop, located on the corner of Bourbon and St. Phillip Streets, is one of the oldest taverns in the United States and allegedly functioned as a front for the pirate's lucrative illicit trade. In this establishment, a diverse set of patrons bought alcohol, gambled, and participated in all manners of illicit activity, including the sale of Africans illegally imported into the territory. The most elite tavern, however, opened in 1814. Located at the intersection of Chartres and St. Louis Streets, the two-story Maspero's Exchange (formerly Bernard Tremoulet's Exchange Commercial Coffee-House) also functioned as a preeminent bar, gambling parlor, and slave auction block. Unlike Lafitte's shop, this tavern appealed only to "commercial gentlemen." According to its initial advertisements, owner Pierre Maspero and manager Philip Alvarez shared a "determination to spare neither pains nor expense, to conduct it in a style of elegance never before witnessed in this place, and to render the house really and permanent [*sic*] useful to commercial gentlemen and the public in general."[24] In exchange for a five-dollar subscription fee, members enjoyed a reading room stocked with the latest political, geographic, and commercial publications, enviable access in such an international city. General Andrew Jackson, the hero of the Battle of New Orleans who leveraged his military success into a political career, became the establishment's most famous patron. The site also attracted merchants and businessmen of European descent. And though enslaved persons undoubtedly performed much of the labor necessary for the establishment's operation, they likely never enjoyed any of its services. Tavern culture therefore permeated all levels of society, though some establishments appealed to exclusive clienteles. Such establishments proved so popular that the 1811 New Orleans city directory listed nearly twice as many publicans as it did doctors. In that listing, men and women, including a Widow Schmidt, described themselves as "cabaretiers" and, according to Berquin, many earned significant sums of money by pouring liquor for any patron.[25]

From colonial times, local leaders fecklessly campaigned to prevent certain people, especially the enslaved, from participating in the city's tavern culture, citing a connection between alcohol, theft, gambling, and social disorder. In 1724, for example, Louisiana's Code Noir stated: "intoxicating liquors shall not be sold to slaves, without a written permission from their master, and . . . any person violating that provision shall incur a penalty; and moreover, be answerable to the owner for all damages which the master may suffer in consequence thereof."[26]

Such legislation notwithstanding, unauthorized enslaved participation in tavern life and culture continued from colonial times through the end of the antebellum period. In a 1790s pamphlet titled "List of Suggested Changes with Regard to the Black Population of New Orleans," one anonymous visionary suggested, "Reduce the great number of taverns, leaving just a sufficient number to furnish drinks to whites. Prohibit the sale of any kind of alcoholic drink to people of color, slaves, or Negroes. Everything that is stolen by our servants is carried to these taverns." The author immediately followed with another, related proposal: "Rid the colony of all [white] vagabonds and habitués of taverns, who are harmful to the colony and who occupy themselves only by stealing and inciting our servants to steal."[27]

Both recommendations reveal a dynamic tavern culture where the so-called dregs of colonial society—slaves, free blacks, and poor whites—drank, bartered, socialized, fought, and scandalized genteel society. The author had good reason to fear this kind of socializing. Decades earlier in New York City, John Hughson's waterfront tavern, which allowed enslaved, free black, and poor white socializing, proved fertile ground for the alleged creation of the Great Negro Plot of 1741. When a series of fires erupted in that year of tense economic and social pressures, English colonists suspected a plot linking poor whites, many of them Irish and Catholic, and the enslaved. After a series of trials, officials executed thirty-four accused persons: thirty black men, two white men, and two white women.[28]

During the transitional years between 1800 and 1804, which marked Louisiana's passage from Spain to France to the United States, the problem of insufficiently segregated revelry increased. Several travelers, including James Pitot, the city's second mayor, expressed outrage at the number of enslaved persons who frequented the spots. In his memoir, Pitot deemed the existence of such taverns evidence of political corruption:

> Hundreds of licensed taverns openly sell to slaves, and, in making them drunk, become throughout the day and night receivers of stolen goods from

their masters. . . . A public ball, where those who have a bit of discretion pre-
fer not to appear, organized by the free people of color, is each week the
gathering place for the scum of such people and of those slaves who, elud-
ing their owner's surveillance, go there to bring their plunder . . . and as a
crowning infamy one finds even some white people who repeatedly battle
with the slaves for places in the quadrilles, and for their share of the household pilferage which they decide by a throw of dice.[29]

Pitot, like the anonymous author writing at the end of the eighteenth century, recognized the relationship between the illicit consumption of alcohol
in taverns, the brisk commerce in stolen goods, and what he considered the
shameful mixing of different populations. As his statement articulated, taverns became particularly sinister because of the many ills they encouraged:
promiscuous socializing, an illegal trade in untaxed goods, and enslaved
truancy from proper surveillance. To Pitot, such activities imperiled the very
foundations of society.

Yet, of all the evils he chronicled, Pitot singled out a "crowning infamy":
white people's eager—and equal—participation in quadrilles with the enslaved
and the divvying of ill-gotten goods with bondpersons. The political tensions
embedded within dances was nothing new in New Orleans, a place where
Anglo-American settlers and French Creoles nearly sparked a violent conflict
over the style of music and dance that would dominate the public ball. Indeed,
Governor Claiborne had to station guards at the venue to prevent nationalist conflict among the "discreet" members of society. But in taverns, people
united not only to drink but also to dance. As such, antebellum taverns must be
added to such sites of memory as Congo Square as spaces of African diasporic
cultural memory and exchange. Indeed, when Pitot wrote, the international
slave trade still flourished legally, and a significant portion of the local enslaved
population was African born. Many of the enslaved persons who frequented
these taverns had memories of rhythms and dances from distant and disparate
geographies and nations. Therefore, just as the jook joints of the postbellum
South receive their due for their role in the creation of jazz, the blues, and a
host of popular dances, their antebellum precursors must also receive attention for their significance in the making of an international musical culture in
antebellum New Orleans.[30]

Governor Claiborne, on the other hand, considered taverns not to be tri-
umphant sites of cultural collaboration and persistence of innovation but as
public nuisances. Indeed, he repeatedly outlawed their existence. Yet those
who patronized these establishments thought them valuable enough to flout
executive orders. In a circular to the commandants of the various districts
dated March 30, 1804, Governor Claiborne prohibited those with liquor
licenses from selling alcohol to enslaved persons unless the bondpersons fur-
nished written permission from their owner. Tavern keepers who disregarded

this protocol risked their licenses and livelihoods, but the enslaved continued to patronize taverns. Two years later, an exasperated Claiborne wrote Mayor John Watkins:

> It was stated to me on yesterday that the Holders of Slaves complained generally of the negligence of the Police. It was said that the Taverns or Cabarets in the City were numerous, that Negroes and free people of colour were licensed as Tavern Keepers, and that their houses were resorted to by Slaves who passed most of their nights in dancing and drinking to their own injury and the loss of service to their Masters.
>
> Near to the residence of Mr. William Brown the Collector I was informed there were several disorderly houses, and it was added that the evil was daily increasing.[31]

It is difficult to verify Williams Brown's account of licensed tavern keepers of African descent, but Governor Claiborne's willingness to believe it possible reflects the extent to which enslaved persons participated in the vibrant nightlife that emerged in colonial and antebellum New Orleans.[32]

Throughout the Territorial Period, local officials attempted to regulate—and profit from—the many taverns that dominated the cityscape through licensing fees that tavern keepers protested as particularly onerous. In *Ramozay et al. v. the Mayor &c. of New Orleans* (1811), "grog-shop" owners complained that the mayor required an annual licensing fee of one hundred dollars for an inclusive license to sell alcohol, operate a pool table, and keep an inn or boarding house. The plaintiffs sought less expensive liquor licenses. The court found in favor of the city, making "inn keeper" (*aubergiste*) and "publican" (*cabaretier*) almost synonymous titles during this period, an arrangement that invited a flourishing prostitution industry. Another absurdity is that when enslaved persons patronized licensed taverns, they indirectly funded the local government charged with governing their enslavement.[33]

Of course, local officials never acknowledged such indirect funding from bondpersons and continued their campaign against unauthorized consumption of alcohol by the enslaved, primarily as a means of preserving the social order that their frolicking threatened to upset. But there was another utility in preventing excessive drinking on the part of the enslaved—the preservation of expensive human investments. Though few leaders cared for the personal safety of enslaved people, their utility for labor and their insurance of future value made the preservation of their lives a critical task for local officials. The case of *Delery v. Mornet* (1822) highlights the intersection of social and material imperatives. In this suit, the plaintiff accused the defendant of selling alcohol to the bondman Jasmin with disastrous consequences. According to court records, Jasmin and other enslaved men went for a ride in a *pirogue* (canoe), stopped at the defendant's home, purchased alcohol, drank it, and then returned to the vessel. Soon after, the intoxicated men began a heated argument. At some point Jasmin fell (or was pushed) overboard and drowned. The court found in favor of the plaintiff and held the defendant liable for Jasmin's death. The court reasoned that since Jasmin was black, Mornet should have assumed he was a slave and, therefore, should have refused to sell him alcohol.[34]

This vignette about the deadly turn that a simple night out might take highlights the blurred boundaries between amusement and danger, particularly when fraternization involved alcohol. According to the case, the men gathered for a night out. It is impossible to say whether they were all friends, but if they joined to seek liquor, an illegal enterprise for bondpersons, there must have been some level of trust uniting them. Whatever their social ties, they began to argue once they consumed alcohol and returned to their vehicle. It is impossible to know what sparked the argument, but it had the perfect ingredients for unnecessary and violent escalation: a set of drunken men confined to a cramped space. Jasmin went overboard, the result of either drunken stumbling or malicious murder. Either way, their simple trip to the defendant's house for a little alcohol turned into Jasmin's final night.[35]

But it was only the beginning of a costly court battle for the defendant, and in light of the financial risks of selling alcohol to the enslaved, one would assume bondpersons had a hard time accessing spirits. They did not. These men and women continued to frequent local taverns, licensed and unlicensed, well into the 1850s. But, as much as alcohol attracted many locals to taverns, enslaved persons included, taverns provided much more than spirits; they housed a bustling commercial culture that allowed people from all levels of society to meet in the market. Of course, enslaved persons regularly participated in legal marketplaces at their masters' command. Enslaved women in particular regularly strolled the streets of New Orleans, peddling their own goods and those produced by their masters, much to the chagrin of local shopkeepers. As early as 1804 irate shopkeepers appeared before the Orleans Legislative Council: "A petition was presented from several store-keepers of New Orleans, representing that negroes and negresses are permitted to sell articles of merchandize about the streets and in the neighborhood of this city, to the injury of petitioners, and of society at large, and praying the council to extirpate such abuse."[36]

If legal vending could provoke such protests, unregulated vending produced a furor. When they earned, bought, and sold without assent, these men and women not only flouted local laws but also enjoyed, even if temporarily, the privileges and equality that money offered. With property, earnings, and winnings, they could patronize establishments, secure goods and the relative status that came with them, save for the future, and, for the enslaved, secure their freedom.[37]

As some prominent historians point out, illicit spaces often prove critical to the creation of multiracial, radical communities and, by extension, politics. Peter Linebaugh and Marcus Rediker, for example, celebrate such spaces—pirate ships, taverns, and the like—as egalitarian and revolutionary sites of resistance to established authority. As compelling as this argument may be, however, it minimizes the raced and gendered risks of participation that some experienced even in such seemingly egalitarian spaces. For example, the black, or illegal, markets in some taverns, such as in Lafitte's Blacksmith Shop, were literally black, as in race, markets, featuring African people on auction blocks as products. And the auction block was not the only place where bodies became commoditized; in local taverns, prostitution flourished alongside the drinking, revelry, gambling, and vending. Women (and, likely, men) from various racial backgrounds offered sexual services in exchange for goods, and this institution, like all others, provided opportunities and risks to those who participated. Both slavery and prostitution, then, offered some participants economic reward and personal satisfaction but others bodily injury and personal exploitation.[38]

Charles César Robin, acute observer and incessant critic of French Creoles, described prostitution on the part of enslaved women at the opening of the nineteenth century:

> The masters encourage . . . the female slaves in their inordinate inconstancy. Often they are encouraged to use their free time in prostitution and to report back each day the amount they have taken. In town, especially, where the servants must behave with more circumspection, they are relieved of this burden, because they have the liberty to make arrangements with generous lovers and the more the servants are indulged in this, the less they are required, to bother their masters with it. The lady of the house, who ordinarily has charge of the matter, grows accustomed to seeing lovers come and go to her Negro servant and she arranges to have them let in at night.[39]

While Robin's account encompasses two of his favorite themes—French Creole libertinage and African hypersexuality—he nonetheless offers an intriguing insight into the intersection of enslaved sexuality and economy. Many slavery studies detail the process of hiring out, which allowed enslaved people, usually men, to labor for others in exchange for compensation. Usually hiring out involved skilled trades, such as smithing, coopering, and so on. Robin's vignette, on the other hand, calls attention to an underappreciated vehicle for enslaved persons to earn money—selling their bodies. In Robin's estimation, these arrangements occurred with masters' permission, encouraging the self-sufficiency of bondpersons who became less of a financial burden to their owners. Indeed, Robin intimates that masters profited from the sexual labor of their bondwomen. The irony is immediately apparent: bondwomen whose bodies are not legally their own must then earn their keep by exchanging their bodies for their master's profit.[40]

In Robin's estimation, enslaved women who sold sexual services benefited tremendously from these arrangements, and some undoubtedly secured monetary advantages and perhaps a measure of financial independence through prostitution. However, sex work cannot be conflated with pleasure or amusement; its costs were far too high for such an interpretation. For example, if a customer received services and chose not to pay, an enslaved woman (and, presumably, her master) had limited legal recourse for securing remuneration. Likewise, enslaved sex workers had little protection from physical abuse, already a routine part of life in the violent city. In addition, New Orleans was a notoriously diseased city, and enslaved sex workers risked contracting sexually transmitted diseases. Robin described the arrival of a shipment of Universal Regenerator, widely considered a cure for syphilis, in New Orleans: "What even the most unabashed libertine would not have done in Paris, here was done by the ladies, who queued up openly in the streets to buy the Regenerator." If the city's elite ladies were so unabashedly diseased, then the rest of the populace must have been downright incurable.[41]

Indeed, a singular set of medical records reveals an enslaved woman's treatment for a sexually transmitted disease. Though there is no indication that she necessarily engaged in prostitution, the records nonetheless reveal the risks of sexuality for all members of society, let alone bondwomen, whose bodies were not their own. On June 16, 1813, surgeon Chevalier submitted an invoice to a certain LaRonde, who lived on a sugar plantation about three leagues upriver from the city. Chevalier sought compensation for the treatment of LaRonde's bondpersons between May 14 and August 20, 1812. The receipt shows the doctor provided a bottle of "balsamic syrup of Tolu," an expectorant that aided in persistent coughs and bronchial infections. But the doctor also treated an enslaved woman afflicted with "*un vice vénérien bien prononcé.*" The doctor treated her advanced sexually transmitted infection with three bottles of purifying syrup and three medicines. These two words, "*bien prononcé,*" penned in the dispassionate language of medical practice and racist distance, summarize what must have been this unnamed woman's extreme duress. Her condition may have included any number of painful manifestations—genital sores, skin rashes, fever, sore throat, and hair loss—but undoubtedly she still performed the tasks assigned by her master. Such corporal risks, not to mention the psychic costs, from prostitution render Robin's flippant assessment of enslaved prostitution strikingly deficient.[42]

Enslaved women, however, did not have a monopoly on prostitution or its risks. Unfortunately, the oldest profession as practiced in early nineteenth-century New Orleans is not easily documented. Instead, one must look to oblique references in accounts like that of Timothy Flint, a congregational missionary from New England who traveled to Louisiana in the 1820s. Flint did not have a high opinion of the Deep South, writing of Natchez, Mississippi: "The town is full of boatmen, mulattoes, houses of ill fame, and their wretched tenants, in short, the refuse of the world." He thought the Crescent City no better: "New Orleans is of course exposed to greater varieties of human misery, vice, disease, and want, than any other American town." That misery included the tippling houses and "temples of fortune," where roulette wheels and alcoholics had "such an aspect of beastliness and degradation, as to render them utterly *unbearable.* . . . Every thing that can tempt avarice or the passions is here."[43]

In the paragraph that immediately follows this fire-and-brimstone assessment of the city comes a curious description:

> Much has been said about certain connexions that are winked at with the yellow women of this city. I know not whether this be truth or idle gossiping. The yellow women are often remarkable for the perfect symmetry of their forms, and for their fine expression of eye. They are universally admitted to have a fidelity and cleverness as nurses for the sick, beyond all other women. When a stranger is brought up by prevailing fever, the first object is to consign him to the care of one of these tender and faithful nurses, and then he has all the chance for life, that the disorder admits.[44]

The missionary's account of "yellow women" as "nurses" who excelled "beyond all other women" in their treatment of men suffering "fever" parallels accounts of the sexualized gaze that European travelers to many parts of the Atlantic World aimed at the bodies of so-called mulatto women. In its vagueness, this description nonetheless boasts of the availability of yellow women's attention to and affection for the men who needed their services. "Yellow women" belonged to any number of racial and economic categories; some were enslaved, while others were free women of color. This relationship might be prostitution or plaçage. Either way, this observer considered women of African descent primarily through the services, whether sexual or medicinal, they offered the male customer or patient.[45]

Finally, women of color were not the only sex workers in antebellum New Orleans, and white male-black female sex was not the only sex across the color line. As Martha Hodes argues, sex between white women and black men was not as unusual as popularly imagined in the antebellum South, and these liaisons undoubtedly occurred under tavern roofs. It is somewhat more difficult to document in earlier periods, but sources from later in the antebellum period may shed light on dynamics that existed in earlier decades. For example, a column in the *Daily Orleanian*, "Snowy White and Sooty," regularly ridiculed white women caught cohabiting with black men. On January 15, 1852, the following story appeared: "Eliza Saucier, or *Liz*, for short, and Mary Darcy, a pair of fallen angels-dwellers in *Sanctity Row*, on *Elysian* Fields street, were arrested for cohabiting with two snow balls one of them Spencer, owned by the Cotton Press Co.; the other Ambrose, the property of Mr. Cucullu. The frail fair ones were sent to the parish prison—the darkies received a half hundred lashes between them."[46] Another example from that period involves two free persons classed into different racial categories, but who likely shared economic circumstances: "Margaret Campbell, a white woman, and Scott, a negro, were arrested for cohabitation, and brought before his Honor of the Second Municipality, who sent 'Snowy White' to the workhouse for a quarter of a year, and ordered 'Sooty' to be flogged. The frail female woman ought to be flogged also."[47]

These articles call attention to the ordinariness of sex across multiple sets of lines: color, gender, and class. But these brief accounts may also invert Robin's model of prostitution, which featured a woman of color, perhaps enslaved, servicing a wealthier, likely white customer. These examples come from a neighborhood where many poor European immigrants settled, some of whom turned to prostitution for survival. Indeed, at the time of these accounts, local officials had declared war on the illicit institution, and newspapers regularly announced raids that netted several arrests in the area. It is quite possible, then, that these white women were prostitutes and the enslaved men customers. Of course these relationships may not have involved prostitution at all. It is impossible to know what defined them, but these examples force a rethinking of the racist, sexist, and heteronormative assumptions that characterize sex and prostitution in the antebellum South.[48]

Considering the many big events that happened in Louisiana between 1791 and 1815—the Louisiana Purchase in 1803, the alleged shift from the international to the domestic slave trade in 1807, the War of 1812—it becomes easy to foreground the "big men" of the period: President Thomas Jefferson, Emperor Napoleon Bonaparte, even the pirate Jean Lafitte. This chapter, on the other hand, presents a microlevel social history of women of color in antebellum New Orleans during a formative period in the region's history. And their lives reveal the importance of social history across not only color lines but also borders of class, geography, nation, language, gender, and sexuality. In other words, these lives provide insight into the workings and limits of macrolevel policies and ideological systems in everyday life. Their stories also reveal the ways in which power differentials permeated even the most mundane and intimate aspects of daily life, highlighting both the possibilities and limits of multiracialism in a society rooted in chattel slavery. Ultimately, this chapter provokes a refinement of conceptions of exceptionalism, hierarchy, and power such that intersecting inequalities of race and gender are detectable in multiracial households, taverns, and even in *les bons temps*.[49]

Notes

My thanks to Carol Faulkner, Alison Parker, Michael Gomez, Walter Johnson, Ada Ferrer, Michele Mitchell, Barbara Krauthamer, Dartmouth College's Department of History, Alexander Chenault, and the anonymous reviewers for all their assistance.

1. Two classic essays on race as category of obfuscation are Barbara Fields, "Slavery, Race, and Ideology in the United States of America," *New Left Review* 181 (1990): 95–118; and Evelyn Brooks Higginbotham, "African-American Women's History and the Metalanguage of Race," *Signs* 17, no. 2 (1992): 251–74. On the multidimensionality of black women's experiences, see Kimberlé Crenshaw, "Demarginalizing the Intersection of Race and Sex: A Black Feminist Critique of Antidiscrimination Doctrine, Feminist Theory, and Antiracist Politics," *University of Chicago Legal Forum* (1989): 139–67. Monographs that take such analyses seriously and therefore serve as an analytic model include, among many others, Leslie A. Schwalm, *A Hard Fight for We: Women's Transition from Slavery to Freedom in South Carolina* (Urbana: University of Illinois Press, 1997); and Dylan C. Penningroth, *The Claims of Kinfolk: African American Property and Community in the Nineteenth-Century South* (Chapel Hill: University of North Carolina Press, 2003). On the importance of individual subjectivity in works that explore southern history, see Nell Irvin Painter, *Southern History across the Color Line* (Chapel Hill: University of North Carolina Press, 2002).

2. Ned Sublette, *The World That Made New Orleans: From Spanish Silver to Congo Square* (Chicago: Lawrence Hill Books, 2008). On interzones, see Kevin J. Mumford, *Interzones: Black/White Sex Districts in Chicago and New York in the Early Twentieth Century* (New York: Columbia University Press, 1997). Queer theory and other critical studies on sexuality and society are often most attuned to the shifting inequalities within and between so-called marginal groups. See, among others, George Chauncey, *Gay New York: Gender, Urban Culture, and the Makings of the Gay Male World, 1890–1940* (New York: Basic Books, 1994); Audre Lorde, *Zami, a New Spelling of My Name* (Trumansburg, NY: Crossing, 1982); and Lorde, *Sister Outsider: Essays and Speeches* (Trumansburg, NY: Crossing, 1984).

3. On plaçage and households headed by free women of color, see Jennifer M. Spear, *Race, Sex, and Social Order in Early New Orleans* (Baltimore, MD: Johns Hopkins University Press, 2009); and Kimberly S. Hanger, *Bounded Lives, Bounded Places: Free Black Society in Colonial New Orleans, 1769–1803* (Durham, NC: Duke University Press, 1997).

4. On the revelry and its subversions and surrogations in New Orleans, see Joseph Roach, *Cities of the Dead: Circum-Atlantic Performance* (New York: Columbia University Press, 1996).

5. For a discussion of the free woman of color and property owner Rosalie Chenault, who was the widow of a white man named Juan (or Jean) Chenau (or Chesneau), see Ben Melvin Hobratsch, "Creole Angel: The Self-Identity of the Free People of Color of Antebellum New Orleans" (master's thesis, University of North Texas, 2006).

6. Earl C. Woods, Dorenda Dupont, and Charles E. Nolan, *Sacramental Records of the Roman Catholic Church of the Archdiocese of New Orleans* (New Orleans: Archdiocese of New Orleans, 1987), 10:151.

7. Gabriel Debien and René Le Gardeur, "The Saint-Domingue Refugees in Louisiana, 1792–1804," trans. David Cheramie, in *The Road to Louisiana: The Saint-Domingue Refugees, 1792–1809*, ed. Carl Brasseaux, Glenn R. Conrad, and David Cheramie (Lafayette: University of Southwestern Louisiana, 1992), 208.

8. Woods, Dupont, and Nolan, *Sacramental Records*, 8:112, 9:121. Demographic data on the migration from Saint-Domingue to New Orleans shows the disproportionate

number of free women of color, indicating that some men of European ancestry brought their mistresses with them. Louisiana governor William C. C. Claiborne's population estimates covering the 1809–10 migration show the high number of free women of color represented in this migration. See William C. C. Claiborne and Dunbar Rowland, *Official Letter Books of W. C. C. Claiborne, 1801–1816* (Jackson, MI: State Department of Archives and History, 1917), 4:381–82.

9. Harriet A. Jacobs, L. Maria Child, and Jean Fagan Yellin, *Incidents in the Life of a Slave Girl: Written by Herself* (Cambridge, MA: Harvard University Press, 1987), 13.

10. On *partus sequitur ventrum* and the larger meanings of race and reproduction during slavery, see, among others, Jennifer L. Morgan, *Laboring Women: Reproduction and Gender in New World Slavery* (Philadelphia: University of Pennsylvania Press, 2004); Kathleen M. Brown, *Good Wives, Nasty Wenches, and Anxious Patriarchs: Gender, Race, and Power in Colonial Virginia* (Chapel Hill: University of North Carolina Press, 1996); Deborah Gray White, *Ar'n't I a Woman? Female Slaves in the Plantation South* (New York: Norton, 1985).

Controversies around erased paternity, black matriarchy, and the hypersexualization of women of color persist into the present day. See, among others, Hortense Spillers, "Mama's Baby, Papa's Maybe: An American Grammar Book," *Diacritics* 17 (Summer 1987): 65–81; Edward Franklin Frazier, *The Negro Family in the United States* (Chicago: University of Chicago Press, 1939); Eugene D. Genovese, *Roll, Jordan, Roll: The World the Slaves Made* (New York: Pantheon Books, 1974); Herbert George Gutman, *The Black Family in Slavery and Freedom, 1750–1925* (New York: Pantheon Books, 1976); Tricia Rose, *Longing to Tell: Black Women Talk about Sexuality and Intimacy* (New York: Farrar, Straus, and Giroux, 2003); Kenneth M. Stampp, *The Peculiar Institution: Slavery in the Ante-Bellum South* (New York: Vintage, 1956); and Rhonda Y. Williams, *The Politics of Public Housing: Black Women's Struggles against Urban Inequality* (New York: Oxford University Press, 2004).

11. Woods, Dupont, and Nolan, *Sacramental Records*, 14:129, 12:125. On Melanie's purchase and sale of Charlotte, see Gwendolyn Midlo Hall, Afro-Louisiana History and Genealogy Database, 1719–1820, accessed June 30, 2009, http://www.ibiblio.org/laslave/index.html.

12. *1811 New Orleans City Directory*, Louisiana Division, Main Branch, New Orleans Public Library. Agnes Mathieu owned several bondspersons prior to 1810, including Bimby, Eufrosine, Louison, Marianne, and Pierre. See Hall, Afro-Louisiana History and Genealogy Database, 1719–1820.

13. The "Lahouze" or "Laheuze" family may have emigrated from Saint-Domingue by way of Cuba. The 1807 list of Cuban coffee farms records a "Lahouze" in Sierra Maestra who owned two enslaved persons. See Gabriel Debien, "The Saint-Domingue Refugees in Cuba, 1793–1815," trans. David Cheramie, in Brasseaux, Conrad, and Cheramie, *Road to Louisiana*, 31–112.

14. On Mathurin Pacaud's freemasonry activities, see Walter Parker, "Secret Orders," in *Standard History of New Orleans, Louisiana*, ed. Henry Rightor (Chicago, IL: Lewis, 1900). Pacaud's fortunes shifted by 1815, a year when creditors sold at least two of his bondmen. See Hall, *Database*.

Incidentally, Pacaud may have been somehow linked to Marie-Louise Pacaud, sister of Pierre Toussaint, the noted Saint-Dominguan ex-slave who became quite wealthy in New York City in the early nineteenth century. Pierre Toussaint's sister

Marie-Louise emigrated to New Orleans from Saint-Domingue by way of Cuba. She resolved never to go back to Saint-Domingue, describing the island as "a country of disorder and tyranny where there is continued fighting." Arthur Jones, *Pierre Toussaint* (New York: Doubleday, 2003), 169.

15. I derived these numbers by manually counting the entries in the 1810 US Census, Population Schedule, New Orleans, LA, Ancestry.com, accessed April 6, 2009, http://www.ancestry.com. For studies that use demographics to produce social histories of US slavery, see Michael Angelo Gomez, *Exchanging Our Country Marks: The Transformation of African Identities in the Colonial and Antebellum South* (Chapel Hill: University of North Carolina Press, 1998); Gwendolyn Midlo Hall, *Africans in Colonial Louisiana: The Development of Afro-Creole Culture in the Eighteenth Century* (Baton Rouge: Louisiana State University Press, 1992); Morgan, *Laboring Women*; and Peter H. Wood, *Black Majority: Negroes in Colonial South Carolina from 1670 through the Stono Rebellion* (New York: Norton, 1975).

16. On the free people of color, see Rodolphe Lucien Desdunes, *Our People and Our History: Fifty Creole Portraits*, trans. and ed. Sister Dorothea Olga McCants (1911; repr., Baton Rouge: Louisiana State University Press, 1973); and Caryn Cossé Bell, *Revolution, Romanticism, and the Afro-Creole Protest Tradition in Louisiana, 1718–1868* (Baton Rouge: Louisiana State University Press, 1997). Where Bell focuses exclusively on the freemen of color, the other works on the Sisters of the Holy Family—the religious order founded by free women of color Henriette Delille, Josephine Gaudin, and Josephine Charles—give greater attention to their female counterparts. See Sister Mary Bernard Deggs, *No Cross, No Crown: Black Nuns in Nineteenth-Century New Orleans* (Bloomington: Indiana University Press, 2002).

17. Adelle v. Beauregard, 1 Mart. (o.s.) 183, 1810 WL 869 (La. Terr. Super. Orleans). On the significance of *Adelle* and *State* in US race making, see Frank W. Sweet, *Legal History of the Color Line: The Rise and Triumph of the One-Drop Rule* (Palm Coast, FL: Backintyme, 2005), 204–5.

18. Hall, "Afro-Louisiana History." On the domestic slave trade, see Steven Deyle, *Carry Me Back: The Domestic Slave Trade in American Life* (Oxford: Oxford University Press, 2005); Walter Johnson, *Soul by Soul: Life inside the Antebellum Slave Market* (Cambridge, MA: Harvard University Press, 1999); Johnson, *The Chattel Principle: Internal Slave Trades in the Americas* (New Haven, CT: Yale University Press, 2004).

19. Slavery in Louisiana Collection, folder 14, MSS 44, Williams Research Center of the Historic New Orleans Collection, New Orleans, Louisiana.

20. On coartación and the creation of a multiracial free black class in Spanish Louisiana, see Hanger, *Bounded Lives, Bounded Places*, 62–70; and Hall, *Africans in Colonial Louisiana*.

21. 1810 US Federal Census; *1811 New Orleans City Directory*. On the notarial records of the purchase of Maria and Staes's other bondpersons, see Hall, *Database*. On governmentality, see Michel Foucault, "Governmentality," in *The Foucault Effect: Studies in Governmentality*, trans. Rosi Braidotti and rev. Colin Graham, ed. Graham Burchell, Colin Gordon, and Peter Miller (Chicago: University of Chicago Press, 1991), 87–104.

To complete Staes's biography, the 1840 US Census lists him as being between seventy and eighty years old, with his wife, presumably their adolescent son, and nine bondpersons, one of whom may have been Louis. Staes died insolvent sometime before 1846, the year *Bertoli v. The Citizens' Bank* (1846) came before the Louisiana Supreme Court. In that case, the Citizens' Bank, which had given Staes a total of three different mortgages on his house and lot, disputed the liquidation of his estate following his death. The mortgages must have been on the land and not the bondpersons, however, because, in the 1850 US Census, Mary Staes, his widow, is listed as owning six bondspersons. See Bertoli v. The Citizens' Bank, 1 La. Ann. 119, 1846 WL 3368 (La.).

22. The application of particular, class-based conceptions of motherhood, virtue, femininity, and love are problematic in the context of chattel slavery. On magnanimous slave motherhood, see Jacqueline Jones, *Labor of Love, Labor of Sorrow: Black Women, Work, and the Family from Slavery to the Present* (New York: Basic Books, 1985). On the difficulties in assessing morality and the enslaved, see Jacobs, Child, and Fagan Yellin, *Incidents*; Morgan, *Laboring Women*; Saidiya V. Hartman, *Scenes of Subjection: Terror, Slavery, and Self-Making in Nineteenth-Century America* (New York: Oxford University Press, 1997).

23. Pierre-Louis Berquin-Duvallon and John Davis, *Travels in Louisiana and the Floridas, in the Year, 1802: Giving a Correct Picture of Those Countries* (New York: Riley, 1806), 53–54.

24. *Courrier de la Louisiane*, November 18, 1814.

25. Herbert Asbury, *The French Quarter: An Informal History of the New Orleans Underworld* (New York: Thunder's Mouth, 2003), 135–40. Lafitte's gained fame in the twentieth century as one of author Tennessee Williams's favorite nightspots. The site was added to the National Register of Historical Places in 1970 for its "briquet-entre-poteaux" (brick-between-post) architecture. Roulhac Toledano and National Trust for Historic Preservation in the United States, *The National Trust Guide to New Orleans* (New York: Wiley, 1996), 19–21. See also *1811 New Orleans City Directory*; Berquin and Davis, *Travels*, 54. On the pirates Lafitte, see William C. Davis, *The Pirates Lafitte: The Treacherous World of the Corsairs of the Gulf* (Orlando, FL: Harcourt, 2005).

26. This section from the Code Noir is quoted in the case of Delery v. Mornet, 11 Mart. (o.s.) 4, 1822 WL 1268 (La.).

27. "List of Suggested Changes with Regard to the Black Population of New Orleans," in *The Favrot Family Papers: A Documentary Chronicle of Early Louisiana*, ed. Guillermo Náñez Falcón and Wilbur E. Meneray, 5 vols. (New Orleans: Howard Tilton Memorial Library, Tulane, 1988), 2:169–70. This pamphlet was preserved only as a copy in a scribe's papers, making it possible to determine its origin in the 1790s, but not its authorship. On the making of colonial Louisiana, see Shannon Lee Dawdy, *Building the Devil's Empire: French Colonial New Orleans* (Chicago: University of Chicago Press, 2008); and Daniel H. Usner Jr., *Indians, Settlers, and Slaves in a Frontier Exchange Economy: The Lower Mississippi Valley before 1783* (Chapel Hill: University of North Carolina Press, 1992).

28. On interracial relationships and their political potential, see Jill Lepore, *New York Burning: Liberty, Slavery and Conspiracy in Eighteenth-Century Manhattan* (New York: Knopf, 2005); Thomas J. Davis, *A Rumor of Revolt: The "Great Negro Plot" In Colonial New York* (New York: Free Press, 1985); and Peter Linebaugh and Marcus Buford Rediker, *The Many-Headed Hydra: Sailors, Slaves, Commoners, and the Hidden History of the Revolutionary Atlantic* (Boston: Beacon, 2000).

29. James Pitot and Robert D. Bush, *Observations on the Colony of Louisiana, from 1796 to 1802* (Baton Rouge: Louisiana State University Press, 1979), 29.

30. On taverns as cultural institutions in antebellum New Orleans, see Sublette, *World*. On the national demographics of enslaved Louisiana, see Hall, *Africans in Colonial Louisiana*; and Gomez, *Exchanging Our Country Marks*. On vagabond internationalism, taverns, and the creation of African diasporic and Atlantic culture, see Claude McKay, *Banjo: A Story without a Plot* (New York: Harper and Brothers, 1929); and Brent Hayes Edwards, *The Practice of Diaspora: Literature, Translation, and the Rise of Black Internationalism* (Cambridge: Harvard University Press, 2003). On jook joints, see Katrina Hazzard-Gordon, *Jookin': The Rise of Social Dance Formations in African-American Culture* (Philadelphia: Temple University Press, 1990); Brenda Dixon Gottschild, *The Black Dancing Body: A Geography from Coon to Cool* (New York: Palgrave Macmillan, 2003).

31. Claiborne, *Official Letter Books*, 3:357.

32. Collector William N. Brown moved to New Orleans as one of the secretaries of the US commission charged with taking possession of Louisiana. Correspondence between secretary of treasury Albert Gallatin, William Brown, and a bank cashier show that by January 1810, William Brown stood accused of embezzling one hundred thousand dollars and absconding. Thus Brown is absent on 1810 census records, making it difficult to identify his exact address (and by extension the exact location of the taverns Claiborne described). Brown's daughter, Louise Adeline Brown Oxnard, married Thomas Oxnard and gave birth to Benjamin Alexander Oxnard, a sugar master and the owner of the Adeline sugar factory company. The Oxnards remained prominent in the Louisiana and larger sugar industry well into the twentieth century. On the Williams-Oxnard family, see Alcée Fortier, *Louisiana: Comprising Sketches of Counties, Towns, Events, Institutions, and Persons, Arranged in Cyclopedic Form 3* (Atlanta: Southern Historical Association, 1909), 3:558–59. On the alleged embezzlement, see Adolphus W. Greely, *Public Documents of the First Fourteen Congresses, 1789–1817: Papers Relating to Early Congressional Documents*, 3 vols. (Washington: GPO, 1900), 538. On Nicholas Trist, see Wallace Ohrt, *Defiant Peacemaker: Nicholas Trist in the Mexican War* (College Station: Texas A&M University Press, 1997). Black Codes eventually outlawed free black ownership of taverns. For example, in 1836 Washington, DC, made it illegal for free blacks to sell alcohol or operate a tavern. See Worthington G. Snethen, *The Black Code of the District of Columbia, in Force September 1st, 1848* (New York: Harned, 1848).

33. Ramozay et al. v. The Mayor &c. of New Orleans, 1 Mart. (o.s.) 241, 1811 WL 1028 (La. Terr. Super. Orleans).

34. *Delery*, 1822 WL 1268. For the case that cemented the presumption of freedom for "mulattos" and enslavement for "Negroes," see *Adelle*, 1810 WL 869.

35. *Delery*, 1822 WL 1268 .

36. "Reports on December 17 Meeting of the Orleans Legislative Council," *Louisiana Gazette*, January 4, 1805.

37. On enslaved participation in markets and its social implications, see Roderick A. McDonald, *The Economic and Material Culture of Slaves: Goods and Chattels on the Sugar Plantations of Jamaica and Louisiana* (Baton Rouge: Louisiana State University Press, 1993); and Penningroth, *Claims of Kinfolk*. See also Shane White and Graham

J. White, *Stylin': African American Expressive Culture from Its Beginnings to the Zoot Suit* (Ithaca, NY: Cornell University Press, 1998).

38. Linebaugh and Rediker, *Many-Headed Hydra*. On the chattel principle, see Johnson, *Chattel Principle*. On prostitution in antebellum and postbellum New Orleans, see Alecia P. Long, *The Great Southern Babylon: Sex, Race, and Respectability in New Orleans, 1865–1920* (Baton Rouge: Louisiana State University Press, 2004); Earl F. Niehaus, *The Irish in New Orleans, 1800–1860* (Baton Rouge: Louisiana State University Press, 1965); and Robert C. Reinders, *End of an Era: New Orleans, 1850–1860* (New Orleans: Pelican, 1964). The most recent work on antebellum prostitution is Judith Kelleher Schafer, *Brothels, Depravity, and Abandoned Women: Illegal Sex in Antebellum New Orleans* (Baton Rouge: Louisiana State University Press, 2009). This legal history chronicles prostitution as recorded in the 1850s in the First District Court of New Orleans.

39. Charles C. Robin and Stuart O. Landry, *Voyage to Louisiana, 1803–1805* (New Orleans: Pelican, 1966), 246.

40. On hiring out, see McDonald, *Material Culture of Slaves*.

41. Robin and Landry, *Voyage*, 41. On libertinage, race, and sex, see Doris Lorraine Garraway, *The Libertine Colony: Creolization in the Early French Caribbean* (Durham, NC: Duke University Press, 2005). "Universal Regenerator" is a curious phrase also mentioned as part of an advertisement on the walls of the gentlemen's restroom in a downtown hotel in New York City. "Our Down-Town Hotel," *New York Times,* January 31, 1853. Around the same time, the phrase gained currency as a synonym for Jesus, who through salvation became the "Universal Regenerator" for humankind. By the 1860s the phrase applied to a deity, a health supplement, or a cure for sexually transmitted disease.

42. *Chevalier v. LaRonde*, folder 532, Manuscript Collection 532, Manuscripts Department, Tulane University. The most prominent Laronde was Pierre Denis de Laronde, who served as captain-commandant of the "Isleños," or the Hispanophone Canary Islanders who settled in present-day St. Bernard Parish. See Sidney Louis Villeré, *The Canary Islands Migration to Louisiana, 1778–1783: The History and Passenger Lists of the Islenos Volunteer Recruits and Their Families* (New Orleans: Genealogical Research Society of New Orleans, 1971), viii. On enslaved healing in the absence of doctors, see Sharla M. Fett, *Working Cures: Healing, Health, and Power on Southern Slave Plantations* (Chapel Hill: University of North Carolina Press, 2002).

43. Timothy Flint and James Flint, *Recollections of the Last Ten Years, Passed in Occasional Residences and Journeyings in the Valley of the Mississippi, from Pittsburg and the Missouri to the Gulf of Mexico, and from Florida to the Spanish Frontier: In a Series of Letters to the Rev. James Flint, of Salem, Massachusetts* (Boston: Cummings, Hilliard, 1826), 295, 300.

44. Ibid., 309–10.

45. The sexualization of so-called mulatto women's bodies occurred with the *signares*, the so-called mixed-race women of Senegal and across the Americas. See, among others, Hall, *Africans in Colonial Louisiana*; Michel Adanson, *A Voyage to Senegal, the Isle of Goreé, and the River Gambia* (London: Nourse, 1759); Gilberto Freyre and Samuel Putnam, *The Masters and the Slaves: A Study in the Development of Brazilian Civilization* (New York: Knopf, 1946); Tita Mandeleau, *Signare Anna, Ou, Le Voyage Aux Escales* (Dakar: Les Nouvelles Editions Africaines du Sénégal, 1991);

Verena Stolcke, *Marriage, Class and Colour in Nineteenth-Century Cuba: A Study of Racial Attitudes and Sexual Values in a Slave Society* (London: Cambridge University Press, 1974); and José Vasconcelos and Didier Tisdel Jaén, *The Cosmic Race: A Bilingual Edition* (Baltimore, MD: Johns Hopkins University Press, 1997).

46. "Snowy White and Sooty," *Daily Orleanian*, January 15, 1852.

47. Ibid., February 12, 1852.

48. On the crackdowns in the Marigny, particularly Elysian Fields (derisively referred to as Sanctity Row), see Schafer, *Brothels*; and Niehaus, *Irish in New Orleans*, 69. On antebellum sex between white women and black men, see Martha Hodes, *White Women, Black Men: Illicit Sex in the Nineteenth-Century South* (New Haven, CT: Yale University Press, 1997); Hodes, *Sex, Love, Race: Crossing Boundaries in North American History* (New York: New York University Press, 1999); and Hodes, *The Sea Captain's Wife: A True Story of Love, Race, and War in the Nineteenth Century* (New York: Norton, 2006).

49. Caryn Cossé Bell, for example, focuses exclusively on the free men of color in antebellum New Orleans. Walter Johnson uses the slave market to map the backgrounds, motivations, and implications of the various actors in that space. Bell, *Revolution*; Johnson, *Soul by Soul*. Key works in the field of feminist geography include Linda McDowell, *Gender, Identity and Place: Understanding Feminist Geographies* (Cambridge, UK: Polity, 1999); McDowell and Joanne P. Sharp, *Space, Gender, Knowledge: Feminist Readings* (London: Arnold, 1997); Pamela Moss and Karen Falconer Al-Hindi, *Feminisms in Geography: Rethinking Space, Place, and Knowledges* (Lanham, MD: Rowman and Littlefield, 2008); and Gillian Rose, *Feminism and Geography: The Limits of Geographical Knowledge* (Oxford, UK: Polity, 1993).

Chapter 3

"There Are Two Great Oceans"

The Slavery Metaphor in the Antebellum Women's Rights Discourse as Redescription of Race and Gender

Hélène Quanquin

The anniversary of the American Equal Rights Association of May 12 and 13, 1869, was a watershed for American reformers. During the meeting, abolitionists and women's rights activists severed personal ties already weakened by the debate over the Fourteenth and Fifteenth Amendments and divided into opposing camps. How did people who had been working side by side for several decades find themselves in the situation of choosing between the two causes—the rights of African Americans and those of women—they had previously fought for almost indiscriminately?[1] Trying to make sense of this rift, women's rights activist Lucy Stone opted for metaphorical language: "Woman has an ocean of wrongs too deep for any plummet, and the negro, too, has an ocean of wrongs that cannot be fathomed. There are two great oceans; in the one is the black man, and in the other is the woman," she said.[2] The image of the ocean, used for both "woman" and "the negro," was meant to show that both groups suffered *equally* from oppression, but it also insisted on the unfathomable depth of their subordination, and the impossibility for any outsider to truly understand it.

Stone's ocean analogy answered Frederick Douglass's speech, made at the same meeting, in favor of the immediate enfranchisement of black men. Despite her lukewarm support for the Fifteenth Amendment—"I will be thankful in my soul if *any* body can get out of the terrible pit," she conceded—she disagreed with the idea brought forward by Douglass that black men were more in need of protection than women: "I want to remind the audience that when he [Douglass] says what the Ku-Kluxes did all over the South, the Ku-Kluxes here in the North in the shape of men, take away the children from the mother, and separate them as completely as if done on the block of the auctioneer." Applied to women's condition and the usual practice of denying them child custody in case of divorce or death of the father, the conflation of two structuring elements of the African American experience in the South before and after the Civil War—the slave auction and the Ku Klux Klan, founded at the end of 1865—showed Stone's belief in the necessity to bring attention to the plight of women, whose enfranchisement, she claimed, was "more imperative" than black men's.[3] But it was also evidence of her failure to describe and convey the reality of women's condition on its own terms.

Stone's speech included ambivalent references to what Elizabeth V. Spelman calls the "generic woman." As Spelman argues, "the description of what we have in common 'as women' has almost always been a description of white middle-class woman."[4] Stone's use of the slavery analogy applied to "woman" was a way to emphasize black men's (or Douglass's) and white women's (or Stone's) commonalities, to promote the rights of white women. Yet it also had a cost, as it erased the experience of one group, black women, including former slave women, for whom both terms of the metaphor had been, and still were, everyday realities: on the one hand, the slave auction and the Ku Klux Klan, the symbols of racist oppression; on the other hand, unjust marriage laws and, more generally speaking, sexism.[5] Stone's discourse was thus part of the "discussions of racism versus sexism" that kept the main actors of the debate over citizenship rights after the Civil War "from seeing ways in which what sexism means and how it works is modulated by racism, and ways in which what racism means is modulated by sexism" and made them oblivious to the intersections of race and gender.[6]

White women's rights activists frequently used the slavery analogy after the Civil War, as evidenced by *The History of Woman Suffrage*, published in 1881 by Elizabeth Cady Stanton, Susan B. Anthony, and Matilda Joslyn Gage.[7] In the introduction, the references to slavery in relation to American women's condition constantly oscillate between the literal and the analogical. Written fifteen years or so after the passage of the Thirteenth Amendment, the very first sentence of the first volume describes slavery as a multifaceted phenomenon: "The prolonged slavery of woman is the darkest page in human history."[8] Slavery was not considered here as a metaphor per se, but rather as a literal descriptive of women's situation. For the authors of the *History of Woman Suffrage*, by abolishing one form of slavery, the Thirteenth Amendment made (white) women's enslavement incomparable because of its permanence. Slavery was then viewed as the most accurate and truthful term to define women's condition and thus legitimized the demand for (white) woman suffrage.[9]

The use of the slavery metaphor after the Civil War should be considered within the context of the abolition of slavery and the debates over the Fourteenth and Fifteenth Amendments, which were structured around the opposition between black men and white women and dissociated race from gender. But it also needs to be studied in terms of both continuity and rupture with the antebellum period, when slavery was the South's "peculiar institution," and abolition and women's rights were seen as joint fights by many reformers.

In her eulogy of William Lloyd Garrison in May 1879, Lucy Stone pointed to "the organic connection between the Anti-Slavery and Woman Suffrage movements, which made the former the inevitable forerunner of the latter."[10] Along the same lines, historians of American feminism have considered the relation between the two movements in the light of women's rights activism's initial dependence on abolitionist "ideology" and "method."[11] More recently, Martha Jones has dealt with this question in terms of the integration of the two issues of race and gender in African American public culture, attesting to "the rich cross-pollinization of the antebellum antislavery and women's rights movement." For Jones, black women offer a unique vantage point, as "they were active at the intersection of those two salient social categories and fashioned their tactics and their aims to suit this circumstance."[12]

Scholars have illuminated the problematic nature of the slavery analogy to describe white women's condition. As early as in 1969 Gerda Lerner claimed that the comparison between women and slaves was "a rhetorical device rather than a factual statement" for reformers, also pointing out its inadequacy as a descriptive of women's condition.[13] More recently, historians have focused on the slavery metaphor as white women's appropriation of the black female body and slave women's experience, as in Lucy Stone's 1869 speech. Karen Sanchez-Eppler has argued that while the slavery analogy used by feminist-abolitionists might have been "mutually empowering," it generally "tend[ed] toward asymmetry and exploitation."[14] According to her, the constant references to the sexual abuse of slave women in white female abolitionists' discourse are an indication of the need "to project the white woman's sexual anxieties onto the sexualized body of the female slave."[15] Studying the example of former slave Sojourner Truth, Teresa C. Zackodnik has also expanded the discussion to include contemporary feminism, contending that "the bondswoman functioned symbolically for all that white women found restrictive in their own condition, never matter that they were free whereas their 'sister slave' was bound for life. . . . For her nineteenth-century white contemporaries, Truth stood as material proof of that rather abstract trope of white woman's condition, 'woman as slave.' However, her symbolic value has been far from limited to her historical time and place. In both the nineteenth and twentieth centuries, *the* black woman symbolically bridges a gap between abstract discourse and the material."[16]

The contribution of white women's use of the slavery metaphor to "their own self-creation as autonomous individuals" through the appropriation of black women's experience and body is crucial to our understanding of the way white female feminist-abolitionists positioned themselves in relation to slavery and intersections of race and gender before the Civil War.[17] Yet the antebellum use of the slavery metaphor has been obscured in part by the post–Civil War debates. The racist attacks some white activists directed at African Americans and their indifference to the plight of black women have led historians to explore the construction of the American women's rights movement as a *white* women's rights movement.[18] From this perspective, the use of the slavery metaphor by white women was another manifestation of their prejudice and appropriation of an experience deeply rooted in racial differences.

Elizabeth Cady Stanton is an example of this continuity throughout the nineteenth century. Her more marginal position in the abolitionist movement might have made her less hesitant to view slavery as a literal description of woman's condition, as suggested by her biographer Lori Ginzberg: "For her, the story of slavery and the emancipation of the slaves would serve primarily as a lesson in women's own status, degradations, and rights."[19] This took on another dimension after the Civil War. As Michele Mitchell points out, Stanton chose to rely on "racialist logic" and "hierarchical rhetoric" to further her goal of woman suffrage after the Civil War.[20] But Elizabeth Cady Stanton did not represent all white women.

As noted by Serena Mayeri, "the political analogies between race and sex are highly context-dependent and historically variable." In addition to focusing on the antebellum context and the racism, both overt and latent, within the reform movement, for white reformers' use of the slavery metaphor, I reassess the analogy through the process that French philosopher Paul Ricoeur has called "redescription." In the metaphor, he notes, both terms of the analogy are "displaced": "to affect just one word, the metaphor has to disturb a whole network by means of an aberrant attribution." Aimed at understanding and making white women's situation visible, the slavery metaphor was a two-way street, a conversation between different conditions as well as different groups. The study of the different trajectories of the slavery metaphor in the antebellum women's rights discourse invalidates the idea that the slavery analogy was consistent among feminist abolitionists. In her analysis of the trajectory of the "abolitionist emblem" of the female supplicant in the nineteenth century, Jean Fagan Yellin shows that it was used to promote different discourses on race and gender and "multiple strategies, alternately addressing and avoiding issues of race, sexual conformity, and patriarchal definitions of true womanhood."[21]

Crucial to understanding the fluidity of the slavery analogy as it was used by white feminist-abolitionists before the Civil War was the challenge of conveying their experience of oppression—"the ocean"—to outsiders. The testimonies that the abolitionist movement relied on contributed to the hypervisibility of the slave's experience among reformers and to the two joint phenomena of what Saidiya V. Hartman has called "the spectacular nature of black suffering and, conversely, the dissimulation of suffering through spectacle." In the case of white women, the incomparable nature of slavery, as well as the near invisibility of their oppression to both themselves and society constituted a challenge that needed to be addressed. The volatility of their use of the slavery metaphor before the Civil War was the complex result of the aggregation of their different experiences as activists, as well as the paradox of white women's condition, which made the slavery metaphor when applied to them at once enlightening and obscuring, both inescapable and unthinkable. As Carole Pateman writes, "when individuals are juridically free and civil equals, the problem is not literally one of slavery; no one can, simultaneously, be human property and a citizen."[22]

Meant to convey a specific experience, the slavery metaphor resonated with white feminist-abolitionists' personal lives. When, at the American Equal Rights Association meeting Lucy Stone compared white women's conditions with the life of African Americans in the South before and after the Civil War, she was not merely trying to make sense of the split among reformers. In 1869 she was also confronted with problems of her own: after years spent looking after her daughter Alice, she had resumed her public work in favor of reform, and was then "los[ing] herself in work, intensifying her already frenetic pace." One of her biographers sees Stone's intense public activity as a way not only to make up for lost time but to deal with her husband Henry B. Blackwell's affair with a certain "Mrs. P."[23] Stone's passionate appeal in favor of white women cannot be considered apart from her personal situation as a married woman dealing with certain personal and emotional issues, as in the other instances analyzed here.

The use of the slavery metaphor by antebellum white female reformers had two important, sometimes contradictory, functions: it helped them explore the interconnectedness of the issues of race and gender, but it also allowed them to try and solve conflicts arising at the juncture of their public and personal lives. I focus on what Nancy Cott calls the "language of politics," relying on women's public and private expressions about women's condition, in conventions, in the press, as well as in letters exchanged by activists.[24] The pervasiveness and fluidity of the analogy reveal not only white female reformers' prejudices and privileges but also the intricacies of antebellum reform culture, which was in theory devoted to universal equality but largely ignored the "complexity of intersectionality" in the process.[25]

The Early Uses of Slavery as a Literal and Metaphorical Descriptive

The use of the slavery analogy to describe women's situation is not specific to antebellum American society: Carole Pateman notes that "the comparison of women and wives with slaves was frequently made from the late seventeenth century onward." In her study of George Sand's literary work and correspondence, Nancy Rogers shows how the French writer used it to convey a specific representation of women's condition. Nor was it then applied only to women. Webster's *American Dictionary of the English language* of 1832 gives four definitions for the word "slave": "1. A person who is wholly subject to the will of another; 2. One who has lost the power of resistance; or one who surrenders himself to any power whatever; 3. A mean person; one in the lowest state of life; 4. A drudge; one who labors like a slave." The word was used metaphorically in the United States in the first half of the nineteenth century to describe different kinds of subjections.[26]

Within the context of the antislavery movement, however, it took on a more complex dimension. A large number of feminist-abolitionists before the Civil War became involved in abolitionism with the belief that slavery was a unique, incomparable institution. The pervasive use of the slavery metaphor attested to the powerful evocation of the "peculiar institution" and allowed antebellum reformers to articulate the joint fight for slavery and women's rights. It also tended to conceal the multiplicity of experiences in relation to slavery within the movement right from the beginning, including those of former slaves who told audiences about their life in bondage; free blacks, whose skin color made them the targets of racism and put them at risk of being captured and sent as slaves to the South; and white activists, who had never experienced slavery and never would.[27] From this vantage point, we can read the many stories of white-skinned women held in bondage, such as Lydia Maria Child's "octoroon," in several ways: while they were meant to create sympathy among a white audience who found it difficult to identify with black slaves, they also played on "the white racism of those . . . incapable of identifying with a black woman."[28] They should also be viewed as expressions of the challenge inherent in fighting for other people's rights and the necessity to bridge the gap between the several experiences present among abolitionists, even at the cost of distorting the reality of slavery. This dilemma explains why, right from the 1830s and the emergence of a women's rights discourse within the abolitionist movement, the use of the analogy to describe white women's condition showed some instability, oscillating between the purely descriptive and the metaphorical.

An early instance of the comparison between the situation of white women and slavery was written by Lydia Maria Child, who was in large part responsible for "the image of the enslaved African American women that took shape in the minds of northern abolitionists in the 1830s and 1840s" and whose writings were central in the integration of the slavery metaphor into feminist-abolitionist discourse.[29] In 1835 Child published a two-volume book titled *The History of the Condition of Women in Various Ages and Nations.* According to Jean Fagan Yellin, "part travelogue, part social history, and part anthropological study, the *Condition of Women* signaled an important moment in the history of American feminism." Its ambitious goal was to give an international and universal perspective on women's condition generally defined as a state of inferiority and subjection. While Child denied in the preface that her book was "an essay upon woman's rights," the lines from Lord Byron's "The Corsair," which she chose as an epigraph, indicated that, for her, subjection was a condition shared by all women and all races: "I am a slave, a favoured slave at best, / At best, to share his splendour, and seem very blest; / When weary of these fleeting charms and me, / There yawns the sack, and yonder rolls the sea. / What! am I then a toy for dotard's play, / To wear but till the gilding frets away?"[30] In keeping with Byron's lines, Child described women's condition in different countries as one of subjection: "The Bedouins consider their wives as slaves"; in Afghanistan, "of course women are considered as property"; in China, a "husband has always a right to sell an unfaithful wife for a slave." Child's depiction of Hindu women contained all the defining features of a state of slavery, without actually using the words "slavery" or "slave": "The *arbitrary* power of a father disposes of them in childhood. . . . If married, their husbands have a *despotic* control over them; if unable to support them, they can lend or *sell* them to a neighbor; and in the Hindoo rage for gambling, wives and children are frequently staked and lost; if they survive their husbands, they must pay implicit *obedience* to the oldest son; if they have no sons, the nearest male relative holds them in *subjection*."[31]

Female bondage and submission might have been universal in Child's eyes, but she also noted that there existed different degrees in this condition: when comparing the lot of African women with that of slave women in Southern states, she wrote that "the domestic slavery of the Africans is altogether of a milder character, and more resembles Hebrew servitude, than the slavery existing among white men." Child was also aware of the specificity of enslaved women, as she devoted a chapter to "women in slave-holding countries." Interestingly, she refrained from using the slavery metaphor in relation to the situation of "women of the United States," which shows that, at the time, it was not systematically used by all abolitionists to describe white women's condition.[32]

In 1837 the English writer Harriet Martineau published *Society in America*, in which she elaborated a complex network of meanings assigned to the word "slavery" in relation to white women. Although not confining her analysis to the female condition, Martineau devoted one section of her book to their "political non-existence," right after a discussion of "people of colour," in the part titled "citizenship." Her comparison of white women with slaves was based on the words of Thomas Jefferson, who believed three categories of people should have been excluded from the "deliberations" of the political process: "infants," "women," and "slaves."[33] The alleged reason for the exclusion of women offered by Jefferson was "to prevent depravation of morals, and ambiguity of issue." Refusing to see the protection of women's morality and paternity rights as the real motive of their marginalization, Martineau wrote,

> If the slave disqualification, here assigned, were shifted up under the head of Women, their case would be *nearer the truth* than as it now stands. Woman's lack of will and of property, is more like the true cause of her exclusion from the representation, than that which is actually set down against her. As if there could be no means of conducting public affairs but by promiscuous meetings! As if there would be more danger in promiscuous meetings for political business than in such meetings for worship, for oratory, for music,

for dramatic entertainments,—and for any of the thousand transactions of civilized life! The plea is not worth another word.[34]

According to Martineau, slavery provided a more accurate rendering of white women's condition, marked by the same characteristics as that of slaves, in particular, their lack of property and of free will. Through what might have been considered as an improbable connection, the comparison with slavery held a specific function in the author's reasoning, that of an eye-opener, allowing the readers to grasp the reality of women's situation. This role was alluded to in several testimonies of feminist-abolitionists when explaining their conversion to women's rights. In a letter addressed to the National Woman's Rights Convention of 1850, Samuel J. May linked his to the words of "a very intelligent woman of that city," called Ruth Olne, who told him after an antislavery lecture he had made in Providence: "I suspect that you do not apprehend how much of your description of the helpless dependence of the Slaves applies equally well to the condition of the whole *female sex*." Struck by "the parallel," May recalled, "then first my eyes were opened to the *Wrongs of Women*."[35] But in *Society in America*, Martineau also showed the ambivalence of the analogy, aimed at making white women's condition visible, while the situation of enslaved women receded into the background. She referred to the existence of female slaves in the United States: "governments in the United States have power to enslave certain women."[36] She did not mention, however, that these "certain women" were black and thus turned slavery into a color-blind institution, thereby making her use of the analogy applied to white women seem less problematic than it was.

Contrary to Martineau, the Grimké sisters never failed to address the ambivalence inherent in the slavery metaphor to describe white women's condition. As Jean Fagan Yellin notes, Angelina Grimké "identified with the slave emblem early," as did her sister Sarah.[37] In 1837 the two sisters published essays in the form of public letters, in which they addressed the situation of white women in relation to slaves' condition. In *Letters on the Equality of the Sexes, and the Condition of Woman*, Sarah Grimké used the work of Lydia Maria Child in two of the letters titled "Women in Asia and Africa" to illustrate the similarities existing between the condition of women in the United States and in other countries.[38] The pronoun "we" used by Sarah Grimké in one of the two letters conjured up the existence of a community of women, linked by the common, universal, experience of enslavement: "We are much in the situation of the slave. Man has asserted and assumed authority over us." The adverb "much," however, suggested that while all women were *like* slaves, not all of them were actual slaves. This distinction was confirmed by Grimké's reference to the particular situation of African Americans: "Here I am reminded of the resemblance between the situation of women in heathen and Mohammedan countries, and our brethren and sisters of color in this Christian land, where they are despised and cast out as though they were unclean. And on precisely the same ground, because they are said to be inferior."[39]

In her *Letters*, Sarah Grimké enlarged the meaning of the term "slavery," from physical to psychological condition, writing that man "has done all he could do to debase and enslave [woman's] mind."[40] In alluding to this idea of psychological dependence and subjection to man's "sensual pleasure," Sarah Grimké pointed to what she saw as one of the specificities of white women's servitude compared with the slave woman's, that is, its voluntary aspect, due to woman's internalization of her own oppression: "Alas! she has too well learned the lesson, which MAN has labored to teach her. She has surrendered her dearest RIGHTS, and has been satisfied with the privileges which man has assumed to grant her."[41] This notion of mental servitude was present at the time in antislavery writings and did not apply only to women, as shown by a piece titled "The Enslaved Mind," published in the *Slave's Friend*, an abolitionist paper from New York: "Men and women have *bodies* and *minds* too; so have children, for they are little men and women. The slaves have their bodies in bondage; but the minds of many of them are free. The mind, you know, is a million times more valuable than the body. We are grieved that the bodies of our fellow men are in slavery, and we are trying to liberate them. Why should we not feel more distressed that so many minds are enslaved?"[42]

For Sarah Grimké, however, the existence of "butterflies of the *fashionable* world" demonstrated that some women had accepted their inferior position to the point that they readily relinquished their status as moral and intellectual beings: "Fashionable women regard themselves, and are regarded by men, as pretty toys or as mere instruments of pleasure."[43] Sarah Grimké's widening of the notion of slavery to encompass self-imposed bondage echoed her own sister's remarks in her *Letters to Catharine E. Beecher, in Reply to an Essay on Slavery and Abolitionism, Addressed to A. E. Grimké*, also written in 1837. Angelina Grimké claimed that "woman has been taught to lean upon an arm of flesh, to sit as a doll arrayed in 'gold, and pearls, and costly array,' to be admired for her personal charms, and caressed and humored like a spoiled child, or converted into a mere drudge to suit the convenience of her lord and master."[44] Reading both sisters' 1837 public letters, it is clear, as noted by Robert K. Nelson, that, for them, it was sex that primarily threatened to enslave women:

> In their use of the term "pleasure," both of the sisters were alluding to the linkage between sexuality and domination in abolitionist ideology. Not only was sex tainted in its association with a hedonistic South where white planters exercised an appalling power over the bodies of black female slaves, sex was more generally suspect because it led a husband to treat his wife as a slaveholder treated his slave: as an object, "an instrument," a "pretty toy," a "pet animal" that he controlled and used for his sensual satisfaction rather than regarding her as a spiritual companion.[45]

In 1837 the Grimké sisters were at the center of an intense network of exchanges, which included abolitionists—black and white, female and male—

but also opponents to abolitionism. In April the black abolitionist activist Sarah Forten was writing Angelina: "We *all* feel deeply sensible of your labors of love for our people."[46] Two months earlier Angelina had confided in Sarah Douglass that her antislavery fight had brought her closer to black people: "The more I mingle with your people, the more I feel for their oppressions and desire to sympathize in their sorrows."[47] That same year the two sisters were also engaged in a correspondence with Theodore D. Weld, their mentor in the abolitionist movement and Angelina's future husband.[48] In 1837 Weld had not yet openly expressed his feelings for Angelina Grimké, although he had probably already fallen in love with her. The tension present in their letters exchanged on the issue of women's rights cannot be considered apart from the growing feelings of affection between the two and, in the words of Gerda Lerner, "that unique fusion of private and public concerns which their entire relationship had manifested."[49] When the Grimké sisters started to advocate for women's rights, they were accused by some abolitionists of leading a "selfish crusade."[50] Weld's letters to Angelina and Sarah Grimké argued that, more than other white women within the abolitionist movement, they had an incomparable responsibility in the fight against slavery. Weld assigned them, as the southern daughters of slaveholders, the role of witnesses and voices for the slaves: "We can only say that our experience of them in the City of New York has led us to bless the God of the oppressed, for having raised up from the very bosom of the slave-holding community, *such* witnesses—*such* pleaders for the mute and stricken-down victims of unrighteous and cruel dominion."[51] Weld argued that the Grimké sisters' primary accountability was to enslaved women more than to white women:

> Besides you are *Southerners*, have been slaveholders; your dearest friends are all in the sin and shame and peril. All these things give you great access to northern mind, great *sway* over it. You can do ten times as much on the subject of *slavery* as Mrs. Child or Mrs. Chapman. Why? Not because your powers are superior to theirs, but because you are *southerners.* You can do more at convincing the north than twenty *northern* females, tho' they could speak as well as you. Now this peculiar advantage you *lose* the moment you take on *another* subject. *Any* woman of your powers will produce as much effect as you on the north in advocating the rights of *free* women (I mean in contradistinction to *slave* women).[52]

According to Weld, any northern (white) woman could advocate women's rights, but only they, as former slaveholders, could fight effectively for enslaved women. For Weld, then, women's rights were a cause for and by white women, which would only distance the Grimké sisters from slaves. This discourse seems quite manipulative, as it laid on the sisters' shoulders the responsibility for slavery and thus the slave. Angelina Grimké denied such statements in different ways. First, she argued that northern white men were equally responsible for slavery: "I am afraid thou art not the only Northern man who thinks I have not lived at the South for nothing, for I do *scold most terribly* when I undertake to tell the brethren *how* the North is implicated in the guilt of slavery; they look at me in utter amazement." She also reminded Weld that she had no intention whatsoever of forgetting slave women in her fight for women's rights, as the antislavery cause was a personal one to her. Crediting a slave for changing her life—"The fact is, I *was* once a great scold and I am indebted to a *slave* for curing me of it"—she strove to fulfill what T. Gregory Garvey has called the "ideal of moral authenticity in the public sphere," composed of "personal risk, public expression of belief, and participation in a committed public dialogue."[53]

In her answer to Weld, Angelina Grimké argued that, as a woman, she would not be able to fight adequately for slave women if she herself felt "fettered": "What *then* can *woman* do for the slave when she is herself under the feet of man and shamed into *silence*?"[54] For her, identification with slave women "came to represent what she concluded was her own oppression as a woman, the oppression of all women, and women's struggle for liberation."[55] The writings of the Grimké sisters in the second half of the 1830s thus show that, right from the beginning, the insertion of women's rights into abolitionist rhetoric raised the question of the relations, or intersections, between the two causes, as well as that of the relations of hierarchy existing between them. Weld quoted a passage from a letter by Angelina Grimké, which asked whether women's rights and antislavery could be considered comparatively or relationally: "Why! Angelina in yesterdays letter says she is doubtful whether womans rights are not the *root*—whether they do not *lie deeper* than the rights involved in our great question!! And adds: 'The slave may be freed and woman be where she is, but woman cannot be freed and the slave remain where he is.'"[56] Grimké argued that, while the two causes and oppressions intersected, abolitionism, in the form advocated by Weld, was more superficial, because it did not necessarily entail the questioning of all relations of authority in society, which she thought was not the case for women's rights.

The way the question was dealt with, however, was also rooted in Grimké's relations with her family and Weld himself. The discussion of women's rights with or against abolitionism allowed them to deal with personal issues arising from their feelings for each other. In a letter written in August 1837, Weld thus tried to convince Angelina and Sarah that his opposition to their advocacy of women's rights in their antislavery lectures was due to the notion that "the abolition question [was] most powerfully preparative and introductory to the *other* question," not to his opposition to the issue. Giving the example of a speech made when he was "a boy" at "a little debating society," he claimed he had then supported the idea that women should not only "make laws, administer justice, sit in the chair of state, plead at the bar or in the pulpit, if she ha[d] the qualifications" but also make "the proposition of marriage."[57] The Grimké sisters' assertion that American women were united by the common experience of subjection took on another dimension, as they had once been part of the master-slave relation, but on the side of the oppressor. Their writings betray their conviction that they had been the double victims of slavery: first, by being involved against their will in the evil institution of slavery; second, by being women, which subjected them to oppression by the men in their family and in American society more generally. This conviction was rooted in the southern context, where, as noted by Nancy Cott, slavery had been "domesticated" by its supporters, who "legitimated the inequalities of slavery by praising all the domestic relations of domination and subordination—master-servant, parent-child, and husband-wife—as one and by seeing the three types as indivisible."[58]

Just as the question of the link between women's and slaves' rights was intensely debated in the antislavery movement in the late 1830s, it was raised again a little more than a decade later at the 1850 National Woman's Rights Convention in Worcester, Massachusetts. On that occasion, Wendell Phillips proposed a resolution about the specific plight of slave women: "That the cause we are met to advocate,—the claim for woman of all her natural and civil rights,—bids us remember the million and a half of slave women at the South, the most grossly wronged and fully outraged of all women; and in every effort for an improvement in our civilization, we will bear in our heart of hearts the memory of the trampled womanhood of the plantation, and omit no effort to raise it to a share in the rights we claim for ourselves."[59] Although the resolution was passed unanimously, it became the object of a controversy in the weeks following the convention. Jane Swisshelm, the white editor of the *Pittsburgh Saturday Visiter*, claimed in an article that "in a Woman's Rights Convention, the question of color has no right to a hearing." Martha Jones saw the controversy as a pivotal moment that showed that "the intersectional character of black women's political identities opened the door to their marginalization in political culture." According to her, "sex and color were emerging as the roots of two mutually exclusive political movements. Even those who defended the Worcester resolution did so in terms that reinforced the perception that issues of race and gender could not be adequately embraced by any one movement."[60]

The "Silken Chains" of Marriage

Generally speaking, it was the situation of married women that made the slavery metaphor more useful in antebellum women's rights discourse, through the comparison between slave codes and marriage legislation.[61] In her *Letters on the Equality of the Sexes*, Sarah Grimké argued that even free women were slaves when considering the condition of married women and marriage laws at the time. In her letter titled "Legal Disabilities of Women," she wrote, "Here now, the very being of a woman, like that of a slave, is absorbed in her master. All contracts made with her, like those made with slaves by their owners, are a mere nullity." But even when referring to the system of coverture, she used an expression that qualified the comparison, showing her awareness of the differences between slavery and marriage: "Her condition resembles, *in some measure*, that of the slave."[62] The idea that marriage laws were metaphorical chains holding women in bondage was recurrent throughout the antebellum period: a memorial presented at the first woman's rights convention organized in Ohio in April 1850 referred to it as "political slavery." At the second National Woman's Rights Convention of October 1851 in Worcester, Massachusetts, Ernestine L. Rose called "on the nation to remove the legal shackles from woman."[63]

The use of the metaphor in relation to married women resonated in white female reformers' personal and public lives in interesting ways. The examples of Abby Kelley and Stephen S. Foster, and of Lucy Stone and Henry Blackwell, are especially telling of the importance of slavery in the way some white female feminist abolitionists considered their own marriage in relation to their public activism and their ideas of female independence. The fact that the women in both couples married antislavery activists or sympathizers after they started working for reform is important, as it allows us to examine the role played by the analogy in coming to terms with a degraded image of the married woman. It also indicates that the slavery metaphor was more of a dialogue between white women and men than a dialogue among black and white women.

Two letters exchanged by Abby Kelley and Stephen S. Foster in August 1843, right after their engagement, show how the slavery metaphor interplayed with issues of personal and marital relations.[64] On August 10 Foster teased his future wife about their future as a married couple: "So you see, I am not going to let you tear yourself from me, under any pretext whatever; nor shall another steal you away, but I shall hence forth claim, & hold you as my <u>own property</u>, which all may be free to enjoy, but none but myself can <u>profess</u>." By calling Abby Kelley his "<u>own property</u>," he jokingly asserted his exclusive power over her. In another passage, he warned her that she "may resign all hope of ever effecting an escape."[65] Foster's allusion to the condition of runaway slaves echoed the public debate over fugitives in Massachusetts at the time.[66] Joel Bernard explains that Foster's "linking of their future domestic life to the South's peculiar institution . . . suggests his sensitivity to the question of his own authority," while alluding to "the important and relatively unexplored connection between the goals of intimacy and social commitment."[67] Abby Kelley had once resisted his courtship, and she had also wanted to "conceal [their] connexion" even after they were engaged.[68] Foster's positioning as the master in their relation might have been a way for him to regain some control. It also demonstrates the way abolitionism resonated with activists, for whom the cause was personal in unexpected ways.

Kelley's answer to Foster indicated what the slavery metaphor meant to her: "I warn you to be careful how you push your jokes too far. I may demand of you, after the fashion of chivalry, that you bring me the trophies of history, shackles broken . . . in the left hand, and a proclamation of emancipation in the right, before your lady love shall give to her good knight the eager hand."[69] Kelley's tone is good-humored enough, but her ironical comparison of Foster to a "knight" cannot hide "the intensity of her own strivings for personal autonomy."[70] This was evident in the way she also resisted the slavery analogy in her public life. Her appointment to the Business Committee of the American Anti-Slavery Society sparked off the "woman controversy" within the abolitionist movement. Significantly, when she chose to compare herself, and all women, to slaves, at the May 1840 meeting of the organization, it was not to show the similarities but rather to insist on the difference between the two conditions: "I rise because I am not a slave," she claimed.[71] Kelley's denial of the analogy shows the way white female abolitionists saw their own activism in the defense of slaves' rights, as a "process of personal liberation."[72] But her denial is also to be read along the same lines as with the Grimké sisters, who acknowledged that white women's "access to political discourse denied the slave, exemplifying the way in which slave labor produces—both literally and metaphorically—even the most basic of freedom's privileges."[73] In some measure, however, it was linked to the way women's rights opponents refused to integrate the woman question into the abolitionist movement in the late 1830s.

In 1839, for instance, Reverend Nathaniel Colver insisted on the specificity of the slaves' experience at the meeting of the Executive Committee of the American Anti-Slavery Society: "the sufferings of the slave are *peculiar in their intensity*. Would that these sufferings, in all their extent, could be presented to our minds again and again with clearer and still clearer light, till the picture should produce a spasmodic effect throughout the community, and our land should throw off from its bosom this hated incubus of hell. The sufferings of the slave are peculiar to himself, as a slave." Coming from an opponent to women's equal participation, such emphasis on what Colver called the "peculiar" sufferings of the slave was a way to disconnect slavery from women's rights, seen as potentially dangerous to the abolitionist cause.[74] From this vantage point, Colver's argument echoed the convictions of some women's rights activists, who, like Lucy Stone before the Civil War, explicitly resisted the use of the slavery metaphor to describe the condition of white women. Like Abby Kelley, she saw the implications of such an analogy in her personal life; like Colver, however, she recognized a difference between the two situations.

Henry B. Blackwell initiated his courtship of Lucy Stone in the spring of 1853, and until their wedding in May 1855, they exchanged several letters on the meaning of marriage. Stone was apprehensive and for a long time refused to commit to a relation that she thought would make her lose her independence because of the marriage laws at the time. Among the arguments serving his goal, Blackwell used the comparison with slavery, but in quite an unexpected way. For him, it was not marriage, but the refusal to commit to another person that condemned a woman to a slave's life: "But for myself I dont see why, in order to do good, you should find it necessary to treat yourself a great deal worse than the Southerners treat their negroes, by depriving yourself of entrance into those personal relations which as you yourself acknowledge are a *want of our nature* & which I regard as a *duty* of our very organization."[75] For Blackwell, the relevance of the comparison lay in the unnatural character of both slavery and "celibacy," except in the latter case, he made Stone her own oppressor—her own master and slave.

Blackwell also resorted to the slavery metaphor when he compared unhappily married women like Elizabeth Cady Stanton and Angelina Grimké with women in bondage, adding that true freedom would be found in happy marriage: "A woman unsuitably married like Mrs. Stanton may find herself fettered—or in difficult circumstances like Mrs. Weld formerly. But a woman who unites herself with a fellow worker with sufficient means & position to prevent the necessity of her drudging—free to be at home when she pleases & to leave it when she thinks it best—with a home of her own to rest & study & with friends to relieve her many responsibilities—is this a position necessarily less influential than your present one?"[76]

A few months after this letter, Lucy Stone found herself at the center of a controversy related to her advocacy of women's rights. On April 21, 1854, the *Liberator* published an anonymous open letter, which had originally appeared in the *Essex County Freeman* from Massachusetts.[77] The author, a woman, attacked what she presented as Lucy Stone's view of marriage.[78] The letter started with a quotation attributed to Stone: "Marriage is to woman a state of slavery. It takes from her the right to have her own property, and makes her submissive in all things to her husband." The anonymous author criticized Stone's ignorance of marriage, a reference to the fact she was single. She then described her own experience of the married relation and what she called "its silken chains." Her own situation, the author insisted, was one of voluntary servitude, transforming a wife's chore into the "right" to please and support her husband. The very end of the letter confirmed this idea: "Can you tell *me* that marriage is slavery! If it is, I thank God that I am a slave—that I have worn its chains for years—that they are still bright and glittering; and I would not exchange them for the monarch's crown!" The letter was followed in the same issue by a reply by William Lloyd Garrison, who called it "sentimental effusion" and argued that the testimony was in no way representative of the majority of women: "If, luckily, the writer of it has found the chains of matrimony in her own case to be silken, there are multitudes of wives who feel them to be iron, and who are as sternly doomed by law to wear them, as are the slaves on the Southern plantations." In a common metaphor, Garrison argued that marriage laws enslaved women: "What Miss Stone demands is, simply, that, in marriage, woman shall be legally the equal of man, so that her personal rights shall not be invaded and she shall have the control of her own property."[79]

Lucy Stone commented on the exchange in a letter to Blackwell written on April 26, 1854. Finding Garrison's reply "very well," she also called the author of the letter "a very stupid being." The publication of the two pieces coincided with a critical moment in Stone's relationship with Blackwell, when the tensions arising from her refusal to marry Blackwell were taking their toll on her, emotionally as well as physically. From her letter, we learn that it was Blackwell who "desired [her] to read" the article, for several reasons, among which probably the curiosity as to how she would react to the public display of the ideas that she was writing him about in private. And Stone's reaction must have been of particular interest to him, as she denied having ever made the remark on which the anonymous text was based: "I never said, however, that marriage is a state of slavery," she wrote Blackwell, adding that a "wife's position is capable of being made horrible enough; but chattelism is a still 'lower depth' to which marriage, bad as it may be made, should never be compared. And I have carefully refrained from doing so."[80] Just as Colver, Stone saw a difference, not necessarily in nature, but at least in "intensity" between slavery and the situation of married women. Her resistance to the direct comparison of white women's condition with slavery was probably due to her years spent at Oberlin, where she taught fugitive slaves and freedmen, who "provided her with firsthand accounts of the evils" of slavery.[81] On the other hand, her remark might also be linked to the fact that she was at that time coming to terms with the idea of marriage and rallying to Blackwell's arguments and courtship.

Another example of Stone's ambivalent relationship with slavery was her encounter with a slave woman a few months after her wedding, which took place on May 1, 1855. In January 1856, a fugitive from Kentucky, Margaret Garner, had killed her three-year-old daughter and injured her three other children for fear they would be taken back in bondage. Lucy Stone visited her in prison and even spoke at the trial, stating in support of Garner that "I would tear open my veins and let the earth drink my blood rather than wear the chains of slavery."[82] Although other abolitionists disapproved of her "dramatization," it was clear that Stone sympathized with the plight of the slave mother, at a time when she was thinking of herself as a potential mother.[83] She wrote Henry Blackwell about "the heroic mother" who had killed her daughter and also referred to a letter by a Mr. Jolliffe, who had asked her if she would "accept the guardianship . . . of one of the little wounded ones."[84] Stone undeniably felt a strong connection with Margaret Garner at a turning point in her life, when she was dealing with issues of matrimony and motherhood.

Despite the bond Stone felt with Garner and other enslaved women, there still seemed to be an intellectual distance that could not be bridged. Retracing the origins of her women's rights activism, at the Conference of the Pioneers organized during the International Council of Women meeting on March 31, 1888, in Washington, DC, she recalled the powerful experience that convinced her to devote her life to women's rights:

> Hiram Powers' statue of the Greek slave was on exhibition in Boston. I went
> up to see it early one morning. No other person was present. There it stood

in the silence, with fettered hands and half-averted face, so emblematic of woman. The hot tears came to my eyes at the thought of millions of women who must be freed. At that evening's meeting I poured all my heart out about it. At the close Rev. Samuel May, who was the general agent of the Anti-Slavery Society, came to me, and with kind words for what I had said, he admonished me that, however true, it was out of place in an anti-slavery meeting. Of course he was right. I said: "Well, Mr. May, I was a woman before I was an abolitionist, and I must speak for women. I will not go any more as a lecturer for the Anti-Slavery Society, but will work wholly for woman's rights.[85]

The *Greek Slave* elicited enthusiastic reactions when it was displayed in the United States.[86] Representing a female slave exposed at a Turkish market, the statue was clearly "influenced by abolitionist iconography." But, in representing a slave woman, carved in the whitest marble, "who through Christian resignation, transcended the tyranny of slavery or of patriarchy," it also distorted it.[87] Stone's reaction to the statue, however, suggests a slightly different story than the one intended by Powers. First of all, Stone depicted her visit to the *Greek Slave* in 1848 as a turning point that led to a change in priorities for her: from then on, she was to fight for who she was, a woman, rather than for ideas, such as abolitionism, that she might have felt strongly about but were disconnected from her immediate experience. Significantly, the *Greek Slave* was not the first representation of slavery or of an enslaved woman that Stone had seen. As an abolitionist, she also had been exposed to the image of the female supplicant, which abolitionists displayed on their letterheads and other items.

The figure elicited strong reactions, even among white male abolitionists, as shown by Theodore Weld's description in a letter to the Grimké sisters: "Ah! Still kneeling, manacled, looking upward, pleading for help! As I caught a sheet at random from a large quantity on the desk of the office to write you a line my dear sisters, I had almost dashed my pen upon it before I saw *the kneeling slave*! The sudden sight drove home a deeper lesson than my heart has learned these many days! The prayer of the slave! Perdition foretokened to the oppressor and deliverance to the oppressed! Blessed be God, '*He* taketh up the needy out of the dust.'"[88]

Weld's intense response to the medallion showed both similarities and differences with Lucy Stone's when she saw the *Greek Slave*. Despite her constant exposure to the image of the enslaved black woman, it was the statue of a white woman in chains that initiated a process of identification that crystallized her identity as a woman. As a white female abolitionist, Stone had maintained an intellectual distance with the institution of slavery and female African American slaves, which the *Greek Slave* disrupted by representing white women's bondage. Her experience confirms the fact that by advocating women's rights, she was fighting for her own rights as a white woman. In a way, her epiphany showed that "the slave, so explicitly an object to be sold, provide[d] feminism as well as abolition with its most graphic example of the extent to which the human body may designate identity."[89] Part of this identity was skin color, which Stone realized was no protection from slavery.[90]

Stone's story about the *Greek Slave* leads us to reconsider the common argument used at the beginning of abolitionism to justify and encourage white women's participation in the movement. The discussion of the legitimacy of women's activism was first grounded in the idea that white women were best able to develop feelings of empathy for female slaves, as shown in this appeal to "ladies" made in the second annual report of the American Anti-Slavery Society in 1835: "The heart of woman can understand, that no political advantages, nor considerations of expediency can, for a moment, justify a system which desolates the *homes* of 450,000 families; which tears the tender babe from the arms of its mother; which makes a million of her own sex the mere property of the highest bidder; which lashes the mother to the toil of a brute, in the presence of, and perhaps by the very hands of her own sons!"[91] For Stone, this feeling of empathy was far from being straightforward; it was in fact based on an intellectual process aimed at integrating race and gender. The call for white women to connect with slaves of their own sex was soon transformed into the notion of white women's empathy for *all* slaves in the name of a condition shared by both groups. This transformation did not come naturally to white women. Some went further when they claimed that white women would become *true* abolitionists on the express condition that they become aware of their own oppression, as noted by Angelina Grimké, and later on by one of Wendell Phillips's correspondents: "How can woman be made to feel the wrongs of the slave, till she is made to realize her own false position? I am convinced that the sympathies and interests of the northern women cannot be brought to bear on the side of true freedom, while she is in her present degraded & indifferent state."[92]

"Redescribing" Race and Gender in Antebellum American Society

Not only did the slavery metaphor provide white feminist-abolitionists with tools to help them understand their own condition, but it also allowed them to engage in a dialogue with white and black men before and after the Civil War. The slavery analogy worked both ways, informing notions of race as much as of gender. Generally speaking, it allowed reformers to think comparatively, though not necessarily relationally.[93] To speak of slavery in relation to women involved a "redescription" as much of gender as of race, but this redescription wavered between identification and separation, for it was based on the impossibility for white female abolitionists of conveying the experience of both enslaved women and white women.

At the foundation of the slavery metaphor was the idea of a possible dialogue between two conditions, but with certain restrictions. First of all, reformers did not view the conditions of both slaves and white women as interchangeable. At the 1869 meeting of the Equal Rights Association, Susan B. Anthony argued, "Mr. Douglass talks about the wrongs of the negro; but with all the outrages that he to-day suffers, he would not exchange his sex and take the place of Elizabeth Cady Stanton."[94] More important, white female abolitionist activists' use of the slavery analogy reveals their difficulty in identifying with slave women. Even if she was hardly mentioned in newspaper reports of women's rights conventions, Sojourner Truth was very active and influential in pointing out the differences between herself and white women.[95] The slave narratives written by both men and women alluded to the contradictions existing between marriage and slavery. Harriet Jacobs thus wrote that marriage protected free women, while it failed to do so for slave women: "the husband of a slave has no power to protect her."[96] When they alluded to the slavery metaphor, white women were not thinking of the situation of slave women as such. The loss of autonomy they were experiencing in marriage mirrored the powerlessness of slaves considered as a group.

This explains in part why, before the Civil War, the dialogue between white women and men concerned white and black men equally. Frederick Douglass articulated the difference between sexism and racism in an 1854 series of articles on Lucy Stone and her decision to speak in front of a Philadelphia audience from which African Americans had been banned. In an answer to one of his readers, Francis Barry from Ohio, who had come to Stone's defense by arguing that Douglass had probably in the past addressed an audience where women had not been admitted, Douglass answered with a clear notion of the dissimilarities between the two examples: "Woman is not excluded with a view to her degradation, or out of a spirit of hate. Nobody will pretend that she is. On the contrary, a sentiment quite opposite to malice dictates her exclusion. It is an error, and one which is to be met with light and truth. Far otherwise is the case of the black man's exclusion from public halls. A malicious determination to degrade, is here self-evident."[97] Douglass alluded to the fundamental difference existing between racism and sexism, suggesting that each stemmed from opposite intentions: while those underlying sexism were noble and aimed at protecting women, those constitutive of racism were meant to degrade African Americans.

When Douglass argued for women's rights in relation to slavery, he sometimes mentioned not so much the common points between the two groups, but rather, as in a *North Star* article about the Seneca Falls convention of July 1848, the fact that the feelings that prompted abolitionists to fight against slavery should go hand in hand with the denunciation of women's condition: "Many who have at last made the discovery that the negroes have some rights as well as other members of the human family, have yet to be convinced that women are entitled to any."[98] Part of the motto of the *North Star*, "Right is of no sex," did not necessarily stem from the idea that the conditions of African Americans and women were identical or that, to use more contemporary terms, racism and sexism were similar, but that both groups should be given the same rights. Moira Ferguson's "metonymic chain of the tyrannized" inherent in the use of the slavery metaphor meant, not the exact equivalence between the two groups, but rather the fact that both slavery and white women's condition informed each other and helped reformers think about the basis of oppression.[99] It also implied that in the dialogue, black women would be left out by both sides.[100]

Despite the claims for sympathy and identification from antebellum reformers, we find numerous references to the impossibility to fully understand the experience of oppression from the outside—Lucy Stone's "ocean"—and to the notion that insiders were their own best spokespersons. At the National Woman's Rights Convention in Worcester of October 1851, Stone expressed the idea eloquently:

> Men cannot fully feel the misery of our lot. They cannot speak what we have *felt*. It is not for the abolitionist, however deeply he may feel the iniquity of the Fugitive Slave Law, fully to portray its wickedness, but the fugitive slave, fleeing from the prison-house of bondage—it is for him to have a realizing sense of its terrors. Who does not feel, when listening to the eloquent and burning words of that heroic slave and noble man, Frederick Douglass, that the bitter wrong of slavery has roused in his spirit the power to do the work he has done so bravely?[101]

Stone argued that race and gender were powerful constitutive elements of identity that could not be bypassed, an idea which Lucretia Mott confirmed in her letter to Elizabeth Cady Stanton in November 1851: "No man can write on Woman's wrongs, as an <u>intelligent</u> sufferer of our own sex."[102]

What the slavery metaphor implied, however, was that servitude was not only a state but also a power relationship between slave and master, involving two individuals. It is clear from the remarks made by reformers about marriage that, for them, it degraded both men and women. Sarah Grimké's commentary that women's oppression was "derogatory to man and woman, as moral and intellectual beings" echoed Thomas Wentworth Higginson's claim at the Seventh National Woman's Rights Convention in New York in November 1856 that "so long as woman is crushed into a slave, so long will man be narrowed into a despot."[103] Henry B. Blackwell went further along those lines, when he tried to assuage Lucy Stone's anxieties about marriage by writing her that unjust relations degraded not the oppressed but the oppressors:

> In your last letter you tell me of the pain you experienced at the idea of being placed in the *legal* position of wife. I am *very sorry* that you should thus suffer. But surely there is no *degradation* in being unjustly treated by *others*. The true

degradation & disgrace rests not with the victim but with the oppressors. In this case the *disgrace* is more *mine* than *yours*. The Law by clothing me with unjust powers puts me in the position of the wrongdoer but it only puts you in that of the wrong sufferer & so my case is morally the most painful.[104]

This eventually led some women's rights activists to think in terms of responsibility: in a relationship based on inequality, but not on physical coercion, who was to be blamed? The question proved one of the most divisive within the antebellum reform movement, between those who placed the sole responsibility on men, and others who laid the blame on both sexes, the two positions being in some measure linked to slavery and abolitionist activism. At the 1851 Woman's Rights Convention in Worcester, Lucy Stone and Abby Kelley Foster were clear in laying the responsibility for white women's oppression on both men and women. Stone adamantly insisted that the responsibility was shared: "The blame is on both sides." Kelley supported a resolution that argued, "Woman lacks her rights because she does not feel the full weight of her responsibilities; that when she shall feel her responsibilities sufficiently to induce her to go forward and discharge them, she will inevitably obtain her rights."[105] This echoed James Russell Lowell's poem "Who Are Slaves," in which he gave his own definition of bondage: the true slaves were those who were free and refused to fight against injustice: "They are slaves who fear to spend / For the fallen and the weak."[106] These three examples show the fluid use of slavery as an extended metaphor to describe both the slave-master relation—the latter being turned into a slave—and white women's condition, but also to put the blame on the free people who did not fight against the bondage of African Americans.

William Lloyd Garrison's different position on the issue suggested, however, a link between slavery and white women's condition in the hands of the same oppressor. As he argued at the Fourth National Woman's Rights Convention held in Cleveland in October 1853, women, just like slaves, could not be held responsible for their own oppression: "Never can it be said that the victims are as much to be blamed as the victimizer; that the slaves are to be as much blamed as the slaveholders and slave-drivers; that the women who have no rights, are to be as much blamed as the men who have played the part of robbers and tyrants." Garrison concluded that it was impossible to consider victims as responsible for their oppression. For him, the analogy was made possible by the fact that both white women and slaves were the victims of the same perpetrator: "I believe in sin, therefore in a sinner; in theft, therefore in a thief; in slavery, therefore in a slaveholder; in wrong, therefore in a wrong-doer; and unless the men of this nation are made by woman to see that they have been guilty of usurpation, and cruel usurpation, I believe very little progress will be made. To say all this has been done without thinking, without calculation, without design, by mere accident, by a want of light; can anybody believe this who is familiar with all the facts in the case?"[107]

White men thus carried the burden of guilt in two crimes: slavery and the subjection of white women. But after the Civil War, Stanton and her supporters put forward the idea that the slavery relation could be changed and make of former slaves, masters—in the same way that masters had been turned into slaves in the antebellum discourse on slavery. Susan B. Anthony thus feared that the Fifteenth Amendment "put two million more men in position of tyrants over two million women who had until now been the equals of the men at their side."[108] The analogy was considered outrageous at the time, and rightly so, but it is still worth considering as it showed that the slavery metaphor did not so much fix the relations between race and gender, but rather both revealed and facilitated the circulation between the two notions. Anthony also noted that, at the time of the debates over the Fourteenth and Fifteenth Amendments, her conviction was that the introduction of a discussion of the merits of each group would open the door to increased discrimination against both African American men and white women. In a letter to William Lloyd Garrison Jr. written in 1905, she presented the prediction allegedly made by Stanton right after the Civil War: "Mrs. Stanton told them plainly then that if they persisted in shutting out women the time would come when the amendment would not protect black men, and that time is here."[109] Stanton's powerful argument was that despite the differences between white women and African American men, the persisting unification of the two causes would have secured rights for both groups.

It is significant that Stanton and Anthony, who expressed their desire to unite reformers in 1869, should have found themselves in the position of further dividing them by advocating the preeminence of gender over race in the following years. Stanton's use of slavery to describe women's oppression after the Civil War is evidence of the instability and ambivalence of slavery as an extended metaphor within the antebellum women's rights movement. The slavery metaphor was a powerful medium for the ideal of universal rights: it allowed reformers to analyze the newly revealed situation of women's oppression in familiar terms and to connect the two fights for the abolition of slavery and women's rights. In this sense, the comparison between race- and gender-based subjections was central to the understanding of the situation of white women, seen not only through the prism of the deprivation of rights but also through the notion of psychological dependence and degradation.

The slavery metaphor also revealed the ambivalence inherent in the universalism of the antebellum antislavery and women's rights movements. While the analogy contributed to the idea that race and gender might be considered comparatively, it did not ensure the effective integration of both causes, often obscuring their specificities, as in the displacement of the experiences of African American women in favor of those of white women. At the same time, the slavery metaphor resonated deeply with white feminist-abolitionists, allowing them to work out intimate issues related to identity and autonomy. These conflicted uses of the slavery metaphor expose the failure of white female activists to bridge the tensions between their personal and collective claims to equality. They also show the impossibility of thinking about the intersections of race and gender without acknowledging the existence of simultaneous situations of oppression and privilege.[110]

Notes

I would like to thank the audience at the conference organized at the University of Rochester on April 16–17, 2010, for their questions and comments. I am also grateful to Carol Faulkner and Alison Parker for their patience and encouragement.

1. For an analysis of the split of the reform movement after the Civil War, see Ellen Carol DuBois, *Feminism and Suffrage: The Emergence of an Independent Women's Movement in America, 1848–1869* (Ithaca, NY: Cornell University Press, 1978).

2. Elizabeth Cady Stanton, Susan B. Anthony, and Matilda Joslyn Gage, eds., *The History of Woman Suffrage*, 6 vols., 2nd ed. (Rochester, NY: Anthony and Mann, 1889), 2:384. Lucy Stone (1818–93), who graduated from Oberlin College in 1847, was an abolitionist activist and women's rights pioneer. In 1869 she was one of the founders of the American Woman Suffrage Association.

3. Stanton, Anthony, and Gage, *History of Woman Suffrage*, 2:382–84. Frederick Douglass (1818–95), a fugitive slave, was a prominent abolitionist and women's rights activist—he attended the Seneca Falls convention of 1848 and signed the Declaration of Sentiments issued on the occasion.

4. Elizabeth V. Spelman, *Inessential Woman: Problems of Exclusion in Feminist Thought* (Boston: Beacon, 1988), ix, 5.

5. At the same meeting, Elizabeth Cady Stanton also left out black women from her argumentation: "We wondered then at the general indifference to that first opportunity of realizing what all those gentlemen had advocated so long; and, in looking back over the many intervening years, we still wonder at the stolid incapacity of all men to understand that woman feels the invidious distinctions of sex exactly as the black man does those of color, or the white man the more transient distinctions of wealth, family, position, place, and power; that she feels as keenly as man the injustice of disfranchisement." Stanton, Anthony, and Gage, *History of Woman Suffrage*, 2:265.

6. Spelman, *Inessential Woman*, 131.

7. *The History of Woman Suffrage* was the first history of the American women's rights movement. Written after the split of the late 1860s, it was also meant to control the movement's narrative.

8. Stanton, Anthony, and Gage, *History of Woman Suffrage*, 1:13.

9. The use of parenthetical modifiers is inspired by Louise Michele Newman, who used them "to signal how nineteenth-century discourses used universalizing language to make generalizations about the 'race,' 'woman,' or 'man,' while intending these generalizations to apply only to people of Anglo-Saxon (or Euro-Protestant) descent." *White Women's Rights: The Racial Origins of Feminism in the United States* (Oxford: Oxford University Press, 1999), 10–11.

10. Lucy Stone, "The Funeral of Mr. Garrison," *Woman's Journal*, May 31, 1879.

11. DuBois, *Feminism and Suffrage*, 22.

12. Martha S. Jones, *All Bound Up Together: The Woman Question in African American Public Culture, 1830–1900* (Chapel Hill: University of North Carolina Press, 2007), 206, 10.

13. Gerda Lerner, "New Approaches to the Study of Women in American History," *Journal of American History* 3, no. 1 (Fall 1969): 3–14, reprinted in *The Majority Finds Its Past: Placing Women in History*, ed. Gerda Lerner (New York: Oxford University Press, 1979), 8.

14. Karen Sanchez-Eppler, "Bodily Bonds: The Intersecting Rhetorics of Feminism and Abolition," *Representations* 24 (1988): 375. The phrase "feminist-abolitionists" is used by Blanche Glassman Hersh to characterize the group of Garrisonian abolitionists, men and women, "who first spoke out and organized for women's rights." In her mind, the phrase also signifies "the important bond between abolitionism and feminism." *The Slavery of Sex: Feminist-Abolitionists in America* (Urbana: University of Illinois Press, 1978), vii, 34.

15. Sanchez-Eppler, "Bodily Bonds," 379. Sanchez-Eppler also adds, "The difficulty of preventing moments of identification from becoming acts of appropriation constitutes the essential dilemma of feminist-abolitionist rhetoric" (377). In the same way, Saidiya V. Hartman's analysis of "empathy" and "its repressive effects" during the antebellum period has shown that "the effort to counteract the commonplace callousness to black suffering requires that the white body be positioned in the place of the black body in order to make this suffering visible and intelligible." *Scenes of Subjection: Terror, Slavery, and Self-Making in Nineteenth-Century America* (New York: Oxford University Press), 19.

16. Teresa C. Zackodnik, "'I Don't Know How You Will Feel When I Get Through': Racial Difference, Woman's Rights, and Sojourner Truth," *Feminist Studies* 30, no. 1 (Spring 2004): 61. A parallel can be drawn between Sojourner Truth and Harriet Tubman. See Milton C. Sernett, *Harriet Tubman: Myth, Memory, and History* (Durham, NC: Duke University Press, 2007). Sojourner Truth (ca. 1797–1883) was born a slave in the state of New York. She took her freedom in 1826 and was freed under New York law in 1827. A preacher, she was an abolitionist and women's rights activist. Harriet Tubman (ca. 1820–1913) was born in slavery in Maryland. She escaped from slavery in 1849 and was known for her role in the Underground Railroad, which gained her the name of the "Moses of Her People."

17. Margaret M. R. Kellow, "The Divided Mind of Antislavery Feminism: Lydia Maria Child and the Construction of African American Womanhood," in *Discovering the Women in Slavery*, ed. Patricia Morton (Athens: University of Georgia Press, 1996), 109.

18. See Newman, *White Women's Rights*.

19. Lori Ginzberg, *Elizabeth Cady Stanton: An American Life* (New York: Hill and Wang, 2009), 47.

20. Michele Mitchell, "'Lower Orders,' Racial Hierarchies, and Rights Rhetoric: Evolutionary Echoes in Elizabeth Cady Stanton's Thought during the Late 1860s," in *Elizabeth Cady Stanton Feminist as Thinker: A Reader in Documents and Essays*, ed. Ellen Carol DuBois and Richard Càndida Smith (New York: New York University Press, 2007), 134. About Stanton, Christine Stansell also notes that "unlike the first generation of women reformers . . . she never worked politically with black

women." "Missed Connections: Abolitionist Feminism in the Nineteenth Century," in Dubois and Smith, *Elizabeth Cady Stanton*, 35. Elizabeth Cady Stanton did not hesitate to use the reference in her letters, for example associating marriage with "plantation slavery" (Elizabeth Cady Stanton to Mrs. Griffing, December 1, 1870, Kalamazoo, copy by Martha C. Wright, Garrison Family Papers, MS 60, Sophia Smith Collection, Smith College, Northampton, MA). Alluding to the verdict in the McFarland trial, she compared it to the *Dred Scott* decision (Stanton to Isabella Beecher Hooker, February 3, 1871, Tenafly, NJ, copy by Martha C. Wright, Garrison Family Papers. In November 1869 Daniel McFarland had shot Albert D. Richardson, who was living with McFarland's wife, while she was trying to obtain a divorce from her violent husband. Mc Farland was acquitted.

21. Serena Mayeri, "'A Common Fate of Discrimination': Race-Gender Analogies in Legal and Historical Perspective," *Yale Law Journal* 110, no. 6 (April 2001): 1046; Paul Ricoeur, *The Rule of Metaphor: Multi-Disciplinary Studies of the Creation of Meaning in Language*, trans. Robert Czerny with Kathleen McLaughlin and John Costello (London: Routledge and Kegan Paul), 7, 21; Jean Fagan Yellin, *Women and Sisters: The Antislavery Feminists in American Culture* (New Haven, CT: Yale University Press, 1989), 25.

22. Hartman, *Scenes of Subjection*, 22; Carole Pateman, *The Sexual Contract* (Stanford, CA: Stanford University Press, 1988), 9. Originally, in the United States, citizenship was disconnected from suffrage. In 1875 the Supreme Court ruled in *Minor v. Happersett* that "suffrage was not coextensive with citizenship and thus that states possessed the authority to decide which citizens could and could not vote." Alex Keyssar, *The Right to Vote: The Contested History of Democracy in the United States* (New York: Basic Books, 2000), 181.

23. Andrea Moore Kerr, *Lucy Stone: Speaking Out for Equality* (New Brunswick, NJ: Rutgers University Press, 1995), 137, 136.

24. Nancy F. Cott, quoted in Linda K. Kerber, Nancy F. Cott, Robert Gross, Lynn Hunt, Carroll Smith-Rosenberg, and Christine M. Stansell, "Beyond Roles, Beyond Spheres: Thinking about Gender in the Early Republic," *William and Mary Quarterly* 46, no. 3 (July 1989): 567.

25. Leslie McCall, "The Complexity of Intersectionality," *Signs* 30, no. 3 (Spring 2005): 1771–800. According to McCall, "the terms *complex, complexity,* and *complexities* appear frequently and are central in key texts on intersectionality, although no text focuses on complexity as such" (1772n2).

26. Pateman, *Sexual Contract*, 120; Nancy E. Rogers, "Slavery as Metaphor in the Writings of George Sand," *French Review* 53, no. 1 (October 1979): 29–35; Noah Webster, *An American Dictionary of the English Language: Exhibiting the Origin, Orthography, Pronunciation, and Definitions of Words . . .* , 9th ed. (New York: Converse, 1832), 762.

27. "By the mid-1840s, Frederick Douglass, Samuel R. Ward, and dozens of other former slaves were lecturing throughout the North." C. Peter Ripley, ed., *Witness for Freedom: African American Voices on Race, Slavery, and Emancipation* (Chapel Hill: University of North Carolina Press, 1993), 9. Ripley notes that "when recounting their personal experiences, former slaves used a rich and emotion-laden variety of methods to convince their listeners of slavery's inhumanity" (9).

28. Yellin, *Women and Sisters*, 71.

29. Kellow, "Divided Mind," 108. Kellow adds that "although utterly committed to ending both slavery and racial discrimination, Child's rhetorical strategies and political objectives shaped her depiction of black American women in ways that tended to flatten, to stereotype, and at times almost to negate the experience of the very women she strove to liberate" (122). Lydia Maria Child (1802–80) was a writer and abolitionist. She helped Harriet Jacobs publish *Incidents in the Life of a Slave Girl* in 1861.

30. Yellin, *Women and Sisters*, 56. "The Corsair" is the story of a pirate who is in love with a slave in a Turkish harem and wants to save her.

31. Lydia Maria Child, *The History of the Condition of Women in Various Ages and Nations*, 2 vols. (London: Simpkin, Marshall, 1835), 1:37; 1:42, 1:148, 1:116 (emphasis added).

32. Ibid., 1:266, 2:212. In the chapter called "Women of United States," Child alluded once to the "tyranny" of New England Puritans toward women and described the specific situation of the "Quaderoons" of New Orleans (2:255, 2:263–64).

33. Harriet Martineau, *Society in America*, 2 vols. (New York: Unders and Otley, 1837), 1:148, 149. Martineau is quoting from Jefferson's correspondence (4:295). Martineau (1802–76) was a prominent English writer and abolitionist. She wrote *Society in America* after an extended visit to the United States.

34. Ibid., 150 (emphasis added).

35. Rev. Samuel J. May to the Woman's Rights Convention to be held at Worcester, Mass., October 23 and 24, Syracuse, Tuesday, Oct. 22, *Proceedings of the Woman's Rights Convention Held at Worcester, October 23d and 24th, 1850* (1851; repr., Charleston, SC: BiblioBazaar, 2010), 54.

36. Martineau, *Society in America*, 148.

37. Yellin, *Women and Sisters*, 29. Sarah (1792–1873) and Angelina (1805–79) Grimké were the daughters of a slave owner from South Carolina. After moving to Philadelphia and becoming Quakers, they got involved in the abolitionist movement in 1835 and started lecturing on slavery and women's rights in 1837.

38. Sarah Grimké's *Letters on the Equality of the Sexes, and the Condition of Woman: Addressed to Mary S. Parker, President of the Boston Female Anti-Slavery Society* (Boston: Knapp, 1838) was written in response to the "Pastoral Letter of the General Association of Massachusetts to the Congregational Churches under Their Care," published during the summer of 1837, condemning, among other things, women's involvement in abolitionism.

39. Sarah M. Grimké, "Letter VI: Women in Asia and Africa," August 15, 1837, Groton, in *Equality of the Sexes*, 33–35.

40. Grimké, "Letter II: Woman Subject Only to God," July 17, 1837, Newburyport, in *Equality of the Sexes*, 11.

41. Grimké, "Letter III: The Pastoral Letter of the General Association of Congregational Ministers of Massachusetts," July 1837, Haverhill, in *Equality of the Sexes*, 17.

42. "The Enslaved Mind," *Slave's Friend* 2, no. 3 (New York: Williams, 1836), 9.

43. Grimké, "Letter VIII: On the Condition of Women in the United States," 1837, Brookline, in *Equality of the Sexes*, 46, 47.

44. Angelina E. Grimké, "Letter XII: Human Rights Not Founded on Sex," October 2, 1837, East Boylston, MA, in *Letters to Catharine E. Beecher, in Reply to an Essay on Slavery and Abolitionism, Addressed to A. E. Grimké* (Boston: Knapp, 1838), 115–16.

45. Robert K. Nelson, "'The Forgetfulness of Sex': Devotion and Desire in the Courtship Letters of Angelina Grimké and Theodore Dwight Weld," *Journal of Social History* 37, no. 3 (Spring 2004): 664.

46. Sarah Forten to Angelina E. Grimké, April 15, 1837, Philadelphia, in *Letters of Theodore Dwight Weld, Angelina Grimké Weld and Sarah Grimké, 1822–1844*, ed. Gilbert H. Barnes and Dwight L. Dumont, vol. 1 (New York: Appleton-Century, 1934), 381. Sarah Forten (1814–83) was a writer and an abolitionist who, along with her sisters and mother, helped found the Philadelphia Female Anti-Slavery Society in 1833.

47. Angelina E. Grimké to Sarah Douglass, February 22, 1837, Newark, NJ, in Barnes and Dumont, *Theodore Dwight Weld*, 1:364. Sarah Mapps Douglass (1806–82) was a founding member of the Philadelphia Female Anti-Slavery Society and a committed educator.

48. Theodore Dwight Weld (1803–95) was an abolitionist responsible for training agents within the American Anti-Slavery Society.

49. Gerda Lerner, *The Grimké Sisters from South Carolina: Pioneers for Woman's Rights and Abolition* (1967; repr., New York: Shocken Books, 1971), 218.

50. John Greenleaf Whittier to Sarah and Angelina Grimké, August 14, 1837, A-S Office of NYC, in Barnes and Dumont, *Theodore Dwight Weld*, 1:424.

51. Ladies' New York City Anti-Slavery Society to "Our Sisters in the Anti-Slavery Cause," March 20, 1837, New York, in Barnes and Dumont, *Theodore Dwight Weld*, 1:374.

52. Theodore Weld to Sarah and Angelina Grimké, August 15, 1837, New York, in Barnes and Dumont, *Theodore Dwight Weld*, 1:426.

53. Angelina Grimké to Weld, August 12, 1837, Groton, MA, in Barnes and Dumont, *Theodore Dwight Weld*, 1:417; T. Gregory Garvey, *Creating the Culture of Reform in Antebellum America* (Athens: University of Georgia Press, 2006), 95.

54. Angelina Grimké to Weld and Whittier, August 20, 1837, Brookline, MA, in Barnes and Dumont, *Theodore Dwight Weld*, 1:430.

55. Yellin, *Women and Sisters*, 32.

56. Weld to Sarah and Angelina Grimké, October 10, 1837, New York, in Barnes and Dumont, *Theodore Dwight Weld*, 1:453–54.

57. Weld to Angelina and Sarah Grimké, August 15, 1837, New York, in Barnes and Dumont, *Theodore Dwight Weld*, 1:426, 1:425.

58. Nancy Cott, *Public Vows: A History of Marriage and the Nation* (Cambridge, MA: Harvard University Press, 2000), 60.

59. *Woman's Rights Convention, 1850*, 17.

60. Jones, *All Bound Up Together*, 92, 93.

61. According to Nancy Cott, both marriage and slavery "were called domestic relations in the law." *Public Vows*, 61. While this legitimated the comparison between the two among the supporters of slavery, it might have had the same consequence among some abolitionists and women's rights activists.

62. Grimké, "Letter XII: Legal Disabilities of Women," September 6, 1837, Concord, in *Equality of the Sexes*, 75, 83 (emphasis added).

63. Stanton, Anthony, and Gage, *History of Woman Suffrage*, 1:105, 1:240. Ernestine Louise Rose (1810–92) was born in Poland and emigrated to the United States in 1836. She embraced abolitionism and women's rights activism, among other causes.

64. Abby Kelley (1810–87) was an abolitionist and women's rights activist. In 1845 she married Stephen Symonds Foster (1809–81), an abolitionist known for disrupting church services in support of the enslaved.

65. Foster to Kelley, August 10, 1843, Utica, Abby Kelley Foster Papers, 1836–91, American Antiquarian Society, Worcester, MA.

66. In 1842 the Supreme Court issued a decision, *Prigg v. Pennsylvania*, declaring that the 1793 Fugitive Slave Law was constitutional and could not be interfered with by state legislation. In 1843 Massachusetts adopted a law forbidding any state action against fugitive slaves.

67. Joel Bernard, "Authority, Autonomy, and Radical Commitment: Stephen and Abby Kelley Foster," *Proceedings of the American Antiquarian Society* 90, pt. 2, annual meeting, Worcester, October 15, 1980, 347–48. Bernard uses Stephen Foster's letter of August 10, 1843, in support of his argument.

68. Kelley to Foster, July 30, 1843, Syracuse, Abby Kelley Foster Papers.

69. Kelley to Foster, August 13, 1843, Waterloo, Abby Kelley Foster Papers. Bernard calls this letter an "emotional rebuttal." Bernard, "Authority," 348.

70. Bernard, "Authority," 348.

71. Quoted in Dorothy Sterling, *Ahead of Her Time: Abby Kelley and the Politics of Antislavery* (New York: Norton, 1991), 104.

72. Keith Melder, "Abby Kelley and the Process of Liberation," in *The Abolitionist Sisterhood: Women's Political Culture in Antebellum America*, ed. Jean Fagan Yellin and John C. Van Horne (Ithaca, NY: Cornell University Press, 1994), 231.

73. Sanchez-Eppler, "Bodily Bonds," 377.

74. *Sixth Annual Report of the Executive Committee of the American Anti-Slavery Society* (New York: American Anti-Slavery Society, 1839), 22 (emphasis added), 23.

75. Henry B. Blackwell to Lucy Stone, August 24, 1853, Walnut Hills, in *Loving Warriors: Selected Letters of Lucy Stone and Henry B. Blackwell, 1853 to 1893*, ed. Leslie Wheeler (New York: Dial, 1981), 56. Henry Browne Blackwell (1825–1909) was born in England, and his family moved to the United States when he was seven. His commitment to abolitionism and women's rights was largely influenced by Lucy Stone, whom he married in 1855.

76. Blackwell to Stone, August 24, 1853, Walnut Hills, in Wheeler, *Loving Warriors*, 57.

77. *Liberator*, April 21, 1854, 1.

78. Stone wrote Blackwell that she did not think the author was a woman. Stone to Blackwell, April 26, 1854, Cleveland, in Wheeler, *Loving Warrior*, 81.

79. This remark is reminiscent of Harriet Jacobs, who in her narrative tells about her daughter, who for her baptism was offered a "gold chain" by her father's mistress. Jacobs writes about her reaction: "I thanked her for this kindness; but I did not like the emblem. I wanted no chain to be fastened on my daughter, not even if its links were of gold. How earnestly I prayed that she might never feel the weight of slavery's chain, whose iron entereth into the soul!" Harriet A. Jacobs, *Incidents in the Life of a Slave Girl*, in *The Classic Slave Narratives*, ed. Henry Louis Gates (1861; repr., Signet Classic, 2002), 528.

80. Stone to Blackwell, April 26, 1854, Cleveland, in Wheeler, *Loving Warriors*, 81.

81. Kerr, *Lucy Stone*, 33.

82. Quoted in Margaret Washington, *Sojourner Truth's America* (Urbana: University of Illinois Press, 2009), 274.

83. Stone was criticized by Lucretia Mott and the women of the Forten and Purvis families. (ibid., 274). Her daughter, Alice Stone Blackwell, was born on September 14, 1857.

84. Stone to Blackwell, February 3, 1856, Richmond, Indiana, in Wheeler, *Loving Warriors*, 155.

85. National Woman Suffrage Association, *Report of the International Council of Women, Assembled by the National Woman Suffrage Association, D.C., U.S. of America*, March 25–April 1, 1888 (Washington, DC: Darby, 1888), 333–34.

86. Linda Hyman, "The Greek Slave by Hiram Powers: High Art as Popular Culture," *Art Journal* 35, no. 3 (Spring 1976): 218.

87. Yellin, *Women and Sisters*, 102, 123.

88. Weld to Sarah and Angelina Grimké, December 15 [1837?], [New York?], in Barnes and Dumont, *Theodore Dwight Weld*, 1:490.

89. Sanchez-Eppler, "Bodily Bonds," 376.

90. For black women, such realization could also be liberating. Mary Church Terrell wrote in her autobiography, "When I grew older, however, the stigma of being descended from slaves had lost its power to sting. For then I discovered that with a single, solitary exception, and that a very small one, no race has lived upon the face of this earth which has not at some time in its history been the subject of a stronger. If history teaches one lesson more than another, it is that races wax and wane." *A Colored Woman in a White World* (1940; repr., Amherst, NY: Humanity Books, 2005), 52. I would like to thank Michelle Kuhl for the reference.

91. *Second Annual Report of the American Anti-Slavery Society* (New York: Dorr, 1835), 50–51.

92. Francis H. Drake to Wendell Phillips, n.d., MS Am 1953, Series 2, 501, Wendell Phillips Papers, Houghton Library, Harvard University.

93. Margaret L. Andersen and Patricia Hill Collins write, "when you think relationally, you see the social structures that *simultaneously* generate unique group histories and link them together in society." "Why Race, Class, and Gender Still Matter," *Race, Class, and Gender*, 6th ed. (Belmont, CA: Wadsworth, 2007), 7.

94. Stanton, Anthony, and Gage, *History of Woman Suffrage*, 2:88. Susan B. Anthony (1820–1906) started her career as an activist in the temperance movement and then became an abolitionist and a women's rights activist. She is well known for her political and intellectual partnership with Elizabeth Cady Stanton.

95. See Nell Irvin Painter, "Sojourner Truth in Life and Memory: Writing the Biography of an American Exotic," in *Abolitionism and Issues of Race and Gender*, ed. John R. McKivigan (New York: Garland, 1999), 35, first published in *Gender and History* 2 (1990): 3–16.

96. Jacobs, *Incidents*, 381. Deborah Gray White writes, "Black in a white society, slave in a free society, woman in a society ruled by men, female slaves had the least formal power and were perhaps the most vulnerable group of antebellum Americans." *Ar'n't I a Woman? Female Slaves in the Plantation South* (New York, Norton, 1985), 15.

97. Frederick Douglass, "Mr. Barry's Letter," *Frederick Douglass' Paper*, March 17, 1854, quoted in Philip Foner, ed., *Frederick Douglass on Women's Rights* (Cambridge, MA: Da Capo, 1976), 72.

98. "The Rights of Women," *North Star*, July 28, 1848, quoted in Foner, *Frederick Douglass*, 50.

99. Moira Ferguson, "Mary Wollstonecraft and the Problematic of Slavery," in *Feminist Interpretations of Mary Wollstonecraft*, ed. Maria J. Falco (University Park, PA: Pennsylvania State University Press, 1996), 137, first published in *Feminist Review* 42 (Autumn 1992): 82–102. A metonymy is a figure of speech in which a thing is called not by its name but by the name of something closely associated with it.

100. Leslie McCall reminds us that this exclusion of black women lies at the core of the study of intersectionality: "Interest in intersectionality arose out of a critique of gender-based and race-based research for failing to account for lived experience at neglected points of intersection—ones that tended to reflect multiple subordinate locations as opposed to dominant or mixed locations. It was not possible, for example, to understand a black woman's experience from previous studies of gender combined with previous studies of race because the former focused on white women and the latter on black men." "Complexity of Intersectionality," 1780.

101. *The Proceedings of the Woman's Rights Convention, held at Worcester, October 15th and 16th, 1851*, 27, American Memory, Library of Congress, accessed on February 10, 2012, http://memory.loc.gov/cgi-bin/query/r?ammem/naw:@field(DOCID+@lit(rbnawsan8287div2)).

102. Lucretia Mott to Elizabeth Cady Stanton, November 9, 1851, Philadelphia [?], Garrison Family Papers.

103. Grimké, "Letter IV: Social Intercourse of the Sexes," July 27, 1837, Andover, in *Equality of the Sexes*, 22; Stanton, Anthony, and Gage, *History of Woman Suffrage*, 1:645.

104. Blackwell to Stone, December 22, 1854, Cincinnati, in Wheeler, *Loving Warriors*, 108.

105. *Woman's Rights Convention, 1851*, 27, 100.

106. James Russell Lowell, "Who Are Slaves," Garrison Family Papers.

107. Stanton, Anthony, and Gage, *History of Woman Suffrage*, 1:137.

108. Ibid., 2:392.

109. Susan B. Anthony to William Lloyd Garrison Jr., January 4, 1905, Rochester, NY, Garrison Family Papers.

110. Margaret L. Andersen and Patricia Hill Collins note that "we all occupy positions of disadvantage and privilege within intersecting systems of race, class, and gender." "Social Change and Sites of Change," in Andersen and Collins, *Race, Class, and Gender*, 481.

Chapter 4

"Grandpa Brown Didn't Have No Land"

Race, Gender, and an Intruder of Color in Indian Territory

Kendra Taira Field

When Thomas Jefferson Brown finally decided to make his home in Indian Territory in 1870, he had been there many times before. For months he had been going in on day trips from Arkansas, his grandson mused more than a century later, learning the Indian languages and becoming familiar with the land, people, and opportunities for economic gain. In spite of national boundaries, promises of federal "protection," and claims to Indian sovereignty, the borders between the nineteenth-century United States and Indian Territory grew increasingly porous, especially following the Civil War. American settlers in and around the territory were scrambling for more and more land, and soon economic and familial relationships across these boundaries began to flourish. During the late nineteenth century, settlement by nonnatives was perceived as the greatest threat to Indian sovereignty in the territory.

While most early American settlers in post–Civil War Indian Territory were identified in government records as white, some were recorded as black or "mulatto," the latter a category still prominent on the federal censuses of this period. Born in Arkansas in the 1850s to an African American man and an Irish woman, Thomas Jefferson Brown was one such settler, and my own great-great-grandfather. Once in Indian Territory, Brown would marry twice to African American descendants of the Creek and Seminole Nations.[1] At least eight of his children were allotted 160 acres of land each due to their mothers' presence on the federal Dawes rolls. This white-looking father was able to secure more than a thousand acres of land, a school, church, and post office, shaping a distinct black and Creek settlement in Indian Territory, known as "Brownsville."

While Brownsville is remembered today as a black settlement, perceptions of Brown when he first arrived in Indian Territory, in the 1870s, were less about his racial identification than about his national (or *non*national) identification; indeed, Brown was initially categorized in Creek national records as a nonnative or an "intruder." Brown's experiences in Indian Territory and Oklahoma reveal that at the turn of the twentieth century, the United States was undergoing a seismic shift of self-definition from "nation" to "race" and from Indian and American national projects to black and white national projects. Indian and black Indian women played a critical role in this transition.

Brown's migration to Indian Territory after the Civil War embodied an attempt to escape racism and claim freedom and American citizenship through the acquisition of land and through relationships with Indians, especially Indian women, as a means to acquire that land. In this context, migration involved African Americans distancing themselves from blackness and connecting themselves, instead, to the project of American national expansion. This chapter thus details the various meanings of Brown's acquisition of Indian land through marriages to two African-descended Creek and Seminole women, and especially the significance of his nonnative or intruder status in the territory. For a time, Brown's position in Indian Territory afforded him myriad privileges associated with American expansion and proximity to Creek national belonging.

Three decades after he arrived, however, circumstances had changed dramatically. Responding to growing pressure from land-hungry American settlers within and beyond Indian Territory, the federal government intervened in the name of Indian "protection." By the early nineteen hundreds all collectively held Indian lands had been individually allotted by the federal Dawes Commission, as in the case of Brown's wife and children; in turn, many of these Indian (and black Indian) allotments were quickly sold or ceded to white and some newer black settlers. In addition, the government offered the remaining "surplus" lands to new settlers. In 1907 the state of Oklahoma was officially founded on most of the same terms of racial segregation and disfranchisement that had driven African Americans out of the South in the first place. In the 1910s Brown—like many African-descended and Creek landowners forced or coerced to abandon their land—lost his family's property to the explosion of land and oil speculation, developments aggressively underwritten by a system of racial classification newly enforced by white settlers, and state and federal governments alike.

As Indian sovereignty was dissolved and notions of racial purity and "blood" acquired growing significance, race soon eclipsed nation as a guarantor of rights and resources in the territory. Two generations later, in the 1920s, in spite of the rich history of African-descended Creeks, Brown's grandchildren were still attempting, with little or no success, to distance themselves from freedpeople and slavery in favor of their Creek lineage. In the end, however, as much as the experience of land acquisition for settlers like Brown had functioned as a national project, the experience of land loss decades later was principally a racialized one. The emergence of a rigid black-white dichotomy thoroughly obscured the more nuanced possibilities of the preceding period in Indian Territory. As a result, the area where Brown had settled has been remembered by descendants as a "black" settlement (connected to Oklahoma's "all-black" town movement), revealing just how complete the twentieth-century erasure of black Indian kinship and property ownership has been. Brown's story thus illuminates an evolving racial hierarchy within the context of an expanding US empire.

Because of my familial connection to Thomas Jefferson Brown, this essay relies deeply on oral testimony and storytelling as well as archival research. I have had access to a handful of family letters from the turn of the twentieth century, as well as extensive genealogical detail and family stories, which may have been otherwise unavailable. I have worked alongside several twenty-first century descendants, and this article references their journeys to ancestral home places in present-day Oklahoma. I have followed these descendants' leads, testing their memories, narratives, and speculation about their ancestors' lives against the archival record and the writings of others who traveled the same routes and encountered similar experiences.

Growing Up with the Country

Thomas Jefferson Brown migrated around 1870, a relatively early point in this migration to Indian Territory, which peaked between 1880 and 1905. At about seventeen years of age, following his father's death in the Civil War, "Jeff" settled in the territory. His hometown of Fort Smith, Arkansas, had begun to play an increasingly critical political and economic role in Indian Territory. Supplies moved in and out of Fort Smith, and from there federal court officials pursued and prosecuted Indian Territory "outlaws."[2] When asked when and how his father, Jeff, came to Indian Territory, Tom Brown, his then 103-year-old son, hinted at a hurried migration: "He was on the run, my daddy was."[3] Indeed, many prospective settlers had begun to view Indian Territory as a place where one could hide from past wrongs; local papers frequently called Indian Territory a haven for "divorce seekers" and other kinds of fugitives.[4]

As he made his life in the Creek Nation, Brown followed in the footsteps of myriad black and "mulatto" frontiersmen who resembled their white counterparts in many respects, but for whom color and racism mattered deeply in their everyday lives in Indian Country. Like many American and African

American frontiersmen before him, Brown would look to build a better life for himself by tying his fate to westward expansion and, especially, to Indians and Indianness.[5] That said, Brown was hardly participating in a deliberately racialized freedom movement, as one might characterize later waves of migration to Indian Territory and, especially, the establishment of the "all-black" towns.

By contrast, the act of migration for earlier travelers such as Brown—who migrated before the emergence of a black emigration movement to Indian Territory—often involved separating oneself from other African Americans and, if not assimilating oneself to an Indian community, then striking out alongside settlers of various backgrounds who relied on one another's support and, through this process, increasingly identified as American. For travelers such as Brown, the act of migration arguably functioned as an escape from blackness—or, perhaps, one's connection to slavery—and, therefore, racism. Historically, such a move has often been achieved by African American and "mulatto" men through participation in conquest, be it military, religious, or both.[6] But what Brown ultimately gained from his relationship to Indians was not merely symbolic or referential—but clearly material.

During the course of his life in Indian Territory, Brown would marry twice, acquiring vast tracts of land through marriage to African American descendants of the Creek Nation and, particularly, through the children of these marriages. In so doing, he followed in the footsteps of African American men who for centuries made their livelihood in Indian Country, often by marrying and linking their fate to Indian and black Indian women, communities, and land. In this way, a degree of freedom was achieved by escaping or denying associations to southern slavery, by illustrating one's proximity to Indianness, and by legitimizing one's relationship to American national expansion and land.

Jeff was considered a noncitizen or an intruder in the eyes of the Indian nations. The Creek, Cherokee, Chickasaw, Choctaw, and Seminole Nations—known by Americans of the period as the "Five Civilized Tribes"—allowed noncitizens to live and work within the territory under a permit system that required the payment of taxes and other fees, under supervision of the US government. Despite mounting complaints by the nations, however, the rules regarding noncitizens were only loosely enforced, if at all, and the difficulty of identifying and removing intruders was widely acknowledged.[7] Some Creek leaders resented the growing role of African Creeks within the nation and used the issue of intruders to bolster their claims. Creek leader George W. Stidham angrily testified that African Creeks had gained undue political influence illegitimately bolstered by African Indian intruders from neighboring nations as well as freedpeople from the states who tried to pass themselves off as African Creeks and gain rights to land and other advantages.[8]

In the face of few restrictions, American settlers of all backgrounds were rapidly launching new lives for themselves in the territory throughout the 1860s and 1870s. In 1938 George Coleman, a seventy-five-year-old Oklahoman of Dutch ancestry, recalled his migration as a young man to what was then known as Indian Territory: "I was born on December 27, 1862," he recounted, "and am almost as native as an Indian. . . . In the spring of 1885, a neighbor and I decided to take Greeley's advice to go west and grow up with the country." George Coleman and his neighbor headed for Kansas and later to Indian Territory, "as a place near the border of civilization." What he called "Greeley's advice" had been circulating since Coleman was a child, when, in an 1865 *New York Tribune* article, editor Horace Greeley advised those young Americans who had survived the Civil War to migrate west. "Go West, young man," he had urged, "and grow up with the country."[9]

Settlers who heeded this advice often depended on their relationships with Indians for survival. E. L. Fisher, who migrated in 1878 and settled near Thomas Jefferson Brown, noted that the territory was still "a very rugged and wild country," including "a great many Indians . . . though not so many white people." Moreover, he noted, "almost all the white people who were here were refugees from some state who had come into the Territory to escape punishment on account of felony which they had committed. Everyone carried a pistol and a Winchester." The country, Fisher added, was "full of wild game and also full of what were called wild Indians though if a white person could gain the friendship of the Indians there were no better friends to be had."[10] Fisher's description of this "rugged" and increasingly tumultuous setting suggests that "friends" were essential to the settlement process.

Indeed, friendship, in this context, could mean economic survival. For his part, when Fisher settled near Brown's eventual homeplace, he "took a lease on some land there from an Indian woman, Sookie McCarty, a widow, and cleared out some of the land, built a log house of hewed logs and planted a small crop of corn."[11] Fred Brown, who came in from Texas in 1886, put it more bluntly: "I ran about seven thousand head of cattle. Of course, it was under an Indian for everyone who held cattle had to be under an Indian. In fact everything was under Indian control at that time. *Hick Harrison was our Indian.* He claimed all land or had charge of it."[12] The contention that all cattle ranchers "had to be under an Indian" indicates that American settlers, by the 1880s, had learned how to navigate and transcend many of the economic and legal obstacles they perceived with regard to the enforcement of Indian Territory borders and sovereignty. The notion of "our Indian," moreover, suggests that in spite of formal "Indian control," at least some of these American men perceived *themselves* to be in control.

When Brown married Aurelia Bruner, he did so fully aware of the myriad benefits of citizenship in Indian society. Brown may have met Aurelia in or around the old settlement of Brunertown, where many Bruners lived prior to allotment. While outside settlers were rarely granted citizenship, a far more common practice was for settlers to marry Indian women. In the 1860s and 1870s such liaisons meant access to new land and markets, as well as a share of government funds designated for Creek and Seminole citizens and families struggling in the wake of war. Moreover, connection to Tecumseh Bruner, Aurelia's Creek father who was a Lighthorseman (a member of the mounted police force in the territory) during this period, may have exempted Brown from rigid law enforcement and eased his incorporation into the territory.[13]

Throughout the history of the southeastern United States, American men frequently gained access to Indian markets and land through marriage to Indian women, who played tremendous economic, cultural, and political roles in historically matrilineal societies such as the Cherokee, Creek, Seminole, Chickasaw, and Choctaw Nations. During the eighteenth and nineteenth centuries, property, including land, was inherited through the matrilineal line, though the US government ultimately encouraged patrilineal inheritance, due to widespread intermarriage between property-holding American men and Indian women. Similarly, in the nineteenth-century US-Mexico borderlands, historian Andrés Reséndez has noted the "inescapable economic dimension" of such transnational unions. As in northern Mexico, marital ties facilitated citizenship and land acquisition in the territory.[14]

Indeed, Brown's marital status and children were of paramount importance for the duration of his life in Indian Territory. When Brown married Aurelia Bruner, he married into the rich history of the Bruner family and the Creek and Seminole Nations, including African-descended members of these nations. The Bruner family had migrated from Alabama in the early 1830s as part of Indian removal. They were among the Upper Creek families, who were generally less assimilated and consistently opposed to removal; following removal, they settled together in the new Indian Territory, near the Canadian River. Creek Freedman William M. Bruner had been told that when his Bruner grandparents came from Alabama in 1835, they traveled in ox wagons along with several families of Creek Indians. William Bruner was one of hundreds of men and women known as *Estelvste*—the Creek word invoked to refer to African-descended people of the Creek Nation. They had lived among the Creeks, as historian Gary Zellar has noted, "since the first Spanish entradas through the Creek lands" of the Southeast during the early sixteenth century. They shared a language, food, worldviews, and kinship ties with the Creeks; by the early nineteenth century, as a portion of the southeastern Indians adopted the agricultural practices of southern planters, many African-descended Creeks ultimately provided slave labor and contributed to the wealth of leading Creek families.[15]

Slavery within the Indian nations was distinct from slavery in much of the US South in important ways. Operating without an overseer, and often supporting themselves with clothing and food by tending to their own "squaw patches," enslaved men and women of the Creek Nation experienced a different sort of enslavement; there is evidence, for instance, of masters borrowing money from their slaves on occasion. Indeed, for much of Native American history, as historian Christina Snyder has argued, "captivity operated on a continuum." Moreover, before and after emancipation, African-descended Creeks—enslaved and free—also served as cultural brokers, ministers, warriors, interpreters, and negotiators, as Creek Indians contended with tribal divisions, Indian removal, and the Civil War. Bolstered by the promise of citizenship and an equal share of tribal funds following emancipation, African-descended Creeks established themselves as subsistence farmers, as well as traders, merchants, and cattle ranchers in Creek country.[16]

Included in this class was a Creek freedman named Paro Bruner. Creek Joseph Bruner recalled that the first time he met Paro was in 1898, until which time he had known "very little of my father's people": "I was a member of the House of Kings in Okmulgee, and there met an old ex-slave named Payro. He was a member from one of the three negro towns of the Creek Nation. When he heard my name called he came over and told me that he had been my grandfather's slave and had come to this country with him. Payro said my grandfather's name was George and that they had been landed people in Alabama." Paro played a prominent role within the Creek Nation and among African-descended Creeks, serving in the 1870s in the House of Warriors and as town chief of the "negro town" known as Canadian Colored. Thomas Jefferson Brown's children referred to Paro as "Uncle Parrow Bruner"; it appears he was a relation, perhaps a brother, of Aurelia Bruner.[17]

But by the time Paro shared this family history with Joseph Bruner in 1898, much had changed for *Estelvste*—increasingly referred to as "colored" or "Negro" citizens of the Creek Nation—just as it had for Joseph, his fellow Creeks, and Indians across the territory. While the treaty of 1866 had granted freedpeople of the Indian Nations citizenship "by adoption" and promised equal protection, this promise held far less weight at the close of the century. In 1890, when Mary Carrer, "a colored citizen of the Cherokee Nation," was tried for assaulting another Cherokee citizen, a local paper reported, "An able argument was made to the point that citizens by adoption were entitled to the same rights under the treaty of '66 as Indians by blood, but the court held that while Indians by blood have the right under that treaty to be tried by their own courts only [,] yet negro citizens are subject to this court also."[18] This verdict reflects a transitional moment in which freedpeople of the Indian nations—many of whom were of Indian, as well as African, ancestry—were subject to two sets of laws (in this case, US and Cherokee) and were prohibited from sharing the same rights and protections as "full-blood" Indians.

Such distinctions were indicative of a broader transformation underway in the territory as a whole. Longtime resident E. L. Fisher noted that around 1890, "the Territory began to be developed very rapidly, people came fast; homes were built; farms cleared and broken out; railroads were being built; townsites were laid out and there was one continual thing following another for the Territory was fast becoming an agricultural country from what was once the best grazing country known to men." At the same time, amid the racially complex history of the Indian Nations and the sudden influx of African American and white settlers, a distinctly multiracial society was fast evolving in this borderland, and politicians and reformers alike increasingly viewed the region as a threat to civilization and Indian "progress." Responding to land-hungry settlers—as well as to benevolent rhetoric about private property as the cornerstone of progress and Indian assimilation—in 1887 Congress passed the Dawes General Allotment Act. By the early nineteen hundreds all collectively held Indian lands had been individually allotted by the federal Dawes Commission; in turn, many of these Indian (and black Indian) allotments were quickly sold or ceded to white and some newer black settlers. Moreover, the government offered the remaining "surplus" lands to new settlers.[19]

In a few short years, the Dawes Act depleted the American Indian land base, forced American Indians into capitalist land markets, and ultimately imposed a patrilineal nuclear household in place of long-standing matrilineal societies. While the Creek, Cherokee, Choctaw, Chickasaw, and Seminole Nations were initially exempted from this act, a decade later the federal government coerced their compliance with the passage of the Curtis Act of 1898.[20] What underwrote, and yet undermined, this staggering decision by the federal government was the presence of so many nonnative settlers in Indian Territory and the related problem of identifying and removing intruders. By 1900 there were more than three times as many non-Indians as Indians in Indian Territory.[21]

"Blood" Sovereignty

Beyond the central violation of Indian national sovereignty by then underway, the most immediate consequence of the Dawes Act in Indian Territory related to enrollment. The government could not begin to allot land until first determining the membership of each of the tribes, and all past attempts at producing rolls of citizenship had largely failed. The commissioners argued that Dunn's roll of Creek freedmen taken in 1867 was a reasonably authentic beginning for identifying freedpeople of the Creek Nation; however, Paro Bruner and other Creeks disagreed, noting that many "good citizens" were left off the roll because Dunn had not made the effort to collect names himself and had sent the roll to Washington before town chiefs were able to collect all the names. Enrolling the Creeks proved to be especially complicated, in part because they were essentially a confederation of forty-four bands, with members living in separate towns, each with a town *micco* (political leader) responsible for keeping track of its citizens. Furthermore, many people operated without surnames, or with multiple names, and there were no official records of vital statistics. Although

Figure 4.1. The Dawes Commission's camps and offices. Headquarters were established in Muskogee, Indian Territory, in the 1890s. Reproduced with permission from the Research Division of the Oklahoma Historical Society.

the commission was meant to be guided by legal standards, its decisions on citizenship were more often led by "the facts known by the Old Settlers" than by written records.[22]

One of the most glaring flaws in this deeply problematic allotment process in Indian Territory lay in the Dawes Commission's emphasis on "blood quantum" and the distinction drawn, or made, between Creeks and freedpeople of the Creek Nation, who may have made up as much as one-third of the Creek population.[23] As Angie Debo noted as early as 1940, none of the rolls taken before 1896, by the Indian Nations themselves, had included a "blood quantum," and only a few recorded whether a person was "full-blood" or "mixed-blood"—"the only distinction most tribes considered important at the time." Even G. W. Stidham and other Creeks who adamantly opposed the political influence of African Creeks had nevertheless long acknowledged that African Creeks with "Creek blood" were, for all purposes, Indians. But determining "blood quantum" for purposes of allotting land was a far more complicated matter. As Silas Jefferson testified in 1895 when asked if he knew any former slaves who were also descendants of Indians, "I have seen many a one." Moreover, he noted that in Creek country it was impossible to tell "whether someone was Indian, white, or black" by appearances. Thus, determining an applicant's "degree of Indian blood" was a major challenge that turned to controversy when property restrictions and eligibility for benefits were made contingent on this very percentage.[24] The federal government's intervention in the shape of the Dawes Commission accounted, in part, for the turn-of-the-century inflation in the value of "blood" in Indian Territory, but so, too, did the federal government's lack of intervention, especially in relation to illegal settlement of the territory prior to allotment.

In short, the focus on "full-blood" status and notions of racial purity expanded exponentially, as more and more white and black nonnatives began to settle the territory, carrying with them experiences of the Deep South. And when Oklahoma became a state in 1907, it did so on the promise of adopting Jim Crow legislation similar to that which by then governed Arkansas and the other southern states. While "blood" had long mattered to privileges within the nation, "blood" identities were now officially sanctioned by the US federal government; "full-blood" status was now linked to the dominant racial categories of an expanding US empire.

Many Creeks, including both Indians and freedpeople, strongly opposed the idea of allotment overall, believing it meant the end of their traditional way of life and their right to govern their own territory. Some of Brown's neighbors resisted allotment, actively participating in what became known as the Crazy Snake Rebellion in 1909. In a brief article on the rebellion, the *New York Times* revealed the racialization and national dismissal of Indian and black Indian resistance in this moment: "After all, though Crazy Snake is a Creek Indian, his murderous band is largely composed of half-breeds and lawless negroes, and though the Creeks have had a grievance since their lands were thrown open to settlers, most of the others are merely cattle thieves whom the Sheriff has been pursuing. The romance of the red Indian is dead and probably Crazy Snake and his lieutenants soon will be in the same safe condition."[25] Notwithstanding the use of "blood" in this dismissal, Joseph Bruner (a relation of Brown's wife, Aurelia) recalled the actual reason behind the rebellion was that the Snake Indians did not want individual allotments but wanted the Creek Nation to "share equally" in the gas, oil, and pasture leases.[26]

Prior to allotment, Creeks of all backgrounds had continued to share in many resources, including, for instance, education. As Brown's grandson, Thurman Brown, recalled, "Well you see. . . . Poppa and them went to school right in here, in Wewoka, a place here called Miccusukki. Creek Indian and black folks went to school together in Miccusukki."[27] Notwithstanding this history of communal resources, by the turn of the century, Brown, like many of those residents versed in the economics of individualized land ownership, urged his children's participation in the allotment process, and quickly things began to change. Many Creeks, freedpeople of the Creek Nation, and savvy intruders tried to negotiate the best deal they could within the new system of allotment and the racial hierarchy codified therein.

Indeed, Brown's marriages to African-descended women—Aurelia Bruner and Julia Simon—of the Creek and Seminole Nations became the basis of his own family's land acquisition. In the case of his first marriage, his wife Aurelia appears to have been descended from both categories of enrollment offered by the Dawes Commission; that is, although her children were placed on the freedmen rolls, her ancestors included freedpeople of the Indian nations as well as Indians "by blood." Brown's second wife was Aurelia's niece and shared this joint lineage on her father's side. But Julia's children were able to claim Creek by blood ancestry because their "full-blood" ancestry was on Julia's *mother's* side, and the commission had decided to "observe the usages and customs of each tribe," in this case that citizenship would follow the mother's status. As Brown's grandson recalled, "See, if your momma was a Creek and your daddy was a Seminole, you was a Creek. If your momma's a Chickasaw and your daddy's a Seminole, he had to live where your momma was. . . . Two miles up from Crumwell, in Seminole County, they call it Sandy Creek, with Seminoles on one side and Creek on the other. All the mommas was born in Creek County, their kids had to be on the Creek side. . . . And they had to follow their mommas."[28] Within the first two years of the twentieth century, all except two of Brown's children by Julia were allotted the promised 160 acres each, due to their maternal enrollment as "Creek by blood" on the Dawes rolls.[29] The Brownsville allotments rested exclusively on Brown's children proving their connection to "full-bloods" or "racial purity," which they could prove only through Julia Simon's mother's family. As the family transitioned from Creek to American citizenship, and from matrilineal to patrilineal inheritance, this process likely involved *not* mentioning the possibility of freed relatives and ancestors, such as those clearly present within Julia's *father's* (and thus Aurelia's) family.

Certainly Brown's children by Julia would have avoided mention of these ancestors by name in the testimony they delivered to the Dawes commissioners in Muskogee in 1901, emphasizing instead their "full-blood" lineage; color and bodily comportment probably played important roles in this process.[30] It was often just as difficult, however, to prove one's citizenship by way of freedmen of the Creek Nation. Indeed, during this same period, Brown's children by Aurelia were working hard to prove their Indian freedmen lineage for purposes of allotment. In a letter between Brown and Aurelia's two daughters, passing on her father's instructions, Chaney (Brown) Wallas desperately urged her sister, Rena (Brown) McNack, to register "at Wonce," to ensure Creek land allotments for all family members. Painfully illustrating the importance of specificity and consistency in the process of substantiating their birthright to the Dawes Commission, Chaney wrote,

I just want to tell you to go and file right away and when you go you must call for realley Brun [er?] and you must tell them about your grandfather name and uncles an aunt name that is on the Dun roll and they will ask you about your Sister and your Brother and you must tell them and you must tell the age of them. So you must tell them that I am 28 year old that you are about 25 or 26 and fred is about 21 or 22 years old and you must tell them Sil is about 18 or 19 years old and you must tell them that Lemmie is about 16 or 17 years old and you must talk one thing. Don't make no mistake in your talking and you must tell them about my children ages and that Washington is 7 years old last October the 24 Day and tell them that Fredonia was 5 years old last august the 30 day and you must tell them Bennie was 3 year old last febuary the 19 Day. So Papa say that you must try and get 25 Dollar this fall for to pay uncle Parrow Bruner for his truble with us to prane our right up and PaPa Say that you must tell Aran to go and file right away at Wonce and Don't Delay for [in fall they . . . ?]. So give my love to all And Try to go right away and file at Wonce and be done with it So you must Do What I tell you for I just got back on the 27 So I will close my short letter from your truly sister, Chaney Wallas.[31]

Here Chaney references their ancestors' presence on the postemancipation Dunn rolls of freedmen, which by 1901 were being used to cross-reference Dawes Commission testimony. Chaney's concern is proving their family's presence on the 1867 rolls. This suggests that her mother was in fact listed as a freedman of the Creek Nation (although, like many Creek freedmen, she may have also been of Creek ancestry).

We do not know what exactly "uncle" Paro Bruner's "truble with us" included, but we do know that he played a valuable role within the Dawes allotment process, particularly for African Creeks. Paro had initially warned in 1894 that "nothing good could come of allotment," predicting that the Creeks would be driven from their land and homes. When allotment began, however, Paro was one of several African Creeks who assisted the Dawes Commission, "seeking out bona fide citizens" and making sure they were "properly enrolled." At the time, some of Thomas Jefferson Brown's fellow African American intruders were being accused of trying to pass as Creek freedmen to gain access to land. Amid rampant suspicion, Brown paid twenty-five dollars to "uncle" Paro, probably to bolster his children's claims to Creek status.[32]

From her letter we know that Chaney had returned home just two days prior, in March 1901, from the Dawes Commission's Muskogee office. By this time, the Muskogee office, at least a day's travel from Brownsville, had become a "mecca" for people of all backgrounds eager to make or improve their lives in Indian Territory. Although the office assigned admission numbers to control the crowds, some developed the practice of buying and selling these tickets to the highest bidder. When an applicant such as Rena McNack finally

Figure 4.2. Paro Bruner, circa 1900. Reproduced with permission from the Research Division of the Oklahoma Historical Society.

Figure 4.3. Paro Bruner, date unknown. Reproduced with permission from the Research Division of the Oklahoma Historical Society.

approached the desk of enrolling clerk Phillip B. Hopkins, she was sworn in and her testimony recorded by the commission's stenographer, D. W. Yancey.[33] If authenticated by previous rolls, as Rena's claim was, the applicant was issued a citizenship certificate and sent on to another office to select land for allotment. Surely they would have been grateful for Paro Bruner's presence throughout this unfamiliar process.

Finally, Thomas Jefferson Brown "with some training and education and many trips to Muskogee saw to it that each child's allotment was joining—so the township was established 'Brownsville' using the family name." According to Brown's granddaughter Marzetta Wesley, "There in this community of Browns was the Post Office, General Store, School and Church."[34] Brown's ability to direct the placement of these individual allotments (an uncommon feat for many allottees), his maneuvering of "Creek by blood" status, and the success, however temporary, of the Brownsville settlement may have raised suspicions for his African Creek in-laws about the motivations of this nonnative. Julia's "full-blood" relatives may have also resented the enrollment of African Creeks on the Dawes rolls; many Creeks resented having been forced by the federal government to grant citizenship to their former slaves. In the years leading up to allotment, Brown and Julia had ten children, and all except two were born before the allotment cut-off in 1907. As their son Tom Brown recalls, "Now my brother Oscar, the baby boy, *he was born too late*. See he come in nineteen seven, when territory went into a state."[35]

Land was certainly a popular point of contention and, especially after the death of his second wife, Jeff's motivation for marrying into the Bruner and Simon families may have been questioned. Just a month after Julia passed away, her two-year-old daughter died. At 103 years old, Jeff's son, Tom Brown, recalled, "I had a sister, a baby sister, her name was Ella Mae. . . . One of the Simons choked her to death. Our daddy, and Ellwood, went out to kill him, kill him, but they couldn't find him." When asked about the source of this conflict, Odevia Field answered, "What she probably did wrong was marrying my grandfather for some reason. Maybe. All I could remember them saying was he married her because of the land and the money. And the more children he had I guess they'd acquire that. It could be all related to land."[36]

Despite tribal resistance, internal conflict, and bureaucratic challenges, the Creek Nation's land was ultimately allotted to those individuals who could prove Creek national membership *or* that they were freedpeople of the Creek Nation, ultimately folding individual allottees into the capitalist land market and releasing the collective "surplus"—and a great portion of the future state of Oklahoma—to the US government and incoming settlers. Since most allottees had little or no experience with private land ownership, the law provided that individual allottees should be protected by making "sufficient land for a good home for each citizen . . . inalienable for twenty-five years," at which point, the commissioners speculated, Indians might be more accustomed to the idea of individual land holding. Dawes agreements with each of the five nations contained provisions to protect a limited (forty-acre) portion, known as the "homestead," against alienation, while the remainder, known as the (individual) "surplus," would soon "pass freely" in and out of Indian control, as Angie Debo noted in 1940.[37] Feeding on what Debo called the "wild, speculative, active spirit of the oil field," oil speculators pushed for the lifting of even these restrictions, and in 1908 Congress acquiesced.

Figure 4.4. Allotments of Julia Brown and six of her children (Charles, Minnie, Madison, Charity, Elwood, Rose). All except two of her ten children were born before the allotment cutoff in 1907. E. Hastain, *Hastain's Township Plats of the Creek Nation* (Muskogee: Model, 1910). Reproduced with permission from the Research Division of the Oklahoma Historical Society.

Figure 4.5. The Dawes Commission's captain Archibald S. McKennon enrolling freedmen at Fort Gibson, circa 1900. Tribal members and officials directed individuals to the "Freedmen" or "By Blood" enrollment sites based on presumed knowledge of one's family, appearance, and other factors. Reproduced with permission from the Research Division of the Oklahoma Historical Society.

But Congress did not do so even-handedly. Instead, it passed legislation that removed nearly all restrictions on the surplus of all Creeks, except "full-bloods," as designated by the Dawes rolls. Because "mixed-blood" allottees—who were in some cases simply children of one Creek and one Seminole parent and were in other cases freedpeople of the Indian Nations—had lived all of their lives among the Indians, in this case among the Creeks and Seminoles, they often understood the concept of individual land ownership no differently than did many Creeks themselves. Within months, most had lost their land to white grafters and oil speculators. With this legislation, more than 1.5 million acres were suddenly available for purchase by speculators near and far, and the vast majority of these acres belonged to freedpeople and "mixed-blood" members of the Indian Nations and their children, such as those residing at Brownsville.[38]

Racialized Land Loss

Surely Brown worried as African Creeks—still faintly recalled as *Estelvste*—were divested of their land and socially and politically segregated from Creeks and white settlers alike through a violent combination of federal allotment policy, state and local Jim Crow policies, and rampant land and oil speculation. The rights of Creek freedpeople were increasingly neglected, as a massive new wave of African American settlers and intermarriage further blurred the boundaries of these populations. In short, race quickly eclipsed national or nonnational status as the leading guarantor of rights and resources in Indian Territory; one's race (and *not* one's historical membership within the Indian nations)—as designated by the Dawes Commission—now determined whether or not one's allotment would be insulated from the rampant speculation, taxation, debt, and foreclosure that immediately transpired. In response to segregation and mounting discrimination, the emergence of the all-black towns also helped to obscure the once distinct position of Creek freedpeople in Indian Territory and thus the Creek origins of such communities. The intensifying of the Jim Crow order and the advent of oil speculation intertwined to muddle the possibility and relevance of black Indian identities. As one historian has noted, the story of the *Estelvste* "tells of the nation choosing a future with no place within it for truly multiracial societies."[39]

Following Oklahoma statehood, in the wake of this transformation, Brown felt the need to communicate to his children (with Julia Simon) their exact status in the Creek Nation in terms that nevertheless reflected the growing significance of race and "blood" in Indian Territory. His son, Charles Brown, passed this on to his own children in the years following Oklahoma statehood. Marzetta Wesley recalled, "Pawpaw always told me, *you are not a freedman.* Others may say they are, but you are not. You are Caesar Simon's great-great-granddaughter. And Charity Simon."[40] The statement reveals Charles Brown's, and likely Thomas Jefferson Brown's, investment in distancing his children, when possible, from slavery and claiming, in its place, Creek lineage. In this way, Brown attempted to link his children's fate not to race, but to nation, and in this case the *Creek* Nation; American national citizenship was no longer the hopeful claim it may have been for African Americans at the time of Brown's initial migration.

Of course, the two categories were not mutually exclusive, and many Creek freedpeople had been both slaves and relatives of their Indian slave owners. Indeed, it seems likely that Brown's wives were both descended from slaves and slave owners. Brown's insistence in this statement clearly reflects the fact that even those who could prove "Creek by blood" heritage along with African ancestry, such as his own children by Julia, were losing traction during this period, particularly in the aftermath of allotment, the massive influx of white and African American migrants from the deep South to the new state of Oklahoma, and the emergence of Jim Crow and oil speculation. Ironically, turn-of-the-century proclamations in local papers about African Creek participation on equal footing in political life had encouraged this influx to the so-called Promised Land; in 1904 in the Muskogee *Cimeter,* Paro Bruner himself would still describe Creek country, relative to the brutality of the surrounding region, as "an island surrounded by land."[41] But by the end of the first decade, the rights of all African descended peoples in the territory were systematically denied. Echoing the Mississippi State Black Codes of 1865 that prohibited African Americans from purchasing or leasing land, white Oklahomans began to limit African American access to land in the early nineteen hundreds. In 1911 white farmers of Okfuskee County (immediately north of the Browns-ville allotments) signed oaths pledging to "never rent, lease, or sell land in Okfuskee County to any person of Negro blood, or agent of theirs; unless the land be located more than one mile from a white or Indian resident." More-over, following a series of Jim Crow laws passed immediately after Oklahoma statehood, disfranchisement and segregation were enforced by both legal and extralegal methods. Racial violence expanded after statehood, and between 1907 and 1930 the victims of lynchings in Oklahoma were almost exclusively African American.[42]

By such tactics, distinctions between Creek freedpeople and the recent wave of state migrants—that is, between black Indians and more recent black set-tlers—were quickly flattened, effectively racializing the whole, allowing black Indians fewer and fewer opportunities to claim national membership within the Indian nations. For the most part, Creek freedmen faced the same dis-crimination imposed on all African Americans of early Oklahoma, and in some cases they expressed resentment toward the newcomers. Their complaints, however, had hardly a place to register, as their particular freedman status had little or no sustaining significance within the new state; there were few oppor-tunities to assign meaning to their unique history within the Creek Nation. Where there had once been social sanctions against a freedman's marriage to a "state Negro," these quickly broke down in the face of white and Indian hostil-ity toward all people of African descent.[43]

In the 1910s, as the Brownsville land was pursued by oil speculators, Brown began urging his children to move away from their rural settlement, closer to the then burgeoning city of Okmulgee, where, in the spirit of racial uplift, African American education, employment, and sheer safety were more eas-ily achieved; soon a new wave of black migration—to cities and beyond the United States—would further obscure the multiracial, multinational origins of this family and community. By 1907 Chaney's sister Rena had already moved to Okmulgee, a then-bustling town, and her siblings soon followed from the Brownsville settlement.

For the Browns and other black and black Indian families facing discrimi-nation throughout rural Oklahoma, the quest for land now transformed into a hunt for jobs and education. Along the way, settlements like Brownsville were leased, mortgaged, and sold to white settlers, speculators, and banks. Before the value of petroleum beneath much of the black and Indian land holdings of Oklahoma was known, and before Oklahoma was ten years old, the Brown family was already gone from the land. Following in the footsteps of his *Estelvste* ancestors who served as negotiators and translators, Brown's son, Charles, ultimately made a living, however uneven, by translating the Muskogee language for white oil speculators and directing them to oil-rich lands throughout the Creek Nation.

Conclusion

In 1870, when Brown settled in Indian Territory, Indian Nations perceived American settlement—black or white—through the lens of national sovereignty. Simultaneously, American frontiersmen—black and white—perceived migration, settlement, and the experience of land acquisition in Indian Territory as a manifestation of freedom and fundamentally an American national project. By the time of Brown's migration, land was the leading incentive for African American settlement in Indian Country, although an explicitly racialized settlement movement had yet to emerge in Indian Territory. During this early period, Indian and American national projects—in the names of sovereignty and freedom—often functioned at odds with each other, particularly within the context of land ownership in Indian Territory.

By 1904, however, when a Mississippi freedman moved his family to the plot adjacent to Brown's, the emerging opposition instead lay largely between black and white national projects. Soon the experience of land loss in relation to Jim Crow and the rise of oil speculation in early statehood Oklahoma bound together black and black Indian families, gradually processing their newly linked fate within the state of Oklahoma. Race and color had so significantly shaped access to resources in the territory that by the second decade of the twentieth century, the reverse was also true: resources could shape perceptions of one's racial and national origins. "When you get as much money as Johnny [a freedman]," one Creek freedman posited, "you're an Indian not a Negro."[44]

A long-standing Creek tradition of cultural integration with regard to African Creeks had been complicated and thoroughly overwhelmed by the racial categories, institutions, and ideas of white Americans, especially ideas about progress and civilization.[45] Indian national sovereignty was undone, and what remained in its wake was a lasting obsession with race and "blood"; for those of African ancestry, race obscured the significance of national versus nonnational status. This shift was not inevitable. Brown resisted, and as Jim Crow and oil speculation plagued Brownsville, he held fast to national belonging—particularly his children's connection through their mothers to the Creek Nation—as a potential escape route within an increasingly racist state. But in the end, as much as the experience of land acquisition for settlers like Brown functioned as a national project, the experience of land loss two decades later was principally a racialized one. Moreover, Brown's mixed racial ancestry played a role, mitigating his initial national status as a nonnative and, throughout his life, mitigating his proximity to blackness.

Brownsville is remembered by twentieth-century descendants as Thomas Jefferson Brown's land, not Julia Simon's or Aurelia Bruner's, and as a black settlement, not an Indian or black Indian one. This is partly because Thomas Jefferson Brown, listed as "mulatto" on the census, appears in most twentieth-century recollections as the patriarch of the family; because it was he who arranged the placement of the allotments adjacent to one another, applied for and received the post office, set up the schoolhouse and church; and because his subsequent wives were nonnative African American women. But it is also because of much broader changes afoot in Indian Territory and Oklahoma in the early nineteen hundreds. Most important, the value of "blood" emerged paramount in turn-of-the-century Indian Territory, beginning with the Dawes Commission's attempt to distinguish between "Indians by blood" and "Creek freedmen," when so many residents were in fact connected to both groups. The resulting rolls nevertheless codified a hierarchy within which "full-blood" Indians were entitled to more land and "protected" from fraud. This shift was ultimately bolstered by a Jim Crow state that soon classified Indians as "white" and African Creeks as "black," and distributed resources accordingly.

At the age of ninety-six, Thurman Brown was one descendant who, having grown up in Brownsville and having been raised by Brown, remembered it the way it actually was. While examining a map of the area, I unthinkingly suggested to him, "This would have been Grandpa Brown's land." He looked up from the map abruptly and said, "You mean Grandma Brown. *Grandpa Brown didn't have no land.*"[46] Having witnessed the first century of Oklahoma statehood, Thurman knew better than most the historical relationship between land and identity. Willfully tying the land to his black Indian grandmother Julia (Simon) Brown, Thurman highlighted the origins of this land as a nineteenth-century Creek allotment, at a time—prior to widespread African American settlement of Indian Territory and the rise of Jim Crow—when African Americans could still *be* Creek.[47] Thus the story of Thomas Jefferson Brown's migration narrates the construction of a new racial order in Indian Territory and, ultimately, the limits of North American escape.

Notes

The author would like to thank the Brown family descendants, Martha Hodes, Walter Johnson, Barbara Krauthamer, David Levering Lewis, Michele Mitchell, Tiya Miles, Celia Naylor, Colin Calloway, Eric Foner, Catherine Allgor, and Khary Saeed Jones for their insight.

1. On the history of African-descended peoples within the Southeast Indian nations, before and after Indian removal, see Tiya Miles, *Ties That Bind: An Afro-Cherokee Family in Slavery and Freedom* (Berkeley: University of California Press,

2005); Celia Naylor, *African Cherokees in Indian Territory: From Chattel to Citizens* (Chapel Hill: University of North Carolina Press, 2008); Theda Perdue, *Mixed Blood Indians: Racial Construction in the Early South* (Athens: University of Georgia Press, 2003); Claudio Saunt, *Black, White, and Indian: Race and the Unmaking of an American Family* (New York: Oxford University Press, 2005); Gary Zellar, *African Creeks: Estelvste and the Creek Nation* (Norman: University of Oklahoma Press, 2007); Barbara Krauthamer, "Blacks on the Border: African-Americans' Transition from Slavery to Freedom in Texas and the Indian Territory, 1836–1907" (PhD diss., Princeton University, 2000); Kevin Mulroy, *The Seminole Freedmen: A History* (Norman: University of Oklahoma Press, 2007); Fay A. Yarbrough, *Race and the Cherokee Nation: Sovereignty in the Nineteenth Century* (Philadelphia: University of Pennsylvania Press, 2007); Circe Sturm, *Blood Politics: Race, Culture, and Identity in the Cherokee Nation of Oklahoma* (Los Angeles: University of California Press, 2002); Daniel Littlefield, *Africans and Creeks: From the Colonial Period to the Civil War* (Westport, CT: Greenwood, 1979); Sarah Deutsch, "Being American in Boley, Oklahoma," in *Beyond Black and White: Race, Ethnicity, and Gender in the U.S. South and Southwest*, ed. Stephanie Cole and Alison M. Parker (Arlington: University of Texas at Arlington, 2004), 97–122; and Ariela J. Gross, *What Blood Won't Tell: A History of Race on Trial in America* (Cambridge, MA: Harvard University Press, 2008), ch. 5, 140–77.

2. See "Interview with Wallace F. Brown," October 27, 1937, interview 7992, Indian-Pioneer Papers, Western History Collections, University of Oklahoma, Norman, 12:203–6. See also Art Burton, *Black, Red, and Deadly: Black and Indian Gunfighters in the Indian Territory, 1870–1907* (Austin, TX: Eakin, 1991); and Kenneth Wiggins Porter, *The Negro on the American Frontier* (New York: Arno, 1971).

3. Tom Brown (Thomas Jefferson Brown's grandson), interview with the author, Okmulgee, Oklahoma, November 23, 2005.

4. Daniel F. Littlefield Jr. and Lonnie E. Underhill, "Divorce Seeker's Paradise: Oklahoma Territory, 1890–1897," *Arizona and the West* (*Journal of the Southwest*) 17, no. 1 (Spring 1975): 21–34.

5. Two African American frontiersmen who preceded Brown in this regard were Peter Caulder and John Marrant. See Billy Higgins, *A Stranger and a Sojourner: Peter Caulder, Free Black Frontiersman in Antebellum Arkansas* (Fayetteville: University of Arkansas Press, 2004); Tiya Miles, "'His Kingdom for a Kiss': Indians and Intimacy in the Narrative of John Marrant," in *Haunted by Empire: Geographies of Intimacy in North American History*, ed. Ann Laura Stoler (Durham, NC: Duke University Press, 2006), 163–88. See also Juliet E. K. Walker, *Free Frank: A Black Pioneer on the Antebellum Frontier* (1983; repr., Lexington: University Press of Kentucky, 1995).

6. African Americans served as soldiers, scouts, and occasionally missionaries in Indian Country throughout the eighteenth and nineteenth centuries. See Higgins, *Stranger and a Sojourner*, xiv; and Miles, "His Kingdom," 165.

7. Kent Carter, *The Dawes Commission and the Allotment of the Five Civilized Tribes, 1893–1914* (Orem, Utah: Ancestry, 1999); "Interview with J. C. Ritter," January 25, 1938, interview 12837, Indian-Pioneer Papers, 76:330–33.

8. Zellar, *African Creeks*, 162–64. See also "Letters Received by the Office of the Adjutant General," 1871–80, roll 471 (rep. 1278; 151–52, 158–59, 197–98), Southwest Region, National Archives, Fort Worth, Texas; and "Records Relating to Intruders," RG 75, Records of the Five Civilized Tribes Agency, National Archives.

9. "Interview with George M. Coleman," April 13, 1938, interview 10449, Indian-Pioneer Papers, 19:271–74. Historians have debated the exact origins of the "Go west . . ." slogan. While the phrase may not have originated with Greeley, he nevertheless popularized the sentiment and encouraged colonization of public lands via the Homestead Act. See Coy F. Cross, *Go West Young Man! Horace Greeley's Vision for America* (Albuquerque: University of New Mexico Press, 1995); "The Homestead Act," editorial, *New York Tribune,* July 13, 1865.

10. "An Interview with Mr. E. L. Fisher," October 25, 1937, interview 8983, Indian-Pioneer Papers, 30:73–78.

11. Ibid.

12. "An Interview with Fred Brown," May 20, 1937, interview 4123, Indian-Pioneer Papers, 12:75–78 (emphasis added).

13. Thurman Brown (Thomas Jefferson Brown's grandson), interview with the author, Okmulgee, Oklahoma, November 24, 2005; "Interview with Caesar Simon," reprinted in Angela Y. Walton, *The Frontier Freedman's Journal: An African American Genealogical and Historical Journal of the South, Indian Territory, and the Southwest* (Baltimore, MD: Walton, 1992).

14. Andrés Reséndez, *Changing National Identities at the Frontier: Texas and New Mexico, 1800–1850* (New York: Cambridge University Press, 2004), 129–30. For the southeast United States, see Perdue, *Mixed Blood Indians*; Richard Godbeer, "Eroticizing the Middle Ground: Anglo-Indian Sexual Relations along the Eighteenth-Century Frontier," in *Sex, Love, Race: Crossing Boundaries in North American History*, ed. Martha Hodes (New York: New York University Press, 1999), 91–111; and Yarbrough, *Cherokee Nation.*

15. Zellar, *African Creeks*, 34; "An Interview with Joseph Bruner" (president of the American Federation of Indians), February 28, 1938, interview 13105, Indian Pioneer Papers, 12:318–28; "An Interview with William M. Bruner," July 20, 1937, interview 6890, Indian Pioneer Papers, 12:334–36; Thurman Brown, interview. Settlement of the "immigrant nations" encroached on the lands and markets of the eastern Comanche. See Pekka Hämäläinen, *The Comanche Empire* (New Haven, CT: Yale University Press, 2008), 152–53.

16. Zellar, *African Creeks*, 34; Snyder, *Slavery in Indian Country: The Changing Face of Captivity in Early America* (Cambridge: Harvard University Press, 2010), 7. See especially Miles, *Ties That Bind*; Naylor, *African Cherokees*; Krauthamer, "Blacks on the Border"; Saunt, *Black, White, and Indian*; Perdue, *Mixed Blood Indians*; and Littlefield, *Africans and Creeks.*

17. "Interview with Joseph Bruner," 318–38; Letter from Chaney Wallas to Rena McNack, March 29, 1901, Wewoka, Indian Territory, in author's possession. Recorded spellings list Paro, Parrow, Pero, and Payro. The "negro towns" mentioned here include Arkansas Colored, Canadian Colored, and North Fork Colored, all three established in the 1870s and 1880s, prior to the development of the all-black towns. See Zellar, *African Creeks*, 98, 159.

18. "Court Notes," *Our Brother in Red* (Cherokee Nation), April 12, 1890.

19. "Interview with Mr. E. L. Fisher," 203–6; Zellar, *African Creeks*, 161–62; Carter, *Dawes Commission*, 33–68. On parallel developments in New Mexico Territory, see Pablo Mitchell, *Coyote Nation: Sexuality, Race, and Conquest in Modernizing New Mexico, 1880–1920* (Chicago: University of Chicago Press, 2005).

20. The Curtis Act of 1898 was an amendment to the Dawes Act of 1887. Carter, *Dawes Commission*, 34–38.

21. "Records Relating to Intruders," National Archives.

22. Congress required that the Dawes rolls be descriptive to ensure positive identifications when assigning allotments; the census card included the applicant's age, sex, and "degree of Indian blood." But many people were known by more than one name and frequently changed names. Commissioners noted, "Surnames are changed overnight . . . in some cases two or more children are given identically the same name." Carter, *Dawes Commission*, 40–42, 49; Letters and Documents Concerning Creek Citizenship, October 11, 1874–December 18, 1895, records 24947 and 24949, Creek National Records 3; and February 28, 1895–October 25, 1910, records 25216, 25411, and 25413, Creek National Records 4, Oklahoma Historical Society, in Carter, *Dawes Commission*, 40–42, 49; Zellar, *African Creeks*, 202, 218.

23. African Creeks constituted 32 percent of the Creek population, according to the census of 1895. The distinction between freedpeople and African Creeks, however, further complicates this calculation. National Council Letters and Documents 1895–1909, document 33317, Creek National Records 13, in Carter, "Snakes and Scribes," in *Dawes Commission*, 387–88; Zellar, *African Creeks*, 201.

24. Superintendent for the Five Civilized Tribes, Annual Report, 1905, quoted in Angie Debo, *And Still the Waters Run* (Princeton, NJ: Princeton University Press, 1940), 47–49; "Lists of Applicants and Docket Books of the Creek Citizenship Commission," 1888–96, 7RA68, roll 2, Report of the Commissioner to the Five Civilized Tribes, RG 75, Records of the Bureau of Indian Affairs, National Archives, quoted in Zellar, *African Creeks*, 162–64, 202.

25. "Crazy Snake's War," *New York Times*, 30 March 1909. "An Interview with Joseph Bruner," July 13 and 23, 1937, 2nd interview 6654, "Seven miles Northwest of Sapulpa," Indian-Pioneer Papers, 12:315–17.

26. This fight to stop allotment was led by Creek Chitto Harjo ("Crazy Snake"). Harjo and his followers were dissatisfied with the 1866 treaties and later laws concerning the Creeks. See Kay M. Teall, *Black History in Oklahoma: A Resource Book* (Oklahoma City: Oklahoma City Schools, 1971), 146–47; Carter, *Dawes Commission*, 56; and David Lewis and Ann T. Jordan, *Creek Indian Medicine Ways: The Enduring Power of Mvskoke Religion* (Albuquerque: University of New Mexico Press, 2002), 19.

27. Here Thurman refers to "Poppa," his father and Thomas Jefferson Brown's son, Lemuel. Thurman Brown, interview.

28. Grandson Thurman Brown hinted that the privileging of matrilineal lineage meant that some parts of the family history were conveniently neglected over time: "See your momma and people [Creek 'by blood'] they didn't know . . . weren't concerned with people, Bruners [freedpeople], around there." Thurman Brown, interview. On Commissioner Bixby's intent to observe matrilineal citizenship, see Carter, *Dawes Commission*, 45. The practice was later attacked by lawyers whose clients wanted to take the status of their fathers.

29. Thurman Brown, interview.

30. Carter, *Dawes Commission*, 45.

31. Wallas to McNack, March 29, 1901, in author's possession.

32. On Paro Bruner's role in the allotment process, see "An Interview with Island Smith," July 17, 1937, interview 6729, *Indian Pioneer Papers*, 85:95–98; Zellar, *African Creeks*, 159, 199, 217; and Carter, *Dawes Commission*, 46.

33. Carter, *Dawes Commission*, 45–46; Dawes Commission to the Secretary of the Interior, April 15, 1899, DC roll 4, microfilm, Oklahoma Historical Society, Oklahoma City.

34. As part of a local history project, in 1985 Marzetta Wesley wrote and submitted a short family history of the Browns to Okmulgee County. See Okmulgee Historical Society and the Heritage Society of America, eds., *History of Okmulgee County, Oklahoma*, vol. 1 (Tulsa, OK: Historical Enterprises, 1985), 587.

35. When Aurelia passed away in the late 1880s Brown married Julia Simon. "Brown Family," in *History of Okmulgee County*, 587; Zellar, *African Creeks*, 53; Tom Brown, interview (emphasis added).

36. Tom Brown, interview; Odevia Brown Field (Thomas Jefferson Brown's granddaughter), interview with the author, Okmulgee, Oklahoma, November 26, 2005.

37. Annual Report of the Dawes Commission for 1894, Records of the Bureau of Indian Affairs, RG 75, Records of the Five Civilized Tribes Agency, National Archives, Southwest Region in Fort Worth, Texas, 82–87, quoted in Debo, *Still the Waters Run*, 36.

38. The Restrictions Bill, passed in May 1908, "removed the restrictions from all lands, except homesteads, of citizens of more than half and less than three-quarters, but it retained restrictions on homesteads of persons, including minors, with more than half blood and all full-bloods until April 26, 1931." The Dawes rolls were to be accepted as conclusive in determining the "quantum of Indian blood." Carter, *Dawes Commission*, 176; Debo, *Still the Waters Run*, 89–90; Charles J. Kappler, ed., *Indian Affairs: Laws and Treaties*, vol. 1 (Washington, DC: Government Printing Office, 1904), 649, 663–64, 764, 772, 788; Teall, *Black History in Oklahoma*, 137–38.

39. Zellar, *African Creeks*, xvii. Like many "all-black" towns in Oklahoma, the town of Boley was founded on the allotment of Creek freedperson Abigail Barnett. For an excellent discussion of Boley's historical significance, see Deutsch, "Being an American," 97–122. On the all-black towns, see Kenneth Marvin Hamilton, *Black Towns and Profit: Promotion and Development in the Trans-Appalachian West, 1877–1915* (Champaign: University of Illinois Press, 1991); Norman L. Crockett, *The Black Towns* (Lawrence: Regents Press of Kansas, 1979); Nell Irvin Painter, *Exodusters: Black Migration to Kansas after Reconstruction* (New York: Knopf, 1977); Hannibal B. Johnson, *Acres of Aspiration: The All-Black Towns in Oklahoma* (Austin, TX: Eakin, 2002); Jimmie Lewis Franklin, *Journey toward Hope: A History of Blacks in Oklahoma* (Norman: University of Oklahoma Press, 1982).

40. Marzetta Brown Wesley, interview with the author, Okmulgee, Oklahoma, November 22, 2005.

41. *Cimeter*, 1904, quoted in Franklin, *Journey toward Hope*; Zellar, *African Creeks*, 237.

42. Painter, *Exodusters*, 7; William Bittle and Gilbert Geis, *The Longest Way Home: Chief Alfred C. Sam's Back-to-Africa Movement* (Detroit: Wayne State University Press, 1964), 54, 56–57; Crockett, *Black Towns*, 167.

43. Bittle and Geis, *Longest Way Home*, 23.

44. Sigmund Sameth, "Creek Negroes: A Study of Race Relations" (master's thesis, University of Oklahoma, 1940); Bittle and Geis, *Longest Way Home*, 23.

45. Zellar, *African Creeks*, 32.

46. Thurman Brown, interview (emphasis added).

47. Nor did Thurman bother to mention that Grandma Julie was categorized Creek "by blood," whereas his own grandmother was designated a freedman. Thurman knew the subtleties of African Creek history, perhaps because he was raised by his grandfather Brown and, in terms of his maternal ancestry, had grown up a Bruner in a house full of Simons, the only Creek freedperson in a house full of Creek "by blood." Several months before he passed away, in the midst of the national controversy over Cherokee membership, he told me, "You know, the Cherokees want 'full-blood' only now," and that the Creeks might follow suit. Then he turned quiet. Thurman Brown, interview, August 2007.

Part 3

Civil Rights and the Law

Chapter 5

Countable Bodies, Uncountable Crimes

Sexual Assault and the Antilynching Movement

Michelle Kuhl

> In the context of the Negro problem, neither whites nor blacks, for
> excellent reasons of their own, have the faintest desire to look back;
> but I think the past is all that makes the present coherent, and further,
> that the past will remain horrible for exactly as long as we refuse to
> assess it honestly.
>
> —James Baldwin, *Notes of a Native Son*

The Cost of Success

On June 13, 2005, the US Senate apologized for filibustering antilynching legislation from the early twentieth century that would have made lynching a federal crime.[1] In essence, the government apologized for failing one of its most
basic functions: protecting its citizens from harm. This apology acknowledged
that victims of lynch mobs, largely southern African Americans killed by whites,
did not receive appropriate protection of law officials to prevent or punish
their deaths. This apology was long overdue and reflects a popular consensus,
perhaps prompted by scholarship, that lynching is unjust.

Had this apology been issued one hundred years ago, however, it might
have been different. It might have included an apology for the government's
failure to protect African American women from white sexual assault. Activists
in the earliest phase of the antilynching movement, the two decades at the turn
of the century, had what we today would call an intersectional understanding.
Lynch critics considered the mob killings of black men and the sexual assaults
on black women to be complementary problems with similar root causes and
faulted the criminal justice system for failing to prevent or punish either crime.

Among white Americans, scientific conclusions and popular attitudes led to the widespread conclusion that black men and women had excessively sexual natures. Thus police did not bother to arrest mob members who killed accused black rapists and similarly did not concern themselves with black women who claimed they were sexually assaulted by white men.[2] Black bodies were unprotected from murder and rape, and in the early phase of the antilynching movement activists challenged both phenomena.

However, as time went on, people found new ways to combat lynching specifically. The biggest obstacle to stopping lynching was the widespread assumption that mobs formed in reaction to black men who raped white women. Over time, black activists found two effective mechanisms for decoupling lynching from the rumors of black rapists. One strategy, martyrdom discourse, grew out of black Christian theology that sacralized suffering to explain oppression. Statistics, the second strategy, flourished as social scientists increasingly looked to hard data to map the accusations that prompted lynching. Statistics on crime undermined claims that lynching was solely a response to black rapists and the martyrdom discourse emphasized the brutality of the mob and the suffering of the victim.[3]

Both strategies proved powerful ways to redeem black manhood from the stereotype of bestial criminality. Ultimately, by the first two decades of the nineteen hundreds, activists drew on both strategies to make the antilynching fight the centerpiece of the black freedom struggle. But the strategies did not apply to sexual assaults on black women, and that issue slowly withered. As the scholar Hazel V. Carby has noted, "The institutionalized rape of black women has never been as powerful a symbol of black oppression as the spectacle of lynching."[4] This chapter examines the cost of success: as antilynching activists found powerful new ways to voice outrage against the murder of black men, they became increasingly silent on the issue of sexual assault against black women. Intersectional awareness did not translate into intersectional activism. To echo James Baldwin's insight, this is a horrible story of murder and humiliation. But, I hope, an honest assessment can make the present more coherent.

The Justification of Lynching

In the late nineteenth century, African Americans were facing many problems—after the brief promise of equal citizenship in Reconstruction, southern white Democrats embarked on a brutal campaign they called Redemption to wrest political control away from the Republican coalition of African Americans and liberal whites. Redeemers had the specific goals of undermining the provisions of the Fourteenth and Fifteenth Amendments that promised the franchise and due process, the essential tools of citizenship, to black men.[5] Redemption was extremely violent, and it is in these decades of the 1880s and

1890s that mob violence rose. Mobs lynched more than twelve hundred victims in the 1880s and more than fifteen hundred in the 1890s.[6]

Starting with Mississippi, southern states rewrote their state constitutions to exclude African Americans from voting, and all over the South Jim Crow barriers were rising. The pioneering African American historian Rayford Logan called this period the "nadir" of black history.[7] After the dizzying promise of emancipation and the hopes of progress during Reconstruction, the old guard of abolitionists were heartsick to see northerners turn a blind eye to southern transgressions. The abolitionist and former slave Frederick Douglass gave an Emancipation Oration in 1883 at a congregational church in Washington DC, where he sadly concluded, "peace with the master class has been war to the Negro."[8] Douglass knew that the government's decisions to dissolve the Freedmen's Bureau, withdraw federal troops from the South, and overturn civil rights legislation left southern African Americans caught in a cycle of vicious labor exploitation under the political leadership of their furious former masters.

The previous era of antebellum slavery inspired a determined abolitionist movement. Although fragmented, the movement at least understood what it was fighting. In the confusion and terror of the 1880s and 1890s, black activists had a hard time deciding how to focus their energies. Some leaders fought for the franchise. Some, like Booker T. Washington, concentrated on industrial education. Some protested the segregation of public transportation, and others, like Bishop Henry Turner, thought conditions were so bad that colonization was the best option.[9] By the second decade of the twentieth century, out of all these issues, lynching became the main focus of the black freedom struggle. Activists recognized that white supremacist violence effectively blocked progress on other fronts.[10] Fear of lynching turned people from the polls, from making speeches calling for political reform, from registering children in school, from publishing problack newspapers, and so on. In 1937 the novelist Richard Wright suggested that Jim Crow was best described by an elevator operator friend of his who said, "Lowd, man! Ef it wuzn't fer them polices 'n' them ol' lynch-mobs, there wouldn't be nothin' but uproar down here!"[11] Indeed, as lynching declined sharply in the 1930s and 1940s black activists could and did turn their attention to other matters, such as school integration and voter registration drives. The civil rights movement achieved many successes in the 1950s and 1960s in part because white supremacist violence, although still a terrifying reality, was nowhere near the levels of the 1880s and 1890s. To paraphrase Wright's perceptive friend, once lynching declined, there was nothing but uproar—civil rights activism—down South.[12]

The antilynching movement began slowly, stymied by the successful white southern public opinion campaign that argued lynching was an understandable punishment for black men who raped white women.[13] Even Ida B. Wells, who became the most famous antilynching activist of the turn of the century, absorbed the hegemonic logic that lynch mobs formed in angry reaction to an incident of rape.[14] Wells held this belief until events shocked her into reex-amining her assumptions. She reflected, "Like many another person who had read of lynching in the South I had accepted the idea meant to be conveyed—that although lynching was irregular and contrary to law and order . . . per-haps the brute deserved death anyhow and the mob was justified in taking his life."[15] But when Thomas Moss, a close friend of Wells, was lynched because his shop threatened white business interests, the reporter used her investiga-tive skills to delegitimize the rape excuse for lynching. With legendary bravery, Wells worked to debunk this stereotype and achieved great successes, but still the myth persisted.

White southern newspapers regularly printed lurid stories of animalistic black men preying on helpless white women. Southern politicians such as Benjamin "Pitchfork" Tillman enthusiastically spread this slander to further their careers. According to his biographer, Tillman longed to maintain law and order in the South but realized quickly that to achieve popularity with the white southern electorate, he had to endorse mob violence. In an 1892 politi-cal speech, Tillman notoriously proclaimed that he would "willingly lead a mob in lynching a negro who had committed an assault upon a white woman."[16] Not only was Tillman successful in whipping southern white crowds into a frenzy, but he spread his tales of sexual outrage in the North. According to the *Record-Herald*, for instance, Tillman gave a speech in Marinette, Wisconsin, in August 1901 and was met with four thousand enthusiastic supporters. Tillman opposed bringing accused black rapists before court since that would unduly shame their delicate white victims. He stressed his resolve that "the white peo-ple of the South would remain on top 'in spite of the devil'" and swore that if need be he would take up arms himself.[17] Tillman's speech was met with great cheers. The standard justification for lynching became a national excuse for ignoring the plague of lynching.

A more powerful national figure than Tillman also blamed lynching on black male rapists, ignoring the revelations of Wells. After a 1903 lynching in Indiana, President Theodore Roosevelt wrote to Governor Winfield Taylor Durbin. First, he condemned the act of the mob: "All thoughtful men must feel the greatest alarm over the growth of lynching in this country." This con-demnation was rare for an American president. However, Roosevelt's words of censure also reinforced the stereotype that black men brought lynching upon themselves by acts of rape. Roosevelt wrote that a black man who raped a white woman "not merely sins against humanity in inexpiable and unpardonable fashion but sins particularly against his own race, and does them a wrong far greater than any white man can possibly do them."[18] With this remark, the president insinuated that whites were not culpable for racism as long as black criminals existed, and he went on to piously suggest that black communities should police themselves to prevent rape. Even a reform-oriented Republican president, who sent shockwaves across the country when he broke protocol and ate lunch with Booker T. Washington in the White House, circulated the myth that black male rapists provoked lynching.

Many of the leading African American activists of this period wrestled with the issue of the rapist stereotype. A Dr. A. L. Winslow in Virginia seemed to genuinely puzzle over the phenomenon and speculated that if black men were raping white women, it must be because they lacked education. He wrote, "Look at the number of lynchings taking place monthly among our people and in almost every case it is some poor fellow who is poorly informed, or not informed at all, and I claim, that if these men in the majority of instances were well informed, and were educated in the proper sense of the term, the offence would not be committed."[19] Winslow went on to condemn lynching, but he clearly had internalized the rationalization that mobs formed in reaction to rape.

In perhaps more cynical fashion, the Reverend William Hooper Councill of Normal, Alabama, expressed his horror of rape in an 1899 symposium on "The Race Problem" in the newspaper *Arena*. Although the other contributor in the symposium was Booker T. Washington, Councill staked out the most conservative position. Councill wrote, "In regard to that terrible crime for which some of the Negroes suffer such horrible deaths, the better class of the Negroes regret it deep down in their souls. Our mortification cannot be expressed in words." Councill even echoed the language of white papers by saying, "We would willingly throw our bodies between these lustful, murderous fiends and their tender, innocent victims." Although Councill ultimately condemned lynching, his antilynching stance was prefaced not only with a reinforcement of the logic that black rapists caused lynching but also with the pungent imagery of brutish black men and chaste white ladies.[20]

Far more sincerely, Rev. W. Bishop Johnson, a renowned Baptist missionary in Washington, DC, and editor of the *National Baptist Magazine*, intoned in an 1899 sermon that it was an ethical imperative for African Americans to prevent rape. Referring to rapists, he wrote, "We must attempt to reach that class of our people, who are moral lepers, spreading their deadly disease far and wide and offering an excuse for much of the injustice that is heaped upon us."[21] Johnson's words predate Teddy Roosevelt's by several years, and yet the black Baptist preacher worked within the same assumptions as the white president: that there was indeed an epidemic of rape and that it was incumbent on the black community to contain the scourge.

In the Northwest, another activist also operated within the paradigm of black rapist criminality but was more inclined to let white institutions solve the problem. Samuel Burdett, a Civil War veteran, veterinary surgeon, and pioneering member of Seattle's African American middle class, wrote a book critical of lynching in 1900.[22] Yet he prefaced his opposition to lynching with the statement, "I believe that Negroes . . . have and may commit the unnatural crime which they are accused of." He moved on to point out that since whites had all the "law-making power," it should not be a problem for them to find justice within the legal system, and thus had no logical reason to resort to mob justice.[23]

Dr. Winslow, Reverend Councill, Reverend Johnson, Samuel Burdett, and others like them were intelligent, well educated, and dedicated to improving race relations. Yet they had internalized the corrosive belief that black male rapists were the catalyst for lynch mobs. In her pamphlet *Southern Horrors*, Wells bemoaned the fact that the "better class" of African Americans "have too often taken the white man's word" and blamed lynching on rape.[24] Although many activists worked with Herculean effort to expose the falsity of the stereotype, there is no one moment in history where the scales were fully lifted from the public's eyes. Despite the heroic campaigns of Wells, enemies of justice had power and privilege on their side and kept renewing this apologia for lynching. Starting in 1913 the Tuskegee Institute sent out statistics every year to prove that lynching was not a response to rape, and every year newspapers reacted with surprise. By the 1910s the National Association for the Advancement of Colored People (NAACP) repeatedly sent journalists to investigate lynching incidents and circulated sensational pamphlets documenting the duplicity of white southerners who blamed lynching on rape.[25] In the 1930s Jessie Daniel Ames and the Association of Southern Women for the Prevention of Lynching carried the same revelation to the shocked ears of earnest white Methodist church ladies.[26] It took time and effort to chip away at this myth.

Fighting the fog of misinformation was dangerous. After the Thomas Moss lynching, Wells published a sensational article in her Memphis paper *Free Speech*, charging that the accusation of rape was just a myth covering up terrorist violence in the service of white supremacy.[27] She also insinuated that many of the rape accusations stemmed from consensual sexual relations between black men and white women. Whites in Memphis immediately retaliated. According to historian Paula Giddings, "Wells's newspaper office was looted and burned to the ground; her co-owners, barely beating the mob were run out of town; and Wells herself was warned that she would be hanged from a lamppost if she were to return."[28] Wells spent the rest of her life crusading against lynching from outside the South.

At least two other journalists, Jesse C. Duke and Alexander Manly, were threatened with death in the 1890s for publishing antilynching editorials that challenged the standard justification for lynching. A reporter for the *Montgomery Herald* in Alabama, Jesse C. Duke wrote about lynching and rape charges and suggested that instead of rape, white women formed complicit relationships with black men.[29] In response, two hundred whites met and signed resolutions denouncing Duke and demanding that he leave town.[30] Alexander Manly was a prominent black journalist in Wilmington, North Carolina, a coastal town that in 1898 had many Republicans and Populists in local offices, such as the mayor and board of alderman. In August of that year, Manly wrote an editorial challenging the assumption that white women had sex with black men only against their will.[31] During the tumultuous November election three months later, white Democrats focused political frustrations on Manly and other leading African Americans, culminating in a riot where a white mob burned Manly's press, tormented scores of people, destroyed property, and ultimately killed ten African Americans.[32]

Political station was no protection. George H. White, a black North Carolina congress representative, made a speech in February 1900 protesting the political support for lynching, saying, "Senators and Representatives have undertaken the unholy task of extenuating and excusing these foul deeds, and in some instances they have gone so far as to justify them."[33] White was referring to Sen. John Sharp Williams of Mississippi and Rep. James Matthew Griggs of Georgia, both white, who had recently given speeches in Congress with accounts of accused black rapists lynched by white mobs, and in both cases insinuated that whites were understandably fighting back against a terrifying wave of black criminals. The Raleigh, North Carolina, paper the *News and Observer* excoriated Representative White for his remarks and ominously warned, "They [North Carolinians] have had enough of Manleyism. They have more than enough of Negro Congressman White. He must be made an impossibility for the future, and will be. The people of this State will not tolerate that sort of thing."[34] The menacing reference to Manly, given the fate of Manly and others in the Wilmington riot, was at worst a death threat and at best encouraged readers to stamp out any last remaining vestiges of black political expression. Thankfully, White remained safe from violence, but he became the last black representative from North Carolina until 1992.[35]

Multiple dilemmas faced those who fought against lynching in the late nineteenth century. Whites were convinced that lynch mobs protected southern whites from a naturally criminal black population. African Americans did not believe criminal tendencies were embedded in their race but seemed willing to dismiss lynch victims as lower-class troublemakers who were not worth protecting, given the black community's limited resources. Those few black activists who spoke out against lynching were threatened with bodily harm by white supremacists. The first resolution to these dilemmas maintained a link between the issues of lynching and rape, but not the link with which most whites were familiar. In the earliest days of the antilynching movement, activists frequently compared the myth of black men assaulting white women with the reality that white men had the power to exploit black women and sexually assault them.

The Early Antilynching Movement

The Reverend Emmanuel King Love of Savannah, Georgia, creatively employed these linked issues when he preached a sermon titled "Lynch Law and Raping" in 1894. Dr. Love had spent many years successfully negotiating the color line. He had worked for both white and black Baptist organizations. His appointment to the Savannah First African Church attracted the notice of white and black newspapers. When he preached this sermon on lynch law and rape, fifteen hundred people were present, at least thirty of whom were white. The *Morning News* of Savannah reported that afterward the church unanimously voted to endorse the sermon "as the sentiment of the church," and the reverend was "congratulated by a number of the white people present."[36] Clearly, the minister had found a successful way to voice his moral outrage against lynching that resounded with both races and did not cause a violent backlash—a rare feat in the Deep South.

Reverend Love did this by first denouncing rape, saying "Rape is a great sin against society and against God. . . . We must insist upon it that our people stop committing the crime for which they are lynched." Love then staked a position against all miscegenation. "If I had my way I would brand and banish with cropped ears everybody who leaves my side of the line and goes to the other side and everyone who comes on my side."[37] This violent imagery raised the flip side of the rape question: the seduction and sexual assault of black women by white men. Love raised this issue by cleverly juxtaposing it with the black rape myth. Once he had all the whites nodding their heads in agreement against black men raping white women, they could not very well fault Love for preaching against white men raping black women. Love then reasoned that even though rape was bad, lynching was not a Christian solution, and he spent the rest of his talk denouncing the sin of mob murder.

At first glance, this strategy might seem to only bolster the corrosive construction of black men as uncontrollable rapists. However, once Reverend Love enacted a ritual acknowledgment of the rape stereotype, he chipped away at its validity. Love suggested that not all the accusations of rape were true and, more important, that lynching was not just a reaction to rape. Many lynch victims had been accused of only petty crimes that would merely bring "a few months on the chain-gang" if tried in court. Using quotes from antilynching editorials in prominent white southern papers, Love argued that "the best white people" were as firmly opposed to lynching as "the best Negroes" were opposed to rape.[38] By carefully choosing these editorials, many from the upper South, Love demonstrated to his white and black listeners that there was not a unified white position on lynching.[39] Whites did not have to support lynching or look the other way; they could also condemn the practice. His mention of the "best whites" cleverly appealed to a class bias, encouraging his white audience to identify with upper-class whites who ostensibly supported law and order, as opposed to the white trash who, according to popular myth, were the instigators of mobs.

Reverend Love's carefully chosen words referred to the present but also tapped into a painful history of white access to black women. Numerous slave narratives published in the antebellum era had testified to the abuses of white masters. In the aftermath of the Civil War, Chaplain Henry McNeal Turner (later to become Bishop Turner) gave a speech commemorating Emancipation and mused on the connections between freedom, white sexual fears, and white sexual crimes:

> It was also said, and Southern fanatics rode that hobby everywhere, "That if you free the negro he will want to marry our daughters and sisters." That was another foolish dream. What do we want with their daughters and sisters? We have as much beauty as they. Look at our ladies; do you want more beauty than that? *All we ask of the white man is to let our ladies* alone, and they need not fear us. The difficulty has theretofore been, *our ladies were not always at our own disposal.*[40]

Turner's words in 1866 reveal that the phantasm of black rapists was rooted in a prophetic fantasy: white southerners had so long equated slave emancipation with black male/white female sexual intermingling that freedom for slaves brought for whites the conviction that black rapists lurked everywhere. As Turner also pointed out, this dystopic vision obscured the distressing reality that during slavery neither the law nor male relatives could protect black women from sexual predators.

Just as Reverend Love's sermon strategically linked the vulnerability of black male and female bodies, almost every antilynching activist in the 1890s connected the issues of lynching and rape. In her 1892 pamphlet *Southern Horrors*, Ida B. Wells cataloged cases of white men who sexually assaulted black women.[41] The renowned black journalist John Edward Bruce published an antilynching book in 1901 and took pains to bring up the recent scandal where white men in New Jersey raped a mill girl of Dutch extraction, Jennie Bosschieter. Bruce noted, "crimes of the character described are not confined to a particular race or class," underscoring the point that rape was not the sole province of black men.[42] Representative George H. White's 1900 speech that discussed lynching included an account of a white sexual assault that he had read about in a recent article from the Raleigh *News and Observer* that chronicled the rape of a crippled black girl by a white man.[43]

When the dominant and widely accepted paradigm of lynching was that it was triggered by black men raping white women, antilynching activists worked within the paradigm to also denounce sexual crimes against black women. The veterinarian Samuel Burdett, as mentioned earlier, thought that maybe lynching did result from black-on-white rape. But Burdett also caustically pointed out that there was a double standard in the treatment of white and black accused rapists:

> What sort of a river of blood would there be if every white man who had despoiled the virtue of the colored woman were killed? The white man of

the south will read this, and I desire he should. If he does not like it, he can change his course. He is bound to admit and glad to confess that it is not the white woman who is the (illegitimate) mother of the half breed, quadroon, and octoroon."[44]

Burdett brings up the uncomfortable point that to see the legacy of white sexual abuse, an individual merely needed to look about a typical black community and see a wide variation in appearance, particularly skin color.[45] Of course, Burdett clearly blamed white men for this mixture. White southerners had often blamed black women themselves for "seducing" their masters. Some African Americans (such as Turner and Burdett) squarely denounced this stereotype, while others (particularly women) quietly buried the painful history in what Darlene Clark Hine calls a "culture of dissemblance."[46]

In 1901 William Hannibal Thomas, a black Civil War veteran and itinerant preacher, violated those two traditions when he published *The American Negro*, which controversially claimed that the period of slavery left black women without any standards of chastity.[47] This stereotype was common to white assumptions, but coming from a black man seemed the last straw for many black leaders, who criticized Thomas as "The Black Judas."[48] The author S. Timothy Tice wrote an entire book refuting Thomas's claims. In it, Tice summarized Thomas's arguments: "Negro marriage is no barrier to illicit sexual indulgence," "Negro women unresistingly betray their wifely honor to satisfy a bestial instinct," and "Negro schools in the South are immoral sanctuaries." Tice then angrily descried, "These infamous charges are an outrage upon fair womanhood of every race, and are without comparison in the annals of history."[49]

In the 1890s and early 1900s, activists linked the issues of the lynching of black men and the sexual abuse of black women. The accusation that black women were unchaste was the flip side of the stereotype of the black male rapist. Both myths painted African descendants as lustful brutes, unable to abide by the mores of civilization and thus unfit for the protection of laws. Black men were not tried in court when accused of rape. Instead, they were "tried," convicted, and punished by lynch mobs. Black women who were raped also did not have their day in court. Whites assumed black women were always sexually available and thus such a crime did not exist.[50] When activists unraveled the stereotype of oversexed black men that led to their extermination, they also took the opportunity to note the similarly unfair stereotype of black women that led to their exploitation. Early in the antilynching movement, the two issues were closely linked.

By the third decade of the twentieth century, however, this link was severed for two main reasons: first, because the antilynching campaign began to draw parallels between lynch victims and martyrs and, second, because of the increased reliance on statistics. Martyrdom discourse became a successful strategy because it drew on a powerful, resonant language and imagery to make meaning from death. However, the martyr discourse's power drew on Christian parallels that explicitly made Christ figures of lynched men. There was no equivalent female imagery to carry the cause of the assaulted black woman. In a different, more analytic approach to antilynching, black leaders began in the 1910s to successfully use tools from the rising discipline of sociology, particularly statistics, to convincingly disassociate lynching from accusations of rape. Using both the martyrdom discourse and statistics, activists worked to sever the crime of lynching from the issue of the rape of white women, but in the process also severed the link between antilynching activism and antisexual assault activism. These new tactics successfully expanded the antilynching movement but swept aside the formerly equivalent issue of black women's sexual assaults.

Martyrdom

The appalling cruelty of many lynchings made them exceedingly difficult for rational, moral people to understand or even discuss. How does one speak of the unspeakable? Upon viewing the burnt knuckles of a lynch victim triumphantly on display in a store window in 1899, the sociologist W. E. B. Du Bois underwent a crisis of confidence. The sight of such a gruesome trophy so disturbed the gentle academic that he concluded, "one could not be a calm, cool, and detached scientist while Negroes were lynched, murdered and starved." Du Bois lost faith in the power of social science to enlighten others and embarked on a path of full-time direct activism, eventually participating in the founding of NAACP.[51]

The entire ritual of lynching was intentionally gruesome, calculated to shock people, just as Du Bois was shocked. The torture of the victim, the actual murder, and the often ritualistic display of the corpse in black neighborhoods or the fetishistic display in stores were designed to frighten and police behavior.[52] Countless people despaired at this horrifying message; many reinterpreted these events by drawing on an older religious model of suffering and martyrdom. To infuse the events with some meaning beyond simple cruelty, many antilynching activists turned to the Old Testament story of the Jews.

The Old Testament established Jews as the chosen people who had a covenant with God. This covenant laid a burden on the chosen tribe to follow God's rules or else suffer penalties such as diaspora and enslavement. According to the historian Lacey Baldwin Smith, "suffering was a sure sign that Yahweh had not broken the terms of the covenant" and that the Jews were still his chosen agents of change in history.[53] Smith makes a convincing argument that, biblically, Jews saw suffering as part of a divine plan. This tradition carried into Christianity, as early Christians willingly died for their faith. Most famously, Christ reputedly died to expiate the sins of humanity. Instead of denoting weakness and loss, suffering could convey an important means of fulfilling

God's divine plan. African Americans drew on this worldview to interpret the suffering of lynch victims and to transform the deaths of accused criminals into martyrs whose suffering would hasten an earthly and heavenly day of reckoning. This interpretation of racialized suffering was not new—it was a common trope in antislavery circles. The pinnacle of suffering and martyrdom imagery in Victorian culture was Harriet Beecher Stowe's 1852 novel *Uncle Tom's Cabin*.[54] This powerful and popular book resonated with Americans of all races. Tom's character was a thinly veiled allegory of Christ. Nonviolent and dignified, he loved his tormentors despite their evil, and he suffered and died for refusing to legitimate an oppressive system.

However, this carefully crafted imagery, along with the larger abolition movement, dissipated with the emancipation of slaves.[55] Abolitionists and slaves who understood the suffering of slaves to be part of a covenant with God interpreted Union victory and emancipation as God's final fulfillment of the covenant. Thus, suffering and violence of the Reconstruction period was interpreted in secular terms. God had fulfilled his end of the bargain through Lincoln, Grant, and Sherman: now African Americans were on their own to grapple with their new situation. And indeed, the suffering and violence of the Reconstruction period had clearly secular goals, such as Republican defeats at the ballot boxes and the restoration of exploitative race-based labor conditions. But lynchings continued after Redemption and actually rose in the late 1880s and early 1890s, when African Americans had the least political power. Perhaps more ominously, lynchings became more ghastly, as mobs devised new tortures for their victims. African Americans at the time were shocked by mob violence and at a loss to explain the brutality.

To make sense of their entire situation, which included economic exploitation, political disfranchisement, and terrorist violence, many religious leaders in the mid-1890s began to revive the abolitionist themes of suffering and martyrdom to make sense of the senseless. The rise of what I call a "martyrdom discourse" began with ministers grappling to understand their relationship with a God who allowed these misfortunes. Although not always specifically connected to discussions of lynching initially, as this discourse grew in power over the 1890s and early 1900s, it eventually became a way to understand lynching and ultimately eclipsed the rhetorical strategy discussed earlier that linked lynching with sexual abuse.

George C. Rowe, the pastor of Plymouth Congregational Church, delivered a lecture to Claflin University in Orangeburg, South Carolina, in 1892 that wrestled with God's apparent neglect. His address, which was subsequently published, contrasted white cruelty with the high moral ground of his own race. Speaking of God's future plans of harmony for the race, Rowe suggested that their suffering would be an object lesson to lead the world to a better state: "God will use largely the spirit of the race under oppression, injustice, and great wrong, as an illustration which the broad-minded and large-hearted of the earth will grasp and wield to the betterment of humanity."[56] Their peaceful suffering under oppression was only temporary, a way for God to demonstrate the ideal of human behavior.

The Reverend Levi Thornton made a more explicit connection between past and present suffering during the 1888 centennial celebration of the Black Baptist Church in Georgia. In Thornton's talk on "The History of the Baptists," he first recounted the tribulations American Baptists faced for their faith:

> The Baptists have furnished quite their share of martyrs and fully their quota of able men fighting for the divorce of church and state, and contending that man should worship God according as he understood the dictates of the gospel. All through the winding ages the Baptists have been called to endure keen sacrifice and terrible suffering. Their sufferings has [sic] tended to develop their strength, and made them search the scriptures, which they have used to the discomfort of their opponents. Let us rejoice that there has been no disposition upon the part of Baptists in any age to shun the hallowed road of suffering, which is the King's highway.[57]

Thornton believed that suffering for a worthy cause was a positive action and that the Baptists' pain had given them an advantage against their opponents on earth and in heaven.

From the history of Baptists in America, Thornton moved to the history of black Baptists in Georgia and put their travails in line with the trajectory of the larger narrative: "Father Andrew Bryan, in much trouble and sheer suffering, planted the first negro Baptist church in this State a hundred years ago. He was whipped until he bled profusely, but his blood was but a heaven-born fertilizer, to enrich and make grow the heavenly plant. His tears were bottled by a covenant-keeping God, and his groans a loving Jesus heard."[58] For Thornton, the flourishing black Baptist church in Georgia was a sign of divine favor. In this narrative Thornton showed the allegorical importance of suffering and blood. Pain was but a sign that God maintained a covenant to help the oppressed, and they would eventually triumph.

The *National Baptist Magazine*, a publication for black Baptists, also tried to elevate pain to a divine mission. In his 1897 article, "Suffering for Christ's Sake," Rev. R. DeBaptiste proclaimed, "Faithful following of Christ involves suffering on the part of true believers for his name's sake. In proportion as persons become 'partakers of the divine nature,' and possess the Spirit of Christ, they become objects of the devil's attacks and the world's hatred and persecution."[59] Instead of feeling abandoned by God, DeBaptiste's followers could understand poverty and cruelty as proof that they truly channeled the Messiah. DeBaptiste concluded that suffering was the road to redemption. In contrast to the social Darwinism of the day, white wealth and power did not mean evolutionary fitness but a sign of Satan.[60]

Drawing on this view of suffering, the Rev. S. B. Wallace, pastor of the Israel Colored Methodist Episcopal Church in Washington, DC, tried to make sense of the scourge of lynching and the indifference of the nation. In an 1894 sermon to his congregation, Reverend Wallace lamented the fall of Reconstruction, saying that when federal troops were withdrawn, "the last ray of hope was gone." Without a military presence, southern whites robbed African Americans of their rights and instituted lynch law. According to Wallace, this time stood out as a stark contrast to slavery. Unlike the sympathy of abolitionists to the plight of the slave, lynchings did not inspire similar social activism, and "the North is impervious to the obligations and duties of the hour." Wallace informed his listeners that this period must have a divine purpose: "The negro is suffering to-day while the dross which depreciates his value as a man is being burnt and purged away, but his day of rejoicing is already breaking; the white man is rejoicing to-day in derision at the negroes' sufferings but the clouds which are to burst in terrible destruction upon him are already gathering in the distance." Rather than despairing, Wallace construed the dire situation as part of God's plan to elevate his race and punish sin. Wallace predicted an earthly triumph for African Americans, in which God would aid them in building a "magnificent empire" whose "temples and buildings of state shall be the pride of our hearts and the glory of nations."[61] Racist southern whites, negligent northerners, and suffering blacks were not hallmarks of racial doom but instruments of God's larger design.

Incubated in sacred soil, the language of suffering and martyrdom increasingly appeared in secular media. This shift from religious institutions to more secular individuals and institutions gave the martyr discourse a broader audience. Robert Charles O'Hara Benjamin, a lawyer who published an antilynching pamphlet, compared the torture of lynch victims to the ordeals of Christian martyrs. John C. Dancy, the editor of the African Methodist Episcopal Zion almanac, the *Quarterly*, cataloged a list of mob victims in his publication. After briefly summarizing a grisly lynching, Dancy stated "The blood of the innocent cries out to Heaven."[62] Dancy also listed Toussaint L. Ouverture as a great race leader and martyr.

At the turn of the century, "various colored societies of Boston" held a mass antilynching meeting at Faneuil Hall. White and black men made speeches and several prominent men were in attendance, including Rep. Elijah A. Morse, Judge Edward Walker, Mayor Edwin U. Curtis, and Father Scully. The honorable George L. Downing offered a resolution against lynching that framed the issue in religious terms: "We condemn this God-defying heartlessness with most indignant feelings, as civilized beings, as citizens, as Christians." Downing also explicitly connected lynching to past crimes of racism: "We invoke the uncompromising spirit of Garrison, of Phillips, of Sumner, of Andrew, and in their names to these defiers of God and humanity, cry out, Stop this brutality, which darkens our nation's fair name, adding that, if it not be stopped, the impetuous spirit of Crispus Attucks, of John Brown, which is still marching on, will in its march, haunt into action."[63] With this invocation, Downing's resolution placed lynching in line with the historic struggle against slavery, a struggle defined in religious and moral terms. The reference to

Crispus Attucks and John Brown explicitly linked the lynching struggle to famous martyrs who died for a worthy cause.

The NAACP formed in 1909 in response to an outrageous spate of racial violence in Springfield, Illinois, the home of the martyred president Abraham Lincoln. From its very beginnings the organization drew on the martyrdom discourse to convince a broad swath of the American public of the moral failings of racism. A 1911 Thanksgiving editorial in the NAACP's magazine *Crisis* intoned, "Let us thank God that we do not profess a religion of human brotherhood which we have not the moral courage to practice."[64] The next month an editorial on Benjamin Tillman characterized the South Carolina politician's race baiting as a "sin against the Holy Ghost."[65] *Crisis*'s talented editor, W. E. B. Du Bois, wrote four short stories between 1914 and 1920 about lynch victims that clearly were parables of Christ's martyrdom.[66]

The discourse of martyrdom proved flexible enough to adjust to changing times. For example, during World War I, *Crisis* writers could blend martyrdom and patriotism. When the United States entered World War I, the NAACP and the writers at *Crisis* supported the move but pointed out the hypocrisy of fighting a war for democracy while oppressing minorities at home. An editorial in *Crisis* encouraged citizens to "enter this war for Liberty with clean hands" and to prevent the outbreaks of lynching and race riots. The same editorial juxtaposed mob violence and international status, stating, "We cannot lynch 2,867 black men and women in thirty-one years and pose successfully as leaders of civilization." The author also suggested that Americans should "bow our shamed heads and in sack cloth and ashes" and decide to destroy the "enemies of mankind" both abroad and at home.[67] *Crisis* printed excerpts from other newspapers, such as the *New York Globe* and the Memphis *Commercial Appeal*, which also merged martyrdom and patriotism and deemed lynching unseemly during a battle for civilization.[68] These sorts of editorials consistently framed racism in religious terms and connected the stature of the United States with its moral track record.

Inspired by the NAACP's campaign against lynching, a group of influential African American women in 1922 formed a committee to raise funds. Mary Talbert and sixteen other women became known as the "Anti-Lynching Crusaders." Their goal was to convince one million women to pay at least one dollar to their fund and then to turn the money over to the NAACP for antilynching work. The very name "Crusaders" emphasized the holy mission of their work. In language reminiscent of early Christian martyrs, the Crusaders implored women to set aside the first week of the winter months as "sacrifice and self-denial weeks" to save money for the cause.[69] In their leaflets and ads, the Crusaders printed a prayer to God reminding him that he created America "to be an example" to other people and warning that lynching diverted the country from its divine purpose.[70] Although the Crusaders did not reach their goal of one million dollars, they did launch an impressive publicity drive, sending out thousands of letters, press releases, and pamphlets. By selling antilynching buttons, they did raise more than ten thousand dollars. In a letter to NAACP headquarters, Mary Talbert concluded, "We believe that women have been awakened who have heretofore been dormant.[71]

Readers of *Crisis* magazine regularly saw excerpts from white newspapers that showed the growing use of the moral perspective nurtured in the black community. In 1914 the *Congregationalist*, a southern religious journal, called a South Carolina lynching "so brutally unjust, so undemocratic, so un-Christian and false to our national ideals that no class of our citizens can long be safe." The editor of the *Independent*, an Elizabeth City, North Carolina, paper declared, "I shudder when I think of the price the white race must someday pay for its sins against colored peoples."[72] Alluding to the southern costs of the Civil War, a Greensboro, North Carolina, paper suggested that lynching would lead to a day of reckoning: "It is the immutable law of the universe that no crime goes unpunished. Our hands are stained with blood, and there is a terrible presumption that some of it is innocent blood. We have paid for it already, paid in more ways than we know and a price greater than most of us imagine. . . . It may easily come to pass that the payment will include another struggle worse than the one of the last generation. Is it not time to quit running up the account?"[73] These white southerners were using language black activists had carefully crafted. The blood spilled in lynching would haunt the region and nation until it had been accounted for, on earth and on Judgment Day.

By imbuing the act of suffering with a holy mission, African Americans made it possible to discuss mob violence in a new light. Still shocking and demoralizing, lynching now had a place in the spiritual order. Certainly people still were sickened and heartbroken at the news of a lynching. But through martyrdom discourse African Americans could transform the pain of a lynching into a renewed belief in their own morality. This discourse was incubated by African American religious leaders in the 1890s and adopted first by black secular writers, then the interracial organization the NAACP. By the late 1910s and 1920s, increasing numbers of white people of conscience drew on the martyrdom discourse to resist the hegemonic paradigm that justified lynching as a punishment for criminal rapists and instead criticized lynching as a crime against humanity.

However, this resistance strategy privileged male victims. The most resonant parallel of martyrdom, Christ's death on the cross, focused attention on black men who were lynched. There was no similarly powerful symbol for the sexual assault of black women. This martyrdom discourse, with its successes and silences, persisted and grew throughout the twentieth century.

Statistics

In addition to the qualitative power of the martyrdom discourse to make sense of lynching, activists harnessed the new tools of social science to prove objectively that lynching was not solely a response to rape. The most power-ful national organization was the National Association for the Advancement of Colored People. Particularly through the pages of its magazine, *Crisis*, the NAACP launched an effective antilynching campaign. Under the direc-tion of its editor, W. E. B. Du Bois, *Crisis* often published statistical tables that broke down lynchings by year and documented the crimes of which victims were accused.[74] These charts showed that lynch mobs killed people for many offenses other than rape.

Beginning in 1910 the NAACP also funded investigators to visit the scene of a lynching, talk to witnesses, and get the story from the black side of town.[75] In the pages of *Crisis*, the NAACP published articles based on such investigations that served as a counternarrative to the white newspaper accounts that always blamed lynching on black criminals. In November 1914, Joel Spingarn, the chairman of the board, sent out a questionnaire to congressional aspirants containing five questions on racial issues. One of the questions asked, "Do you under any cir-cumstances justify lynching?"[76] A summary of the responses was published in *Cri-sis*. Readers could choose candidates who answered favorably on race issues and also see the spectrum of opinions on lynching. This tactic became customary. Whenever election season rolled around, NAACP journalists would pepper poli-ticians with questions about their position on antilynching legislation and *Crisis* would publish the results. Famously, the NAACP's legal experts supported the drafting of the 1921 antilynching Dyer Bill and hired lobbyists to pressure Con-gress to make lynching a federal crime. Their materials drew heavily on statistics showing the number of lynch victims and the crimes of which they were accused. Although the bill passed the House in 1922 only to be filibustered by the Senate, the campaigns gave people a focus and a cause to rally around.[77] The NAACP's antilynching legislation campaign encouraged people of conscience nationwide to condemn lynching as a moral outrage.

As the NAACP launched its courageous antilynching campaign out of New York City, another campaign was quietly orchestrated out of Tuskegee, Ala-bama. It was headed by Monroe Work, the director of Records and Research at Tuskegee Institute, a conservative black school dedicated to industrial educa-tion. Its principal, Booker T. Washington, was popular with southern whites and northern white industrialists for his accommodationist approach. Wash-ington did not favor agitation on the issue of black votes or social equality, preferring to focus his energies on what he saw as more attainable goals, such as land ownership and jobs in the skilled trades. Many scholars dismiss Wash-ington and Tuskegee as a failed experiment, particularly in contrast with the NAACP's emphasis on integration, but the antilynching campaign conducted out of the school is one example of its persistent, eventually successful efforts to chip away at oppression.[78]

Monroe Work earned a master's degree in sociology in 1903 from the Uni-versity of Chicago, the first black man to do so. He worked at Georgia State

Industrial College in Savannah and occasionally collaborated with another sociologist working in Georgia, W. E. B. Du Bois, on projects in the area and the short-lived Niagara Movement. Monroe Work was deliberately courted in 1909 by Booker T. Washington to begin a department of research and records at Tuskegee Institute, ostensibly to keep track of alumni. But Work, with the tacit approval of Washington, began an antilynching campaign. It was not as bold and emotional as the NAACP campaign, but it was aimed at, and squarely hit, white southerners.[79]

The campaign was brilliant in its simplicity. Work subscribed to newspaper clipping services to gather data on lynching. He specifically chose to limit his data to white newspapers to stave off any charges of racial bias. Then he sorted the cases by state, gender, and initial alleged offense (such as murder, rape, etc.). He compiled a statistical table and brought his work to Booker T. Washington's attention. According to Work, the principal "immediately became interested and wanted to send out a report several times a year." During 1913 Tuskegee sent out reports after three, six, and twelve months. Washington made "numerous comments" throughout each report and signed his name at the bottom.[80]

Building on that success, in 1914 Work composed another report and sent it out to three hundred daily papers, the Associated Press, and "the leading Colored papers." The lynching report became a yearly event, going out every January to chronicle the record from the previous year. Tuskegee became the accepted authority on lynching statistics. The *World Almanac* in 1915 began publishing the Tuskegee lynch record in its annual editions. Work carefully composed a format in the press releases designed to maximize their impact. He used an objective language of statistics, with a hidden transcript of injustice. By listing the offenses of which lynch victims were accused, Work made a silent point that lynching was not about rape. Indeed, his 1938 summary of his antilynching work explained, "In the Tuskegee Reports it was especially emphasized that only a small percentage of the persons put to death was for the alleged crime of rape." But if lynching was not about rape, what was it about? Work included all the petty offenses people were lynched for, such as "slapping boy" or "making boastful remarks."[81] Instead of the sentimental, righteous sorrow of earlier antilynching language, Work arranged hard data to point the reader to the same conclusion: innocent people were being killed for resisting white supremacy.

Tuskegee preferred their press releases to contain only hard data and let readers draw their own conclusions. The NAACP took no such chances. For example, the February 1911 *Crisis* data on lynching was accompanied by a short verse: "If blood be the price of liberty, If blood be the price of liberty, If blood be the price of liberty, Lord God we have paid in full."[82] The data and poem clearly point the reader to interpret lynching statistics through the prism of martyrdom. Every death would be part of a heavenly accounting of righteousness. Even though Tuskegee never paired its data with similar kinds of interpretation, it is quite possible that Tuskegee press releases prompted similar readings.

The tactic of statistical press releases proved successful with the target audiences. African Americans reading the release in a newspaper could feel a number of emotions: relief at the dissolution of the rapist stereotype, outrage at the injustice, and confidence that they were now armed with hard evidence to defend the reputation of their race. The press releases were also effective in reaching white southerners, inclined to be receptive to a Tuskegee message. The white press reports that Tuskegee used as evidence were clearly not an outside attack by Yankee agitators. The report represented a calm rejoinder from a respected group. Tuskegee's reputation as a conservative school earned it scorn from more radical critics such as Du Bois and Monroe Trotter but also gave them impeccable credentials as ambassadors to the white South. The lack of overt indictment in the press releases meant white southerners were not put on the defensive. They were free to draw their own conclusions about lynching, rape, and injustice and take the initiative to criticize the phenomenon.

And criticize they did. There was not an immediate end to lynching but a slow process of national and regional discussion, which led to a growing condemnation. First, a wide variety of newspapers printed the Tuskegee statistics. The Tuskegee archives are filled with newspaper clippings that carried the 1914 press release in its entirety. A partial sample includes *Freeman*, *Topeka Plaindealer*, *Atlanta Independent*, *Nashville Globe*, *Nebraska State Journal*, *St. Louis Globe Democrat*, *Chicago Examiner*, *New York American*, *Minneapolis-Tribune*, and *Schenectady Union Star*.[83] Even if such newspapers did not comment on the data, readers had plenty of information from which to draw their own conclusions.

Nationwide, papers that carried the Tuskegee press releases began editorializing on the ostensibly newfound observation that lynching was not exclusively a response to black rape. In 1915 the *Outlook* of New York City printed the Tuskegee numbers and stated, "As the public mind apparently still continues to assume that a majority of the cases in which lynching takes place are for rape, it is right to point out that less than a quarter of these cases had this origin."[84] On the other coast, a California paper wrote,

When Northerners criticise the Southern habit of lynching Negroes a frequent Southern rejoinder runs something like this: "You don't know anything about the negro problem, because you don't have to live with it. How would you have felt if it had been YOUR wife or sister?" . . . Now it happens that a large number of the lynchings in the South are not for crimes against women. Petty offenses, which in San Francisco would be punished with six months in the county jail, are often an excuse for lynchings in the South.[85]

This national conversation on lynching, prompted by the Tuskegee releases, slowly eroded the sense of complacency that southern mobs were justly retributive against African Americans.

The most compelling evidence that white leaders in southern states were shamed by the Tuskegee lynch records is the reaction of southern governors. Between 1916 and 1936 at least eight southern governors wrote to Work, requesting that he lower the lynching numbers for their states.[86] White southerners regarded Tuskegee as the authority on lynch records, and politicians were concerned about the effect the press releases had on the reputation of their states. In one such instance, after an ugly lynching in 1927, Virginia and Kentucky leaders fought over who should be saddled with the lynching that occurred on their border. Prominent Virginia politicians wrote to Monroe Work pleading that he assign the lynching to Kentucky, since the border was dubious and Virginia had been lynch-free for several years. However, Work stood firm and pointed out that although the victim was shot and fell over dead in Kentucky, those who shot him were standing in Virginia, which was then saddled with the dubious credit of having a mob lynch another black man.[87]

Gradual Erosion of Lynching

The simultaneous antilynching campaigns of the NAACP and Tuskegee Institute, and the ongoing efforts of individual activists, increasingly gained traction as the regional and national climate shifted. Local city boosters increased efforts to attract business and industry to the "New South." During World War I, white southerners, who had long taken their huge pool of cheap black labor for granted, began worrying as it drained north. Many newspaper reporters, organizational heads, and other race leaders used the Great Migration as leverage to argue for better treatment of African Americans in the South. During the 1920s and 1930s, lynching slowly but steadily declined. The South continued to use violence, but that use was far less frequent. The NAACP famously shifted its focus toward school integration, and other reform issues steadily followed. It was now safer for leaders in the black freedom struggle to pursue a wide array of goals.

Uncountable Crimes

The wretched practice of mob violence became overwhelmed by a powerful social movement that exposed it to the cold light of scientific study and shamed white southerners. But its former twin, sexual assaults against black women, remained in the shadows. It is difficult, and maybe inadvisable, to write a history of why something did not happen. But a few possibilities may be explored. One clue comes from the dynamic of campaigns to protect white women from assault. In her book *Southern Horrors*, Crystal Feimster makes the insightful and persuasive argument that white women were willing to publicize charges against alleged black rapists as a way to challenge white men's power in the public sphere and shame them into using their privilege on behalf of women.[88] As a 1919 letter to *Crisis* magazine shows, black women faced a different landscape. An anonymous woman wrote of her heart-wrenching dilemma: "Only colored women of the south know the extreme in suffering and humiliation. We know how many insults we have borne silently, for we have hidden many of them from our men because we did not want them to die needlessly in our defense."[89] Far from wanting to challenge black men to share their privilege, black women wanted instead to avoid calling attention to black men's powerlessness, their inability to protect the women in their lives. The historian Darlene Clark Hine suggests that black women developed a "cult of secrecy" around the many difficulties caused by sexual violence to protect their innermost selves.[90] This self-imposed silencing, coupled with the notorious callousness the southern police force showed to black women, indicates that most assaults went unreported.[91]

Even the assaults that were reported did not become a major social movement. The very tools that the antilynching movement found most successful, the martyrdom discourse and the use of statistics, were not translatable to sexual assault. The issue of sexual assault was not buried, but powerful institutions never put their formidable resources into antiassault strategies. Many activists still referred to the problem and condemned it strongly. For example in his 1920 essay "The Damnation of Women," W. E. B. Du Bois confessed he was willing to "forgive the white South" for slavery, the Confederacy, the Civil War, its pride and posturing but swore he would never forgive "its wanton and persistent insulting of the black womanhood which it sought and seeks to prostitute its lust."[92] Yet Du Bois did not mobilize the NAACP to launch a resistance campaign against this one unforgivable sin. There were no lawyers hired to write legislation making the sexual assault of black women a federal crime. There were no silent parades to protest rape. There were no journalists sent South to investigate specific cases of devastated women.[93] There were no fund-raising campaigns. Tuskegee similarly was concerned about the issue of sexual abuse but did not risk a public campaign. A visitor to the Tuskegee Archive can find newspaper clippings on the sexual assaults of black women. The Records and Research Department meticulously tracked these stories and filed them within the lynching data, showing the persistent belief that these issues were linked. But Tuskegee did not send out annual press releases on sexual assault statistics broken down by state. No white newspapers were shamed into editorializing against the custom. No governors quarreled with Tuskegee over what state bore the stigma of a sexual assault incident.

Concerns about sexual assault became channeled into public efforts by club women to elevate black women's reputation and maintain community standards of respectability and private attempts at self-defense.[94] Despite these efforts, black women remained vulnerable. In her interviews of black domestics, Elizabeth Clark-Lewis revealed that young girls were warned about the possibility of sexual assault before they went to work in white homes. One woman, Ora Fisher, revealed the broad concern of the entire family: "My mama told you first. Next was aunts and all. Now, then just before I was to leave with the family, my daddy just gave me a razor and he said it's for any man who tries to force himself on you. It's for the white man. He gave us *all* one."[95] In contrast to the massive institutional resources brought to bear on the problem of lynching, Clark-Lewis's accounts reveal that African American women faced the problem of sexual assault armed only with warnings. And perhaps a razor.

Part of the problem is the nature of sexual assault and how it differs from murder. In a lynching, no matter what disagreements there were over what first sparked the rage of the mob, at the end of the day there was a dead body that could be counted. There is no such certainty in sexual assault. Even today DNA testing can objectively establish sexual contact, but the issue of consent is subjective.[96] At the turn of the century, sexual assault simply was not countable the same way that lynching was.

I found the 2005 Senate apology in part heartening as a way of acknowledging the past, and in part empty. It is harder to acknowledge and apologize for other past historical crimes that are not as easily quantified. In this instance, it is the crimes against men that are more easily documented. We can count the bodies of the victims of lynching denied the basic protections of citizenship, but we can never count the women whose bodies were also not protected by their local, state, or national government. We cannot scientifically measure some events that have happened, and we cannot measure the lost possibilities. I certainly favor continuing scholarship to determine the wrongs of the past to make as full an accounting as possible for the inequities of the present. But I think we should also be humble before the vast amount of what we cannot know, what is not countable. We will never know the exact volume of the dream deferred.

Notes

Michelle Kuhl would like to thank the University of Wisconsin Oshkosh Women's Studies brown bag lunch series for hearing the first incarnation of this talk, the Western Association of Women's Historians for giving feedback on the second incarnation at their 2007 conference, Jeffrey Pickron for his encouragement, and the editors of this volume for their patient guidance.

1. Rep. George White first introduced antilynching legislation in 1900. Subsequent efforts include the Dyer Bill of 1911 and the Wagner-Costigan Bill introduced

in 1934. For more on these legislative debates, please see Philip Dray, *At the Hands of Persons Unknown: The Lynching of Black America* (New York: Random House, 2002), 259–60, 341–44.

2. Deborah Gray White pointed out that the Mississippi and Tennessee courts did not recognize any law that criminalized the rape of a slave women. White, *Ar'n't I a Woman: Female Slaves in the Plantation South* (New York: Norton, 1985), 152. Crystal Feimster documented the sexual violence against black women during the postemancipation period: "Thus, while emancipation deprived wealthy white men of easy sexual access to and greater control over black women, black women remained vulnerable to sexual and racial violence at the hands of white men." *Southern Horrors: Women and the Politics of Race and Lynching* (Cambridge: Harvard University Press, 2009), 52. In her work on sexual assaults, Danielle McGuire discusses the incredibly slow process by which activists convinced the courts to prosecute white men for assaults on black women during the post–World War II period. *At the Dark End of the Street: Black Women, Rape, and Resistance—A New History of the Civil Rights Movement from Rosa Parks to the Rise of Black Power* (New York: Knopf, 2010).

3. This emphasis on the innocence of the victim directly inverted the logic of the mob. As the historian Amy Louise Wood has documented, the ritual of spectacle lynching drew heavily on evangelical Christian beliefs and practices and "constructed a symbolic representation of white spiritual and moral superiority." *Lynching and Spectacle: Witnessing Racial Violence in America, 1890–1940* (Chapel Hill: University of North Carolina Press, 2009), 49.

4. Hazel V. Carby, *Reconstructing Womanhood: The Emergence of the Afro-American Woman Novelist* (New York: Oxford University Press, 1987), 39. This essay focuses on the period from 1890 to 1940. Danielle L. McGuire argues that the issue of sexual assaults were an important part of the civil rights movement in the period 1940–75, but that story has been erased from history. *Dark End*, xix.

5. For general works on Reconstruction and Redemption, please consult the following: Eric Foner, *Reconstruction: America's Unfinished Revolution, 1863–1877* (New York: HarperCollins, 1988); Nell Painter, *Standing at Armageddon: The United States, 1877–1919* (New York: Norton, 1987); and Michael W. Fitzgerald, *Splendid Failure: Postwar Reconstruction in the American South* (Chicago: Dee, 2007).

6. Monroe N. Work, *Thirty Years of the Tuskegee Lynching Records, 1908–1938*, Monroe N. Work files, Tuskegee Archives, Tuskegee, AL, 3. For secondary works on lynching, please see W. Fitzhugh Brundage, *Lynching in the New South: Georgia and Virginia, 1880–1930* (Urbana: University of Illinois Press, 1993); Dray, *At the Hands*; and James R. McGovern, *Anatomy of a Lynching: The Killing of Claude Neal* (Baton Rouge: Louisiana State University Press, 1982).

7. Rayford W. Logan, *The Negro in American Life and Thought: The Nadir, 1877–1901* (New York: Dial, 1954). See also David M. Oshinsky, *Worse Than Slavery: Parchman Farm and the Ordeal of Jim Crow Justice* (New York: Free Press, 1996).

8. Frederick Douglass, "Address by Hon. Frederick Douglass, Delivered in the Congregational Church, Washington, D.C., April 16, 1883, On the Twenty-First Anniversary of Emancipation," Daniel Murray Pamphlet Collection, Library of Congress, Washington, DC, accessed February 10, 2012, http://memory.loc.gov/ammem/aap/aaphome.html.

9. Robert J. Norrell, *Up from History: The Life of Booker T. Washington* (Cambridge, MA: Harvard University Press, 1999); Edwin S. Redkey, *Black Exodus: Black Nationalists and Back-to-Africa Movements, 1890–1910* (New Haven, CT: Yale University Press, 1999); Michele Mitchell, *Righteous Propagation: African Americans and the Politics of Racial Destiny after Reconstruction* (Chapel Hill: University of North Carolina Press: 2004).

10. The issue of resistance in the Jim Crow era is controversial. Leon Litwack's 1998 book *Trouble in Mind* documented the awful effectiveness of oppression but provoked a firestorm of criticism from scholars who argued that protest and agency should be foregrounded. I recognize the existence of courageous resistance, but I also agree with Litwack that violence, brutality, and intimidation did choke off widespread, organized action. *Trouble in Mind: Black Southerners in the Age of Jim Crow* (New York: Knopf, 1998).

11. Richard Wright, *The Ethics of Living Jim Crow* (New York: Viking, 1937), 39–52.

12. I do not mean to suggest that the 1950s and 1960s were entirely free of violence. Certainly, the lynching of Emmett Till; the murder of Schwerner, Chaney, and Goodman; and the many acts of brutality and intimidation visited upon civil rights workers were horrific. But a hard look at statistics show there were far fewer murders and lynching than in earlier decades, and the regional and national reaction to white supremacist violence indicated a far different sort of atmosphere.

13. Many historians have written about the trope of black rapists terrorizing the South. Jacquelyn Dowd Hall, *Revolt against Chivalry: Jessie Daniel Ames and the Women's Campaign against Lynching* (New York: Columbia University Press, 1979); Paula Giddings, *When and Where I Enter: The Impact of Black Women on Race and Sex in America* (New York: Bantam Books, 1984); Glenda Gilmore, *Gender and Jim Crow: Women and the Politics of White Supremacy in North Carolina, 1896–1920* (Chapel Hill: University of North Carolina Press, 1996); and most recently Feimster, *Southern Horrors*, 7–8, 47–55.

14. Two excellent biographies of Ida B. Wells are Paula Giddings, *Ida: A Sword among Lions: Ida B. Wells and the Campaign against Lynching* (New York: Amistad, 2008); and Mia Bay, *To Tell the Truth Freely: The Life of Ida B. Wells* (New York: Hill and Wang, 2010).

15. Giddings, *When and Where*, 28.

16. Steve Kantrowicz, *Ben Tillman and the Reconstruction of White Supremacy* (Chapel Hill: University of North Carolina Press, 2000), 168, 169.

17. *Record-Herald*, 1901, Tuskegee Lynching File, Discussions, Tuskegee Archives, 49.

18. "[Illegible] Sounds Note of Warning: Letter to Governor Durbin of Indiana Points Out the Danger Which Menaces Civilization," *Chicago Daily Tribune*, October 10, 1903, Tuskegee Lynching File.

19. A. L. Winslow, "The Growing Demand for Educated Men and Women among the Colored People," *Baptist Magazine* (Lynchburg, VA: National Baptist Magazine, 1897), 553.

20. William Hooper Councill, Normal, AL, quoted in "Washington and Councill on the 'Race Problem'" *Richmond Planet*, April 29, 1899, 43, item 47, microform, Hampton University Newsclippings File (Alexandria, VA: Chadwyck-Healey, 1987). For a discussion of the rivalry between Councill and Washington for white patronage in Alabama, please see Norrell, *Up from History*, 87–88.

21. W. Bishop Johnson, "The Church as a Factor in the Race Problem," *Sermons and Addresses* (Lynchburg: Virginia Seminary Steam Print, 1899), 45.

22. Esther Hall Mumford, *Seattle's Black Victorians, 1852–1901* (Seattle: Ananse, 1980).

23. Samuel Burdett, *A Test of Lynch Law, an Expose of Mob Violence, and the Courts of Hell* (Seattle, 1901).

24. Ida B. Wells, "Southern Horrors," in Wells, *On Lynchings* (New York: Arno, 1969), 14.

25. For information on the NAACP's antilynching campaign, please see Robert Zangrando, *The NAACP Crusade against Lynching, 1909–1950* (Philadelphia: Temple University Press, 1980); Dray, *At the Hands*; and Michelle Kuhl, *Modern Martyrs: African American Responses to Lynching, 1880–1940* (PhD diss., Binghamton University, 2004).

26. Hall, *Revolt against Chivalry*.

27. Ida B. Wells, editorial, *Free Speech*, May 21, 1892, in Wells, *On Lynchings*, 4.

28. Giddings, *When and Where*, 29.

29. Jesse C. Duke, editorial, *Montgomery Herald*, August 13, 1887, as described in Allen W. Jones, "The Black Press in the 'New South': Jesse C. Duke's Struggle for Justice and Equality," *Journal of Negro History* 64, no. 3 (Summer 1979): 221.

30. Martha Hodes, *White Women, Black Men: Illicit Sex in the Nineteenth-Century South* (New Haven, CT: Yale University Press, 1997), 188.

31. Alexander Manly, editorial, *Daily Record* (Wilmington, NC), August 18, 1898.

32. Gilmore, *Gender and Jim Crow*, 105–14.

33. George H. White, "Trade of Puerto Rico: Personal Explanation; Speeches of the Hon. George H. White, of North Carolina, in the House of Representatives, Monday, February 5 and Friday, February 23, 1900," 4, Murray Collection.

34. White, "'Trade of Puerto Rico," 14–15.

35. North Carolina sent Eva M. Clayton to Congress in 1992. Mildred L. Amer, "Black Members of the United States Congress: 1870–2005," Congressional Research Service, July 23, 2008, http://www.senate.gov/reference/resources/pdf/RL30378.pdf.

36. Emmanuel King Love, *A Sermon on Lynch-Law and Raping* (Augusta: Georgia Baptist Print, 1894), 4.

37. Ibid., 6–7, 8.

38. Ibid., 13. Love used the *Memphis Daily Commercial, Roanoke Times, Petersburg Daily Index Appeal*, and *Jacksonville Daily Times-Union*.

39. In *Lynching in the New South*, Brundage demonstrates that the Upper South (such as Virginia) had far fewer lynchings than the Deep South (such as Georgia).

40. Henry McNeal Turner, "On the Anniversary of Emancipation," 1866, in *Respect Black: The Writings and Speeches of Henry McNeal Turner*, ed. Edwin S. Redkey (New York: Arno, 1971), 10.

41. Ida B. Wells, *Southern Horrors and Other Writings: The Anti-Lynching Campaign of Ida B. Wells, 1892–1900*, ed. Jacqueline Jones Royster (Boston: Bedford Books, 1997). For analyses of Wells and sexual assaults on black women, please see Giddings, *When and Where*, 31, 86; Gail Bederman, *Manliness and Civilization: A Cultural History of Gender and Race in the United States, 1880–1917* (Chicago: University of

Chicago Press, 1995), 58–59; Giddings, *Ida*, 223–26; and Feimster, *Southern Horrors*, 91–92.

42. John Edward Bruce, *The Blood Red Record: A Review of the Horrible Lynchings and Burning of Negroes by Civilized White Men in the United States, as Taken from the Records* (Albany: Argus, 1901), 12.

43. White, ""Trade of Puerto Rico," 9.

44. Burdett, *Test of Lynch Law*, 37.

45. Malcolm X effectively used this technique while a preacher for the Nation of Islam. Malcolm X, *The Autobiography of Malcolm X as Told to Alex Haley* (New York: Ballantine Books, 1964), 206.

46. Darlene Clark Hine, "Rape and the Inner Lives of Black Women in the Middle West: Preliminary Thoughts on the Culture of Dissemblance," *Signs* 14 (Summer 1989): 912–20.

47. William Hannibal Thomas, *The American Negro: What He Was, What He Is, and What He May Become; A Critical and Practical Discussion* (New York: Macmillan, 1901).

48. The fiction author Charles Chesnutt found the book so repugnant that he made it a personal quest to destroy Thomas. Chesnutt spent months investigating Thomas and sent the MacMillan publishing company a list of Thomas's many financial and moral transgressions. Chesnutt claims this caused MacMillan to withdraw Thomas's book from circulation. Joseph R. McElrath Jr. and Robert C. Leitz III, eds., *To Be an Author: Letters of Charles W. Chesnutt, 1889–1905* (Princeton, NJ: Princeton University Press, 1997), 207.

49. S. Timothy Tice, "The American Negro: What He Was, What He Is, and What He May Become: A Critical and Practical Rejoinder to William Hannibal Thomas" (Cambridgeport: Facey, 1901), 35–36, Murray Collection.

50. Hazel V. Carby argues that during antebellum slavery, ideologies of womanhood were constructed in racial contrasts. White women (especially plantation mistresses) were characterized as chaste and pure, while black women were associated with unrestrained sexuality. *Reconstructing Womanhood*, 32.

51. W. E. B Du Bois, *Dusk of Dawn* (Millwood, NY: Kraus-Thomson Organization, 1975), orig. published 1940 by Harcourt, Brace; David Levering Lewis, *W. E. B. Du Bois: Biography of a Race, 1868–1919* (New York: Holt, 1993), 226.

52. For more on the ritual nature of lynching, please see Stewart Emory Tolnay and E. M. Beck, *Festival of Violence, an Analysis of Southern Lynchings, 1882–1930* (Urbana: University of Illinois Press, 1995); and Grace Elizabeth Hale, *Making Whiteness: The Culture of Segregation in the South, 1890–1940* (New York: Pantheon Books, 1998).

53. Lacey Baldwin Smith, *Fools, Martyrs, Traitors: The Story of Martyrdom in the Western World* (Evanston, IL: Northwestern University Press, 1997), 43.

54. Harriet Beecher Stowe, *Uncle Tom's Cabin* (1852; repr., New York: Dodd, Mead, 1952). For scholarly criticisms of Stowe's book, please see Eric J. Sundquist, ed., *New Essays on Uncle Tom's Cabin* (Cambridge: Cambridge University Press, 1986); and Cindy Weinstein, ed., *The Cambridge Companion to Harriet Beecher Stowe* (Cambridge: Cambridge University Press, 2004).

55. For an account of how abolitionist energy was rechanneled into Reconstruction-era uplift, please see Carol Faulkner, *Women's Radical Reconstruction: The Freedmen's Aid Movement* (Philadelphia: University of Pennsylvania Press, 2004).

56. George C. Rowe, *The Aim of Life: Live, Learn, Labor, Love* (Charleston, SC: Kahrs and Welch Printers, 1892), 21.

57. Levi Thornton, "The History of the Baptists," in Love, *Sermon on Lynch-Law*, 237.

58. Ibid.

59. R. DeBaptiste, "Suffering for Christ's Sake," in *National Baptist Magazine* (Lynchburg, VA: National Baptist Magazine, 1897), 458, Murray Collection.

60. On social Darwinism, see Carl N. Degler, *In Search of Human Nature: The Decline and Revival of Darwinism in American Social Thought* (New York: Oxford University Press, 1991); Robert W. Rydell, *All the World's a Fair: Visions of Empire at American International Expositions, 1876–1916* (Chicago: University of Chicago Press, 1984); and Bederman, *Manliness and Civilization*.

61. S. B. Wallace, *What the National Government Is Doing for Our Colored Boys: The New System of Slavery in the South* (Washington, DC: Jones, 1894), 51, 54, 56.

62. Benjamin, *Southern Outrages*, 38–39; John C. Dancy, *The "Quarterly" Almanac* ([Wilmington, NC?], [1893?]), 19, Murray Collection.

63. George L. Downing, quoted in Harvey Johnson, *The White Man's Failure in Government* (Baltimore: Press of Afro-American, 1900), 16.

64. NAACP, editorial, *Crisis* 3, no. 1 (November 1911): 21–22.

65. NAACP, editorial, "The Sin against the Holy Ghost," *Crisis* 3, no. 2 (December 1911): 68.

66. See Michelle Kuhl, "Resurrecting Black Manhood: Du Bois's Martyr Tales," in *The Souls of W. E. B. Du Bois: New Essays and Reflections*, ed. Edward J. Blum and Jason R. Young (Macon, GA: Mercer University Press, 2009), 160–87.

67. "Awake America," *Crisis* 14, no. 5 (September 1917): 216–17.

68. "The Protest of a Nation," *Crisis* 16, no. 4 (August 1918): 182.

69. NAACP, *Minutes of the Meetings of the Board of Directors, 1901–1950* (Frederick, MD: University Publications of America, 1982), September 11, 1922, 3.

70. Leaflets and ads, *Crisis* 25, no. 1 (November 1922): 8.

71. NAACP, *Minutes*, December 11, 1922, 3.

72. *Congregationalist*, quoted in "A Follower of Jesus Christ," *Crisis* 7, no. 6 (April 1914): 284; *Independent*, quoted in "A Lynching Talk-Fest," *Crisis* 11, no. 5 (March 1916): 233.

73. "Mob Murder," *Crisis* 12, no. 1 (May 1916): 24.

74. For an early example, see "The Burden," *Crisis* 1, no. 3 (January 1911): 26.

75. NAACP, *Minutes*, November 29, 1910, 3.

76. Joel Spingarn, "Where Does Your Congressman Stand?," *Crisis* 9, no. 1 (November 1914): 22.

77. Dray, *At the Hands*, 258–72.

78. For an excellent discussion of Washington's academic critics, such as C. Vann Woodward and Louis R. Harlan, please see Norrell, *Up from History*, 433–38. For a particularly negative view of Washington, please see Houston A. Baker Jr., *Turning South Again: Re-thinking Modernism/Re-reading Booker T.* (Durham, NC: Duke University Press, 2001).

79. For a fuller discussion of the Tuskegee antilynching campaign, please see Kuhl, *Modern Martyrs*.

80. Work, *Thirty Years*, 4.

81. Work, "An Autobiographical Sketch," February 7, 1940, box 1, folder "Auto-biographical Sketches," Monroe Work Papers, Tuskegee Archives, 2, 9. For other discussions of the Tuskegee lynching statistics, please see Linda O. McMurry, *Recorder of the Black Experience: A Biography of Monroe Nathan Work* (Baton Rouge: Louisiana State University Press, 1985), 121–27; and Norrell, *Up from History*, 371.

82. "The Burden," *Crisis* 1, no. 4 (February 1911): 29.

83. Overview of 1915, Tuskegee Lynching File, 1915.

84. *Outlook*, 1915, Tuskegee Lynching File, 267.

85. *Bulletin*, 1915, Tuskegee Lynching File, 242.

86. Work's overview of his antilynching campaign contains typed copies of all the letters from governors and his responses. *Thirty Years*, 30–44, 47–48, 52–53, 56–57, 58–61.

87. Ibid., 59.

88. Feimster, *Southern Horrors*, 126.

89. "A Southern Colored Woman," *Crisis* 19, no. 1 (November 1919): 339.

90. Clark Hine, "Rape," 915. In the same article, Hine lamented the impact of the culture of dissemblance on history: "Undoubtedly, these fears and suspicions contribute to the absence of sophisticated discussion of the impact of rape (or threat of rape) and incidences of domestic violence on the shape of Black women's experiences" (916).

91. Multiple instances of the failures of the criminal justice system can be found in McGuire, *Dark End*.

92. W. E. B. Du Bois, *Darkwater: Voices from within the Veil* (New York: Harcourt and Brace, 1920), 172.

93. As McGuire documents in *Dark End*, the NAACP did begin investigating sexual assault cases, but not until later in the twentieth century.

94. For readings on club women and the politics of respectability, see Giddings, *When and Where*; Darlene Clark Hine, *A Shining Thread of Hope: The History of Black Women in America* (New York: Broadway Books, 1998); Deborah Gray White, *Too Heavy a Load: Black Women in Defense of Themselves, 1894–1994* (New York: Norton, 1999); Victoria W. Wolcott, *Remaking Respectability: African American Women in Inter-war Detroit* (Chapel Hill: University of North Carolina Press, 2001).

95. Elizabeth Clark-Lewis, *Living Inn, Living Out: African American Domestics in Washington, D.C., 1910–1940* (Washington: Smithsonian Institution Press, 1994), 25.

96. The most recent illustration of this dilemma: Nafissatou Diallo, a black hotel maid in New York City, accused Dominique Strauss-Kahn, the head of the International Monetary Fund, of sexual assault. He maintains it was a consensual encounter. At the time of final revisions to this chapter, DNA tests established sexual contact between the two, but people cannot determine the truth of the competing accounts. Jim Dwyer, William K. Rashbaum, and John Eligon, "Strauss-Kahn Prosecution Said to Be Near Collapse," *New York Times*, June 30, 2011, http://www.nytimes.com/2011/07/01/nyregion/strauss-kahn-case-seen-as-in-jeopardy.html?ref=dominiquestrausskahn.

Chapter 6

Persecuting Black Men and Gendering Jury Service

The Interplay between Race and Gender in the NAACP Jury Service Cases of the 1930s

Meredith Clark-Wiltz

On October 13, 1936, the sheriff read aloud the jury's verdict: "We, the jury, find Joe Hale, the defendant, guilty of the first degree of murder, fix his penalty death in the electric chair."[1] Hale probably stood as each white juror nodded, affirming for the judge and record that he had supported that decision. An all-white grand jury had indicted him, and this all-white petit jury convicted Hale, an "illiterate, destitute" nineteen-year-old, of the murder of a forty-year-old white man, W. R. Toon. Hale had admitted he confronted—but did not kill—a white man to protect black women. Hale claimed he approached Toon to demand that he stop "accosting" black women walking along the street. According to the defense, he insisted that Toon "quit stopping these colored women."[2] The NAACP defense team, which included Charles H. Houston, Leon A. Ransom, and Thurgood Marshall, appealed this case to the Supreme Court.

The NAACP, guided by Charles Houston, led a jury service campaign in the 1930s that produced two successful Supreme Court decisions, one nationally publicized case, and a model litigation strategy for other black defendants.[3] In these cases the overt contestations over the existence of racial inequality between the NAACP defenses and the state prosecutions relied on interconnected racialized and gendered understandings of criminality, victimization, and citizenship and reaffirmed jury service as a masculine duty. While the NAACP attorneys and state prosecutors intentionally used discussions of race for their own ends—arguing against racial discrimination or reminding the jury of the importance of racial difference—both relied on gendered assumptions in arguing the cases.

The prosecutors often referenced the white female victims and called for the men of the jury to provide justice, ultimately reinforcing racist notions of sexual interactions between black men and white women. In contrast, the NAACP defenses, though making gendered assumptions about criminals and victims, did not endorse the prosecutions' association of *white* "manhood" with jury service obligations. Instead, the NAACP relied on, with more subtlety, connections drawn between masculinity and jury service. The NAACP even suggested a need to protect black women (from white men) as a potentially mitigating factor in the *Hale* case.[4] These arguments met the state's more forcefully promoted arguments about the need to protect white women from black men (never black women from white men) and ultimately resulted in the reiteration of a racist and paternalistic justification for the all-white, all-male jury.

The *Hale* case, like other NAACP jury service litigation, illustrates the various ways that race and gender mutually shaped understandings of citizenship, performance of its duties, and access to judicial institutions. While other historians have shown black women litigants used gendered arguments to pursue equitable treatment as "ladies," black men became central litigants in jury service cases.[5] Jury service, while not entirely limited to men in every state in the 1930s, remained predominantly a bastion of masculinized citizenship and associated with the obligations of men and the female privilege that exempted white women.[6] These cases also showcase how, for many white southerners, gendered and racialized identities overlapped and intersected, carving out well-defined roles for individuals in the justice system, including the black rapist, the white female victim, and her chivalrous white male protectors.[7] As other historians have also noted, the construction of the figure of the black rapist gave white men a means not only to deny black men's citizenship rights but also to exert control over black and white women.[8] Scholars have shown that black and white women organized antilynching campaigns and promoted the use of legal institutions.[9] These campaigns offered women new avenues for political participation.[10] But these cases indicate that as chivalry transferred to courtrooms, women remained largely outside the justice system as a class of "protected" citizens. In fact, these cases often condoned, or even necessitated, women's exclusion.

Interconnected understandings of race and gender undeniably shaped individual citizens' access to the justice system and experiences of citizenship. Race and gender assumptions also intersected and mutually sustained one another in larger socially constructed narratives of rape and chivalry. In most cases, white women's assumed delicacy and helplessness generated the perceived need for the protection of paternalistic white men from sexually deviant and violent black men. The interlocking and intersecting nature of these stereotypical categories informed the legal proceedings in trials of black men. The protection afforded white women because of their race and gender through "female privilege" encouraged their absence from the justice system except as passive victims. In contrast, the legal rights of black men offered an illusion of masculine citizenship that crudely masked their vulnerability in a racist system. Black women, denied the chivalrous protection because of their race, also did not often appear as defendants who claimed citizenship rights to jury service because of their gender. White men thus gained status and power through being the protectors and punishers. Race *and* gender identities of an individual together informed his or her position and power within trial proceedings. Female privilege and white supremacy in tandem influenced the workings of legal institutions, notions of civic fitness, and activists' strategies.

This article examines the three most prominent cases in the NAACP's 1930s jury service campaign to reveal how overlapping categories of race and gender influenced individuals' experiences in the justice system and their access to citizenship. After an explanation of the turn-of-the-century precedents and early arguments made for black men's equal access to juries, I analyze the NAACP's strategy and the gendered narratives in the nationally publicized 1933 *Crawford* case, the 1935 appeal of Jess Hollins to the Supreme Court, and the 1938 *Hale* case. These cases demonstrate the racial injustices of the southern court system and the centrality of gender to black men's citizenship claims and white men's defense of the racial order.

Since the Reconstruction era, black men had demanded jury service obligations as a means to protect black defendants and to procure citizenship rights. Having secured federalized rights in the 1870s and 1880s, black men after Reconstruction campaigned against race discrimination that prevented their access to juries. By the turn of the twentieth century, Wilford H. Smith, an advocate for racial equality and Booker T. Washington's lawyer, became one of the most outspoken advocates for ending racial discrimination in jury service policy at the time. In the southern justice system, he asserted, blacks were "denied all voice, except as parties and witnesses, and here and there a negro lawyer is permitted to appear." African Americans could occupy relatively powerless or passive positions in the courtroom, not the ones that decided the fates of others. Smith contended that southern states removed black men from grand and petit juries (among other institutions) because of concerns that social equality would follow equal access. Smith added that jury commissioners excluded blacks from jury panels, despite the laws against it. Arguing that representation on juries was more "serious" than exclusion in other areas, he expounded, "One vote on the grand jury might prevent an indictment, and save the disgrace and the risk of public trial; while one vote on the petit jury might save a life or a term of imprisonment, for an innocent person pursued and persecuted by powerful enemies."[11]

In addition to his calls to protect black defendants by ending race discrimination on juries, Smith drew correlations between citizenship obligations and masculinity. In his short pamphlet "A Negro's Right to Jury Representation," he advised southern blacks to continue to fight for their constitutional rights to juries selected without racial discrimination. Smith "strongly urged" them to "insist, through their attorneys, upon this right to be represented upon juries in all cases where their interests are at stake." Smith wanted this information to permeate the black communities and pleaded that the "information contained in this circular be circulated as widely as possible through the agency of the press, the pulpit, and in all ways where it will reach the masses of the Negro people." He called for social activism, expounding on the importance of black participation in the administration of law. Yet Smith also reaffirmed gendered understandings of citizenship in his claims to the rights and protections afforded by it. "This is no contention for social equality," he wrote, "but for manhood rights under the law, which you cannot neglect with safety to the liberties of yourselves and your children." Smith rhetorically tied jury service to notions of masculine obligation and the idea that it provided black men a means for the protection of their dependents.[12] These gendered notions of jury service operating as a patriarchal duty undertaken by male citizens in their need to protect the weak in the community shaped Smith's discussions of race discrimination in jury service in the early twentieth century.

Wilford H. Smith acted on his conviction to achieve equality for black defendants by bringing two jury service cases to the Supreme Court. Both of these cases—*Carter v. Texas* (1900) and *Rogers v. Alabama* (1904)—garnered limited victories in the form of Supreme Court decisions that favored black defendants' appeals for new trials. In 1900 Smith won the appeal of his client Seth Carter, who was convicted of murdering his recently divorced lover, a black woman named Bertha Brantley.[13] Before the trial the defense motioned to quash the indictment on grounds that otherwise qualified African American men, who made up one-quarter of the population of the city and county of Galveston, were intentionally left off of the list of prospective jurors because of their race or color. The lower court denied the motion without allowing the defense to produce witnesses or evidence supporting the accusation of race discrimination in the jury process. The Supreme Court determined that the lower court had failed to authorize the correct procedure for allowing the presentation of evidence and "whenever, by any action of a state, whether through its legislature, through its courts, or through its executive or administrative officers, all persons of the African race are excluded solely because of their race or color from serving as grand jurors in the criminal prosecution of a person of the African race, the equal protection of the laws is denied to him, contrary to the Fourteenth Amendment."[14]

Here, the Supreme Court noted the danger of race discrimination in jury selection for black defendants in particular, not simply its unconstitutionality regardless of the race of the defendant. Additionally, the court ignored the lower court's argument that racial discrimination had no bearing on the trial, since both the defendant and the victim were black. Intriguingly, this argument presumed that race discrimination in jury selection had an impact only on cases where the race of the defendant and the victim were different and that race discrimination in selection was not alone a real problem. This argument supposed that an all-white jury would have no reason to unfairly judge the defendant if the victim was a black woman and not a white woman. This rationale implied recognition of the possibility that a white male jury might be more incensed by a crime against a white woman and therefore less objective in its deliberations.

In 1904 Wilford H. Smith again presented arguments about race discrimination in jury selection on behalf of a black defendant, Dan Rogers. Smith contended that a recently revised section of the Alabama Constitution disfranchised more than seventy-five thousand African Americans statewide and as a result disqualified them from jury service. The outcome of reducing the number of black men on juries, he claimed, infringed on his client's ability to have a fair trial. Having been charged with and convicted of murder and given a life sentence, Rogers appealed to the Supreme Court to rectify the violations to his Fourteenth Amendment right to equal protection of the laws. In a brief decision, the Supreme Court reaffirmed its earlier decision in *Carter*, applied it to the case here, and reversed the lower court's decision.[15]

Neither of Smith's cases, according to Benno C. Schmidt Jr., signified a change in the Supreme Court's narrowly construed arguments about the burden of proof needed by defendants to prove discrimination.[16] The defense had to show explicit acts of discrimination by state officials in the process of selecting jurors. Other cases heard by the Supreme Court before the 1930s about race discrimination in jury selection continued a "theme of deference to state court fact-finding" and failed to make substantial gains for black defendants from the South.[17] In both *Carter* and *Rogers*, the court ruled against the state because of procedural issues that prevented the defense from pursuing arguments against race discrimination in jury selection. In *Carter* the court found it unacceptable that the state prohibited the defense from calling witnesses to testify about the exclusion of blacks from juries. The short decision in *Rogers* contended that the state could not throw out the defense's motion to quash the indictment because of race discrimination in the selection of the grand jury by calling it "prolix," or superfluous and irrelevant.[18] Outside of the *Carter* and *Rogers* decisions, the Supreme Court resisted reversing state court decisions for black defendants, arguing that the juries that indicted or convicted them excluded blacks from serving.

By the 1930s black activists' litigation strategy found a more receptive court. The NAACP became a principal reform organization, focused on achieving legal equality for black men in courtrooms during this period when African Americans, particularly in the South, faced discrimination, segregation, and outright violence. As Manfred Berg suggests, the NAACP's focus on defendant's rights and its litigation strategy were means of protecting the black community, and black men in particular, against the injustices of a racist criminal justice system.[19] The NAACP developed the criteria for deciding which defendants to represent in this campaign for jury service. First, the *man* had to be innocent. The case also had to center on an injustice based on race or color. Finally, the case had to be able to set a national precedent that would help African Americans.[20] These standards—which sought to increase protection for black communities while, perhaps inadvertently, recognizing the gender specificity of their clientele—guided the NAACP's selection of cases.

Charles Houston was instrumental in promoting the NAACP's reliance on black lawyers.[21] As the early to mid-1930s marked a shift in the makeup of the NAACP's national legal circle from one consisting of primarily white lawyers to one that featured predominately African American lawyers, most notably Charles Houston, Leon Ransom, and, later, Thurgood Marshall, jury service became a prominent component of the NAACP's litigation strategy.[22] In fact, Charles Houston believed *Crawford v. Commonwealth of Virginia* (1933) would be especially important not only because it raised the issue of race discrimination in jury selection but also because it would be the first NAACP case to be brought by an all-black defense team.[23] He ignored the suggestion that a white woman lawyer should assist in the defense and the ACLU should become involved to "offset the prejudices against the NAACP as an organization of colored people."[24] Black men would provide the defense on behalf of the NAACP in this case, regardless of the potential fallout from the community or jury because of their race or sex.

Before the trial in Virginia, Houston, along with local trial attorneys Butler R. Wilson and J. Weston Allen, hoped to prevent Crawford's extradition from Massachusetts by arguing against the systematic exclusion of black jurors on the grand jury in Virginia that indicted him. Wilson asserted that he wanted evidence that blacks had been excluded from juries in Virginia for decades and hoped he "could depend on the citizens of standing (colored men) to testify to the custom."[25] In a letter to Walter White, Houston asked, "Would an intelligent Negro (the type of man whom the Judge stated he selected for his grand juries from the white list) have permitted the authorities to load the crime on Crawford," considering the state of the evidence against him?[26] Wilson and Houston both indicated the existence of an association between jurors and male citizens.

Houston's arguments against the extradition of Crawford hinged on the presence of race discrimination on Virginia juries. He, with Edward P. Lovett, investigated the situation in Virginia, producing an affidavit confirming the existence of race discrimination in its jury system. In his correspondence to White, Houston revealed his hope that this extradition case might transform the jury system of the South, noting, "It strikes me more and more that here is something big if properly handled in Boston." He explained that if this case set precedent, the South would be unable to extradite black men from the North without ending race discrimination in jury selection.[27] Houston's affidavit uncovered that the court officials in Virginia knew that only white men appeared on juries. Those officials attributed the practice to custom and deemed that black defendants had not complained about the justice they received at the hands of these juries. The affidavit also revealed that these officials kept two racially segregated lists of tax payers, drawing jurors only from the white list.[28] The defense saw initial success with the decision of the trial judge to prevent extradition. Newspapers reported that immediately following this portion of the trial that a black man was selected to serve in a trial and that a Virginia clerk of court announced the addition of twenty black men to the jury list.[29] The NAACP reported that black jurors had been added in four southern states and that a white man had been fined for refusing to serve alongside a black man in Virginia.[30] But the appellate court reversed the favorable decision and the Supreme Court refused to hear the case. When the final attempt to stop Crawford's extradition failed, he returned to Virginia to stand trial.

In the fall of 1933 the NAACP all-black defense team began preparing to defend Crawford. Though suspected of killing two women, Crawford faced charges of murdering only a wealthy white woman, Agnes Ilsley.[31] As chief council, Houston sought to quash the indictment of the grand jury by proving race discriminatory practices unconstitutionally excluded black men from the jury. He argued before the court that blacks were not on the lists of potential grand jurors and provided evidence that several qualified blacks lived in the area. The defense called numerous witnesses; Houston claimed they had 350 people to testify unless the prosecution admitted that there were qualified black men in the area.[32] The Circuit Court overruled the defense's motion, finding that since the jury commissioner did not deliberately consider race when making the lists his actions did not constitute racial discrimination.[33] The indictment against Crawford stood, and the trial began with the voir dire of the petit jury.

The underlying racial elements of this case, namely the charges against a black man of killing white women, first surfaced in the voir dire of the petit jury. Leon A. Ransom, for the defense, questioned the pool of potential jurors, "May I ask you gentlemen whether . . . you believe you could give the evidence in this case, in which a Negro is charged with the crime of murder against a white woman, the same impartial treatment as if the situation were reversed."[34] None of the men responded, indicating that they believed themselves to be impartial. Additionally, the defense probed whether potential jurors belonged to any racist organizations, such as the Ku Klux Klan. Moreover, Ransom asked these men whether they would trust the testimony of a white person over that of a black person (93). These first interactions between the defense and the jury showed the disadvantaged position of the defense because of race discrimination in the jury selection. The defense felt they had to ask these racially charged questions to the prospective jurors to protect the defendant from discrimination and, perhaps, highlight the increased possibility for unequal treatment of a black defendant by an all-white jury.

The defense, the prosecution, and the judge returned to discussions of race throughout the case. The defense interjected a discussion of race into the proceedings to probe the impartiality of the system and to question the fairness of the trial for the defendant. The prosecution used race to feign impartiality while constantly drawing attention to the blackness of the defendant and the whiteness of the victim. Additionally, Judge James L. McLemore opened the case by stating that he had "no doubt" that the defense, implicitly noting their race, would "be treated exactly like the white people" in this courtroom "if they conduct themselves properly" (102). The judge noted the hardships the defense council faced from the community and the potential for their inequitable treatment by the courts generally. Specifically referencing a newspaper article that discussed the case, McLemore warned that "any man or set of men or any of those who undertake to form public sentiment are doing a distinct disservice to the community when they attempt to raise the question of race hatred or race feeling in the conduct of this case."[35] Yet he also said he could not "imagine the good people of this county giving themselves over to any sort of incendiary remarks or statements that would bring disrespect upon the county and shame and disgrace upon its name," calling for them to remember that this case was "simply the trial of a man for murder to determine whether he is guilty, the same as in any other case of murder" (101). Only these statements indicate that it was not like a case involving a white defendant; the judge believed he needed to make these remarks for this trial of a black man.

The opening statement of the prosecutor vividly described the criminal offense, illuminating the prosecutor's gendered and racialized understandings of the event (101).[36] John Galleher, commonwealth attorney for Loudoun County, described the brutal death of "a most charming lady" in their "quiet little town." He explained that her blood-covered body lay face up with her arms extended over her head and "nude from her breast down." Her skull and chest were beaten, and the coroner found under her fingernails "Negro skin and Negro hair"—which one doctor, Oscar B. Hunter, later described as "two little crinkly hairs" that were "not the same structure as [the victim] Mrs. Ilsley's hair." After being questioned further about the skin cells he discovered under the fingernails, Hunter explained that the pigment is the only difference between white men's and black men's skin, but one can "look at it and immediately differentiate the skin of a white man from that of a colored man." He continued by creating a dehumanizing comparison between black skin and animal hide: "You probably might have some difficulty if you had a black animal," though he failed to follow up with more discussion other than stating that this understanding becomes "too technical to go into here" (145).

Finally, Hunter was asked repeatedly about how he collected the material, studied it, and determined whether it came from one of only two options—

"a white man or a black man." He said with certainty, "It was a black man."
During his cross-examination, Hunter modified his earlier statements about
race, claiming the skin was that of someone from a "dark-skinned race" that
could potentially include the "Indian." He continued by saying that the skin
he found was not that of "a very black man but a moderately dark-skinned individual" and made comparisons to others in the courtroom to demonstrate the
shade of skin to which he was referring (145). Of course, according to the
doctor and prosecution, the color of the perpetrator was scientifically proven
through tests, but the sex of the perpetrator was an assumption made without
question by all involved in the proceeding.

Also revealing contemporary understandings of gender stereotypes, the
coroner was questioned and cross-examined about the placement of the bodies, the injuries that caused the death, and the general occurrence of events.
Perhaps trying to undermine the myth of the black rapist or at least its application here, Houston asked if there was a "sex element" to the crime, and the
coroner answered, "I understand not." Moreover, Houston asked the coroner
to describe the physicality of the "ladies." He described them by height, weight,
and age and, additionally, mentioned one of them to be "fair" and both to be
"healthy" or "apparently healthy" (129). Even though the testimony in the trial
centered on women, their bodies, and the looming question of sexual impro-
priety or assault (strengthened by the universally accepted assumption that
the perpetrator was male), no statement presented questioned the absence of
women from the trial process. Instead, the proceedings positioned women as
passive victims, individuals needing protection not through participation but
through state intervention. Those in the courtroom believed that the perpetrator must have been a man, even though they questioned whether sexual violence occurred or not. The women were voiceless victims, described in detail
as submissive entities whose only hope at justice was through the prosecution
of the defendant. The all-male jury had a duty to ensure crimes like this one,
especially man against women, did not happen without consequence. The
court became a paternalistic arm shielding women from (possible or potential) sexual violence.

Despite the increased presence of black lawyers, the justice system most
often positioned black men in less powerful roles—those of witnesses and
defendants. Even when black men served as lawyers, they did not wield the
same control as a judge or jury. Yet unlike white women, black men in the
courtroom stereotypically faced persecution, not protection—being viewed
as threatening or criminal. Houston articulated the importance of pursuing
cases of racial discrimination at the end of this case, stating that African Americans "can only hope to rise by convincing you [the white community] that we
are entitled to and are able to share in your institutions without endangering
them." He continued by stating that he realized that the community had to
be behind such a transformation and that he did "not expect to see things

completely changed overnight" (129). After less than three hours, the jury convicted George Crawford of murder, sentencing him to life in prison rather than to death. Houston and others believed the defense saved Crawford from a death sentence. Because of this outcome and Houston's failed motion for a second trial, Crawford decided not to appeal and plead guilty of the second murder to advert the risk of being tried by a less sympathetic jury and sentenced to death.[37] Houston and the rest of the defense respected and understood Crawford's decision; however, others questioned whether the decision not to appeal would hurt the fight for constitutional protections regarding the jury question.[38]

For Crawford the decision was a success, in so far as it saved him from a death sentence. Yet the decision also reveals the compromised position black men faced in the judicial system and the continued need for activism to secure in actuality the constitutional protections that had already legally been granted to them. The NAACP, especially Houston, noted that the fight was far from over.[39] Houston and Ransom used their experience in this case to outline particular procedures for other attorneys wishing to raise questions about jury selection in their trial, eventually distributing 112 copies to states in the South or border-South.[40] These suggestions noted the importance of knowing the state's jury qualifications (specifically noting sex as one) and advised that the best citizens be called on to testify first. The NAACP would continue to make efforts to protect black male defendants from unconstitutionally selected juries.

Virginia v. Crawford revealed how overlapping racialized and gendered assumptions of the defense and the prosecution informed legal proceedings. Both state prosecutors and defense attorneys shared gendered notions of criminality and victimhood. Men perpetrated crimes, and women (coded as white for state prosecutors) easily fit the position of victim. Neither the prosecution nor the defense questioned these underlying assumptions, despite their debates over the definition of race and its relationship to notions of criminality and citizenship. Similarly to those gendered and racialized conceptions apparent in the *Crawford* case, the subsequent jury service case filed by the NAACP amplified these connections between masculinity and citizenship while also prompting the state and defense to contest the connections drawn between black maleness and criminality as well as those drawn between white maleness and jury service obligations.

The first 1930s jury service case the NAACP argued before the Supreme Court concerned black-on-white rape and provided the most obvious platform for the prosecution to rely on white men of the jury to secure white supremacy and protect white womanhood by convicting a black man. As part of the first all-black defense team to present a case before the Supreme Court, Houston appealed *Hollins v. Oklahoma* in 1935. Jess Hollins, the black defendant charged and convicted of the rape of a seventeen-year-old white girl, Alta McCollum, became, for the prosecution, the quintessential black rapist that represented the gravest danger to white womanhood.[41] Sentenced to death by electrocution, Hollins relied on his defense to appeal to the Supreme Court to save his life.[42]

The local newspaper editor and Oklahoma NAACP branch president, Roscoe Dunjee, became highly involved in publicly defending Hollins and coordinating with the NAACP's local white lawyers and national office in the trial's appeal to illuminate the racial inequalities black men faced in the justice system, especially in trials with white women victims.[43] He believed, "Jess Hollins happened to have an illicit relationship with a white girl who grew angry with him," but he was not guilty of rape. Additionally, he noted the inequitable standards by which a white man and a black woman caught in an affair faced only misdemeanors. Dunjee expounded, "Before judge, jury, and sheriff, a horrible crime has been committed when a Negro man is found even to be associating with a white girl, while great derision and laughter are vented when the same immoral relationship is exposed between a white man and a colored girl." Not only does Dunjee use "girl" to describe adult women in an effort, possibly, to reduce their culpability in these scenarios, but he also characterized this case as "the fight of the NAACP . . . to insure for black men the same type of justice in the courts as is meted out to other citizens."[44] Furthermore, Dunjee published in the *Black Dispatch* that the trial showed real "progress and the growth of manhood spirit," underscoring the importance of this trial and discrediting the black rapist myth as a victory for black men.[45]

In the 1934 trial two white lawyers, W. N. Redwine and E. P. Hill, defended Hollins by pointing to the race discrimination that inhibited him from equal participation in the southern criminal justice system and worked to insulate his client from the racial double standard that presumed black men culpable in rape cases with white women victims. Hill argued that mob violence and the local context prohibited him from getting a fair trial.[46] Because Hollins was black "and the crime [was] alleged to have been committed upon a white woman, and that naturally great feeling and prejudice existed at the time, and still exists in Creek County, Oklahoma, where this cause [was] pending, to such an extent that he cannot secure a fair and impartial trial guaranteed to him."[47] In voir dire Hill asked each potential juror two questions: whether he could give a black defendant the same consideration he would give a white defendant in this case and whether the notion that a black man allegedly assaulted a white woman would cloud his ability to render an impartial verdict. To both of these questions, each juror responded that race would not play a role in his decision making (120–48). Finally, the defense also maintained that since no black jurors were called for service and the victim of the crime was a white woman, Hollins could not have an impartial trial. The district court granted his request for a change of venue, moving Hollins to another county in Oklahoma.

At trial the defense used demographics of the county and the testimony of white and black male residents to show black men had been excluded from the jury. Hill argued that "more than one-fourth of the inhabitants and more than one-fourth of the legal electors of Okmulgee County are persons of color or African descent, known as negroes, and are qualified jurors" but are excluded from service on the basis of race or color by the commissioners of the county. In presenting evidence of this discrimination, Hill first called the trial judge, Mark L. Bozarth, to the stand, asking him how many black jurors he had seen in his courtroom or known about in other courtrooms and how jury commissioners select jurors. Bozarth admitted that he had never had a black man serve as a juror in his courtroom and could not recall any others serving. He stated that he relied on jury commissioners to select jurors from tax rolls (43–45). Hill then moved on to question the sheriff, John Lenox, who confessed he had never called a black man for service. He reasoned that none had been called, because "we had better qualified jurors in the ones I sum- moned." He explained that by "better qualified" he meant they had "a higher sense of citizenship—not talking about color, just talking about special fitness" (47). Hill also relied on the testimony of two black men, a newspaper editor and an attorney, from the area about the absence of black jurors. The black attorney responded to one of the prosecution's questions by estimating that only about a fifth of the black voters registered in the area were women (and therefore not eligible for jury service), implying that more than enough black men could qualify for jury duty. All this testimony provided the defense with the grounds for appeal (74). Additionally, it illustrates the push to show black men as qualified and rightful recipients of full citizenship and white officials' refusal to extend full citizenship to black men.

In his argument for the state, Sebe Christian constructed a narrative that conformed to familiar accounts of black-on-white rape. He explained he wanted the jury to know that the prosecution of Hollins was not "because he is a negro and the girl he assaulted, a white girl." He followed up this point by indicating that "rape is rape, whether committed by a negro man upon a negro woman, or upon a white girl" (309–11). Christian mentioned that the race of the woman did not matter in rape cases but failed to mention that the race of the defendant would not matter in these cases either. He also appealed to the conventional stereotypes in his narrative, stating "When he [Hollins] held that little girl with brute strength . . . [he] raped her not one time not two times, but three times" (314). Finally, Christian also presented a lengthy ora- tion about how McCollum did not have consensual sex, claiming that the use of force, her screams, and the lack of witness testimony to deny it proved the rape "stands unimpeached and undenied" (316).

Christian also appealed to the jury as men. He flattered the jury, claiming the men were model jurors and complimenting them on the quality of their service. He proclaimed, "You are all intelligent men, reasonable men" (309).

Emphasizing the need to protect the fragile female victim, Christian appealed to the jurors' masculinity and urged them to meet their civic obligation: "If you bring in a verdict, as American citizens, with the sting of truth on your lips, and the gleam of manhood in your eyes, that a man, white or black, can't do these things, and expect to get any sympathy from juries in this county, you can retire to your homes with contentment and peace of mind, before God, that under your oath as jurors, you had the intelligence to see your duty, and the manhood to do your duty" (319). He focused on the sense of man-hood and duty to protect this woman and other white women from the violent acts of men through the state-sanctioned, legitimate process of rendering a jury verdict. The alternative to a conviction with a death sentence, Christian believed, was the possibility the defendant might escape, be freed, or killed by those outside the justice system. According to his statement, the legal sys-tem could defend innocent white women, promote the citizenship of white men (through their service on juries), and legitimately (at least in appearance) punish black men—in other words, sustain and reproduce conventional race and gender hierarchies.

The closing statements for the prosecution also illuminated the wide impact race and gendered assumptions had on shaping this trial. While Christian men-tioned race several times in his opening remarks, Sam Cunningham, the assis-tant county attorney of Creek County, also did so in his closing in ways that were seemingly to discourage jurors from using race as a factor in the case—all the while reminding them of it. Yet, near the end of his closing, he interjected, "but you know the laws of this state don't permit whites and blacks to marry or inter-marry. There is too much difference in nationality there, too much difference. They are of African descent, [*sic*] we are Caucasians, and the law says we shall not cohabit" (326). Cunningham emphasized the "differences" between the races and confirmed the appropriateness of race segregation and the importance of legal restrictions on the relationships, especially romantic or sexual ones, between blacks and whites. He promoted the idea of the defenseless, young *white* woman who needed protection from this man and his brutal attack:

> Listen, my fellow citizens! A woman's virtue is the most precious thing on earth to her. Rob her of that, you rob her of the most precious thing God Almighty gave her—rob her of that, and these ravishers of woman's virtue, will follow her like dogs after a hot bitch, and you know it. What would you feel like doing, if it was a white man, meeting an innocent girl—what would you feel like doing? You might give him the death penalty, if it is one of the cases you feel like doing it, all right. This is a white girl over there. . . . She was as pure as any woman in Oklahoma. (326)

He insisted on the quality of her reputation and stressed her "purity" as a fac-tor in recognizing that a crime was committed against her. Also, in response to the testimony of black men and a black woman for the defense, Cunningham showcased the supposed damage the *white* victim endured: "that her good name has been dragged in the mire . . . that she has been accused of associating with negroes, drunk, sprawled out on a nigger dance floor" (328). Dismissing the testimony of African Americans in the case, he emphasized the added harm to her reputation done by the defense, which insisted that she willingly associated with blacks.

The defense argued that the exclusion of black men from juries and highly racialized remarks by Christian and Cunningham prevented Hollins from obtaining a fair trial. With the state supreme court ruling that the defense failed to meet its burden of proof, the defense, now headed by Charles Houston and backed by the NAACP, filed an appeal with the Supreme Court in 1934. In this appeal Houston explained that the jury commissioners excluded any qualified black men from serving and accused the state, sanctioned by the court, of making "repeated inflammatory appeals to race prejudice," despite the defense's objections. He stated that proof of exclusion had been made by the defense, including a notation of the demographics of the area: Okmulgee County was 17 percent black, contained eight hundred or nine hundred black voters, of whom about only one-fifth were women. Furthermore, Houston cited the prosecution's statements as appealing to racial prejudice. He noted Christian's plea—"I am not asking for the death penalty because he is a Negro, and the girl a white girl. Those are just circumstances for you to consider"— and his discussion of "defenseless little white girls" like "your girls or mine, or our wives" who might be "assaulted by some Negro or white man, taken in the woods, at the point of a gun, and raped and ravished and torn."[48] Houston illuminated the import of the use of racial difference by the state, implicitly in the discrimination against black men in jury selection procedures and explicitly in the discourse of state officials during the trial. Though Houston did not discuss the gendered elements apparent in these statements, the prosecution's closing arguments relied on emphasizing interracial, sexualized encounters to promote the need to protect stereotypically represented white women from black men, with the intention of reinforcing racist presumptions about black men and the consequence of reinforcing the patriarchal role of the legal system, especially the white male jury, to protect white women.

For Hollins, however, the success of the 1935 Supreme Court decision was quickly tempered by the outcome of his third trial. The Supreme Court decided this case by issuing a per curiam decision, reversing the decision of the appellate court and noting the defendant's Fourteenth Amendment rights had been violated.[49] Hollins was entitled to a new trial—one free of racial discrimination in the selection of its juries. In 1936 another all-white jury in Oklahoma convicted him, sentencing him to life in prison. He remained imprisoned until his death in 1950. The NAACP campaign, however successful in setting precedent, still failed to change the circumstances for Hollins. He got a new trial but still faced an all-white jury in a racially charged atmosphere. The precedent itself would not be enough to ensure fair trials or discrimination-free jury decisions.[50] States could circumvent real changes to the system by adding the names a few blacks to jury lists and either rarely calling them, using preemptory strikes to remove them, or intimidating them to keep them from serving.[51]

The *Hollins* case exemplified how racialized and gendered understandings of citizenship, criminality, and victimhood worked together to reproduce stereo-typical narratives of black-on-white rape that underpinned justifications for the patriarchal power of white men. The subsequent NAACP jury service case in *Hale v. Kentucky* threatened that scenario of black male perpetrators, white women victims, and white male protectors by introducing black women into the center of the trial. This atypical case reflected and had the potential to expose the historical abuse of black women at the hands of white men. It challenged the dominant story found in *Hollins,* but the legal and social confines of the 1930s courtroom and the overriding concern for the defendant stunted the power of its use as a contrasting view of interracial interactions between the sexes.

Not long after *Hollins*, the NAACP entered *Hale v. Kentucky*, a case that inverted the typical scenario of black male defendant as aggressor, white woman as passive victim, and white male jurors as paternalistic protectors.[52] Unlike the prosecutor's elaborate narrative of black-on-white rape in the *Hollins* case, this case only subtlety presented an account of Hale's chivalrous attempt to protect black women from a white man's advances. According to transcripts of the trial, the police found Toon, dazed and bleeding, hunched over in the front seat of a car. The stabbing occurred shortly after Toon had allegedly shouted at black women along the street and called to one, "Hello, girlie. Let's go riding."[53] Hale admitted to insisting that Toon "quit stopping these colored women," but he maintained that he had not hurt Toon.[54]

The potential sexual connotations of the white man enticing black women into his car, however, did not have the same power in court as the scenarios where black defendants were accused of attacking white women (say, as that in the *Hollins* case). The prosecution seemed to question whether Toon had actually harassed these black women. The state would not have stressed the defendant's intention of protecting black women, since those claims would have weakened the case against Hale. The defense did offer testimony of two black women who said they were harassed by a white man the night of the murder. Novella Nailing stated that a white man called out to her on the street and asked her to get into his car twice in one night. Bertie Mae Bradfort also testified that a white man told her to "come here" that night and followed her slowly in his car as she walked along the street.[55] The prosecution successfully moved to exclude the testimony of the two defense witnesses, claiming these women could not absolutely identify the man who approached them as Toon.[56] The prosecution also elicited the testimony of another black woman, Eugenia Hamilton, who claimed Toon said only "Howdy" to her twice and that Hale admitted to her that he confronted Toon. Hamilton also testified that Hale had a knife.[57] Hamilton's testimony supported the prosecution's position—Hale had the means to commit the crime and black women did not need protection from Toon. With the ruling to exclude the testimony of the defense witnesses, the information in the record about Toon's actions that night remains scant. Because of these limits, the defense could not place much emphasis on the situation as it pertained to race and sex stereotypes or the position of black women in society.

Instead, the defense argued against the race discrimination they believed to be apparent in the selection of jurors, while highlighting the qualifications of black men as citizens. Kentucky permitted, but did not require, women to serve on juries. Women, even though allowed to serve, did not serve often or regularly, and no women served in this trial.[58] Still, the defense efforts to show race discrimination in the selection process relied on the testimony of only black men from the community. In addition to court officials who confirmed that no black jurors had served in the past decades, the defense produced multiple statements from local citizens. Those from the community were white and black men—among them a college professor, an undertaker, a bank president, and newspaper publisher—who testified that no black juror served in the county in at least the previous fifty years.[59] In this case, men still dominated the jury as well as the place of informed citizen discussing jury composition.

Charles Houston appealed the case to the Supreme Court, hoping for it to reaffirm the constitutional protection that guaranteed black men equal jury service obligations regardless of race or color. In 1938 the NAACP lawyers, including Houston, Leon Ransom, and Thurgood Marshall, argued that Hale's constitutional rights to equal protection of the laws under the Fourteenth Amendment had been violated by the McCracken County's exclusion of qualified blacks from the jury pool. Relying on the trial evidence that included the testimony from male resident citizens, the defense showed that McCracken County had forty-eight thousand people, of which approximately eight thousand were black. Of that population, six thousand whites and seven hundred blacks were qualified for jury service, though blacks virtually never became jurors in the previous fifty years.[60] Statements of sheriffs and jury commissioners serving in the county between 1906 and 1936 bolstered the defense by confirming that no black men had served on a jury in the county over those thirty years.[61] Furthermore, the defense argued that no potential juror disqualified from serving for statutory reasons was black, showing that blacks were left out of the process intentionally and entirely. In each of these points, the question of women's elective inclusion in 1928 as potential jurors was not mentioned.

Despite earlier jury service cases reversed by the Supreme Court, it agreed to hear this case on appeal in 1938. In a per curiam decision, it decided that the evidence offered by the NAACP, because it was not adequately countered by the state, showed "a systematic and arbitrary exclusion of negroes from the jury lists solely because of their race or color." Citing earlier decisions in *Neal*,

Carter, and *Norris,* the court reversed the decision, claiming that the jury selection process violated Hale's right to equal protection of the laws.[62]

Hale demonstrated not only that the *Norris* and *Hollins* cases would not change the actual experience of black men in the courtrooms of the South but also that the defense—as did much of society—connected jury service with notions of male citizenship. This case underscored that even permissive jury laws and an inverted scenario that removed any focus on white women still was not sufficient to challenge gendered assumptions about the judicial system, victimhood, or juries. Facing little response from the prosecution and little resistance from state courts, defendants effectively made arguments about the unconstitutionality of race discrimination and promoted black men's citizenship rights. The case also offered a chance to invert the familiar southern scenarios of black-on-white rape to reveal, if only partially, the experiences and exploitation of black women by white men.

The NAACP in the 1930s became a major player in the campaign to secure jury service obligations for blacks—a necessary venture for making the criminal justice system, particularly in the South, fair for black defendants. Under the guidance of Houston and with the aid of Thurgood Marshall, the NAACP supported several cases, some of which made it to the Supreme Court. Black men led this campaign, which contested racial discrimination while reinforcing gendered notions of citizenship and its obligations. Though the Supreme Court reaffirmed the constitutional rights of black men to fairly constructed juries, the continued resolve of the NAACP to push these cases to the Supreme Court indicates the importance of the issue and the constant need to legitimize these rights because of their lack of enforcement.

Although equal obligations to jury service regardless of race or color came from Reconstruction-era policy, the 1930s cases continued to reaffirm African American men's constitutional rights to a jury trial free of racial discrimination. They revived the Supreme Court's commitment to securing black rights to jury service obligations. In contrast, women could not count on the Supreme Court to mandate that they serve on juries under the same obligations as men. White women would have to delegitimize notions of gender difference and female privilege, such as the ones reaffirmed in these cases, which positioned them as innocent, vulnerable, and passive victims reliant on the paternalistic legal system and male jury for protection. These notions underpinned the sexually discriminatory policies impeding white women's access to the jury and equality before the law. Moreover, gendered assumptions and sexual stereotypes often reinforced notions of racial difference or the importance of racial segregation (as emphasized through sexual relationships between men and women of different races). Most of these cases also revolved around violence against women, generally white women, which showcases the assumptions made (or manufactured) about violent black men and vulnerable or victimized white women. These cases reaffirmed gendered assumptions—some of which perpetuated inflammatory and racially charged scenarios and all of which reinforced gendered notions of white women being weak, vulnerable, and innocent.

Racialized and gendered notions of citizenship and criminality worked in tandem in each of these cases. Contestations over racial difference relied on gendered understandings of citizenship. Black men relied on their own masculinity to lay claim to jury obligations as male citizens, while white men associated jury service with white men's protection of innocent white female victims. Black women receded in these trials, not obtaining privileges or pedestals bestowed on white women, nor joining black men as peers in the fight for equal citizenship. The interconnected nature of racial hierarchies and gendered citizenship informed all perspectives in the 1930s cases.

Black women were the most marginalized in these cases, because of their race *and* gender. Their gender eliminated them from the NAACP's strategy to affirm black men's jury service rights and prevented them from appearing as criminal menaces that prosecutions made black men out to be. Their race excluded them from the purview of state prosecutors, who imagined all women to be white and in need of protection. The general absence of black women from these cases and the marginalization of their appearance as witnesses and potential victims in these trials reveal the effects that overlapping categories of gender and race had on individuals' experiences with the justice system. Race and gender identities shaped where individuals fit in most of these proceedings and left little room for black women at all.

These cases also uncover how legal institutions work against producing outcomes reflective of an understanding of the overlapping and often murky facets of individuals' identities. Instead, the legal system encouraged adherence to precise standards and procedures, and it recognized fixed, distinctive (rather than overlapping or social constructed) categories. As a result, it discouraged more holistic approaches of understanding the complexity of constructing individuals' identities or how those identities shaped citizens' interactions with the courts or the law. This rigidity and indifference seems to provide a sense of authority to the legal system and to its supposed impartiality that creates a sense of fairness and objectivity that belies the justice of actual process or its outcome. This chapter reveals the centrality of black men and their claims to a gendered citizenship in early twentieth-century litigation and the effects of legal lynching on conceptions of juries.

Both groups—black men and all women—ultimately lost with these decisions. These cases were hollow victories for black defendants and the campaign for racial equality in jury service obligations. Reentrenching gendered understandings of criminality, victimization, and justice, these trials reproduced racist notions through gendered and sexualized scenarios of interracial interaction, reaffirmed the need for masculinized juries to protect white women, and marginalized the position and protection of black women provided by the court system. Not until the 1960s, when black women produced a direct assault on race and sex discrimination, did gendered, racialized conceptions of citizenship—particularly jury service—effectively change to ones more inclusive and democratic.

Notes

In writing this chapter, I have benefited from the comments of many individuals, including Paula Baker, Susan M. Hartmann, Lawrence Bowdish, Kevin Boyle, Audra Jennings, Martha S. Jones, Lindsey Patterson, Jessica Pliley, and David Stebenne. All the conference participants, and especially Carol Faulkner, Alison Parker, and Victoria Wolcott, helped improve my work. I am grateful for all of their advice, criticism, and encouragement.

1. Hale v. Commonwealth of Kentucky, 303 US 613 (1938), transcript of record, filed January 8, 1938, 80 pp., term year 1937. Transcripts and court records of the *Hale* and *Hollins* cases in this paper have been collected from the *U.S. Supreme Court Records and Briefs, 1832–1978* database, accessed March 18, 2008, http://galenet. galegroup.com.proxy.lib.ohiostate.edu/servlet/SCRB?uid=0&srchtp=a&ste=14&rc n=DW103704439, 17.

2. Leon A. Ransom, Charles H. Houston, Thurgood Marshall, and Edward P. Lovett, "Petition for Writ of Certiorari to the Court of Appeals of the Commonwealth of Kentucky and Brief in Support Thereof," *Hale*, 303 US 613, 1–33, 24.

3. The NAACP also assisted other cases pursuing the jury service question by producing resources for other lawyers and providing some financial support. The best-known jury service case of the 1930s was one of the famous Scottsboro cases, *Norris v. Alabama* (1935). The NAACP competed with the International Labor Defense, a more leftist workers' organization that strove for racial equality and equity, for the position of defending the eight black boys convicted and sentenced to death for the rape of two white women. The NAACP divided internally over the decision of whether or not to join the case by affiliating with the ILD. Ultimately, the NAACP backed away from the case, and the Scottsboro decision revealed the Supreme Court's determination to protect the constitutional rights of African Americans to juries constructed without race discrimination. The *Norris* decision became part of the precedent relied on by the NAACP court cases in *Hollins* and *Hale*. For more on the Scottsboro decision, see Dan T. Carter, *Scottsboro: A Tragedy of the American South*, rev. ed. (Baton Rouge: Louisiana State University Press, 1979); James Goodman, *Stories of Scottboro* (New York: Vintage Books, 1994); and James A. Miller, *Remembering Scottsboro: The Legacy of an Infamous Trial* (Princeton, NJ: Princeton University Press, 2009).

4. The case in which a white man approached several black women was the 1938 case, *Hale*, 303 US 613.

5. Barbara Young Welke, *Recasting American Liberty: Gender, Race, Law, and the Railroad Revolution, 1865–1920* (Cambridge: Cambridge University Press, 2001), 295.

6. For scholarship on women's jury service obligations, see Linda K. Kerber, "Woman Is the Center of Home and Family Life: Gwendolyn Hoyt and Jury Service

in the Twentieth Century," in *No Constitutional Right to Be Ladies: Women and the Obligations of Citizenship* (New York: Hill and Wang, 1998), 124–220; Gretchen Ritter, "Jury Service and Women's Citizenship Before and After the Nineteenth Amendment," *Law and History Review* 20, no. 3 (Fall 2002): 479–515; Ritter, *The Constitution as Social Design: Gender and Civic Membership in the American Constitutional Order* (Stanford, CA: Stanford University Press, 2006).

7. For the literature on black-on-white rape and its gendered, racialized context, see Martha Hodes, *Black Men, White Women: Illicit Sex in the 19th-Century South* (New Haven, CT: Yale University Press, 1997); Diane Miller Sommerville, *Rape and Race in the Nineteenth-Century South* (Chapel Hill: University of North Carolina Press, 2004); and Lisa Lindquist Dorr, *White Women, Rape, and the Power of Race in Virginia, 1900–1960* (Chapel Hill: University of North Carolina Press, 2004).

8. Crystal N. Feimster, *Southern Horrors: Women and the Politics of Rape and Lynching* (Cambridge: Harvard University Press, 2009), 5, 158.

9. Jacquelyn Dowd Hall, *Revolt against Chivalry: Jessie Daniel Ames and the Women's Campaign against Lynching*, rev. ed. (New York: Columbia University Press, 1993), 197–201. Hall mentioned that Ames and the Association of Southern Women for the Prevention of Lynching discussed legal lynchings and, in particular, the *Scottsboro* case. Despite its understanding of legal lynchings, the ASWPL still made arguments about restoring law and order in its antilynching campaign.

10. Feimster, *Southern Horrors*, 157.

11. Wilford H. Smith, "The Negro and the Law" in *The Negro Problem: A Series of Articles by Representative American Negroes of Today*, ed. Booker T. Washington (New York: Pott, 1903), 127–59, 135, 143, 136.

12. Smith, "A Negro's Right to Jury Representation," *Committee of Twelve for the Advancement of the Interests of the Negro Race*, ca. 1909, Cheyney, PA, Library of Congress Collection of Books by Colored Authors, Washington DC.

13. August Meier and Elliot Rudwick, "Attorneys Black and White: A Case Study of Race Relations within the NAACP," *Journal of American History*, 1976, 941n106.

14. Carter v. Texas, 177 US 442 (1900), Motion to Quash the Indictment, Error to the Court of Criminal Appeals of the State of Texas, transcript of record, filed January 20, 1899, in the US Supreme Court, October 1899, no. 193, 4.

15. Not every jury service case that went before the Supreme Court in the early twentieth century was decided in favor of the black defendant. The evidence had to persuade the court that discrimination had occurred (often through the use of testimony and demographic statistics) and not simply that the fact that no black men were on the jury meant that they were discriminated against in the process.

16. Benno C. Schmidt Jr., "Juries, Jurisdiction, and Race Discrimination: The Lost Promise of *Strauder v. West Virginia*," *Texas Law Review* 61, no. 1401 (1983): 1471. See also Christopher Waldrep, *Jury Discrimination: The Supreme Court, Public Opinion and a Grassroots Fight for Racial Equality in Mississippi* (Athens: University of Georgia Press, 2010). His book reveals the plight of black men in the early twentieth-century southern justice system, their fight for trials by their peers, and the Supreme Court's inaction to prevent or punish race discrimination on juries.

17. Schmidt, "Juries," 1471–72. The cases referred to here are *Martin v. Texas*, 200 US 316 (1909) and *Thomas v. Texas*, 212 US 278 (1909).

18. Ibid., 1470–71.

19. Manfred Berg, *"The Ticket to Freedom": The NAACP and the Struggle for Black Political Integration* (Gainesville: University of Florida Press, 2007), 71. Berg argues that the NAACP found the legal system to be the best place to reform, since, especially in the South, the black community had extremely limited ability to mobilize politically en masse or to open protest without fear of violence. Berg has also argued that unlike the "bold sense of grand expectations" of the movement for racial equality in the 1960s, "the prevailing mood among racial reformers in the early twentieth century was largely defensive" (11).

20. In fact, the NAACP mentioned the prospect of black women serving on juries only in one 1937 memorandum about how black women could make themselves available and eligible to serve on juries in New York; see Thurgood Marshall to Joseph A. Tolbert, November 27, 1939, frames 310–12, reel 16, pt. 8, series A, microfilm edition, NAACP Papers, Library of Congress, Washington, DC.

21. Genna Rae McNeil, *Groundwork: Charles Hamilton Houston and the Struggle for Civil Rights* (Philadelphia: University of Pennsylvania Press, 1983), 6; In part, the NAACP could rely more on black lawyers because more African Americans became lawyers. By 1925 black lawyers created a separate American Bar Association, and by the 1930s the civil rights movement depended on the services of most of the 1,175 black lawyers in the country; see Meier and Rudwick, "Attorneys Black and White." But J. Clay Smith Jr. notes that there was a decline in the numbers of African American lawyers in some southern states in the 1930s; see *Emancipation: The Making of the Black Lawyer, 1844–1944* (Philadelphia: University of Pennsylvania Press, 1993), 17, 341. Berg, *Ticket to Freedom*, 85; Mark V. Tushnet, *Making Civil Rights Law: Thurgood Marshall and the Supreme Court* (New York: Oxford University Press, 1996), 57. The legal network of the NAACP, particularly in the South, was somewhat limited in the 1930s and 1940s. Lawyers often looked to the NAACP for financing, but they faced severe challenges and violence by defending black men in the courts. Black attorneys faced even more hardship than their white counterparts. For example, Tushnet describes that Leon A. Ransom, a NAACP advocate, referred to the NAACP contact in South Carolina as "the lawyer in South Carolina." See Tushnet, *Making Civil Rights Law*, 58.

22. Meier and Rudwick, "Attorneys Black and White," 913–46; Kenneth A. Mack offers a glimpse at the experiences of black female lawyers of the 1920s, 1930s, and 1940s by exploring the life of Sadie Alexander as well as her correspondence with the small group of black women lawyers of her generation. His article reveals a difference in the perspective of this earlier generation of black women lawyers and the later generation that included more equal rights feminists, like Pauli Murray. See "A Social History of Everyday Practice: Sadie T. M. Alexander and the Incorporation of Black Women into the American Legal Profession, 1925–1960," *Cornell Law Review* 87 (September 2002): 1405–74. Pauli Murray's interactions with Howard Law School and even her mentor, Leon A. Ransom, reveal a gendered understanding of the legal profession and women's roles in society that complement the approach speared by the NAACP in these trials. See Pauli Murray, *Song in a Weary Throat: An American Pilgrimage* (New York: Harper and Row, 1987).

23. "Crawford to Have Defense by All-Negro Council," NAACP press release, November 10, 1933, reel 7, NAACP Papers, 166–67; Charles Houston to Walter

White, October 17, 1933, in "Crawford to Have Defense," 6–7; McNeil, *Groundwork*, 90.

24. RNB [Roger Nash Baldwin] to undesignated, August 25, 1933, reel 6, NAACP Papers, 871. Other pleas for interracial council because of concerns about a black lawyer questioning white witnesses, "particularly white women," are in Walter White to Dr. Dennis Freeman, October 31, 1933, reel 7, NAACP Papers, 104–5.

25. Butler R. Wilson to Walter White, February 20, 1933, reel 6, NAACP Papers, 406.

26. Houston to White, March 12, 1933, reel 6, NAACP Papers, 465–69.

27. Houston to White, March 10, 1933, reel 6, NAACP Papers, 486.

28. Charles H. Houston and Edward P. Lovett, "Affidavit on the Exclusion of Negroes from Jury Service in Loudon County, State of Virginia," March 10, 1933, reel 6, NAACP Papers, 488–93.

29. "Colored Man Is Seated on Jury for First Time," *Star*, June 12, 1933, reel 6, NAACP Papers, 753.

30. Walter White to the Branches, re. Crawford Case, October 20, 1933, reel 6, NAACP Papers, 916; "Stay Granted Crawford Pending Appeal to Supreme Court," July 17, 1933, reel 6, NAACP Papers, 863.

31. Crawford faced trial for the murder of one woman, though another woman was found dead in the same place at the same time, and he could have faced charges for that murder as well, though he did not during this trial. In fact, he declined an appeal after conviction because he worried that he might be tried for the second crime and sentenced to death. Along with Houston, Leon A. Ransom, Edward P. Lovett, and James G. Tyson composed the defense team.

32. "Crawford to Have Defense," 166–67.

33. McNeil, *Groundwork*, 91–92.

34. "*Commonwealth of Virginia v. Crawford*: Transcript of the Shorthand Report of the Proceedings, etc., December 12 to 16, 1933," prepared for Charles Houston (1933), no frame numbers available, reel 17, NAACP Papers, 94–95 (hereafter cited in text).

35. Black lawyers in the South, especially those fighting cases for the NAACP or racial equality, faced violence during their activities, sometimes requiring protection from white community members.

36. Charles Houston waived his opening statement.

37. McNeil, *Groundwork*, 92–95; McNeil details the problems the defense had with confirming Crawford's story, and the difficult position Houston and the other NAACP lawyers faced during the trial when Crawford's story changed, threatening the case. The alibi witness, a black woman and former girlfriend of Crawford's named Bertie de Neal, changed her testimony, helping the prosecution. Eventually, Houston felt Crawford was not a completely sympathetic figure or one perfectly situated for the NAACP's campaign.

38. While Walter White extolled the case as a success, Houston was not as thrilled with the outcome, finding out that Crawford had lied about his alibi. For more discussion on Houston's position and the publicity of the case, see McNeil, *Groundwork*, 90–95.

39. Ibid., 103–4. McNeil outlines the disagreement and growing rift between the NAACP and the International Labor Defense, citing the aftermath of the

Crawford case as one of the sites of contention apparent through contemporary media coverage.

40. Charles Houston and Leon Ransom, "Suggested Outline of Procedure for Attack upon an Indictment by Reason of the Unconstitutional Exclusion of Negroes from the Grand Jury (Based upon the Procedure Followed in Commonwealth of Virginia v. Crawford," reel 7, NAACP Papers, 797–802. For information about the promotion of this document, see "Jury Exclusion Target of County-Wide NAACP Drive," *Baltimore Afro-American*, October 20, 1934.

41. Hollins v. Oklahoma, 295 US 394 (1935), transcript of record, October term 1934, no. 686, 629–50. In 1932 the court of appeals in Oklahoma granted Hollins a new trial, finding that he had been intimidated by a mob and could not voluntarily waive his constitutional rights. This trial was his second trial.

42. McNeil, *Groundwork*, 122; For an overview of the *Hollins* case, see Roger W. Cummins, "'Lily-White' Juries on Trial: The Civil Rights Defense of Jess Hollins," *Chronicles of Oklahoma* 63 (1985): 166–85.

43. "Jess Hollins Granted Stay 30 Hours before Execution," reel 9, NAACP Papers, 313–14. Houston secured the stay in August 1932, and the NAACP defended Hollins thereafter. At this point, the ILD left the defense. Hollins's first trial, with defense by the ILD, was voided because of its questionable nature, having taken place in a jail without defense council. See "Hollins' Death Sentence to US Supreme Court," *New York Age*, March 3, 1934, reel 9, NAACP Papers, 287.

44. Roscoe Dunjee, "Honest Indictments," ca. 1934, reel 9, NAACP Papers, 474–75.

45. Dunjee, quoted in Cummins, "Lily-White," 176.

46. Smith supposed that "between 1935 and 1944, the number of black lawyers in Oklahoma declined, perhaps because of the continued exclusion of blacks from juries." He also mentioned that he found no record of a black woman being admitted to the Oklahoma bar before 1945; see *Emancipation*, 510–11.

47. *Hollins*, 295 US 394, 12 (hereafter cited in text).

48. Charles Houston, William L. Houston, and Edward P. Lovett, "Petition for the Writ of Certiorari to the Supreme Court of the State of Oklahoma and Brief in Support Thereof," in *Hollins*, 295 US 394, 2, 12, 15.

49. A per curiam decision is an unsigned one issued by the court as a whole. This decision referred to the precedents set in Neal v. Delaware, 103 US 170 (1881) and one of the Scottsboro decisions, Norris v. Alabama, 294 US 587 (1935).

50. Cummins, "Lily-White," 166–86.

51. Michael J. Klarman, *From Jim Crow to Civil Rights: The Supreme Court and the Struggle for Racial Equality* (New York: Oxford University Press, 2004), 154.

52. Ransom et al., "Petition for Writ," transcript of record, no. 680.

53. *Hale*, 303 US 613, 61; Leon A. Ransom, Charles H. Houston, Thurgood Marshall, and Edward P. Lovett, "Petitioner's Brief on Argument," *Hale*, 303 US 613, transcript of record, 9.

54. Ransom et al., "Petition for Writ," 24.

55. *Hale*, 303 US 613, 60–61.

56. Ransom et al., "Petition for Writ," 26–27; *Hale*, 303 US 613, transcript of record, 60–63.

57. *Hale*, 303 US 613, 39–41.

58. The instructions to the jury began with a gendered greeting: "Gentlemen of the Jury," and from the names appearing in the record, I believe it is a fairly good assumption that the individuals on the trial jury were all men; ibid., 4–5, 16.

59. Ibid., 6–14; Ransom et al., "Petitioner's Brief on Argument," transcript of record, 14.

60. Ransom et al., "Petition for Writ," transcript of record, 2. The defense stipulated that allegedly only blacks served on a special jury in 1921 that was summoned to try an African American. However, the names of these jurors were not a part of the regular jury list and were not selected in the regular fashion.

61. Ransom et al., "Petitioner's Brief on Argument," transcript of record, 14.

62. *Hale*, 303 US 613.

Part 4

Sexuality, Class, and Morality

Chapter 7

A "Corrupting Influence"

Idleness and Sexuality during the Great Depression

Michele Mitchell

Anna Pauline Murray found herself fighting to remain in college, pay for a room at the Harlem YWCA, and eat on a regular basis during a time when the economy of the United States was itself under considerable strain. A young woman of African descent, Murray had moved to New York City from Durham, North Carolina, in the fall of 1926 due to her determination not to attend a segregated institution in the South. Murray lived with a cousin in Brooklyn during the 1926–27 academic year, mainly so that she could supplement her education to meet Hunter College's entrance requirements and establish residency in New York, which would allow her to attend Hunter—"the poor girl's Radcliffe"—without paying tuition. Economic necessity forced the resourceful, determined Murray to go back to North Carolina for a year to work. Murray nonetheless returned to New York in the fall of 1928 for what would be "the only carefree year" that she would have as a university student.[1] Carefree times would soon end for other members of Murray's generation. Both financial security and a life relatively free from responsibility had already been elusive for many children, adolescents, and young adults during the 1920s, especially those whose families tried to make a living off of the land. If the mid- to late 1920s witnessed a widening income gap between the working poor and wealthy, the 1930s would bring trying times to a stunning range of people living in the United States.[2]

By the fall of 1930, Murray had been forced to drop out of school, after which she routinely competed with "hundreds of men" for "a half-dozen jobs posted in hastily scrawled handwriting" on employment bureau boards.[3] That "the vast majority of unemployed Black women" in Manhattan were generally "marginalized in separate unemployment offices in Harlem" certainly did not help matters.[4] Perhaps the fact that the city's unemployment offices rarely offered jobs to women—let alone women of color—encouraged Murray to get married, only to find her union to William Wynn a "dreadful mistake." The marriage lasted but a few months. Murray's fortunes looked upward when she found office work, but once she lost that job, she headed to California during the spring of 1931 in an attempt to begin anew.[5]

As luck would have it, Murray was able to catch a ride with an acquaintance in New York who was driving back home to Vallejo, California. Shortly after making the trek across country, however, Murray received news that her Aunt Pauline—the woman who raised Murray following her mother's untimely death when Murray was just three years old—had become ill and "wanted [her] to come home to Durham as soon as possible." With precious few resources of her own and no money forthcoming from relatives for a return trip to the East Coast, Murray donned androgynous clothing that "made [her] appear to be a small teenaged boy," went to an Oakland rail yard, jumped on a train, and joined the ranks of youthful "products of the Depression, who rode freights or hitchhiked from town to town in search of work." She also, at some point, started calling herself "Pauli."[6] A few years later, following a brief stint working for the Urban League, Murray would again share an experience that thousands of young women and men had during the 1930s: she attended a federally sponsored camp. Race, class, and gender certainly shaped Pauli Murray's young adulthood, yet the moment in which she came of age would ultimately result in Murray having experiences not altogether dissimilar from others of her generation who hailed from markedly different backgrounds.

This chapter focuses largely on transiency among youth during the initial years of the Great Depression and explores attendant discourses about idleness in the process. Transiency was "one of the earliest open sores of the depression" according to Harry Hopkins, a one-time settlement worker who directed the Federal Emergency Relief Administration (FERA), the Civil Works Administration (CWA), and then the Works Progress Administration (WPA) between mid-1933 and the end of 1938.[7] Other administrators, policy makers, and activists believed that transiency would lead to undesirable and permanent changes, especially among Americans between sixteen and twenty-four years of age.[8] The Children's Bureau reported that "over 200,000 transient boys" existed during the early 1930s. A chief inspector for the Nashville, Chattanooga, and St. Louis Railway offered a higher, more inclusive estimate in the fall of 1933 when he claimed that, "200,000 women and perhaps one-half million boys between the ages of 15 and 25 are daily hitch-hiking about the country and hoboing on passenger and freight trains." Transiency and homelessness were linked in discourse as well as quotidian lives, despite the fact that homeless persons did not always leave their communities and regardless of the reality that some people who hit the road actually had someplace that they could call home. As difficult as it was to arrive at precise figures when it came to transients and the dispossessed during the early 1930s, an estimated one and a half to two million homeless existed by 1933 when Franklin Delano Roosevelt's New Deal began.[9]

Young Americans in their teens and twenties, many who simply could not afford to continue their education or whose schools were closed due to insufficient funding, faced a notable predicament during the 1930s: they entered the labor market during a moment of economic calamity and then competed for scarce jobs with older adults, who typically had longer work histories and more experience. People born roughly between 1907 and 1922 in the United States also grew to maturity or entered adulthood when the Great Depression created a new population of people adrift. Activists, intellectuals, government officials, and pundits often viewed this burgeoning, often peripatetic group as being distinct from dissolute vagrants, street-corner habitués, "professional idlers," and "incurable tramps and bums" who lived hand-to-mouth long before the stock market crash of 1929.[10] All the same, many academics, journalists, administrators, policy makers, and businesspeople in the United States shared overriding concerns about idleness and the idle between late 1929 and the onset of World War II. They worried that inactivity resulting from unemployment could be nothing less than toxic, that idleness led to vice, crime, degeneracy, and debilitating rootlessness.[11]

I am particularly concerned in this chapter with camp programs established during the Roosevelt administration. In addition to Civilian Conservation Corps (CCC) camps for unemployed young men, New Deal camps also served transients of various ages and migrant workers; Pauli Murray attended one of the short-lived camps for women. Government-funded camps did not serve every person in need. Still, New Deal camps attempted to alleviate widespread misery and encourage productive activity on a mass level. The camps were also a form of social control meant to curb transiency and discourage the careworn from succumbing to subversive behaviors and ideologies. Ironically, perhaps, the camps themselves attracted controversy. Some detractors claimed that camps promoted deviant behaviors, incubated radical tendencies, facilitated an indifferent attitude toward work as well as moral propriety, and even enabled idleness itself.

Since this chapter emerges out of a work-in-progress, my arguments are somewhat preliminary.[12] My analysis pivots to an extent on the experiences of Pauli Murray for two reasons, one of which is evidentiary and the other historiographical. I have found precious few girls or women of African descent thus far who produced accounts about either life "on the road" or in a New Deal camp during the Depression.[13] Pauli Murray might not have written extensively on these fronts, but she did publish a veiled account of her exploits on the road. Murray additionally incorporated brief reminiscences of her experience with what she termed "a female counterpart to the CCC camps" into an autobiography, *Song in a Weary Throat*.[14] She purposefully saved ephemera and mementos from this period of her life as well. Although I hardly presume to make overarching claims based on a woman who was, in many regards, a singular individual, I attempt to situate Murray within a specific context. Such contextualization results in a noticeable tension: this chapter is both about black women and *not* about black women. This seeming paradox exists in part because it comes from work that shall consider "race" in a fairly capacious manner, but it also exists because women of African descent are generally not discussed at length in either Depression-era texts or recent historiography about transiency and government-funded camps.[15] Moreover, work programs during the New Deal tended to prioritize men, as did federally sponsored camps. People of color in the United States faced various forms of discrimination when it came to relief efforts as well.[16] I therefore feel that it is critical to consider how Pauli Murray and other young African-descended women experienced transiency and an important but ultimately failed New Deal effort to meet the needs of women. Just as significantly, analyzing aspects of Murray's life enables me to speak to a range of dynamics and discourses of the 1930s, only some of which are about race.

Depression-era commentators could (and did) infuse idleness with racialized undertones. While African Americans were certainly rendered as unmotivated and lazy in both racialist discourse and popular culture during the 1930s, herein I shall primarily consider overarching moral and sexualized valences of supposed idleness. At a time when "leisure became a battleground for widespread ambivalence about technology, social change, economic change, and new social habits," idleness—whether loafing, aimless wandering, going to a beer parlor to wile away hours once spent at work, or waiting around an employment agency hoping that a job might materialize—retained its longtime association with sloth, personal failing, and immorality.[17] To be sure, the indifference typically associated with idleness could be considered particularly problematic when it came to the occasionally overlapping minority populations of American Indians, Latinas/os, Asians and African-descended Americans. Indifference and idleness were nevertheless also considered problematic in terms of people considered white, especially if they were poor.[18]

Idleness, like leisure, assumed various meanings during the Depression, some of which had gendered and generational implications; "idleness" became convenient shorthand for a host of social problems. Social workers, reformers, sociologists, activists, physicians, and ministers pointedly associated prolonged inactivity among idle youth, women, and men with increased alcohol consumption, delinquency, promiscuous behavior, mental instability, domestic discord, and desertion.[19] Commentators could be quick to make overarching arguments about what they believed idleness would do to the nation's moral fiber. In 1930, for example, the veteran activist, educator, and African American club woman Nannie Helen Burroughs feared that escalating unemployment and mass inactivity were metastasizing into moral cancers as the United States sank deeper into economic depression. "The homes of the masses are packed with idle men who are resorting to every kind of vice to fill up their idle hours and satiate their lower passions," Burroughs wrote. "No people can live in enforced idleness without succumbing to the vile, lustful, imbruting all-destroying power of it."[20] A minister named James M. Boston put the matter in more euphemistic but no less evocative terms five years later. For Boston, idleness was simply sin—"the bane of body and mind, and the nurse of naughtiness."[21] When Burroughs and her contemporaries referred to unemployment as "enforced idleness," such a reference not only captured a condition endured by millions during the Great Depression but could also be suffused with implications that mass inactivity was at once a situational imposition, an unnatural state, and morally corrosive.[22]

The relationship between work, workers, and time was undergoing significant transformation in the United States when the Great Depression hit. Adult workers found it increasingly difficult to secure—let alone retain—steady, full-time jobs after the stock market crash of 1929, as ongoing mechanization both eliminated jobs and reduced workers' hours.[23] Due to the confluence of a rapidly sagging economy with an increased reliance on technology in various employment sectors, unemployment rates soared during the early 1930s. "Between 13 and 15 million people were unemployed" during the winter of 1932–33; at the peak of the depression in 1933, approximately 25 percent of the nation's workers had no gainful employ.[24] An unemployment rate around 40 percent in Los Angeles fueled hysteria in California that resulted in the mass expulsion of Mexican immigrants and Mexican Americans from that state. Anywhere from thirty-five thousand to six hundred thousand people of Mexican descent, including individuals born as US citizens, were repatriated to Mexico from the United States during the Depression. Indeed, "in virtually every locale in which [Mexican workers] lived in substantial numbers," people of Mexican descent were blamed for high unemployment levels, particularly by nativists. Several cities in the East and Midwest had markedly high unemployment rates, and black workers were hit particularly hard. In Harlem, for example, the unemployment rate for blacks was about 50 percent in 1932; in Philadelphia it stood at 56 percent. Approximately 55 percent of black women in Chicago and perhaps more than 70 percent of black women in Detroit were jobless during the early thirties; 40 percent of black men were unemployed in Chicago, and 60 percent of black men were unemployed in Detroit. In southern cities such as Norfolk and Atlanta, between 65 and 80 percent of unemployed and underemployed black workers were forced to turn to relief to survive.[25]

As African Americans streamed toward cities where relief networks were stronger than in the rural South, the Philadelphia-based *Brown American* contended that the combination of relief programs and mass unemployment was resulting in hosts of inactive black workers sitting about on neighborhood stoops or in "the corner taproom" with "nothing to look forward to but the weekly check."[26] The *Chicago Defender* actively discouraged both continued migration to the city during the Depression and idle, dissolute association in black neighborhoods. In a 1931 editorial cartoon that depicted "uncouth youth . . . loiter[ing] all over the steps and on . . . balustrades" in front of an urban apartment house, the *Defender* archly implied that such young men did little more than insult women and compromise neighborhoods by creating "breeding places for crime."[27] Idleness was linked to urban unrest as well. For example, in the wake of a March 1935 riot in Harlem that started after policemen beat a teenager accused of shoplifting, one journalist noted that while some "observers [were] . . . certain that the disturbance was fostered by radical white men," the root causes of the riot could actually be found in "the corrupting influence of idleness."[28]

Whereas one writer quipped in the *Los Angeles Times* during the summer of 1933 that "all idleness and no play . . . make[s] Jack a dull boy," many more commentators worried that inactivity nurtured dangerous sentiments and loathsome activities.[29] Idleness was frequently associated with fomenting communism or socialism. A 1933 letter to Harry Hopkins of FERA from a railway inspector named Frank Fitzpatrick contained such an assertion. Fitzpatrick claimed that "communists, radicals, and anarchists" were routinely indoctrinating transients who rode "hither and yon in aimless fashion upon the freight and passenger trains of the nation," either looking for work or seeking escape. Along similar lines, a *Los Angeles Times* reader opined in 1935 that the idle had "too much time in which to develop Communistic ideas and leisure in which to spread them to their fellow loafers." As late as 1939 Mary McLeod Bethune contended that an underutilized "rising army of trained Negro youth" could well "prove fertile ground for the seeds of resentment and of false political and economic doctrine."[30] As much as idleness could prove worrisome from an ideological and political standpoint for some observers, it was just as frequently portrayed as having a deleterious impact on morals.

Indeed, the "corrupting influence of idleness" arguably had the power to penetrate sites where workers congregated in attempts to secure gainful employment. For example, in a 1935 *Crisis* article on domestic workers, Ella Baker and Marvel Cooke noted that black women who waited around for work in urban "slave markets" did so in the proximity of women engaged in prostitution. Whereas one Harlem journalist claimed in 1933 that few unemployed black women were "resorting to the 'pick-up game,'" Baker and Cooke subtly implied two years later that "economic necessity" eventually compelled at least a few black women unable to secure jobs to offer "human love [as] . . . a marketable commodity" instead.[31] Some out-of-work women across the country from a range of racial and ethnic backgrounds who chose temporary prostitution over seemingly perpetual unemployment were probably able to make a few dollars. A *New Republic* article by Emily Hahn nonetheless claimed that such women who turned to sex work "found the field overcrowded."[32]

The *Crisis* and *New Republic* articles likely alarmed more than a few readers, but an item in the *New York Times* from August 28, 1933, sounded a tocsin of its own. The *Times* article stressed that young workers had been especially hard hit by the Depression; it additionally maintained that the majority of idle individuals were under the age of twenty. Although this article based its claim about youth and idleness on merely two surveys, both "technological advances and changing economic conditions" during the 1930s did indeed create an increased "period of idleness [for] . . . American youth" between the time that they left school until they could find consistent, paid work.[33] When the Depression peaked, an estimated seven million workers between the ages of sixteen and twenty-four were jobless and more than a quarter of a million young people were roaming the United States looking for sustenance, shelter, and work. Unemployment rates for young women and men between sixteen and twenty-four were more than 40 percent in some states and 50 percent in others.[34] Whereas some young transients sought adventure when they hit the road, and others might be classified as "runaways," many young people left their communities to look for work and to ease the economic burden on their families. As one woman who wrote to FERA in 1933 put it, many of the "youngsters" who "struck out for distant fields" were actually ambitious and loathed the prospect of "remain[ing] in idleness and dependence at home."[35] Transient or not, New Deal or not, many young people remained underemployed or unemployed throughout the 1930s. As late as 1937, when the New Deal engaged millions of Americans in work projects, almost four million youth remained out of work.[36]

If young men and women with nothing but time on their hands were often considered more problematic than underoccupied middle-aged and elderly people, idle youth also stoked a host of anxieties that swirled around sexuality. Some public health officials went so far as to claim that unoccupied youth were more likely to engage in "'wrongful' sex activity," namely masturbation, homosexuality, and premarital intercourse. Concerns about masturbation primarily focused on boys and young men, but anxieties about premarital sex were more general. One pamphlet, for example, suggested that exercise and sport would give girls a "healthy tired feeling" that would effectively curtail any sexual urges that they might have.[37] Creating jobs and building recreational facilities therefore assumed particular importance for activists, reformers, and politicians concerned about policing both youth and their sexuality.[38] Significantly, "wholesome" activities for people in their teens and twenties, such as chaperoned dances, hiking, sports, and work projects, all encouraged physical movement; such physical activity was viewed as being a healthy way to maintain idle bodies, channel sexual urges, and provide constructive activity for millions of young women and men at risk of becoming an "army of disillusioned, bewildered youth" that constituted "a potential menace to the social order of the nation."[39] A young University of Minnesota researcher named Thomas Minehan studied this "potential menace," focusing on a particular cohort of ostensibly idle youth whose activities generated both commentary and concern during the Hoover administration and throughout the first two terms of Franklin Roosevelt's presidency.

In 1932 Thomas Minehan was working on a master's thesis that stemmed out of his interest in "men who went down with the boom in 1929." Whereas Minehan had already collected oral histories, he felt that the "truth in regard to the homeless . . . could never be ascertained" by approaching down-and-outers as a sociology graduate student. That November, Minehan dressed in tattered clothes that he hoped would make him look like a vagrant and huddled "in a bread line in the cold and rain." This one experience convinced Minehan that masquerading as an unemployed transient gave him prime access to "opinions and attitudes" that simply could not be "ascertained by other methods." Somewhere along the way he also decided not to limit his study to males, and he turned his attention toward youth in general; Minehan eventually estimated that "about one child tramp in twenty is a girl." Minehan hit the open road and lived as a transient so that he could "experience in all seasons and under all conditions the daily life of a boy or girl living in box cars." Minehan roamed through six states (mostly in the Midwest) whenever he could over the next two years. He claimed to have collected "500 life histories of boys and girls . . . on the bum" during his fieldwork, in addition to having conducted more than 1,400 interviews. Minehan published his provocative findings as *Boy and Girl Tramps of America* in 1934. Given the book's compelling and even sensational content, Minehan took pains to assert that he neither embellished nor "substantially changed" any "incidents" or dynamics described in his work.[40] *Boy and Girl Tramps* was generally well received and most critics were convinced that Minehan's text was neither exaggerated nor fiction.[41]

Minehan's book tapped into popular interest that persisted throughout the Depression about young people on the road. Periodicals such as *Survey*, *Harper's*, and *Literary Digest* ran stories about transients of various ages; narratives—be they fictionalized, attributable, pseudonymous, or dubious—and novels addressed the phenomenon of youthful migrants roaming the road. Pauli Murray even published an account in Nancy Cunard's edited collection, *Negro: An Anthology* (1934) of how she encountered "veteran hoboes, suckers, gamblers, murderers, cowboys" and other assorted characters when she hopped freights from California back to the East Coast in 1931. Murray did not reveal that she was a woman in her account but she did briefly address the hostility and danger that black freight hoppers could face.[42]

In addition to print sources, at least three Depression-era movies other than the film adaptation of John Steinbeck's *The Grapes of Wrath* portrayed the trials and travails of young transients: *Wild Boys of the Road*, *Boy Slaves*, and *Girls of the Road*.[43] These three films all underscore that sexual assault was a likely fate for young women who were on the road, homeless, or otherwise victimized by economic hardship. In *Wild Boys of the Road*, a railway brakeman rapes a girl who is temporarily left alone in a boxcar by other young transients. The lone adolescent female character in *Boy Slaves* is the sexual prey of a handsome, young, yet brutish turpentine camp overseer who ultimately seems intent on forcing himself on her. And, in addition to its palpable lesbian subtext, *Girls of the Road* features young female transients who endure predatory men, sexual degradation, assault, and untimely death. Both *Wild Boys of the Road* and *Boy Slaves* emphasize that teenaged boys who hit the road looking for work faced their share of bodily peril. A major character in *Wild Boys of the Road* undergoes a partial leg amputation following an accident in a rail yard, and an incidental character is hospitalized after eating rancid food "fit for a dog." In *Boy Slaves*, wandering youth are reduced to backbreaking peonage with dire results: extreme dizziness causes one malnourished teen to fall from a tree, which results in the loss of an arm; another boy dies—albeit heroically—from being hit in the back by a stray bullet.[44]

Wild Boys of the Road, Girls of the Road, and Boy Slaves each tried to dissuade young people from roaming in search of work by portraying transiency in a relatively gritty and grim manner. The attempted realism in *Wild Boys of the Road* might have been meant to discourage youngsters from leaving home, but the film did not necessarily have such an effect on its viewers.[45] Robert Symmonds, who was a teenaged transient during the Depression, later claimed that *Wild Boys of the Road* was anything but a deterrent for him and many of his contemporaries. "Kids loved the movie," Symmonds recalled, "it put ideas in your head. . . . Nothing was going to happen to you, you thought."[46] At least some youthful filmgoers at decade's end likely had similar reactions to *Girls of the Road* and *Boy Slaves* in that these films also contained plucky (and at times naive) characters willing to cast about for work rather than expect financial support from parents with dwindling, few, or no resources. If *Wild Boys of the Road* was the only film in release when *Boy and Girl Tramps of America* was published, some of Minehan's young informants might have been intrigued themselves by other portrayals of life on the road in popular culture, some of which were textual and had been published between the 1890s and the late 1920s.[47] Significantly, Minehan's book—not unlike *Wild Boys of the Road* and its filmic successors—made it abundantly clear that many young women and men who actually became transients had rather compelling reasons to leave home.

Boy and Girl Tramps of America covered a range of subjects, including life before the Depression. Many of Minehan's subjects had either turbulent or unstable home lives before economic calamity hit. Some had been abandoned, their parents had married multiple times, or they had been shunted from home to home; others had lost a parent to death, were the children of alcoholics, endured physical (and probably sexual) abuse, or witnessed routine domestic violence.[48] If a number of Minehan's young subjects had known domestic discord or even privation before the Depression hit, life at home only became harder with rising unemployment, both in terms of their parents' inability to make enough money and their own unemployment. Not all of Minehan's young informants came from violent or hardscrabble backgrounds, but "hard times" helped "dr[i]ve them away from home," too.[49]

As Minehan explored the forces that pushed youth onto the road, he significantly concluded that idle urban youth were especially susceptible to vagrancy. Rather than "wait around cities for a job," youth on the road hoped that they could improve their situation by looking beyond their own communities.[50] Minehan discussed how they traveled by rail and road, as well as how they obtained food, shelter, and clothing. He additionally covered young transients' "religious life," "political and social philosophy," and what he called "their tribal life." Not only did Minehan believe that the young transients he encountered "should be in high schools and homes" instead of "box cars and hobo jungles," he also concluded that many of them were having inappropriate experiences, especially those who had barely entered their teen years.[51] Minehan therefore wrote a fairly frank chapter on sexuality, which he opened by noting that "on the road now boys in great numbers and girls in lesser ones are learning about life—and who can learn about life and ignore sex?" Minehan made relatively fleeting references to venereal disease and masturbation. His discussion of attempted rape between older men and boys as well as consensual sexual relationships between "wolves and their little 'lambs'" was somewhat more detailed.[52] Minehan was all but silent on lesbian relationships in this chapter on "Sex Life."

Thomas Minehan had decidedly more to say about heterosexual practices, dynamics, and interactions among transient youth, not to mention between young people and older adults. According to Minehan, many young and presumably heterosexual transients who were sexually active with one another "pose[d] as brother and sister on the main stem . . . [but lived] as man and wife in the jungle." Pretending to be siblings was often beneficial to unmarried transient couples. At times, rail men allowed fictive sister-brother pairs to ride trains when they refused single-sex groups or individuals; local residents and shop owners could also be more willing to provide clothing and edibles to ersatz siblings. Young women who traveled in such pairs—or even in larger mixed-sex groups—were probably somewhat less vulnerable to sexual assault by strangers as well. Although Minehan acknowledged that some young women in couples were eventually abandoned, he said little about unplanned pregnancy. Beyond his acknowledgment that some young male transients "were suddenly forced" to pick up and head out if they impregnated a girl, Minehan maintained—if not completely convincingly—that none of the girls he encountered "feared pregnancy."[53]

Minehan explicitly addressed promiscuity among girls on the road. He described "maverick" girls who were "available to any and all boys in the camp including adults," who associated with boy groups and had sex with most or all of them or who went "from jungle to jungle and from box car to box car without discrimination."[54] Minehan could be sympathetic toward girls who turned to prostitution on the road out of hunger and desperation, yet transient girls who had serial sexual encounters perplexed him:

On a freight pulling South one night a skinny little girl of sixteen with dishwater eyes and matted fair hair left the company of three boys . . . , who were perhaps a little slow, for a box car of older and more vigorous males. All night she entertained them. . . . Two of us, fearing the child might be murdered, complained to the brakie. . . . He went to the car and demanded the girl. . . . "You big fat fool," she called him. . . . "Why can't you let a girl alone when she isn't hurting you? Everything was fine . . . and now you've spoiled it all."

This young woman was, according to Minehan, "a little bit drunk and very undressed" when the brakeman separated her from her apparent sexual partners and placed her in a separate boxcar. Minehan also claimed that she soon escaped her imposed isolation, only to be pursued by "two dozen men"—men with whom she would presumably have serial or group sex.[55]

Minehan was hardly alone in noticing that some young women transients engaged in fairly frequent sex on the rails. In 1933, for example, an assistant probation supervisor in Washington, DC, Edgar Gerlach, wrote to a FERA administrator who dealt with transient camps about a teenaged girl from Kansas who had been charged with violating the Mann Act. This particular sixteen-year-old "started out hitch-hiking . . . through Oklahoma, New Mexico, and Colorado," and she allegedly "ha[d] been rather generous in her co-habitating activities along the road." For Gerlach—and perhaps for Minehan as well—such a young woman was a vexing sort of transient who merited assistance, supervision, shelter, and possibly corrective measures if it was not practical or possible for her to return home.[56]

When Minehan briefly addressed race in his chapter about sexuality, he observed that whereas young African American and Filipino males he met "boasted of relations with white girls or women," none of the white male transients he encountered would "admi[t] to sex relations with a colored girl." He said nothing explicit about sex lives of young women transients of color. In fact, many of Minehan's descriptions of girl transients that he met suggest that they were white; one of the only references to women of color in *Boy and Girl Tramps* appears when Minehan noted that black women had a reputation among transients as being relatively generous in terms of sparing food and small change. Whether one young white man who claimed that he "never asked a black woman for anything . . . that [he] didn't get" was also referring to sex was left to the reader's imagination.[57]

The relative absence of young African American women (not to mention other young women of color) in Minehan's text is not necessarily surprising. During both the late nineteenth and early twentieth centuries, both homelessness and transiency were typically gendered as male in popular discourse as "widely shared values about sex roles prevailed to render the transient woman . . . [as] marginal . . . in an already marginal culture." "Tramp" could be gendered in that its meanings for women could "denote not a transient worker, as it did for men, but rather a sexual outcaste [*sic*]." The very term "hobo" was also firmly associated with whiteness for many Americans. And, quite significantly, "unattached women comprised only one to three percent of the general transient population" during the Depression.[58] If "the female drifter remained an anomaly" during the early twentieth century and if some Depression-era observers claimed that the majority of transients were white, public acknowledgment of transient African American women could be fleeting, if not infrequent.[59]

When, for example, the Emergency Relief Administration of New Jersey published a short study titled *Negroes on the Road* in 1935, "the female Negro transient" was—without explanation—excluded from the report's statistical analysis and commentary.[60] Perhaps the report omitted black women because they were considered statistically insignificant; perhaps the investigators encountered no black women or mistook women who cross-dressed as male. Unattached women of various racial and ethnic backgrounds might have avoided registering at transient bureaus in New Jersey and other states because they assumed that single women might not receive assistance. Such an assumption would not have been totally unfounded, given that single women were somewhat of an afterthought when it came to New Deal efforts for transients. Activists, reformers, and New Deal administrators seemed reluctant overall to establish all-female transient camps due to beliefs that such camps could undermine desires for chaste domesticity within women or even facilitate prostitution. Young women transients therefore might have been resourceful in ways that their male counterparts generally were not. It is additionally possible that young women on the road continued to rely on local Travelers Aid societies even after New Deal programs were in place.[61] Women might also have been loath to register at transient bureaus due to fears that such an action would compromise their respectability. And, if female hoboes and transients tended to hitchhike more frequently than men and if "hitchhiking . . . may have contributed to the relative invisibility" of these teens and women, investigators possibly overlooked black females on the road.[62] Whatever the case, the investigators refrained from claiming that no black female transients existed, if only for the reality that the state probably contained some transient families.

In contrast, African American newspapers occasionally ran stories pertaining to black women on the road. As early as September 1929, the *Chicago Defender* ran an item about three young black women who "donned male attire and flipped a train out of Birmingham, Ala[bama]" to Chicago. In 1936 the *Baltimore Afro-American* warned girls from "small home-towns" intent on heading to New York City that Harlem was already "over-populated with girls who are both economic and moral hoboes . . . hoping for . . . [a] rainbow that may never come." If the *Afro-American* implied that transient girls faced sundry dangers in New York City, a May 1935 *Chicago Defender* story about two teenaged hoboes from Mississippi acknowledged that young women faced sexual danger on the road, when it reported that a transient man attempted "to outrage" the girl hobo while another man restrained her male cousin. Three years later, a June edition of the *Chicago Defender* contained an article about an unemployed eighteen-year-old from Tennessee who "hoboed her way" to Illinois in search of work, because friends assured her that jobs could be found in Chicago. One story published in the *New York Amsterdam News* even claimed that three Spelman College sophomores "from good stock" hitchhiked from Georgia to New York because they were convinced that prospects were better "on the ill-famous Bronx 'Slave Mart'" than they were in Atlanta. The *Amsterdam News* stressed that the three girls had secured part-time employment, planned to enroll in night school, and were intent on remaining in New York.[63]

If policy makers concerned with transiency could overlook black women, black newspapers noted their presence for a variety of reasons. Some newspapers, including the *Afro-American*, published stories intended to discourage young black women from hitting the road. Others, such as the *Defender*, published stories because young hoboes had local connections through relatives. Black newspapers additionally published stories about hitchhiking young women as human-interest items that dramatized the impact of the Depression on African Americans. Indeed, the *Amsterdam News's* report that three Spelman sophomores were desperate enough to seek domestic work provocatively suggested that economic matters led some black youth to make unexpected decisions. The Spelman women were not unlike Pauli Murray in critical regards: they migrated as necessary to earn money that would enable them to continue their education, and they were willing to travel "minus train or bus fare." And, they—like Murray and the three cross-dressing young women from Birmingham who hopped freights to Chicago in 1929—might have hitchhiked for the sheer adventure of it.[64]

Pauli Murray did more than hobo across country in 1931 when she unexpectedly needed to return from California due to her aunt's illness. She also made at least one visit to "Shanty-Town" while living in New York City and hitchhiked on at least two occasions during the 1930s.[65] On one of those occasions, Murray's exploits made it into the press. On her way back to New York City from Rhode Island in the spring of 1931, police at a Bridgeport, Connecticut, train station briefly detained her. At least one newspaper reported that Murray and her traveling companion, Dorothy Hayden, both had "boyish bob[s]" and were "garbed in Boy Scout hiking outfits" when they were stopped and questioned. The reason why the two young black women were questioned in the first place—and probably why their story was considered newsworthy—was that Hayden used the women's room and an observer mistakenly thought Hayden was a young man. A Travelers Aid worker in the train station subsequently discovered that Murray "was not the boy she pretended to be."[66] Significantly, a few years before Murray's and Hayden's cross-dressing caused them momentary delay, an item in *Scribner's* proclaimed that "lady hobo[es]" were "angular-bodied, flint-eyed, masculine-minded travest[ies]." The *Scribner's* article thus associated women who made a life on the road with lesbianism.[67] It is possible, then, that Murray and Hayden were questioned partially because authorities wanted to ascertain whether they were a couple.

Murray, Hayden, and other cross-dressing women on the road likely opted to wear men's clothing out of sheer practicality and safety, but their sartorial choice could—and often did—indicate sexual preferences as well.[68] Murray, for one, apparently reveled in passing as male during her journeys and recognized her own sexual desires for women during the 1930s. Cross-dressing could constitute transgressive behavior or indicate sexual preference, to be sure, but appearing to be male instead of female also did something else for women on the road: it provided them with a modicum of protection from sexual assault from heterosexual and bisexual men.[69] As Murray herself later acknowledged, appearing to be "a small teenaged boy like thousands of others on the road" protected her from gendered dangers.[70] Adolescent boys and young men in their twenties were hardly immune from sexual advances and assault by other men, and black boys and men on the road certainly faced sexualized dangers of their own, but it is nonetheless possible that Murray would have encountered specific indignities and violence if she was discovered to be a woman of color.

Young black women were, then, part of the nationwide body of youthful transients that Minehan documented in *Boy and Girl Tramps of America*. It is quite possible that Minehan interviewed some black female transients and that he did not, for whatever reason, feature their stories in the book. Perhaps Minehan included young black women and other women of color in some of his chapters without mentioning their race. Whatever the case, young black women were on the road during the Depression—some seeking adventure, others looking for work, others escaping bad situations, and still others who were homeless. Since black women generally experienced "diminished work opportunities" during the 1930s, unemployment was likely acute among black women in their teens and twenties. Above and beyond the reality that "eight or nine out of every ten [Depression-era] black households" teetered on the brink of "complete economic disaster," both gender and racial bias limited black women's access to federal New Deal benefits, especially if they lived in the South. In other words, if domestic conditions pushed many of Minehan's young informants on the road, young and unattached black women might have been especially motivated to strike out on their own to improve their situations.[71]

As increasing numbers of unattached youths and families hit the road during the Depression out of homelessness and desperation, the Roosevelt administration actively tried to address transiency. The short-lived Federal Transient Program (FTP) existed from 1933 to 1935; it created transient camps primarily for boys and men that provided a distinct alternative to the informal hobo jungles, box cars, underpasses, and shanties inhabited by people on the road.

Because many Americans associated transiency with promiscuity, perversion, and prostitution, those very associations made the FTP one of the least popular New Deal initiatives. FTP administrators even fought the common public perception that federal transient camps were, as Margot Canaday puts it, little more than "a state-sponsored haven for sex perverts."[72] Administrators' efforts aside, young men and perhaps some young women at federal transient camps had a range of sexual experiences, just as they did at other camps established by the New Deal that offered temporary shelter and sustenance for the transient, the jobless, and the worry-worn.

One of the most popular New Deal initiatives on this front was the Civilian Conservation Corps. The CCC, established in 1933, put young men between the ages of eighteen and twenty-five to work in reforestation projects, flood control, and road and state park construction, as well as a variety of other rural projects; the age range for enrollees was expanded to encompass ages seventeen to twenty-eight in 1935. Some camps were racially segregated and a "separate [division] for Native Americans on Indian reservations" was referred to as the Indian Emergency Conservation Work (IECW) program. CCC camps were intended to serve primarily unmarried men, although married men could enroll on a select basis; camps for American Indians were envisioned, in part, as family camps and the IECW therefore enrolled married men on a much wider scale.[73] Not only was the CCC one of the New Deal programs established by President Franklin Roosevelt during his first one hundred days, it was also created in large part due to anxieties that unemployed young men concentrated in cities would roam the streets, engage in crime, and produce social unrest.[74] In a March 1933 address in which he introduced his plans to establish the CCC, Roosevelt announced that he hoped the corps would help "eliminate . . . the threat that enforced idleness brings to spiritual and moral stability."[75] Roosevelt's announcement suggested that enforced idleness among young men had especially combustible potential. The fact that the CCC was limited primarily to adolescent males and younger men and that attempts to establish a similar program for young women would be beleaguered only underscored that dangers associated with idleness were more strongly associated with unbridled masculinity.

If the very establishment of the CCC emerged largely out of anxieties about the potential mayhem that idle young men might create in cities, idleness in CCC camps could generate somewhat different anxieties about enrollees' sexuality. Two authors of one text about the CCC published in the early 1940s noted that they were "startl[ed]" over the "prevalence of sex relations with women" among CCC enrollees:

> Not one boy in a dozen stated that he had never had sexual intercourse; most enrollees clearly regarded intercourse as a normal if sometimes infrequent practice. . . . Some admitted visiting prostitutes. . . . It should be added that

masturbation seemed to be fairly common among CCC youth, but those admitting the habit usually asserted that camp had a tendency to break or lessen its hold upon them.

The authors, Kenneth Holland and Frank Hill, expressed relative astonishment that few enrollees admitted to being virgins; that said, the fact that CCC enrollees slept with girlfriends, visited prostitutes, and masturbated was not presented as being particularly problematic. Holland and Hill said little about same-sex intimacy beyond a brief claim that most "enrollees despised homosexuality, and only a few cases of it were reported."[76] But, as historian Eric Gorham has pointed out, just because homosexual activity in CCC camps was "rarely acknowledged in writing" at the time hardly means that it did not occur or that New Deal administrators were not aware that CCC enrollees had homosexual encounters and relationships. Gorham even asserts that camp administrators "'shipped in' young girls by bus" for dances and socials to discourage same-sex activity when CCC enrollees had downtime.[77]

Historians have provocatively demonstrated that both homoeroticism and homosexuality were part of life in the CCC.[78] Scholars have focused far less on a smaller yet nonetheless allied New Deal initiative: camps and resident centers for homeless women, unemployed women, and women on relief. Women's camps were nowhere nearly as extensive or popular as were CCC camps for young men. According to conservative estimates, women's camps and resident centers served only between 8,000 and 10,000 women between 1933 and 1937, in comparison to the approximately 3 million young men who enrolled in the Civilian Conservation Corps between 1933 and 1942, approximately 250,000 of whom were African American and 85,000 American Indian.[79] According to Diane Galusha, the CCC did include an extremely limited number of women who "were assigned indoor jobs at CCC camps and were paid 'allowances' of 50¢ a week."[80] Both Lois Scharf and Gwendolyn Mink have rightly stressed that women's camps served a mere fraction of unemployed women. Moreover, as Margot Canaday has recently argued, "the paltry number of CCC-type camps that were designated for women were incredibly short-lived, with FERA administrator [Harry] Hopkins [ultimately] declaring them too expensive."[81] Historian Susan Ware observes that "camps for unemployed women . . . [never] caught the imagination of the American public as had the Civilian Conservation Corps," yet examining New Deal–era women's camps nonetheless provides useful insights into idleness, gender, and sexuality during the 1930s.[82]

Franklin Roosevelt's abiding interest in environmental conservation made the CCC especially dear to him, and Eleanor Roosevelt had a vested interest of her own in creating a similar program for women. Indeed, the realization of New Deal camps for women was largely due to the efforts of the First Lady, secretary of labor Frances Perkins, and workers' education specialist Hilda Worthington Smith.[83] Although Eleanor Roosevelt hoped that a network of women's camps akin to the scale of the Civilian Conservation Corps would become a reality, and while she believed that women could be used for conservation work, the First Lady also realized that most federal bureaucrats viewed CCC-style camps where women would engage in reforestation and horticultural projects as neither practical nor desirable.[84] Indeed, some bureaucrats and commentators derided the very creation of camps for women due to what was then a contested notion—"that government ha[d] a responsibility in meeting women's education and job-related needs."[85] If gendered notions about work, education, and vocational training fueled opposition to women's camps, news articles claiming that women's camps would offer "vacations" for unemployed women certainly did not help matters, either.[86]

Skeptics aside, Camp TERA (Temporary Emergency Relief Administration) opened in June 1933 at a vacation facility owned by a life insurance company located in Bear Mountain State Park, in easy driving distance from both New York City and Hyde Park.[87] The camp quickly garnered nationwide attention as the first "federally-sponsored camp for unemployed women" created by the New Deal. A number of other states (including New Jersey, Ohio, Indiana, Georgia, South Carolina, California, and North Dakota) subsequently announced that they, too, were eager to host their own New Deal-funded women's camps.[88] If Camp TERA was somewhat experimental, it was also a template for the twenty-eight camps and schools devoted for women that the Federal Emergency Relief Administration operated by the summer of 1934, many of which were located in former CCC campsites that had been abandoned after particular CCC projects were completed.[89]

Camp TERA and other women's camps might have been dismissively referred to as "she-she-she" camps, but they differed from the CCC in one key respect—enrollees did not engage in large-scale work projects.[90] Women attended camps anywhere from a period of weeks to months; "unlike the CCC camps, where the young men were paid wages, the women received only small allowances."[91] Camp TERA—and women's camps in general—instead stressed rest and physical rehabilitation "in preparation for a return to normal employment." Such rehabilitation was necessary, the *New York Times* observed, for young women who had endured "the strain of months, and in some cases years, of fruitless job hunting on minimum rations of food."[92] Such language clearly invoked late nineteenth-century rhetoric regarding neurasthenia, a state of nervous collapse typically gendered as female. As Elaine Abelson convincingly argues, when unemployment was associated with psychologically induced physical distress during the Depression, it was women who were usually viewed as being prone to "near breakdown from worry," whereas the "mental state" of unemployed men more frequently went without extended comment.[93]

When an exhausted Pauli Murray arrived at Camp TERA in late 1934 upon the advice of her physician, Dr. May Chinn, she went more to restore her body and less because she was unemployed.[94] Murray, along with most of the other campers she met, found Camp TERA to be "a sanctuary from the pressures of unemployed city life." Although Murray was quite pleased that the camp was not segregated, she clashed with the camp's director, Jessie Mills, who Murray found to be a "raw-boned, gray-haired, authoritarian person who . . . attempted to run the camp on semimilitary lines."[95] Perhaps Jessie Mills deemed it necessary to run Camp TERA in such fashion because she was primarily dealing with young women under twenty-five. Whereas Camp TERA's initial target group was rather broad—between the ages of eighteen and forty—and while one instructor at the camp claimed that the very first seventeen enrollees were in their thirties, the majority of attendees from the summer of 1933 until the camp's final closure during the fall of 1937 hailed from New York City and were in their late teens and twenties.[96] Out of the reported two hundred women who attended Camp TERA during the summer of 1933, fewer than twelve were of African descent; at least one of these women, Regina Fuentes, might have identified as Latina.[97] During Pauli Murray's stay between November 1934 and March 1935, at least one of her coresidents might have been Latina and another Asian American. There was, at minimum, one woman in camp with Murray from the Caribbean, "Pee Wee" Inness. Since Inness bunked with Murray, it is quite possible that Inness also had African heritage.[98] Camp TERA was not segregated as were women's camps in the South and parts of the Midwest and Mid-Atlantic. Women of color were apparently not abundant at the Bear Mountain facility, either.[99] Racial composition of the camp aside and despite her disdain for Jessie Mills, Murray found that Camp TERA provided her with welcome respite. Not only did Murray find the setting rejuvenating, but her health improved as well. Murray also met a white counselor at Camp TERA named Peg Holmes who was "in charge of hiking and other outdoor activities." Holmes and Murray formed a quick bond and eventually embarked on an intimate relationship.[100]

Organized leisure activities at women's camps—swimming, hiking, parlor games, playacting, crafts, tap and folk dancing, campfire sing-alongs—were certainly wholesome.[101] These activities were intended to restore body, mind, and spirit, yet some camp activities could be woefully out of step with the needs and interests of young female enrollees. If, for example, Murray and other campers enjoyed outdoor activities, they might have been less enchanted with activities such as table setting.[102] According to one teacher at the camp, Harry Gersh, the campers he worked with during his tenure were primarily "slum-raised, street-wise women" who were "neither Girl Scouts nor YW girls." Some of these young women were quite likely virgins, but the campers, at least in Gersh's eyes, "came out of sexually aware and sexually stimulating environments" and sought outlets for their sexual desires. One director of the camp—probably Mills's predecessor, Marion Tinker—reportedly responded to this reality by proclaiming that "she would 'put tin pants on every one of th[e] girls' before she 'allowed one of them to get knocked up.'"[103] Any woman desiring entrance to Camp TERA—not to mention all other New Deal camps for women—had to undergo screening for venereal disease, as did CCC enrollees.[104]

Administrators at women's camps acknowledged on some level that enrollees were sexual beings but certainly did not expect enrollees to have sex while in camp. Toward the end of the camp's existence, however, administrators did eventually loosen their rules so that men from a nearby CCC camp could attend regular dances.[105] Still, the fact that "sexual isolation"—at least when it came to heterosexual desire—might be a problem for some campers was a reality that New Deal administrators apparently did not consider when devising plans for women's camps.[106] They nonetheless did wonder whether placing groups of women in camps "would raise 'serious questions of discipline,'" as detractors openly insinuated that isolated groups of underoccupied women out in the woods would only incubate degenerate behavior.[107]

Sex and sexuality shaped life at women's camps in ways that raised both eyebrows and hackles. For one, New Deal administrators could be extremely reluctant to locate resident camps with "white girls" near segregated camps for "Negro boys" due to both local prejudices and fears about potential interracial socializing. Women's camps attracted local young men on the prowl. Some administrators responded to this "objectionable" fact by calling on local law officials to dissuade young men from cruising by women's camps and "blowing . . . [car] horns to attract the attention of girls." On a related front, administrators at a segregated camp in Florida for black women resorted to seeking police protection for one camper being stalked by a dubious character who was convinced that he had "a claim of some sort" on the young woman.[108] If administrators' decisions to turn to local law enforcement protected some campers, other enrollees probably chafed at efforts to control or even prohibit their interaction with potential and actual suitors.

Camp TERA had its share of controversies and conflict over sex. Jessie Mills was outraged, for example, when one white woman in residence openly discussed her affair with a married black man, by whom she reportedly had a child. Mills alleged that this young woman's behavior encouraged other campers to seek illicit love over the color line. As proof, an exasperated Mills claimed that "a number of girls . . . at camp" were going to the young woman's home to "mee[t] other colored men." The young woman's affair and conduct apparently resulted in her being dismissed from Camp TERA. Whereas Murray perhaps left Camp TERA of her own volition shortly after she clashed with Mills over her possession of a copy of *Das Kapital* and because she apparently failed to show proper deference during one of Eleanor Roosevelt's visits, it is also quite possible that Murray was asked to leave Camp TERA because Mills suspected that Murray was involved in a sexual relationship with Peg Holmes. Mills frowned on and all but prohibited socializing between staff and campers outside of organized, sanctioned activities. Murray found Mills's policies regarding campers and staff to be both needlessly restrictive and infantilizing.[109] Significantly, Mills dismissed at least one woman from camp as a result of rumors about "homosexual relations between two girls," only to be accused of having a lesbian relationship with one of her own staffers. Whether Mills had same-sex desires and intimate partnerships is hard to know. Perhaps to protect her own reputation, Mills went out of her way to establish that she both disapproved of interracial sex and "stood for nonhomosexuliaty" when she spoke to New Deal administrators and sent letters to Eleanor Roosevelt.[110] Despite Mills's public protestations and actions, some young women at Camp TERA—not to mention other women's camps—were likely attracted to one another and some of these women probably acted on those desires.

Sexuality was therefore an issue at women's camps, as it was in transient and CCC camps. Because the purpose behind women's camps was somewhat ill-defined and women in camps did not participate in large-scale work projects, enrollees in women's camps arguably had more time on their hands than did CCC enrollees. To be sure, women's camps had both educational and vocational programs during the day, and attendees were required to do chores that helped maintain camps. Some women reportedly "mad[e] ... hospital supplies and recreational equipment" or performed "labor in tree nurseries." The ostensible primary purpose of Camp TERA was, moreover, "the rebuilding of health and morale in preparation for a return to normal employment."[111] But, as Gwendolyn Mink has pointed out, some of the work and activities at women's camps "mimick[ed] the homemaking lessons maternalists had imparted to girls and women during the Progressive Era." Indeed, one woman who had attended a New Deal camp for women reportedly told Hilda Smith that "most of us got the impression that they wanted to teach us something useful if we got married immediately." Young women who attended New Deal camps could, then, come to the conclusion that they should prepare for marriage but not act on their sexual urges until they got married.[112] It is possible, however, that efforts to police socializing and enforce heterosexual marriage within women's camps ultimately could not eradicate sexual dynamics and behaviors among women in camps that were as carnal as the erotic activities of CCC "peavies" and controversial as alleged sexual predilections and behaviors of girls and women on the road.[113]

After Pauli Murray left Camp TERA in early 1935, she and Peg Holmes hitch-hiked their way to Nebraska and back to New York during a sojourn that lasted a little over a month. Murray and Holmes lived by their wits during their time on the road:

> We discovered that if we did not have to pay for lodgings and used a little ingenuity, we could see the country as inexpensively as we could live in one place. We carried light knapsacks and the equipment we needed for cooking outdoors, traveled at a leisurely pace, and avoided large cities, and never accepted a ride that left us on the road at night. Around dusk we would stop off in a town or village and seek free shelter from the local police or the

Salvation Army. We were bedded in jails, courthouses, hostels, and once in a hotel at the town's expense. Often we were given breakfast before we left in the morning.

The time that Murray and Holmes spent with each other beyond the confines of Camp TERA also enabled the women to deepen their intimacy. Murray kept a diary of their trip in which she detailed when they caught rides, where they slept, how they ate, and the work that the pair did to earn money or obtain food; she noted when Holmes rinsed out their undergarments and when the pair discussed their relationship. Murray and Holmes found "free shelter" on occasion, but there were also numerous times that they did miscellaneous chores or "washed dishes" so that they could pay for food and lodging. If Murray and Holmes encountered helpful and even generous souls along the way, they were also "refused service in [the] small town of Roseville, Ill[inois]," where the women were subsequently detained and "questioned" by authorities. Murray perfunctorily wrote "race again" at the conclusion of her diary entry for the day, but a combination of race and gender—perhaps assumptions about sexual preference as well—might have played a role in this particular incident and others.[114]

Holmes and Murray were once again "stopped by [two] sheriffs and [two] state cops" on their way to Maple Park, Illinois, and they were additionally "held . . . for questioning" by a "woman Probation Officer" in Plattsmouth, Nebraska. The interracial pair did attract negative attention on occasion, then, but for Murray life on the road "about the countryside was one way of relieving the monotony of having nothing to do." A cryptic reference in Murray's diary regarding her hope that the journey might solve the "problem" between her and Holmes additionally suggests that Murray hoped that life on the road would strengthen their relationship.[115]

The fact that Murray made relatively few explicit references in her trip diary to negative reactions and questioning by officials suggests that both women either cross-dressed at the same time or simultaneously presented themselves as women on occasion. In other words, Murray probably did not wear masculine clothing while Holmes dressed as a woman lest they be mistaken as a heterosexual interracial couple. By 1935 both Murray and Holmes would have known about the infamous Scottsboro case involving nine young black men who had been riding the rails looking for work, only to be accused of raping two young white women on the same train. African American newspapers also published stories about black youths on the road who feared being entangled in a similar situation. Murray eventually compiled a souvenir photo album "chronicl[ing] herself as the romantic 'Pete' enjoying life on the road with Peggie," but it is relatively unlikely that the women risked passing themselves off as a sexually involved couple while they were actually thumbing rides, riding in boxcars, and seeking shelter. Two women on the road who were perceived as lesbians could well encounter harassment—and worse. Even a platonic, het-eronormative, interracial pair made up of two men or two women could face danger if they tried to receive service at establishments that did not welcome clientele of color. Murray might have circumvented some problematic situa-tions by allowing people to believe that she was a minority other than "Negro." "Salesmen for Indian herbs," who gave Holmes and Murray a ride in the Mid-west, for example, assumed that Murray was Indian. Capricious racial violence was hardly reserved for black people during the 1930s, yet being perceived as belonging to another minority population possibly allowed Murray to trade one set of prejudices for another. Murray may even have received assistance from people of color who were not classified as "Negro" but who believed that Murray shared a common heritage with them.[116]

However they presented themselves, Holmes and Murray took pains to appear "neatly dressed" when they sought odd jobs that would provide them with money for food and lodging.[117] The very way in which Murray described her time on the road with Holmes underscored that life on the road was actu-ally work and that the effort required to stay fed and alive meant anything but being idle. Thomas Minehan's *Boy and Girl Tramps of America* similarly sug-gested that life for transient youth involved concerted effort to survive, as it argued that a number of young women and men actually hit the road as a means of finding work and easing financial burdens for their families. Still, a range of activists, commentators, and politicians during the Depression viewed the phenomena of youth hitching rides, hopping trains, and living in hobo camps as indicating mass inactivity and constituting a significant social prob-lem. New Deal programs such as the CCC, women's camps, and a host of other programs eventually run by the National Youth Administration (NYA) were intended to replace inactivity among young women and men with productive activity. Yet some of the very activities negatively associated with both idleness and transiency—namely "wrongful" sexual activity such as promiscuity, premar-ital sex, and homosexuality—occurred in facilities and programs sponsored by the New Deal.

As a young woman who hitchhiked for adventure, acted on sexual attraction to other women, routinely cross-dressed, and kept a scrapbook that contained photographs presenting herself as male (some of which were taken when she was on the road), Pauli Murray cannot necessarily be considered representa-tive of other young women of African descent who lived and struggled during the Great Depression, let alone young women from other racial groups who had histories of their own with racism, colonialism, containment, immigration, and segregation.[118] Murray's experiences nonetheless speak to ways in which attempts to respond to mass inactivity among a particularly worrisome group—youth—did not necessarily curtail some of the very sexual activities ostensibly enabled or fueled by idleness. Murray's experiences also provide intriguing context in which to situate the choices and decisions of other black women who hit the road during the 1930s, such as the three young women who wore men's clothing when riding the rails from Alabama to Illinois and the group of three young Spelman students who hitchhiked from Atlanta to New York City so that they could find employment.

Many of my arguments are indeed tentative. I am still processing how race, ethnicity, gender, class, generation, and region informed notions about transiency, work, and leisure in Depression-era thought. I am in the admittedly early stages of analyzing the experiential contradictions of conditions, behaviors, and lifestyles associated with idleness as well. Idle individuals, for example, could be itinerant because they chafed at the prospect of living in one place and holding down a steady job, even in the midst of mass upheaval and privation. Transients or migrants in search of gainful employ typically spent a fair amount of time in motion; they were neither still nor was their movement completely footloose and without purpose. The unemployed and the underemployed often expended considerable energy pounding the pavement, visiting employment bureaus, pleading for a day's work. Transients, migrants, homeless, and destitute unemployed found themselves working in some form or fashion for what food they could get, whether by performing odd jobs, soliciting charity, or relaying accounts of their lives in ways that would produce sustenance if not sympathy. Even hoboes, vagrants, and tramps who panhandled, bummed rides, and hopped freights were not utterly inactive, including those who resorted to theft to procure material goods and relied on stealth to avoid arrest.[119] To an extent, portrayals of transiency in popular culture as well as texts produced by intellectuals, journalists, activists, and administrators (some of whom were New Dealers) could recognize this reality.

I cannot yet make sweeping arguments regarding young black women and other youth who either experienced life on the road or attended New Deal camps. I instead hope that the research presented herein suggests that examining young black women's lives on the road and in government-funded camps has potential to deepen our understanding of what might have been distinctive about African American women's lives during the Depression. For example, the same racial attitudes that kept some black men out of hobo "jungles" probably resulted in black women being fairly rare in those same spaces as well. Some young women openly entertained sexual partners in hobo camps, but they also had reason to fear sexual assault in hobo encampments regardless of their race or ethnicity. The confluence of race, sexualized stereotypes, and gender possibly (and even probably) made various women of color particularly vulnerable to rape when they were on the road. Women from minority populations might have pointedly avoided hobo encampments due to such a reality. On another front, if gendered assumptions about idleness informed the Roosevelt administration's decision to prioritize the organization of the Civilian Conservation Corps, raced notions about the ostensible "corrupting influence" of idleness might well have shaped how administrators at women's camps monitored the activities of women from minority populations and policed their sexual behavior.

The decision to expand my analytic optic so that I can consider "race" in ways not limited to blackness will hopefully enable me to interrogate specific ways in which anxieties about idleness had a particular impact on women of African descent during the 1930s. In turn, such an approach shall perhaps allow me to discover how young African American women's experiences both diverged from and converged with other young people who weathered the Depression—white, American Indian, Latino/a, and Asian, native-born and immigrant, male and female. Still, I remain mindful of Gloria Anzaldúa's warning in *This Bridge We Call Home.* "In our efforts to rethink the borders of race, gender, and identity, we must guard against creating new binaries. . . . Though most of us live entremundos, between and among worlds, we are frustrated by . . . hybridities and ambiguities, and by what does not fit our expectations of 'race' and sex."[120] As I conduct additional research for the larger book project and proceed further with writing, it is imperative that I be as attentive as possible to the specific histories of different racial and ethnic groups in the United States, not to mention how racial categories themselves are constructed, imprecise, inadequate, and problematic.

It would, for one, be nothing less than problematic to assume that different minority populations during the interwar period experienced unemployment, transiency, and New Deal relief efforts in similar ways. Likewise, if there were some racialized stereotypes about sexuality within Depression-era thought that could apply to more than one ethnic or racial group, there were arguably others that tended to be used in connection with a specific population. I shall also need to analyze the experiences of Pauli Murray and her contemporaries with care: Murray's racial heritage was complex, as were her gender and sexual identities; other people who lived in the United States or elsewhere during the 1930s had complex racial, gender, and sexual identities, too. As I continue work on the larger book project, I therefore might engage more thoroughly with literature on intersectionality, which can be productively used to avoid conflating, flattening, or oversimplifying people's lived experiences.[121] Transiency may or may not have functioned as a metaphor for race and gender during the Great Depression. That allowed, contemporaneous anxieties about idleness were infused with potent racialized, gendered, and sexualized meanings for young black women and other youths alike.

Notes

I very much wish to thank George Chauncey and Joanne Meyerowitz for inviting me to Yale University, where I presented the first iteration of this chapter in the fall of 2009. I also thank audiences at Yale and the University of Rochester as well as the 2010 and 2011 meetings of the American Historical Association for their extremely productive feedback. George Lipsitz, Martin Pernick, Annelise Orleck, and Adolph Reed Jr. each provided invaluable insights and suggestions that helped me clarify and strengthen critical aspects of the narrative in addition to my overarching argument. Lastly, I am most grateful indeed to Carol Faulkner and Alison Parker for their engaged comments, graciousness, patience, and collegiality.

1. Pauli Murray, *Song in a Weary Throat: An American Pilgrimage* (New York: Harper and Row, 1987), 64–77, esp. 67, 71; Glenda Gilmore, *Defying Dixie: The Radical Roots of Civil Rights, 1919–1950* (New York: Norton, 2008), 252. Gilmore succinctly explains both why Murray's secondary education in North Carolina fell short of Hunter College's entrance requirements and how Murray initially reacted to this reality: in short, Murray was "astonished to discover that northern states required twelve, not eleven, years of secondary school." See Gilmore, *Defying Dixie*, 252. See also Sarah Azaransky, *The Dream Is Freedom: Pauli Murray and American Democratic Faith* (New York: Oxford University Press, 2011), 6–8, esp. 8. Murray had declined a scholarship to Wilberforce University in Ohio because that scholarship "barely covered tuition for one semester." She originally set her sights on Columbia University in terms of going to school in New York City. Upon visiting Columbia and learning that its college enrolled only male students, Murray was "referred to Barnard College," where, she later recalled, "it became evident that I had neither the money nor the qualifications to enter that institution." *Weary Throat*, 64–66.

2. Robert S. McElvaine, *The Great Depression: America, 1929–1941* (1984; repr., New York: Three Rivers, 2009), 38–41; Donald L. Parman, "The Indian and the Civilian Conservation Corps," *Pacific Historical Review* 40, no. 1 (February 1971): 39–56, esp. 39–40; David H. Dinwoodie, "Indians, Hispanos, and Land Reform: A New Deal Struggle in New Mexico," *Western Historical Quarterly* 17, no. 3 (July 1986): 291–323; Harry A. Kersey Jr., "Florida Seminoles in the Depression and New Deal, 1933–1942: An Indian Perspective," *Florida Historical Quarterly* 65, no. 2 (October 1986): 175–95; Steven Mintz and Susan Kellogg, *Domestic Revolutions: A Social History of American Family Life* (New York: Free Press, 1988), 133–49, esp. 134–36; Sucheng Chan, *Asian Americans: An Interpretive History* (New York: Twayne, 1991), 116; Eiichiro Azuma, *Between Two Empires: Race, History, and Transnationalism in Japanese America* (New York: Oxford University Press, 2005), 95, 114; Natalia Molina, *Fit to Be Citizens? Public Health and Race in Los Angeles, 1879–1939* (Berkeley: University of California Press, 2006), 126–57; Valerie J. Matsumoto, "Japanese American Women and the Creation of Urban Nisei Culture in the 1930s," repr. in *Unequal Sisters: An Inclusive Reader in U.S. Women's History*, ed. Vicki L. Ruiz, with Ellen Carol DuBois, 4th ed. (New York: Routledge Taylor and Francis Group, 2008), 379–89, esp. 380–81.

3. Murray, *Weary Throat*, 76.

4. Elaine Abelson, "'Women Who Have No Men to Work for Them': Gender and Homelessness in the Great Depression, 1930–1934," *Feminist Studies* 29, no. 1 (Spring 2003): 105–27, esp. 109.

5. Murray, *Weary Throat*, 71–81. Doreen Marie Drury, "'Experimentation on the Male Side': Race, Class, Gender, and Sexuality in Pauli Murray's Quest for Love and Identity" (PhD diss., Boston College, 2000), 61–64; Gilmore, *Defying Dixie*, 252. Some scholars have identified Murray as being a "daughter of the African American middle class." Scholars have nonetheless acknowledged that members of her

extended family "lived among those Murray termed the 'respectable poor'" and that she endured poverty as a college student. Examples of scholarly claims about Murray's class background and economic status may be found in Doreen Drury, "Love, Ambition, and 'Invisible Footnotes' in the Life and Writing of Pauli Murray," *Souls* 11, no. 3 (2009): 295–309, esp. 298; Drury, "Experimentation," 64; Gilmore, *Defying Dixie*, 251–52; and Leslie Brown, *Upbuilding Black Durham: Gender Class, and Black Community Development in the Jim Crown South* (Chapel Hill: University of North Carolina Press, 2008), 1–8, 254, 343–44. In Murray's own writings, she made a concerted effort to establish just how precarious her economic situation was during her years at Hunter on at least two occasions; see *Weary Throat*, 74–77; and "A Working Student," *Hunter College Echo*, Christmas 1932, 42–44, scrapbook, vol. 83, RG MC 412, Pauli Murray Papers, Schlesinger Library, Radcliffe Institute for Advanced Study, Harvard University, Cambridge, MA.

6. Murray, *Weary Throat*, 78–79; Drury, "Invisible Footnotes," 298. Murray wrote the following in a letter to her brother, Bill, during the late 1930s: "Now, Brother Love, about this 'Anna Pauline' business. I may be 'Pollyanna' to you, but it is still Pauli to me. . . . Best love and luck to all—Pauli. (little-brother-sister-or what have you)." Pauli Murray to William Murray, February 9, 1939, folder 238, box 10, RG MC 412, Pauli Murray Papers.

7. Harry L. Hopkins, *Spending to Save: The Complete Story of Relief* (New York: Norton, 1936), 127; Henry H. Adams, *Harry Hopkins: A Biography* (New York: Putnam's Sons, 1977); George McJimsey, *Harry Hopkins: Ally of the Poor and Defender of Democracy* (Cambridge, MA: Harvard University Press, 1987).

8. "Youth" was generally defined as encompassing the ages between sixteen and twenty-four, but the category could assume different parameters and instead cover ages fourteen to twenty-four, fifteen to twenty-four, or even sixteen to twenty-one. Examples of how Depression-era commentators defined youth may be found in Clinch Calkins, ed., *Youth Never Comes Again* (New York: Committee on Unemployed Youth, 1933); Homer P. Rainey, *How Fare American Youth?* (New York: Appleton-Century, 1937); Bruce L. Melvin, *Rural Youth on Relief* (Washington, DC: Government Printing Office, 1937); Leonard V. Harrison and Pryor McNeill Grant, *Youth in the Toils* (New York: Macmillan, 1938); and Betty Lindley and Ernest K. Lindley, *A New Deal for Youth: The Story of the National Youth Administration* (New York: Viking, 1938).

9. "Statement of E. L. Worthington, Chairman of the Farms Committee of the Cleveland Employment Commission and President of the Cleveland Boys' Bureau," in *Relief for Unemployed Transients: Hearings before a Subcommittee of the Committee on Manufactures, United States Senate, Seventy-Second Congress, Second Session on S. 5121 . . . January 13 to 25, 1933* (Washington, DC: Government Printing Office, 1933), 104–10, esp. 105; Frank Fitzpatrick (Chief Inspector, Nashville, Chattanooga and St. Louis Railway, Nashville, Tennessee) to Harry Hopkins (Director, Federal Emergency Relief Administration), September 25, 1933, box 80, Old General Subject Series, FERA Central Files, 1933–36, Records of the WPA, RG 69, National Archives, College Park, Maryland; "Statement of Nels Anderson, Instructor in Sociology, Columbia University, New York City," in *Relief for Unemployed Transients*, 63–71, esp. 65, 67; Hopkins, *Spending to Save*, 128. Todd DePastino argues that certain terms for marginal, migratory, and often homeless individuals

tended to predominate during different eras in the United States. He contends that there was "the 'tramp' of the Gilded Age, the 'hobohemian' of the Progressive Era, the 'transient' and 'migrant' of the Great Depression, and the skid row 'bum' of the postwar period." Lynn Weiner offers another interesting observation along these lines: "Jack MacBeth, president of Chicago's Hobo College, suggested . . . [during the mid-1930s that] 'A hobo is a migratory worker, a tramp is a migratory nonworker, and a bum is a nonmigratory nonworker.'" DePastino, *Citizen Hobo: How a Century of Homelessness Shaped America* (Chicago: University of Chicago Press, 2003), xix; Weiner, "Sisters of the Road: Women Transients and Tramps," in *Tramps in America, 1790–1935*, ed. Eric H. Monkkonen (Lincoln: University of Nebraska Press, 1984), 171–88, esp. 185n2.

10. See, for example, "Encouraging Idleness," *Washington Post*, March 22, 1931, S1; "Statement of Miss Grace Abbott, Chief, Children's Bureau, Washington, D.C.," in *Relief for Unemployed Transients*, 23–35, esp. 31; "Statement of Mrs. Margaret Ford, Executive Secretary Travelers Aid Society, Washington, D.C.," in *Relief for Unemployed Transients*, 60–62, esp. 60; "Statement of Maj. J. Arthur Fynn, Field Secretary of the Salvation Army in the Southern States, Atlanta, GA," in *Relief for Unemployed Transients*, 144–48, esp. 145 and 146; and Hopkins, *Spending to Save*, 126.

11. See, for example, Alfred Kram (Egg Harbor City, New Jersey) to Harry L. Hopkins (Director, Federal Emergency Relief Administration), September 25, 1933, FERA Central Files, 1933–36.

12. This chapter is part of my current book project, tentatively titled *Idle Anxieties: Race and Sexuality during the Great Depression*.

13. I have located an account of one "mixed" woman from Texas, Clydia Williams, who "went on the road because [she] . . . felt [she] . . . was not wanted" when she was but seven years old. Sometime in 1932 Williams started "hopping freights with her cousins, two boys of eight and a half and ten years," and she continued to do so until 1935. Based on the content of her account as well as a photograph, I have surmised that Williams likely has (or had, if she has passed away) some African ancestry. Williams's interview was recorded in 1994 and appears in part in Errol Lincoln Uys, *Riding the Rails: Teenagers On the Move During the Great Depression* (New York: TV Books, 1999), 201–5, 284. Errol Uys's book is a companion piece to the independent documentary, *Riding the Rails* (Artistic License Films, ca. 1997), by Lexy Lovell and Michael Uys.

14. Murray, *Weary Throat*, 95.

15. Elaine Abelson notes that Depression-era discussions of the "New Poor" routinely excluded people of color. Abelson further contends that "if homeless women as a group were not readily visible, African American women were almost wholly invisible to the mostly white investigators." See "Women," 109. "Negro" girls are discussed briefly in a study of the National Youth Administration published during the 1930s. See Lindley and Lindley, *New Deal For Youth*, 48, 93, 104. In terms of recent scholarship on hoboes, transiency, and homelessness, African American women are effectively absent from DePastino's *Citizen Hobo*. DePastino does carefully establish that transiency was gendered as male during the late nineteenth and early twentieth centuries. He also convincingly demonstrates that popular discourse and culture during this period generally portrayed transients and hoboes as white. Depression-era black transient women receive either

fleeting or no attention in other texts. See, for example, Lynne Marie Adrian, "Organizing the Rootless: American Hobo Subculture" (PhD diss., University of Iowa, 1984); Tim Cresswell, *The Tramp in America* (London: Reaktion Books, 2001); Kenneth L. Kusmer, *Down and Out, On the Road: The Homeless in America* (New York: Oxford University Press, 2003); and Roberta Ann Johnson, "African Americans and Homelessness," *Journal of Black Studies* 40, no. 4 (March 2010): 583–605. Lastly, existing studies that touch on women's camps tend to mention black women in passing or overlook them altogether. See, for example, Susan Ware, *Beyond Suffrage: Women in the New Deal* (Cambridge, MA: Harvard University Press, 1981); Lois Scharf, "'The Forgotten Woman': Working Women, the New Deal, and Women's Organizations," in *Decades of Discontent: The Women's Movement, 1920–1940*, ed. Lois Scharf and Joan M. Jensen (Westport, CT: Greenwood, 1983), 243–59; Gwendolyn Mink, *The Wages of Motherhood: Inequality in the Welfare State, 1917–1942* (Ithaca, NY: Cornell University Press, 1995); Thomas W. Patton, "'What of Her?' Eleanor Roosevelt and Camp Tera," *New York History* 87, no. 2 (Spring 2006): 229–47. Susan Wladaver-Morgan does discuss black women at some length, but her analysis largely occurs when she discusses National Youth Administration programs that followed the attempt to establish women's camps. See "Young Women and the New Deal: Camps and Resident Centers, 1933–1943" (PhD diss., Indiana University, 1982), 163–68.

16. In the West, for example, "Chinese and Filipinos on relief were given a food budget that was 10 to 20 percent lower than that given to whites, because the relief agencies believed that Asians could subsist on a less expensive diet." Chan, *Asian Americans*, 115. Steven Mintz and Susan Kellogg note that in rural Texas "black families received a quarter less aid than white families on relief." *Domestic Revolutions*, 142.

17. Susan Currell, *The March of Spare Time: The Problem and Promise of Leisure in the Great Depression* (Philadelphia: University of Pennsylvania Press, 2005), 1–11, esp. 2 and 10. Steven M. Gelber similarly notes that hobbies—a "socially sanctioned subset of leisure"—assumed new meanings during the 1930s. See "A Job You Can't Lose: Work and Hobbies in the Great Depression," *Journal of Social History* 24, no. 4 (June 1991): 741–66, esp. 741. Examples of claims from the 1930s that the leisure hours of US workers were increasing may be found in John Gilmore, "Let's Have a Ministry of Leisure," *Los Angeles Times*, November 24, 1935, I11; and John Clarence Wright, "From My Study Window," *Atlanta Daily World*, June 24, 1939, 2. Whereas neither Currell nor Gelber focus on idleness in quite the manner that I do here, their respective analyses do touch on the state of purposeless inactivity. Gelber (who is less concerned with gender dynamics than Currell) notes that "hobbies were [increasingly viewed as] a way to redeem idleness with constructive activity" during the thirties. For her part Currell contends that not only did social scientists warn that "the unemployed worker would be led astray in his or her increased leisure hours," but leisure itself could also be "described in terms of a pathological illness." Gelber, "Job You Can't Lose," 747; Currell, *March of Spare Time*, 6.

18. The literature on racial mixing in the United States—not to mention how "racial" categories have been both fluid and entrenched throughout North American history—is fairly extensive at this point. Two recent analyses of these complex

subjects during both the nineteenth and twentieth centuries are Ariela J. Gross, *What Blood Won't Tell: A History of Race on Trial in America* (Cambridge, MA: Harvard University Press, 2008); and Peggy Pascoe, *What Comes Naturally: Miscegenation Law and the Making of Race in America* (New York: Oxford University Press, 2009). Nayan Shah offers critical analyses of race, migrant workers, transiency, and sexuality in his article, "Between 'Oriental Depravity' and 'Natural Degenerates': Spatial Borderlands and the Making of Ordinary Americans," *American Quarterly* 57, no. 3 (September 2005): 703–25. See also Shah, *Stranger Intimacy: Contesting Race, Sexuality, and the Law in the North American West* (Berkeley: University of California Press, 2012). For incisive and wide-ranging analyses of race in the United States in terms of work, unemployment, spatial mobility, and ostensibly problematic populations, see Ruth Wilson Gilmore, *Golden Gulag: Prisons, Surplus, Crisis, and Opposition in Globalizing California* (Berkeley: University of California Press, 2007).

19. Examples of such arguments include the following: "Find Idleness in U.S. Causes Increase in Liquor Consumption," *Chicago Daily Tribune*, January 23, 1933, 13; "Idle Husbands Told Not to Stay Home Too Much," *Chicago Daily Tribune*, January 24, 1933, 14; Dr. Irving S. Cutter, "The Mental Hazard of Idleness," *Chicago Daily Tribune*, February 9, 1936, 14; "A Growing Menace," editorial of the day, *Chicago Daily Tribune*, February 20, 1936, 10; and Taschereau Arnold, "A Message to Idle Folk," *Atlanta Daily World*, November 9, 1940, 2. See also Richard Ian Kimball, "Enforced Leisure: New Deal Recreation in Indiana," *Mid-America: An Historical Review* 79, no. 1 (Winter 1997): 47–69, esp. 49–50. A columnist whose work appeared in an African American newspaper, the *Atlanta Daily World*, even linked idleness to diminished attractiveness in women. See Helen Jameson, "Beauty Hints," *Atlanta Daily World*, September 5, 1937, 3.

20. Nannie Helen Burroughs, "What Negro Leaders Can Do about Idleness," box 46, Papers of Nannie Helen Burroughs, Library of Congress, Washington, DC. A slightly altered, published version of this paper appeared in the *Baltimore Afro-American*: "Leaders Mark Time with Many Idle, says Nannie Burroughs," December 6, 1930, 5. Similar arguments on her part may be found in Burroughs, "Philanthropy, Which Provides Colleges, Hospitals, Closes Its Shops and Factories," *Baltimore Afro-American*, January 24, 1931; and Burroughs, "Nannie Burroughs Favors a Back-to-the-Farm Movement," *Baltimore Afro-American*, August 31, 1932, 21. For critical analyses of Burroughs, see Victoria W. Wolcott, "'Bible, Bath, and Broom': Nannie Helen Burroughs's National Training School and African-American Racial Uplift," *Journal of Women's History* 9, no. 1 (Spring 1997): 88–110; and Audrey Thomas McCluskey, "'We Specialize in the Wholly Impossible': Black Women School Founders and Their Mission," *Signs* 22, no. 2 (Winter 1997): 403–26, esp. 418–23. See also Linda Gordon, "Black and White Visions of Welfare: Women's Welfare Activism, 1890–1945," repr. in Ruiz, *Unequal Sisters*, 221–47.

21. James M. Boston, "The Danger of Rearing Children in Idleness," *Atlanta Daily World*, October 12, 1935, 2.

22. For discussions of unemployment as "enforced idleness," see the following: "Hoover on Unemployed," *Wall Street Journal*, March 10, 1930, 1; "How Many Mexicans," *Wall Street Journal*, March 27, 1930, 1; "The Sooner the Better," *Wall Street Journal*, August 15, 1932, 6; "City Finds 80 Jobs for 2,000 Seekers," *New York Times*, August 16, 1930, 8; "Annual Wage Plan Proposed by Green," *New York Times*, Sep-

tember 2, 1930, 16; "Old Five Points Mission Faces New Tax on Efforts," *New York Times*, October 26, 1930, X20; "White-Collar Girls," *New York Times*, December 6, 1930, 14; "Lists Labor's Gains in Survey for Year," *New York Times*, January 1, 1931, 8; W. H. Glazer, "Benefits of Depression," letters to the editor, *New York Times*, September 29, 1931, 24; "A Mental Health Problem," *Los Angeles Times*, March 13, 1933, A4; "Roosevelt in Message Asks for Jobless Relief," *Los Angeles Times*, March 22, 1933, 2; "Domestic Peril Seen in Enforced Idleness," *Atlanta Constitution*, March 24, 1933, 8; "Warns Idle Labor Is Losing Its Skill," *New York Times*, March 7, 1935, 25; "Benefits for the Unemployed," *Washington Post*, November 27, 1937, 6; Ernest K. Lindley, "A Word for Youth," *Washington Post*, December 12, 1938, 11; and "The Political Arena: Rep. Edith Rogers Blames New Deal for 'Enforced Idleness' of 10,000,000," *Washington Post*, October 7, 1940, 3. In addition to "enforced idleness," unemployment was also referred to as "forced idleness" or "enforced leisure" during the 1930s. See, for example, Burroughs, "Philanthropy," 3; and Kimball, "Enforced Leisure." Relevant analyses of how sexuality, gender, and race shaped moral panics and social control efforts in the United States during the early twentieth century may be found in the following select works: George Chauncey, *Gay New York: Gender, Urban Culture, and the Making of the Gay Male World, 1890–1940* (New York: Basic Books, 1994); Martin Summers, *Manliness and Its Discontents: The Black Middle Class and the Transformation of Masculinity, 1900–1930* (Chapel Hill: University of North Carolina Press, 2004); Pippa Holloway, *Sexuality, Politics, and Social Control in Virginia, 1920–1945* (Chapel Hill: University of North Carolina Press, 2006); and Cheryl D. Hicks, *Talk With You Like a Woman: African American, Justice, and Reform in New York, 1890–1935* (Chapel Hill: University of North Carolina Press, 2010).

23. Along these lines, Lizbeth Cohen points out that "mechanization . . . contribut[ed] to speed-ups and hiring cuts" during the thirties. See *Making a New Deal: Industrial Workers in Chicago, 1919–1939* (Cambridge: Cambridge University Press, 1990), 316. Examples of Depression-era arguments regarding the relationship between mechanization and unemployment may be found in "Annual Wage Plan," 16; and "Causes of Idleness Revealed in Census," *New York Times*, August 1, 1931, 26. During the 1930s labor organizers in the International Workers of the World (IWW) connected unemployment with mechanization, capitalism, and a "class of idle, arrogant, and overfed parasites" who owned the means of production but ultimately contributed nothing in terms of labor power. Significantly, however, IWW organizers also contended that machines could benefit rather than displace workers. The IWW even argued that machinery should facilitate a shorter, less burdensome workday and that shortening the workday would actually enable greater numbers of people to be employed during slack times. See *So, You're Out of a Job!* (Chicago: International Workers of the World, 1933), esp. 7–9, 16. Similar arguments may be found in *Where Do We Go From Here?* (Chicago: Chicago Branch No. 1, General Recruiting Union for the IWW, ca. 1930s); and C. B. Ellis, *Unemployment and the Machine* (Chicago: Industrial Workers of the World, 1934).

24. Robert S. McElvaine, ed., *Down and Out in the Great Depression: Letters from the "Forgotten Man"* (Chapel Hill: University of North Carolina Press, 1983), 21; McElvaine, *Great Depression*, 75.

25. George J. Sánchez, *Becoming Mexican American: Ethnicity, Culture, and Identity in Chicano Los Angeles, 1900–1945* (New York: Oxford University Press, 1993), 209–26, esp. 210–17; David G. Gutiérrez, *Walls and Mirrors: Mexican Americans, Mexican Immigrants, and the Politics of Ethnicity* (Berkeley: University of California Press, 1995), 71–74, esp. 72; Vicki L. Ruiz, "'Star Struck': Acculturation, Adolescence, and Mexican American Women, 1920–1950," repr. in Ruiz, *Unequal Sisters*, 363–78, esp. 372; Molina, *Fit to Be Citizens?*, 126–27; Daniel M. Johnson and Rex R. Campbell, *Black Migration in America: A Social Demographic History* (Durham, NC: Duke University Press, 1981), 92–93; Mintz and Kellogg, *Domestic Revolutions*, 141; E. Franklin Frazier, "Some Effects of the Depression on the Negro in Northern Cities," *Science and Society* 2, no. 4 (Fall 1938): 489–99, esp. 490–91; New York Temporary Commission on the Condition of the Colored Urban Population, *Second Report of the New York State Temporary Commission on the Condition of the Colored Urban Population to the Legislature of the State of New York, February, 1939* (Albany: Lyon, 1939), 33–36; Mink, *Wages of Motherhood*, 133; Cohen, *Making a New Deal*, 242; Victoria Wolcott, *Remaking Respectability: African American Women in Interwar Detroit* (Chapel Hill: University of North Carolina Press, 2001), 170–72; Mark Naison, *Communists in Harlem during the Depression* (Urbana: University of Illinois Press, 2005), 31. See also William H. Harris, *The Harder We Run: Black Workers since the Civil War* (New York: Oxford University Press, 1982), 106–7; Raymond Wolters, *Negroes and the Great Depression: The Problem of Economic Recovery* (Westport, CT: Greenwood, 1970), 90–92; and Alfred Edgar Smith, "Reasons for the Disproportionate Number of Negroes on the Relief Rolls," April 1935, folder 1, box C122, Work Projects Administration Records, Library of Congress, Washington, DC.

26. "Relief: A Survey . . . II," *Brown American* 1, no. 4 (August 1936): 9–11, esp. 11.

27. "Folks We Can Get Along Without," editorial cartoon, *Chicago Defender*, May 9, 1931, repr. in *Stylin': African American Expressive Culture from Its Beginnings to the Zoot Suit*, by Shane White and Graham White (Ithaca, NY: Cornell University Press, 1998), 231. For a discussion of how—and why—the *Defender* discouraged continued black migration to Chicago during the 1930s, see Felicia G. Jones Ross and Joseph P. McKerns, "Depression in 'The Promised Land': The *Chicago Defender* Discourages Migration, 1929–1940," *American Journalism* 21, no. 1 (2004): 55–73.

28. Edmund Gilligan, "Idleness, Harlem's Chief Threat," March 22, 1935, reel 10, Harlem scrapbook, vol. 40, Alexander Gumby Collection, Rare Book and Manuscript Collection, Columbia University, New York. I thank Laura Helton for bringing this article to my attention.

29. "Athletic Idleness," *Los Angeles Times*, July 8, 1933, A4.

30. Fitzpatrick to Hopkins, September 25, 1933, FERA Central Files, 1933–36; Grace Cadigan, "The Bread of Idleness," *Los Angeles Times*, February 24, 1935, 10; Mary McLeod Bethune, "Summary Statement of the Evaluation of Committee Reports," in *Proceedings of the Second National Conference on the Problems of the Negro and Negro Youth* (Washington, DC: Department of Labor, 1939), 31–33, esp. 33.

31. Ella Baker and Marvel Cooke, "The Bronx Slave Market," *Crisis* 42, no. 11 (November 1935): 330–31, 340, esp. 330; "The Feminist Viewpoint," *New York Amsterdam News*, May 17, 1933, 5.

32. Emily Hahn, "Women without Work," *New Republic* 75 (May 31, 1933): 63–65, quoted in Patton, "What of Her?," 229–47, esp. 234.

33. "Most Idle Found to Be Less Than 20," *New York Times*, August 28, 1933, 15; "Report from Committee on Youth and Its Problems," in *Second National Conference*, 59–63, esp. 59.

34. Wladaver-Morgan, "Young Women," 32–33; Uys, *Riding the Rails*; Robert Cohen, ed., *Dear Mrs. Roosevelt: Letters from Children of the Great Depression* (Chapel Hill: University of North Carolina Press, 2002), 6.

35. [Mrs.] B. M. Carstairs (Portland, Oregon) to Harry L. Hopkins, October 14, 1933, FERA Central Files, 1933–36. For a similar assertion, see "Statement of Gen. Pelham D. Glassford," in *Relief for Unemployed Transients*, 125–34, esp. 125–26.

36. Robert Reiman, *The New Deal and American Youth: Ideas and Ideals in a Depression Decade* (Athens: University of Georgia Press, 1992), 174.

37. Kimball, "Enforced Leisure," 56–57.

38. See, for example, E. Franklin Frazier, *The Negro Family in the United States* (1939; repr., Notre Dame: University of Notre Dame Press, 2001), 271–390, esp. 342–75; W[illis] D. Weatherford, ed., *A Survey of the Negro Boy in Nashville, Tennessee* (New York: Association Press, 1932), 81–104; Elaine Ellis, "Our Delinquent Children," *Crisis* 44 (December 1937): 12; Kimball, "Enforced Leisure," 56–57; and Rufus S. Watson, "I Work with Youth," *Brown American* 3, no. 3 (September 1939): 15–16.

39. "5,000 Boys Found Adrift in the City," *New York Times*, November 13, 1932, 26. See also "Will Ask Youth to Stay in School," *New York Times*, August 7, 1931, 2; Father E. J. Flanagan (Omaha, Nebraska) to Harry L. Hopkins, September 26, 1933, FERA Central Files, 1933–36.

40. Thomas Minehan, *Boy and Girl Tramps of America* (1934; repr., Seattle: University of Washington Press, 1976), xxii–xxviii, esp. xxii, xxv, xxvi, xxviii, 133. Minehan published yet another—albeit considerably shorter and comparatively sanitized—book based on his time "living with hobos" in 1941. See Minehan, *Lonesome Road: The Way of Life of a Hobo* (Evanston: Row, Peterson, 1941).

41. Donald W. Whisenhunt, introduction to *Boy and Girl Tramps*, xi–xxi, esp. xviii; J. F. Lennon, "Thomas Minehan's Quest for Fact and Fellowship in Depression America," *Journal of American Studies* 19, no. 2 (August 1985): 263–66. William Stott offers a more critical reading of Minehan. See *Documentary Expression and Thirties America* (Chicago: University of Chicago Press, 1973), 168–69.

42. A. Wayne McMillen, "An Army of Boys on the Loose," *Survey* 68 (September 1932): 389–93; Elizabeth Wickenden, "Transiency = Mobility in Trouble," *Survey* 73 (October 1937): 308–9; Joseph Fulling Fishman, "Bum's Rush," *Harper's* 168 (May 1934): 750–51; "Ladies of the Road," *Literary Digest*, August 13, 1932, 33; Pauli Murray, "Three Thousand Miles on a Dime in Ten Days," *Negro: An Anthology*, ed. Nancy Cunard (1934; repr., New York: Continuum, 2002), 67–70, esp. 67. Quite significantly, Murray wrote this article as though she was traveling with a young man named "Pete," when in fact she—as the narrator—and "Pete" were one and the same person. The text itself gave no indication that the narrator was female. And, since the byline indicated that "Pauli Murray" wrote the article, some readers likely assumed that the author was male. Indeed, there is evidence that Murray wanted readers to assume that she—as the author—was male. See Nancy Cunard to Pauli Murray, January 15, [1932?], folder 84, box 4, RG MC 412, Pauli Murray Papers; and Drury, "Experimentation on the Male Side," 69–78. Murray herself revised

"Three Thousand Miles" in *Weary Throat*, 77–81. See also Azaransky, *Dream Is Freedom*, 11; and Kevin K. Gaines, *American Africans in Ghana: Black Expatriates and the Civil Rights Era* (Chapel Hill: University of North Carolina Press, 2006), 113.

43. John Steinbeck, *The Grapes of Wrath*, directed by John Ford (Twentieth Century Fox, 1940); *Wild Boys of the Road*, directed by William Wellman (First National, 1933); *Boy Slaves*, directed by P. J. Wolfson (RKO, 1939); and *Girls of the Road*, directed by Nick Grinde (Columbia, 1940). *Wild Boys of the Road* does feature adolescent female transients who cross-dress as male. Interestingly, *Girls of the Road* is the only film out of the three that does not feature at least one character easily identifiable as African American. *Wild Boys of the Road* features young men of African descent and *Boy Slaves* also has a black male character. Both *Wild Boys* and *Boy Slaves* also feature characters who can arguably be considered "white ethnics." None of the films contain dialogue, implication, symbolic cues, stereotypes, or close-ups that indicate—from my multiple viewings, at least—the presence of Latino/a, Asian, or American Indian characters.

44. Fiction though they were, the screenplays for *Wild Boys of the Road* and *Girls of the Road* were undoubtedly influenced by contemporaneous journalists' coverage of child, teen, and young adult transients; both films contained montages of possibly real (but presumably fake) newspaper headlines pertaining to the plight of young transients as well. For evidence that *Wild Boys* was inspired by news items (not to mention a 1931 Russian film, *The Road to Life*), see William Troy, "Forgotten Children," *Nation* 137 (October 18, 1933): 458. *Boy Slaves* was apparently inspired by peonage in Florida's turpentine camps during the 1920s and 1930s as well as by contemporaneous investigative exposés that detailed brutality and death within those camps. See Jerrell H. Shofner, "Postscript to the Martin Tabert Case: Peonage as Usual in the Florida Turpentine Camps," *Florida Historical Quarterly* 60, no. 2 (October 1981): 161–73, esp. 170; and "Hedda Hopper's Hollywood," *Los Angeles Times*, March 4, 1939, A7. In a My Day column titled "'Boy Slaves' Shown for the President," Eleanor Roosevelt wrote of her "hope that many people will have an opportunity to see this film." See *Atlanta Constitution*, February 2, 1939, 14.

45. Thomas Doherty, *Pre-Code Hollywood: Sex, Immorality, and Insurrection in American Cinema, 1930–1934* (New York: Columbia University Press, 1999), 89–92. A fleeting but telling reference to the film's relatively bleak content may be found in Paul Buhle and Dave Wagner, *Radical Hollywood: The Untold Story behind America's Favorite Movies* (New York: New Press, 2002), 24. For a contemporaneous review that at once describes the film as a "rare expositio[n] of the persecution of youth" and warns that young viewers could potentially interpret the film as depicting teenagers on "a great lark," see "Roaming Youth Dramatized on Earle Screen," *Washington Post*, October 7, 1933, 11.

46. See "Robert Symmonds, 1934–42," in Uys, *Riding the Rails*, 264–69, esp. 265.

47. For evidence along these lines, see Uys, *Riding the Rails*, 18–20. Analysis of both the film version of *The Grapes of Wrath* and contemporaneous migration narratives may be found in Michael Denning, *The Cultural Front: The Laboring of American Culture in the Twentieth Century* (London: Verso, 1998), 259–82.

48. Minehan, *Boy and Girl Tramps*, 21–36, esp. 26, 29, 28.

49. Minehan, *Boy and Girl Tramps*, 48–53, esp. 48.

50. "The Open Road Is Home to the Starving Waifs of America's Dark Jungles," *Washington Post*, July 1, 1934, SM8; Minehan, *Boy and Girl Tramps*, 59.

51. Minehan, *Boy and Girl Tramps*, xxvii. Lynn Weiner notes that hobo jungles were "transient settlements on the side of railroad junctions." Similarly, Margot Canaday observes that "jungle" was a reference to "large camps where transients congregated" and that they were typically located "at railroad crossings." See Weiner, "Sisters of the Road," 178; and Canaday, *The Straight State: Sexuality and Citizenship in Twentieth-Century America* (Princeton, NJ: Princeton University Press, 2009), 98, 98n25. If this term was fairly common during the 1930s, DePastino suggests that referring to unofficial transient encampments as "jungles" had emerged by the 1910s. See *Citizen Hobo*, 68.

52. Minehan, *Boy and Girl Tramps*, 133–43, esp. 133.

53. Ibid., 133–38, 61, 169, 48. For additional albeit brief commentary regarding travel and young female transients, see "Statement of Prof. A. W. McMillen, University of Chicago, Chicago, Ill.," in *Relief for Unemployed Transients*, 38–50, esp. 45.

54. Minehan, *Boy and Girl Tramps*, 139, 140.

55. Ibid., xxvi, 38–39, 46, 139–41. Minehan relayed similar anecdotes about the ostensibly heterodox behavior of "girl tramps" in an article that he published the same year as *Boy and Girl Tramps*. See Thomas Minehan, "Girls of the Road," *Independent Woman* 13 (October 1934): 316–17, 335.

56. Edgar M. Gerlach (Asst. Supervisor, Probation System, US Courts, Washington, DC) to Morris Lewis (Director, Federal Transient Program), November 24, 1933, FERA Central Files, 1933–36. A notably different portrayal of "the numerous women who . . . join[ed] the ranks of hoboes"—one that discusses, in part, middle-aged women—may be found in "Ladies of the Road," 33. DePastino asserts that if "'ladies of the road' were rife in journal, magazine, and newspaper stories through the early 1930s," they were also portrayed as "taking on multiple sex partners as they traveled." *Citizen Hobo*, 202–3.

57. Minehan, *Boy and Girl Tramps*, 138, 124. Curiously (or not), Minehan mentions venereal disease within his rather short section on interracial sex; see 139.

58. Cresswell, *Tramp in America*, 87–109; Weiner, "Sisters of the Road," 172, 177, 178; DePastino, *Citizen Hobo*, 13, 81–83, 202. As DePastino points out, there were key ways in which indigent African Americans faced particular risks on the road due to racism and racially motivated violence during the late nineteenth century; see *Citizen Hobo*, 14. Such a reality continued into the twentieth century and was dramatically underscored when in March 1931, nine young black men who had been riding the rails were apprehended outside of Paint Rock, Alabama, due to accusations that they sexually assaulted two young white women on the same train. Their arrest happened despite the fact that "none of the black men shared the same boxcar as the women." See Robin D. G. Kelley, *Hammer and Hoe: Alabama Communists during the Great Depression* (Chapel Hill: University of North Carolina Press, 1990), 78. One of the most compelling treatments of this infamous case remains James Goodman's *Stories of Scottsboro* (New York: Vintage, 1995). Vital historical context regarding "unattached women" during the period leading to the Great Depression may be found in Joanne Meyerowitz, "Sexual Geography and Gender Economy: The Furnished-Room Districts of Chicago, 1890–1930," repr. in Ruiz, *Unequal Sisters*, 325–41.

59. Abelson, "Women," 106; Canaday, *Straight State*, 105.

60. Nelson C. Jackson, *Negroes on the Road: A Survey of the Negro Transient in New Jersey, January–June, 1934* (Trenton: New Jersey Emergency Relief Administration, 1935), 4.

61. Evidence regarding contemporaneous beliefs regarding all-female transient camps as well as Travelers Aid providing assistance to young women on the road may be found in "Statement of Miss Grace Abbott," 33; Morris Lewis (Director, Federal Transient Program) to Walter C. Reckless (Nashville, Tennessee), November 8, 1933, FERA Central Files, 1933–36; "Statement of Miss Bertha McCall, Director National Association of Travelers Aid Societies, New York City," in *Relief for Unemployed Transients*, 50–57. Significantly, Reckless was a sociologist who published an article about transient women. See "Why Women Become Hoboes," *American Mercury* 31 (February 1934): 175–80. In terms of Travelers Aid, Weiner notes that during the 1930s its "governing principle . . . changed from moral protection to social casework as the organization began to cooperate with the Federal Transient Program." See "Sisters of the Road," 183. For insight into why activists, reformers, and administrators largely tended to view concentrated groups of female transients as undesirable, see Meyerowitz, "Sexual Geography," 326, 328.

62. Hopkins, *Spending to Save*, 128–33; Weiner, "Sisters of the Road," 177, 183. Weiner stops short of arguing that FERA's transient policy either favored boys and men or underserved girls and women. Canaday, however, pointedly contends that FERA's "Federal Transient Program . . . created a national system of camps and shelters for mostly male migrants." Canaday additionally refers to both FTP and CCC camps as "gender-segregated institutions" for men. I agree with Canaday's conclusion that "female transiency was not a problem that the federal government felt it had to solve." See Weiner, "Sisters of the Road," 184; and Canaday, *Straight State*, 92, 127. See also Suzanne Mettler, *Dividing Citizens: Gender and Federalism in New Deal Public Policy* (Ithaca, NY: Cornell University Press, 1998), 45. For a critical analysis of working-class women during this period, consult Annelise Orleck, "'We Are That Mythical Thing Called the Public': Militant Housewives during the Great Depression," repr. in Ruiz, *Unequal Sisters*, 401–16.

63. "Young Girls 'Hobo' Way from Alabama to Chicago," *Chicago Defender*, September 21, 1929, A10; Ralph Matthews, "Girl Hoboes," *Baltimore Afro-American*, February 29, 1936, 12; "Boy, 14, Girl, Also 14, Hobo From Mississippi," *Chicago Defender*, May 11, 1935, 24; "Memphis Girl, 18, Hoboes to Chicago, But Can't Stay Unless She Gets Job," *Chicago Defender*, June 4, 1938, 2; "3 Girls Hitch-Hike Here from Atlanta," *New York Amsterdam News*, August 20, 1938, 4. Examples of more general commentary on black hoboes may be found in Milton Velasco, "The Colored Hobo," *Chicago Defender*, December 23, 1933, 11; and "Race Man Lifts 'Jim Crow' Bar at Hobo Camp," *Chicago Defender*, April 13, 1935, 1.

64. "3 Girls Hitch-Hike," 4; "Young Girls," A10.

65. Although Murray uses the term "Shanty-Town" as well as "hobo-camps" in this letter, it is not altogether clear whether she is referring to temporary camps set up by transients or homeless persons or whether she visited hobo jungles. For Murray's brief description of her visit to "hobo-camps on the [river] bank right in the shadow of wealth and power" near Riverside Church and Columbia University, see

Pauli Murray to Pauline Dame, October 3, 1933, folder 238, box 10, RG MC 412, Pauli Murray Papers.

66. "Slip Brings Halt to Tour of Two Girls; Garbed in Boy Scout Outfits" (n.p., n.d.), scrapbook, vol. 83, RG MC 412, Pauli Murray Papers. Further discussion of this incident may be found in Drury, "Experimentation," 64–66. In March 1940 Murray was arrested while traveling with another friend, Adelene McBean, in Petersburg, Virginia; police officers claimed that the pair was guilty of "disorderly conduct and creating a public disturbance." McBean and Murray's attempt to move to more comfortable seats while they were on the bus was also interpreted by local officials as violating a segregation ordinance. Murray, *Weary Throat*, 138–49, esp. 142 and 146; Drury, "Experimentation," 226–35, esp. 231. Glenda Gilmore makes the critical observation that Murray was apparently wearing men's clothing on this occasion as well. *Defying Dixie*, 316–29, esp. 324.

67. DePastino, *Citizen Hobo*, 202; Cresswell, *Tramp in America*, 104–5. See also Weiner's discussion of "Boxcar Bertha" in "Sisters of the Road," 174–76, 178; and *Sister of the Road: The Autobiography of Box Car Bertha as told to Dr. Ben L. Reitman* (1937; repr., Edinburgh: AK/Nabat, 2002).

68. The literature on cross-dressing is fairly extensive and cuts across disciplines, geographic fields of specialization, and temporalities. Select work that speaks to my analysis herein, the Great Depression, and US history more generally includes the following: John D'Emilio and Estelle B. Freedman, *Intimate Matters: A History of Sexuality in America* (New York: Harper and Row, 1988); Elizabeth Lapovsky Kennedy and Madeline D. Davis, *Boots of Leather, Slippers of Gold: The History of a Lesbian Community* (New York: Penguin Books, 1994); Marjorie Garber, *Vested Interests: Cross-Dressing and Cultural Anxiety* (New York: Routledge, 1997); Amy Dockser Marcus, "The Adventures of Loreta Janeta Velázquez: Civil War Spy and Storyteller," with Virginia Sánchez Korrol, in *Latina Legacies: Identity, Biography, and Community*, ed. Vicki L. Ruiz and Virginia Sánchez Korrol (New York: Oxford University Press, 2005), 59–71; Alison Oram, *Her Husband Was a Woman! Women's Gender-Crossing in Modern British Popular Culture* (London: Routledge, 2007); Linda A. Morris, *Gender Play in Mark Twain: Cross-Dressing and Transgression* (Columbia: University of Missouri Press, 2007); Judy Tzu-Chun Wu, "Was Mom Chung a 'Sister Lesbian'? Asian American Gender Experimentation and Interracial Homoeroticism," repr. in Ruiz, *Unequal Sisters*, 467–82; and Kathleen Bridget Casey, "Cross-Dressers and Race-Crossers: Intersections of Gender and Race in American Vaudeville, 1900–1930" (PhD diss., University of Rochester, 2010).

69. Weiner, "Sisters of the Road," 177–79; Drury, "Experimentation," 66–69. In addition to Doreen Drury's analysis of Murray's sexuality in "Experimentation" and "Invisible Footnotes," documentation of Murray's recognition of her same-sex desires may be found in "PM-Medical . . . 1937–43," n.d., folder 71, box 4, RG MC 412, Pauli Murray Papers.

70. Murray, *Weary Throat*, 79.

71. Jacqueline Jones, *Labor of Love, Labor of Sorrow: Black Women, Work, and the Family, from Slavery to the Present* (New York: Oxford University Press, 1985), 197, 221, 231.

72. Canaday, *Straight State*, 92–93, 100–101, esp. 93; DePastino, *Citizen Hobo*, 85–91, 200–209.

73. Neil M. Maher, *Nature's New Deal: The Civilian Conservation Corps and the Roots of the American Environmental Movement* (New York: Oxford University Press, 2008), 106, 254n19. Canaday argues that "CCC camps were intended almost exclusively for unmarried men . . . as the 'separation of married men from their families would be undesirable.'" She additionally notes that "an exemption allowed up to five married men to enroll in each camp." *Straight State*, 117, 117n. Maher writes that the CCC made an "exception" for "a small number of World War I veterans, Native Americans, and what the CCC called 'Local Experienced Men,' all of whom could be married and over twenty-five." *Nature's New Deal*, 82. In terms of the Indian Emergency Conservation Work program, Donald Fixico observes that "the CCC . . . marked a significant moment in the integration of Indian people into the wage labor economy." "Federal and State Policies and American Indians," in *A Companion to American Indian History*, ed. Philip J. Deloria and Neal Salisbury (Malden, MA: Blackwell, 2004), 379–96, esp. 386. See also Parman, "Civilian Conservation Corps," 40–41; Kenneth R. Philp, *John Collier's Crusade for Indian Reform: 1920–1954* (Tucson: University of Arizona Press, 1977), 120–21; and Graham D. Taylor, *The New Deal and American Indian Tribalism* (Lincoln: University of Nebraska Press, ca. 1980), 18 and 131. Discussion of Indian Emergency Conservation Work camps may be found in the following select primary sources: Charles H. Taylor (Assistant Director) to John Collier (Commissioner, Office of Indian Affairs), March 30, 1934, Correspondence with Office of Robert Fechner, vol. 1, box 2, Records of the Bureau of Indian Affairs, National Archives, Washington, DC; William Zimmerman Jr. (Assistant Commissioner, Office of Indian Affairs), memo dated November 8, 1933, Correspondence with Office of Robert Fechner; *Indians at Work: An Emergency Conservation News Sheet for Ourselves* 1, no. 1 (August 15, 1933): 1–13, esp. 9; *Indians at Work* 1, no. 2 (September 1, 1933): 1, 19–24.

74. Reiman, *American Youth*, 76. Key information about the corps may be found in Maher, *Nature's New Deal*. See also Eric Gorham, "The Ambiguous Practices of the Civilian Conservation Corps," *Social History* 17, no. 2 (May 1992): 229–49.

75. "Roosevelt in Message," 2.

76. Kenneth Holland and Frank Ernest Hill, *Youth in the CCC* (Washington, DC: American Council on Education, 1942), 216–17.

77. Gorham, "Ambiguous Practices," 242.

78. Colin R. Johnson, "Camp Life: The Queer History of 'Manhood' in the Civilian Conservation Corps," *American Studies* 48, no. 2 (Summer 2007): 19–35; Canaday, *Straight State*, 91–134.

79. Wladaver-Morgan, "Young Women," 100–101; Diane Galusha, *Another Day, Another Dollar: The Civilian Conservation Corps in the Catskills* (Hensonville, NY: Black Dome, 2009), 37; Maher, *Nature's New Deal*, 252n2; Harvard Sitkoff, *The Depression Decade*, vol. 1 of *A New Deal for Blacks: The Emergence of Civil Rights as a National Issue* (New York: Oxford University Press 1978), 74; Parman, "Civilian Conservation Corps," 54; Philp, *John Collier's Crusade*, 122. According to Harry Gersh, who taught at the very first women's camp established by the New Deal, perhaps as many as fifty-six thousand women attended women's camps. Gersh claims that "total women served varied with who did the counting and at what period. There are no hard figures." "The She-She-She Camps: An Episode in New Deal History," unpublished term paper, 20–21, file 292, RG A-76, Hilda Worthington Smith Papers, Schlesinger

Library, Radcliffe Institute for Advanced Study, Harvard University, Cambridge, MA. Gersh, a one-time labor union leader, taught at Camp TERA, apparently after it had been renamed Camp Jane Addams in March 1936. See Bernice Miller (Director, Camp Jane Addams) to Hilda Smith (Specialist, Workers' Education) June 6, 1936, folder 321, box 2, RG 119, Correspondence, Camps, 1935: New York, Records of the National Advisory Committee on Educational Camps for Unemployed Young Women, New York–West Virginia, Records of the National Youth Administration, National Archives, College Park, MD. After a lengthy career as a journalist, Gersh enrolled in Harvard College during his sixties and received his bachelor's in 1980. He submitted this particular term paper in the spring of 1979.

80. Galusha, *Another Day*, 36.

81. Scharf, "Forgotten Woman," 246; Mink, *Wages of Motherhood*, 128.

82. Ware, *Beyond Suffrage*, 114.

83. Gersh, "She-She-She Camps," 5–6, 12; Wladaver-Morgan, "Young Women," 49–55; Joyce L. Kornbluh, *A New Deal for Workers' Education: The Workers' Service Program, 1933–1942* (Urbana: University of Illinois Press, 1987), 79–82; Ware, *Beyond Suffrage*, 111–12; Scharf, "Forgotten Woman," 246.

84. "Women's Forest Camps May Be Set Up If Enough Ask Them, Says Mrs. Roosevelt," *New York Times*, May 24, 1933, 1.

85. Kornbluh, *Workers' Education*, 95.

86. See, for example, "Camp for Needy Women Will Be Enlarged to Give Summer Vacations to 200 at Once," *New York Times*, April 15, 1932, N2; Mark Barron, "A New Yorker at Large," *Washington Post*, June 27, 1933, 17.

87. New York's Temporary Emergency Relief Administration was itself established during the summer of 1931 when Franklin Roosevelt was still the state's governor. Adams, *Harry Hopkins*, 44; Galusha, *Another Day*, 23.

88. The camp was administered largely by New York's State Conservation Department on behalf of the Federal Emergency Relief Administration. Patton, "What of Her?," 231–33. Evidence of public interest in the establishment of a large network of women's camps akin to the CCC may be found in the following: Lillian R. Sire, "Camps for Women," *New York Times*, May 28, 1933, E5; letter to the editor, *Happy Days*, September 9, 1933, 4; "Jobless Camp Greatly Helped by First Lady," *Washington Post*, July 7, 1933, 12. See also Wladaver-Morgan, "Young Women," 51–52.

89. Wladaver-Morgan, "Young Women," 54, 56–57.

90. Evidence that opposition to CCC-style camps for women persisted well after the opening of Camp TERA may be found in J. W. Hull (Director, Division of Educational Camps, Arkansas) to Richard R. Brown (Deputy Executive Director, National Youth Administration), April 8, 1936, folder 231, box 1, Records of the National Advisory Committee on Educational Camps for Unemployed Young Women, Arkansas–New Mexico. For a very brief yet important mention of "she-she-she" as a term of derision used by detractors, see Gersh, "She-She-She Camps," 20; and Kornbluh, *Workers' Education*, 79.

91. Dorothy Gurin, "Camp Tera: An Experiment in Rehabilitation" (master's thesis, Columbia University, 1936), 10–11; Wladaver-Morgan, "Young Women," 62; Ware, *Beyond Suffrage*, 111.

92. Gurin, "Camp Tera," 2, 6, 9; "17 Jobless Women Enter New Camp," *New York Times*, June 11, 1933, N1.

93. Abelson, "Women," 108.

94. Murray, *Weary Throat*, 94–95; Drury, "Experimentation," 83. Whereas both Murray and Drury render the physician's first name as "Mae," most sources end Chinn's first name with a *y* and not an *e*. Chinn was a legendary African American physician who practiced in New York City.

95. Murray, *Weary Throat*, 96. See also Gilmore, *Defying Dixie*, 253.

96. Gurin, "Camp Tera," 16, 35; Wladaver-Morgan, "Young Women," 61n45; Gersh, "She-She-She Camps," 2.

97. Genevieve Forbes Herrick, "Mrs. Roosevelt Visits U.S. Camp for Idle Girls," *Chicago Tribune*, August 8, 1933, 3; "Seven Negro Women at Roosevelt Camp," *New York Amsterdam News*, August 30, 1933, 16. When Harry Gersh taught at Camp Jane Addams, he recalled the enrollees as follows: "they were heavily Italian, Irish, fewer Slavs, a few Jews, and, as I remember, no Blacks." "She-She-She Camps," 16. In her master's thesis on Camp TERA, Dorothy Gurin discusses diversity among campers primarily in terms of religion and ethnicity and whether they were the children of immigrants. Gurin claims that "60% . . . was Jewish and 24% Catholic, with only 16% Protestant"; these figures likely apply to women who attended Camp TERA in either 1934 or 1935. See "Camp Tera," 13, 16–18, 41–52. Additional commentary regarding the enrollment of women of African descent at Camp TERA/Jane Addams may be found in Patton, "What of Her?," 238.

98. This speculation on my part is fairly tentative in that it is based on the names (Mary Figueroa and Carmen Tong) on a Christmas list that Murray produced in camp—and surnames can be a rather unreliable indicator of ethnicity and race. Not only is it quite possible that this list does not include all the women in residence between November 1934 and March 1935, it is also not clear whether Murray's list matched the complete roster of all the women in attendance at Camp TERA that December. See "Camp List (Christmas, 1934)," scrapbook, vol. 83, RG MC 412, Pauli Murray Papers. Information regarding the dates when Murray attended Camp TERA may be found in "Chronology of Events in PM's Life (1910–39)," folder 2, box 1, RG MC 412, Pauli Murray Papers.

"Pee Wee" Inness might have been Margaret Inniss, who had at least two Harlem addresses during the late 1930s. Inniss, like Pauli Murray, corresponded with Eleanor Roosevelt. As Thomas Patton points out, a "'Pee Wee' Inness" encouraged Murray to "star[t] corresponding with Eleanor Roosevelt in 1938." "What of Her?," 240; Copy of undated e-mail correspondence from Franklin Delano Roosevelt Presidential Library, Hyde Park, New York (in author's possession).

99. Some camps in the Southwest apparently were integrated in that they housed both Anglo and Latina campers but others were segregated; there was at least one camp—apparently segregated—for Native American women in North Dakota. Wladaver-Morgan, "Young Women," 63, 72, 102. See also Ella Ketchin (Director, Division of Educational Camps) to [Richard] Brown (Deputy Executive Director, National Youth Administration), June 24, 1937, box 1, NC-35, Records of the Division of Educational Camps and Educational Aid, Records of the National Youth Administration.

100. Murray, *Weary Throat*, 94–95; Drury, "Experimentation," 84–85.

101. Gurin, "Camp Tera," 4–5; Wladaver-Morgan, "Young Women," 50; Gersh, "She-She-She Camps," 16–17; Mary B. Perry (Director of Women's Work, New

Mexico) to Clinton Anderson (State Youth Administrator, New Mexico), August 23, 1935, folder 321, New Mexico, box 1, Records of the National Advisory Committee on Educational Camps for Unemployed Young Women, Arkansas–New Mexico; Frank Glick (Director, Direct Relief Division, Illinois) to Illinois County Relief Administrators, memo, December 18, 1935, folder 321, Illinois, box 1, Records of the National Advisory Committee on Educational Camps for Unemployed Young Women, Arkansas–New Mexico; "Educational Camps for Unemployed Girls," May 1, 1936, memo, National Youth Administration of Missouri, folder 321, Missouri, box 1, Records of the National Advisory Committee on Educational Camps for Unemployed Young Women, Arkansas–New Mexico.

102. Mink, *Wages of Motherhood*, 157.

103. Gersh, "She-She-She Camps," 18. The ambiguity regarding which director made this statement is due, in part, to an inconsistency in Gersh's text: at one point, he mentions three directors (the first two female and the last male); at other junctures, he explicitly mentions Camp TERA's very first director, Marion E. Tinker (whose first name Gersh renders as "Marian"), and Bernice Miller, who replaced Jessie Mills in early 1936. Tinker herself was replaced by Mills, who first served as dietician and supervised camp finances. See pages 2–3, and 10. See also Patton, "What of Her?," 235, 242–43.

104. See, for example, Ketchin to Dorothea de Schweinitz (Director, Division of Educational Camps), October 1, 1936, box 1, NC-35, Records of the Division of Educational Camps and Educational Aid, Records of the National Youth Administration.

105. Kornbluh, *Workers' Education*, 89; Gersh, "She-She-She Camps," 18.

106. Gersh, "She-She-She Camps," 18.

107. Wladaver-Morgan, "Young Women," 56n28; Gersh, "She-She-She Camps," 12.

108. Ketchin to Smith, November 20, 1937, box 1, NC-35, Records of the Division of Educational Camps and Educational Aid, Records of the National Youth Administration; Ketchin to Brown, June 24, 1937, Records of the National Youth Administration.

109. Drury, "Experimentation," 85–88.

110. Jessie Mills (Director, Camp TERA) to William A. Welch (General Manager, Palisades Park Commission), November 27, 1935, Camp TERA Folder, Suffern, New York, folder 321, box 2, Records of the National Advisory Committee on Educational Camps for Unemployed Young Women; Correspondence of the chair and the deputy executive director of NYA with state youth and camp directors on camp policies and problems, 1935–36, New York–West Virginia, Records of the National Youth Administration; Mills to Eleanor Roosevelt, December 22, 1935, folder 321, Camp TERA, Suffern, New York, box 2, Records of the National Advisory Committee on Educational Camps for Unemployed Young Women; Smith to Aubrey Williams (Executive Director, National Youth Administration), January 20, 1936, folder 321, Camp TERA, Suffern, New York, box 2, Records of the National Advisory Committee on Educational Camps for Unemployed Young Women; Mills to Eleanor Roosevelt, January 8, 1936, folder 321, Camp TERA, Suffern, New York, box 2, Records of the National Advisory Committee on Educational Camps for Unemployed Young Women.

111. Melvin, *Rural Youth on Relief*, 52; Gurin, "Camp Tera," 2.

112. Mink, *Wages of Motherhood*, 157.

113. Johnson notes that the "term 'peavie' refers to a tool used in logging." See Johnson, "Camp Life," 20, 30n5.

114. Murray, *Weary Throat*, 98; Diary, April 30, 1935, and May 7, 1935, folder 25, box 1, RG MC 412, Pauli Murray Papers.

115. Murray, *Weary Throat*, 98; Diary, May 18, 1935; May 8, 1935; and April 27, 1935, Pauli Murray Papers.

116. "'Don't Play Us Scottsboro,' College Boys Tell Southern White Girls Seeking Shelter," *Pittsburgh Courier*, June 3, 1933, A1; "'I Ain't No Ruby Bates,' White Girl Says, Resents the Comparison," *Pittsburgh Courier*, July 8 1933, 5; "'Scottsboro' Re-Enacted in West Virginia," *Pittsburgh Courier*, August 19, 1933, A3; Drury, "Invisible Footnotes," 298–99; Diary, May 6, 1935, Pauli Murray Papers.

117. Murray, *Weary Throat*, 99.

118. Drury, "Experimentation," 78–80; Drury, "Invisible Footnotes," 298–99.

119. In January 1933, for example, Nels Anderson observed that when it came to "vagrants," it was possible to "look at their hands and bodies . . . [to] see that they have been working." See "Statement of Nels Anderson," 63–71, esp. 71. The author of *The Hobo: The Sociology of the Homeless Man* (Chicago: University of Chicago Press, 1923), Anderson was a pioneer in participant-observer ethnography and eventually served as a WPA administrator.

120. Gloria E. Anzaldúa, "Preface: (Un)natural Bridges, (Un)safe Spaces," in *This Bridge We Call Home: Radical Visions for Transformation*, ed. Gloria Anzaldúa and AnaLouise Keating (New York: Routledge, 2002), 1–5, esp. 3.

121. "Intersectionality," as initially articulated by Kimberlé Crenshaw more than twenty years ago, is a theoretical approach meant to facilitate analysis of the "unique compoundedness" of race, gender, sexuality, class, and other politicized identities as they function on individual and collective levels. Crenshaw uses the term to apply to people belonging to racialized populations (especially black women) and social groups who tend to face varying levels of discrimination and oppression in their quotidian lives. See "Demarginalizing the Intersection of Race and Sex: A Black Feminist Critique of Antidiscrimination Doctrine, Feminist Theory and Antiracist Politics," *University of Chicago Legal Forum*, 1989, 139–67, esp. 150. In a second landmark essay, Crenshaw contends that intersectional approaches reveal why "ignoring differences within groups contributes to tension among groups." See "Mapping the Margins: Intersectionality, Identity Politics, and Violence against Women of Color," in *Critical Race Theory: The Key Writings That Formed the Movement*, ed. Kimberlé Crenshaw, Neil Gotanda, Gary Peller, and Keller Thomas (New York: New Press, 1995), 357–83, esp. 357. Some scholars, theorists, and practitioners have criticized the very concept of "intersectionality" as actually reinforcing categories that are potentially limiting, reductionist, or otherwise problematic. Leslie McCall outlines three general approaches to the complexities implicit within the notion of intersectionality itself. McCall notes that some theorists and practitioners have adopted views regarding "anticategorical complexity" and thereby question whether "categories [can be used] . . . in anything but a simplistic way." Others, McCall argues, think in terms of "intercategorical complexity" and "provisionally adopt existing analytical categories to document relationships of inequality among social groups." Still others continue to embrace notions of "intracategorical complexity [that] inaugurated the

study of intersectionality . . . [and they] interrogat[e] the boundary-making and boundary defining process itself." "The Complexity of Intersectionality," *Signs* 30, no. 3 (2005): 1771–800, esp. 1773–74. See also Dorthe Staunæs, "Where Have All the Subjects Gone? Bringing Together the Concepts of Intersectionality and Subjectification," *NORA: Nordic Journal of Feminist and Gender Research* 11, no. 2 (2003): 101–10, esp. 103–5; and Nira Yuval-Davis, "Intersectionality and Feminist Politics," *European Journal of Women's Studies* 13, no. 3 (2006): 193–209, esp. 195, 197.

Chapter 8

What Women Want

The Paradoxes of Postmodernity as Seen through Promise Keeper and Million Man March Women

Deborah Gray White

On the morning of October 4, 1997, members of the National Organization of Women (NOW) greeted the hundreds of thousands of Promise Keepers (PK) who gathered for the Stand in the Gap assembly on the National Mall with shouts of "Ominous!" and "Dangerous!" and with placards that read "Patriarch Keeper."[1] It was a familiar sight, one that had been repeated at almost every Promise Keepers gathering since Bill McCartney founded the organization in 1990, and one that would be repeated at every Promise Keepers gathering through the remainder of the 1990s. "They're a very sexist, racist and homophobic organization," said Sondra Sinke, the Nebraska chapter coordinator of the National Organization for Women, when the Promise Keepers gathered in Omaha in 1999.[2] Later that year, at the PK meeting in Hartford, Connecticut, the protest was the same. In an editorial titled "Much to Fear from Promise Keepers," Alice Lambert, the president of the Connecticut NOW, wrote, among other things, "We feminists believe that women control their own bodies and lives. Bill McCartney . . . opposes women's rights."[3]

Feminist opposition to the Million Man March (MMM) was similarly insistent. Julianne Malveaux, the future president of Bennett College, asked, "When men are 'stepping up,' we have to ask, will the first step be onto a woman's back?"[4] Another black woman, Rhonda Williams, could also not support the march: "If it means that more men are capitulating to a type of thinking that says black families are simply broken and pathological, unaffected by economic and cultural change, and simply needing some more good ole-fashioned male supremacy—I can't sign on."[5] Neither could activist Jewel Jackson McCabe, who declared that African American "needs are not served by men declaring themselves the only 'rightful' leaders of our families, or our communities and of our ongoing struggle for justice." Justice, she said, "cannot be achieved with a march that offers a distorted racist view of black manhood with a narrowly sexist vision of men standing degrees above women."[6]

Whether they knew it or not these black and white women had a lot in common. For sure, they rejected both Bill McCartney, the founder of the Promise Keepers, and Louis Farrakhan, the convener of the Million Man March, both of whom were associated with antiwomen, antifeminist, and homophobic positions. Even though both Farrakhan and McCartney at one time or another disavowed their critics' claims with proclamations on the equality of men and women, and men's responsibility to share parenting responsibilities with women, both drew heavy skepticism.

Also, black and white feminists did not buy into the idea propagated by march leaders that these large gatherings gave men a chance to bond and thus be emotionally reborn into kinder, gentler human beings. Rather, to feminists, this was just another instance of what one scholar has called "male romance," the phenomenon that "involves men going off with other men, ritually bonding with each other, and being 'reborn' within a community of males," a process which throughout American history has allowed men to consolidate power while they eliminated women from the centers of political, social, and economic control. Rather than allay feminists fears, "the preponderance of tears and repentance . . . on the National Mall constituted a symbolic claim on the capital itself." Men's mourning, it was feared, signaled little more than a softer expression of male domination. According to *New York Times* columnist, Maureen Dowd, when men explore their fragilities, "it usually leads to trouble."[7]

Most women, however, rejected the view put forth by NOW.[8] On the morning of October 16, 1995, activist and self-avowed feminist, E. Faye Williams, had only good things to say about the multitude of black men who gathered in Washington, DC, for the Million Man March. "There is an African proverb that it is the women who hold up the sky," said Williams. "I have a feeling that from this day on, it's going to be a whole lot easier. . . . You have come to help us hold up the sky."[9] Williams, a DC lawyer and chair of the district's MMM organizing committee, was joined in her support of the march by countless other black women who could be heard along the sidelines shouting, "Black man. Black man. We applaud you, black man. Black sunshine! Black sunshine! We love you, Brothers!"[10] For them, October 16 marked a new beginning. They were not offended by Farrakhan's instruction that women stay home and mind black children so that men could march alone. It would not, as Dowd predicted, lead to trouble, but to a new era where black men claimed leadership of neighborhoods and of families, where black men recognized the strength of black women and where the abuse of black women was henceforth tolerated by no one.[11] So supportive were many black women of the Million Man March that a *Washington Post* poll found that more black men than women objected to the exclusion of women. Only 18 percent of the black men polled said the march ought to be single-sexed while fully half of the black women polled supported the men-only restriction.[12] Similarly, black male academics were more likely than their female counterparts to think that black women should have been included.[13]

The elation expressed by these black women was not unlike that of the wives of most Promise Keepers. When Jeanne Parrott's husband left for a 1994 gathering in Boulder, Colorado, Parrott "prayed that God would open the floodgates and that Dale would come home touched by the Spirit in a new way."[14] When he did, she was overjoyed. So was Karen Jensen. "Women have gone through years of tears, and God is answering their cries," she proclaimed. "Promise Keepers is teaching men how to become servants to their families, and to society," she said.[15] Jensen's sentiment was seconded by syndicated columnist Suzanne Fields, who found a lot to admire about both the Promise Keepers and Million Man Marchers. "It's unfair to call them anti-feminist because they don't bash women or women's issues, but like the Million Man March participants, insist on meeting without women . . . to reevaluate themselves from within, with other men."[16]

Why did these women support these male-centered gatherings? Why were they not threatened by them? Because the Promise Keepers are a predominantly white group and the Million Man March was a predominantly black event, answering these questions allows for a rare comparison of the way these two select groups of black and white women view men and male-female relationships. It also allows for a look at the different way that feminism figures in the lives of these black and white women. Besides exploring why feminist arguments like that promoted by NOW missed the mark with these women, this chapter explores the similar and different needs and desires of these black and white females. It looks at what was important to them and explores their perspectives in both historical and contemporary contexts. Finally, this chapter suggests that these women had more in common than we might expect, beginning with the fact that their responses to their men's organizing was calculated to help them cope with, and even overcome, the profound societal dislocations of the 1990s.[17]

The Promise Keepers, Million Man March, and the Postmodern 1990s

By the 1990s Americans were reeling from all of the dislocations associated with late twentieth century capitalism, what some scholars call "postmodernism."[18] The nation's shift from a producer to a consumer or service economy had decreased the number of manufacturing jobs that had made it possible for a single male wage earner with limited education to earn enough money to support a wife and children. In the 1990s the effects of the global nature of the economy were fully visible. As blue- and white-collar jobs were exported over-seas, and corporations downsized to be more competitive, lay-offs in all sectors were common and job security disappeared. Increasingly, women entered the labor market to compensate for the lost earnings of men. Though the fem-inist movement had supplied an ideological basis for women's work outside the home by postulating all of the benefits that accrued to economically inde-pendent women, it was economic hardship that forced the majority to work to keep their families afloat.

Men, women, and families felt the pressure of the new economy and the social order that flowed from it. African Americans suffered disproportion-ately because racism made their lives more precarious than whites, but whites suffered also. Young white families earned less in 1986 than comparable families in 1979, and they had little prospects for homeownership, a prin-ciple signifier of middle-class status. The thirteen year period between 1973 and 1986 that saw real earnings for young men between the ages of twenty and twenty-four drop by 26 percent also saw the price of a mortgage for a medium-priced home rise to about 44 percent of an average male's monthly earnings. Alone, most men had a hard time purchasing and maintaining a home. On average, women fared worst. Most did not enter the labor force as professionals, well paid or not. Rather, they were fast becoming the nation's postindustrial proletariat, and poverty was increasingly feminized. As white women worked at jobs that made their unpaid homemaking more burden-some, many joined the majority of African American women who, after cen-turies of being stuck at the bottom of the labor ladder, still questioned the benefits of female labor force participation.[19]

The new economy played havoc with American culture, especially family culture. It demanded that men and women change their ideas about masculin-ity and femininity, about motherhood and fatherhood, and about the purpose and value of the "traditional" two-parent family. Once held together by the family wage that made women dependent on men's wages, men were the first to detether themselves from the economic burdens of their wives and children, followed by women who preferred singleness and single parenthood to unsat-isfying and sometimes abusive relationships. Although feminism and women's self-sufficiency made it possible to imagine a truly democratic marriage where household duties, childrearing, and emotional sharing became the responsi-bility of both parents, the reality was that it was hard to change the entrenched patriarchal patterns, which by custom and institutional structure placed emo-tionally distant men at the head of the family. As divorce and rates of singleness rose, the end-of-the-century traditional two-parent heterosexual family became more unsettled and insecure. Households containing married couples with children were fast becoming a minority. The blended household of divorced and remarried adults, single-mother households, and single-sexed households were becoming prominent. As one scholar put it, the family was a "contested domain," and the "postmodern family condition of diversity, flux, and instability" was a fact of end-of-century life.[20]

This very disorder, which characterized so many aspects of postmodern American life and culture, was the catalyst for the mass gatherings of the 1990s, including the numerous Promise Keeper gatherings and the Million Man and Woman Marches of 1995 and 1997, respectively. Critics bemoaned these gatherings as identity marches, because they emphasized the differences that separated Americans rather than the commonalities that brought them together. Indeed, Americans did gather in distinct groups to try to congeal around what they considered the most important part of their identity. But they did so, ironically, not to be divisive but in an attempt to make sense of a fractious world that was increasingly unfamiliar. They gathered with people they perceived to be like themselves in hope of providing stability in a world where a new economic order had combined with a series of rights movements to make, among other things, class mobility uncertain, gender roles confusing, and community, however previously conceived, precarious. Promise Keepers used their maleness and Christianity to anchor themselves in the ever-changing turn-of-the-century environment. Million Man Marchers found their moorings in their maleness and blackness. Both groups gathered to explore and pronounce a new understanding of themselves as men, fathers, husbands, and leaders, and both groups chose to do so without women present. Neither group grumbled excessively about the new structure of the economy, nor did they petition the state for help. Both the Promise Keepers and Million Man Marchers turned inward and embraced a self-help ethic. As we have seen, for the most part they were supported by the women in their respective communities. That support is the subject to which this chapter now turns.

The Promise Keepers and the Women Who Supported Them

Like their men, Promise Keeper wives (and female relatives and friends) wanted stable, functioning families.[21] They thought the two-parent, heterosexual family was the core unit of American society and believed that the dislocations of the seventies and eighties had weakened it. No doubt they were disturbed by the almost 10 percent drop in white women's marriage rate between 1950 and 2000 and a corresponding increase (nearly 10 percent) in the divorce rate.[22] Like PK men, they thought that the family was in trouble because men were not emotionally involved in the unit. Some were just absent, but most men, PK wives believed, did not know how to be in the family or relate to other family members.

PK wives endorsed the Promise Keepers because in showing men how Christ loved his disciples and other people, PK showed Christian men how to befriend other men in supportive, sensitive ways, and in so doing taught them how to relate to their wives and children. This is the message that comes through the strongest in PK wives' testimonials. For example, Jennifer McDonald of Wayzata, Minnesota, thanked her husband for attending a PK convention and "learning how to be a better husband and father and sharing your faith." Fellow Minnesotan, Allyson Jelinski, likewise thanked her spouse for making "our family the top priority in his life." Although another Minnesotan, Kristine Harley, dissented, finding all the rant about men making family a priority akin to endorsing a "benevolent tyranny." Others, like Sally Becker of Milwaukee, found it the salvation of their marriage: "Now there's more give and take. . . . He's more understanding of my needs and I'm more understanding of his."[23] Connie Schaedel of LaMirada, California, was similarly thankful of PK: "Our relationship, our marriage, became even more complete, even more whole, as a result of the way he felt he could express himself."[24]

PK wives found that Promise Keeper teaching led to a marked improvement in the way their husbands related to their children. Veronica Gonzalez, for example, said that her husband Efrain, a Kansas City pastor, "spends more time with their five children and they love it."[25] Minnesotan Sarah Richards reported that her husband, Brian, came home from a rally determined to spend more time with their three- and five-year-olds. Although his job as a CPA forced him to bring work home, PK taught him the value of "making more time for the family."[26] Likewise, Houston resident Gary Blackmon was married twelve years and had four children before he attended his first Promise Keepers gathering. According to his wife, Kintra, it was that first meeting that made him "more sensitive to the needs of the family." "Every husband needs to be part of Promise Keepers," said Blackmon.[27] Michigan insurance agent Ron Bodine's wife agreed. Promise Keepers, she maintained, "opened up more time for talking with . . . [his thirteen-year-old son] and doing things with him."[28]

Most PK wives wanted men in the household, because they believed it made the family stronger and changed the family chemistry. In short, they thought that men and women are fundamentally different, particularly in matters of relationships and emotions, and that this difference balanced the family in a positive way. Karen Tucker, for example, felt that her husband needed to build relationships with men to better communicate with her: "Men are just not as good at building relationships as women are."[29] Annette Cox, of Liberty, Kansas, felt similarly: "It is easier for women to find other women. It seems harder for men to find each other." Kimberly Francisco of Kansas City saw men and women in complementary ways. She thought that women, more than men, often put more effort into finding ways to improve themselves, their spiritual lives, and their families. "Men find value in their jobs, and women find value in the way someone treats them."[30] The Reverend Peggy Jones, a black woman who had nothing but praise for the Promise Keepers, thought PK was a blessing because she knew "how difficult it is for them [men] to open up."[31] And when her friends suggested that she would be made subservient if she continued dating her Promise Keeper boyfriend, Kathy Finnell of Kansas City scoffed as she expressed the essentialist idea that "men need to be leaders." She added, "To the extent that you are in a relationship with a man, if you don't trust his decisions and yourself in his hands, you need to look elsewhere."[32]

At first glance it seems that these women had conceded decision-making autonomy and assumed a subordinate role in the household in return for masculinist protection, something NOW leaders decried. That the Promise Keepers projected a kinder, gentler, in fact gallant and chivalrous, masculinity did not mask, they argued, the fact that PK men wanted women to play subordinate roles in the households so that they could assert their authority through their role as protector. Political scientist Iris Marion Young explained this very well when she argued that feminine women are more likely to concede to masculine dominion when men are loving and self-sacrificing and not selfish, violent, and aggressive. Since the feminine woman wants healthy, safe homes, and "masculine protection is needed to make a home a haven," the logic of masculinist protection is the submission of women.[33] Scholar Deniz Kandiyoti calls this dynamic the "patriarchal bargain." Women, she argues, consciously and unconsciously weigh their life chances against the patriarchal system of their society and constantly strategize according to the benefits that accrue from submitting to male domination. Even when that system does not yield economic or emotional security for women, their perception that it does or their sense that resistance will not empower them is enough to keep the patriarchal bargain in place.[34] Critics of PK wives supposed this kind of bargain was at work. To them, these Christian women were making a deal with patriarchy which was just as bad as making one with the devil.

And this was maddening. "They want to subjugate women," said Mary Celeste, a spokesperson for the Colorado Legal Initiatives Project.[35] "SMART WOMEN DON'T BUY YOUR PROMISES," read a banner that flew over the fifty-two thousand men who met in a stadium in Boulder, Colorado.[36] Diana Butler, an editorialist who attended a Los Angeles PK rally, put the argument succinctly. She found the Promise Keepers to be unobjectionable on the level of individual transformation. The overall ethos and agenda, however, was objectionable, because PK "implicitly and sometimes explicitly—opposes women's leadership in the home and in the church." Butler took exception to one PK minister who interpreted Ephesians 5:22, "Wives, be subject to your husbands as you are to the Lord," claiming that "he urged men to 'out-serve' their wives." To Butler, there was something wrong with this Christian definition of marriage as a "competition in which the best servant wins."[37] Butler was also disturbed by what she thought was PK's greater sensitivity to racial matters than to sexism. That PK failed to denounce the sins of "pornography, demeaning women verbally, abuse, sexual sin, power manipulation, lack of emotional support" was "belittling" to women. Butler summed up the PK philosophy this way:

"Promise Keepers envisions life as a football game. A great team on the field cheered by women on the sidelines."[38]

Most Promise Keeper wives disagreed with the likes of Butler, and they would not have used the scholarly arguments of Young and Kandiyoti. They took exception to the idea that they were being submissive and would not abide the notion that they had somehow bought protection. "Critics don't understand. They're speaking out of ignorance," said Kathy Simmons of Independence, Missouri. "I haven't heard anything that suggests that the woman is inferior in any way."[39] Valerie Bridgeman Davis, a black woman who described herself as "a happily married womanist," had an entirely different interpretation of Ephesians 5:22. She and her PK husband, Don, read mutuality into the verse. "I believe in submission, but as us submitting to each other," she heard her husband say.[40] Laurie Beyer, a PK wife from Milwaukee, would agree with Bridgeman: "To me there is nothing more equal than the way God designed marriage relationships and families to be."[41]

PK wives felt this way for several reasons. To begin with, they understood equality not in the sense of sameness but in the vein of equal complementary roles. Since they believed that men and women were inherently different, it followed that men and women brought different qualities to the relationship and had different roles to fulfill in the household. "It's called teamwork," said Marilyn Kenaga. While some feminists might see female subordination written all over her directive that "Men are to work and provide for their families and bathe them in the word of God," while women "are to help the husbands by taking care of what God has given them," PK wives saw this as equality based on the complementarity of men and women.[42] This is how Kim Bruder of Milwaukee interpreted marriage roles. Her seemingly contradictory statement that "I do feel the husband is head of the household, but we're equal," makes the most sense if viewed in this light.[43] Similarly, this is what Texan Lynda Vaughan meant when she said, "men are leaders of the family, but that doesn't mean they step all over us and we are doormats. . . . That means we work together."[44] Donna Schaper, a minister with the Massachusetts Conference of the United Church of Christ, summed up this sentiment this way: "We want our men to dance. We don't even mind being led—in fact some of us want to be led. We don't want to be led everywhere and we won't be. We won't let ourselves be led out of the benefits of partnership marriage. . . . Women are tired of being both mother and father. We want strong men as much as men want to be strong; Strength in men is not a rival to our strength; it is a complement.[45]

This perception of equality rooted in complementarity was in direct rebuttal to the feminist's critique of the Promise Keepers. In this counternarrative, PK women were not duped into making a naive bargain with willful patriarchs, nor had they succumbed to a nationalist project that had them safely ensconced in the private sphere of the home, protecting the hearth for the good of the nation.[46] Rather, feminists were the problem. Feminists, they would argue, were uncompromising, man hating, angry, shrill women who did not value the family or the communities that families made strong. Feminists were all about self, whereas they, Christian women, were about God, family, and community.

Nothing demonstrates this better than the critique of feminism offered by Promise Keeper women who were critical of PK and yet still tried to distance themselves from feminism. One woman, who described herself as an evangelical Episcopalian, agreed with feminists that PK "is dangerously close to reversing many hard-won gains." She quickly added, "although not that I am a feminist." Sarah Peterson, a woman who sought a divorce from her husband because his Promise Keeper teachings led him to become too assertive, was also sure she was not a feminist, one of those "strident bitter women who have placed their careers above all else." Said Peterson, "You do not have to be a feminist . . . to have some say-so in what happens in your own house." Another woman, from Rhode Island, grounded her objection to the Promise Keepers in scripture. She took her cues from the strong women in the Bible. When her PK husband tried to push her into a subordinate role, she screamed at him, "Did you miss Mary and Martha? Jesus told her to get out of the kitchen, and come sanctify herself at his feet. He told her Mary had made the better choice. Tell me where that is in these sermons you're hearing?" Yet another woman, quoting from her *Study Bible for Women*, took aim at those Promise Keepers who did not read mutuality into Ephesians. The verse in her study Bible read, in part, "Rather than meaning the mutual acceptance and endorsement of woman and man, it has been used to evoke the idea of male dominance and female submission. Similarly, the terms 'equal but different' have often been twisted to mean 'unequal and hierarchical.'" When she finished reading, she turned to her interviewer and pointed out the obvious: "for goodness sakes!" she said of her study Bible, "It's not exactly radical feminist!"[47]

The important point here is that Promise Keeper women believed in the equality of men and women, but they did not want to be associated with feminism, especially with what some perceived as radical feminism. In this they were like the women from various denominations who in 1997 signed "A Christian Women's Declaration," a concise statement of theology that attempted to carve out a middle ground between Christian fundamentalists who advocated women's submission to men, and feminist positions that were perceived to be anti-Christian. These women sang the praises of women of previous generations who made it possible for women to enjoy more opportunities and respect than ever before. They claimed as their foremothers the women who first bore witness to the risen Christ. They proclaimed equality with men based on the fact that Jesus Christ made "freedom and dignity possible for all human beings—for women as well as for men," as well as on the fact that women were created in God's image, "and the grace of God is extended equally to women." These women affirmed the Triune God, meaning that although they addressed God by the name Father, they "acknowledge that God, who created sexuality,

238 DEBORAH GRAY WHITE

is neither male nor female." The human race, they claimed, was constituted not by a continuum of sexes but by two complementary sexes, both created in God's image and created to mutually serve each other. All that these women asked of their fellow Christian women they also asked of men. They were especially aggrieved, because they were "conscious of how often women have been the targets of such disrespect, abuse, prejudice, and oppression." They pledged themselves "to stand in solidarity with all who have been denied justice, freedom and opportunity."[48]

Needless to say, in their declaration these Christian women took aim at what they perceived to be radical feminism's faults, particularly what they perceived to be its endorsement of detrimental cultural trends. Among the many faults they attributed to radical feminists were the latter's interpretation of gender as a social construct. They claimed that while they recognized the force of cultural influence on individual choice and on concepts of maleness and femaleness, they affirmed "that sexuality is rooted in the biological designation of the two sexes—male and female." These Christian women rejected what they claimed was the radical feminist notion of "equality" as "identical." They also discarded the idea that women have been "victims" or "empty vessels" shaped by patriarchy, and they discounted the "exaggeration of women's suffering." They claimed that there have been "countless women of vision and tenacious faith who, through prayer and perseverance, overcame limitations of every variety to influence the shaping of human history." Rather than complain about the innate superiority, inferiority, or radical differences between men and women, these Christian women claimed to celebrate the commonalities of men and women as well as their "unique differences." Of course, in their view, radical feminists were to be faulted for the glorification of "sexual lifestyles without limits or consequences and views of marriage and family that contradict biblically-based faith and time-tested moral behavior." In other words, radical feminists had to be opposed because of their support of abortion, homosexuality, and same-sex marriage, cultural practices that they believed destabilized the family.[49]

Because Promise Keeper wives are a diverse group of women, it is impossible to know whether they all endorsed "A Christian Women's Declaration."[50] But given the similarity of positions on the centrality of marriage and the family, the equality of men and women, the complementarity of men's and women's roles, the mutual service of husbands and wives, and the folly of radical feminism, "A Christian Woman's Declaration," does help us position PK wives theologically and understand the theology that underpinned their support of their husbands. It is also helpful to understand that the women who supported the kind of equalitarianism endorsed by PK wives were considered to be to the left of Christian fundamentalists, who blasted the declaration. These critics excoriated women who "equivocate on the masculinity of God and the maleness of Jesus, neuter language, and separate the man from his proper office as head of the church and family." These more conservative Christians opposed what most PK wives supported. Above all, they believed that "among Christians rule is given to the man, who is to lay down his life for the woman, who for her part is to submit to him."[51] This is not the portrait of PK wives presented in interviews and testimonials, a portrait made clearer when placed not just in the secular context many, including NOW leaders, placed them in, but also in the Christian context, where they appear far more liberal or progressive than their more conservative counterparts.

The work done by sociologist Judith Stacey on evangelicalism and feminism also helps us understand Promise Keeper women. During the course of her 1980s fieldwork in Silicon Valley, California, Stacey found that with the exception of ideas about homosexuality and abortion, "feminist ideas and practices have diffused broadly throughout evangelical Christian discourse in the United States." Many of the evangelical women she came in contact with expressed sentiments similar to those of PK women. "We are not doormats," said one woman who espoused submission in the context of mutuality. Despite the diversity of the evangelical community, Stacey still found that Christian women and secular feminists had much in common. For example, Christian women's magazines took working outside the home for granted, counseled women against tolerating abuse, and held men as responsible as women for failed relationships. Using the term "postfeminism" to denote the fact that feminism had in fact transformed evangelical interpretations of the Bible such that ministers and journals provide "information on rape self-defense, criticisms on social pressures for thinness and youth and reviews for books celebrating friendships between women," Stacey interpreted the choices made by evangelical women as a response to the unsettling dislocations imposed by America's new economy, an economy that, as she put it, has "intensified cravings for security and spirituality."[52]

Stacey's work dovetails with that of religious scholar R. Made Griffith, who studied members of Women's Aglow Fellowship International, an evangelical women's organization dedicated to prayer and women's fellowship. Careful not to leave the impression that her subjects are feminists, Griffith nevertheless demonstrates the affinities between them and Aglow women. Both, for example, denounce the irresponsibility shown by many husbands toward their families and express distrust of men. Like feminists, Aglow women are woman centered and use their communities to help women build self-esteem and love for themselves independent of male relationships. In her words, both evangelicals and feminists "want to see women's cultural and social labor revalued, celebrated, and elevated in status." The difference, Griffith argues, is partly in the way Aglow members define womanhood. In essence, Aglow women ascribe different characteristics to women and men, and they believe feminism forces women to act, unnaturally, like men. Like Promise Keeper women, Aglow women want women to be able to embrace power grounded, not in the sameness of men and women but in a powerful womanness.[53]

What then can we conclude about why most female relatives of Promise Keepers supported their men's efforts to change themselves? For sure they espoused a nonfeminist and sometimes antifeminist position, but Promise Keeper women, like other evangelical women, were nevertheless profoundly wary of male supremacy and supremely confident in women's abilities. Yet because they supported their men's efforts to change themselves, PK women wanted men back in the household in a meaningful way, not just as providers but as emotionally involved, responsible husbands and fathers. They wanted to share responsibilities with them in the home, a home made stable by the equal complementary contribution of husbands and wives and mothers and fathers. This was their strategy for dealing with the high divorce rates, rising singleness, and other insecurities of postindustrialism. They were past deciding whether some of the basic precepts of feminism were good or bad; they needed a strategy for dealing with postmodern culture, and they were willing to work with men who looked to the Promise Keepers for help in navigating the new status quo.

Million Man Marchers and the Women Who Supported Them

Like Promise Keeper wives, the black women who supported the Million Man March believed in the viability of the two-parent heterosexual family and the necessity of making it central to African American community life. "Place," however, was what differentiated these women from their white counterparts, because African American women did not talk about the family apart from discussions about race, also understood as "the community." They believed that the family had to remain strong because, historically, it had been *the* bulwark against racism and its economic effects. Its weakening, they believed, had left black people more vulnerable than usual. Typical of the sentiments expressed were those of Linda Greene, a national fundraiser for the march, who declared, "I knew this was going to restore family values in our fragmented African American race."[54] Freddie Groomes, executive assistant for Florida State University's Human Resources Department, said something similar: "I think that the strength of the black family equals the strength of the race."[55] Frances Murphy, the publisher of the *Washington Afro-American*, opined that "almost all of us agreed that the goal was to reverse the balance in the black family and create a partnership with our men, like it was originally, before slavery." Cora Barry, the wife of the former mayor of Washington, DC, went so far as to deny that the march was about "division by gender." Despite the call for a "men's only" march and despite the official exclusion of women, Barry declared the march to be about "the liberation of our people."[56]

Barry was, no doubt, thinking about the state of the black family and the literal absence of men. In the 1990s half of all African American children lived in single-parent female headed households, and the marriage rate among African Americans was such that at the end of the 1990s only about a third of African American women of marriage age were married. The black male firearm homicide rate was two to four times higher than that of any other socioeconomic census strata, accounting for 42 percent of all young black male deaths. And although African Americans composed only 11.4 percent of the total US population, African American males accounted for almost 31 percent of all prison inmates.[57]

This made Faye Williams's statement about holding up the sky more than a mere metaphor. As Williams subsequently elaborated, "Just the thought of a million black men coming together makes the job easier for me and other black women who are out there every day working. Maybe we do finally get to bow out for a little while and get a little rest." Williams took her support a step further when she suggested that black women, who have the highest single rate in the nation, might finally be able to find a man and get married. "Just think," she said half tongue in cheek, "we could observe all these black men in Washington in October and be married by Christmas."[58]

Black women's support for the Million Man March was therefore steeped in a desire to reverse a particularly harsh postmodern condition faced by African American women. Chicago alderman Dorothy Tillman spoke for a lot of black women when she said, "I've been on the front lines all my life. It does my heart well to see our men go forward.[59] A San Francisco woman had the same feeling: "I myself raised my three oldest sons alone for 10 years. There comes a time when you have to stand up and take responsibility. . . . Men can no longer sit back and say it's the white man's fault."[60] For the millions of women who had been the financial backbone of their families, Linda Greene's statement that "they are recommitting their lives to us as a provider of their families" represented the real hope perched behind black women's support of the march. For others, like Geneva Smitherman, a University Distinguished Professor at Michigan State University, Greene expressed the desperation of many. Smitherman added, "The fact of the matter is we *can't* do it alone. Sisters have been climbing up the rough side of the mountain. . . . Unless we do something quick, this will be the plight of the next generation of African Americans in the 21st century."[61]

As steadfast as was most black women's support of the march, it was not uncritical. Just like the support that PK wives extended to their emotionally absent Promise Keeper men, black women were angry that black men had abandoned their familial responsibilities and had fomented so much of the violence in black communities. In fact, because so many black women agreed with the goals of the march—the atonement of black men for their sins against women and the family—many did not hide their frustration. Alderman Tillman, for example, was pleased to see black men go forward, but she also expressed anger over the fact that "the men are killing each other and the men in our community need to address that."[62] Two Cleveland area women hinged their support for the march on what happened when the men returned home. One woman, the associate director of the Interchurch Council of Greater Cleveland warned, "this better not be a case where they feel all this emotion in Washington and go back home and do the same things that cause problems when they get back home." Another woman, activist Grace Jones, thought it would be a wasted effort if when the men returned home they did not "seriously address the problems of the African-American community." If the march turned out to be just a "symbolic march," she said, "they can all fold their tents and go away as far as I'm concerned."[63] A forty-nine-year-old New York woman who attended the Million Woman March was like-minded. When she compared the Million Man and Woman marches she found the difference in each march's purpose: "the brother's march was atonement; the sister's march is affirmation," she declared. Explaining further, she said, "We didn't do anything wrong. . . . We've got nothing to atone for, we were there keeping the family together while they were out doing whatever they were out doing."[64] Even a fifteen-year-old had imbibed this opinion. About the Million Man and Woman marches she said, "We didn't need this march as much as the men did. Women always stick together. But men, if they got into it today, tomorrow they'd talk about killing each other."[65]

This criticism is significant, since historically African American women have been cautious about criticizing black men for fear of being accused of dividing the race. The trope of the black woman as race traitor has a history that goes back at least until the 1830s, when Maria Stewart, an African American activist, was forced to leave her Boston community for publicly questioning the effectiveness of black men's leadership on the question of slavery and abolition. When women like Sojourner Truth argued for female suffrage on the grounds that they did not want to be subject to any man, white or black, it seemed again that some black women were willing to sacrifice race unity and, worse yet, sacrifice black male suffrage, which was seen by many as the key to African American citizenship. Whether cast as a Mammy, an overweight black woman who loved her whites more than her blacks; a Jezebel, a woman who never refused the white man's sexual advances; or a Sapphire, a woman who usurped the black man's power in the home and community, the historical stereotypes of black women revealed them as women who could not be trusted to support black men. Several high profile events of the 1990s, most notably the testimony of Anita Hill against Supreme Court nominee Clarence Thomas, seemed to reinforce the notion that black women were race traitors.[66]

Obviously, this trope circumscribed black women's responses to the Million Man March and helps to account for the complexity of their feelings. Although support for the march did not preclude criticism, that criticism was tempered with understanding. The same woman who supported the march because she was pleased that black men were finally proactive could be angry about black

WHAT WOMEN WANT   243

men's past failures and yet still find reason to absolve black men of responsibility for those failures. For black women who supported the Million Man March, race and racism made all the difference. Promise Keeper wives believed that men and women were different because God made them so. Black women supporters of the Million Man March believed black men and women to be different because racism made it so.

This sentiment extended across the generations and was overwhelming. Twenty-nine-year-old Chicagoan Kristen Anderson said, "I think the black men in this country deserve my support. . . . [They] have an entirely different set of problems that are unique to both their malehood and their race."[67] An older woman, Pauline Tarver, Cleveland's NAACP executive director, opined the very popular view, the one that surfaced effectively during the 1991 Clarence Thomas Supreme Court hearings, that historically racist measures were directed mostly at black men. "You have to understand that, historically, black men have been held down while black women have been held up as the positive, strong force in black households."[68] "Black men as a whole are in more of a crisis right now," said Crystal Herrod of Silver Springs, Maryland.[69] In Prof. Charshee McIntyre's opinion, the crisis was racism. She supported the march because she thought young black males had been targeted for extinction.[70] As if to agree, the day after the march, sixteen-year-old Jamilla James told her Washington, DC, high school class about her efforts to keep her brother occupied with house cleaning and homework to keep him away from the drug dealers who stalked her neighborhood. Her classmate, Martrelle Pyatt, chimed in with stories of how her family always made a "special effort to support the men in the family." When someone found a job in the suburbs listed in the newspaper, the whole family would chip in to get the male out to the job.[71]

The prevalence of these ideas demonstrates that political scientist Nikol Alexander-Floyd's observations about the Black Cultural Pathology Paradigm have a lot of currency among black women. Alexander-Floyd argues, convincingly, that in the past twenty-five years contemporary black politics has developed a masculinist emphasis centered on "ideological assumptions about wounded Black masculinity (alternately described as the plight of the Black male/endangered Black male or the black male in crisis) and the breakdown of the Black family." According to Alexander-Floyd, assumptions about the black male crisis have caused both blacks and whites to endorse ideas about black family pathology and deviance and seek to reverse it by endorsing public policy aimed at restoring black patriarchy. Besides noting the similarity between conservative white politics, which likewise addresses patriarchy, specifically the absence of fathers, Alexander-Floyd posits that the combined black and white conservative agenda spells trouble for black women, whose own particular personal and familial burdens are scapegoated, trivialized, or ignored.[72]

As indicated here, and in Alexander-Floyd's work, the Million Man March was a perfect example of the heightened emphasis in black America on black masculinity. Not only did the march exclude black women but, as happened so often in the past, black women who pressed for inclusion were accused of being traitors to the race, and not just any traitor but *feminist* traitors, out of touch with rank-and-file black Americans who did not have the luxury of concerning themselves with sexism because black male unemployment and homicide were wreaking havoc in their lives. Black women, cautioned Smitherman, "had to be wary of the seductive feminist trap." Black men might be sexist, she argued, but because white men held all of the power and control over the nation's institutions, it was they who needed to be opposed, not black men. To oppose the march, "the first mass-based, sorely needed, long overdue, positive effort by black men on the grounds of sexism is to engage," she said, "in a misguided, retrogressive brand of feminism."[73] Abdul Allah Muhammad, in the *Final Call*, the Nation of Islam newspaper, accused black women who opposed the march of "merely parroting the white feminist party line."[74] More scathing than Muhammad or Smitherman was writer Ishmael Reed's commentary of black women who opposed the march. He found them in league with "right wing white males who controlled the media" and white feminists who were singularly opposed to black men, especially, Mike Tyson, O. J. Simpson, Clarence Thomas, and Mel Reynolds, black men who, he claimed, had been either excoriated in the press or set up and denounced by black women in the justice system. According to Reed, "Unlike the grievances of black mothers who must face drastic welfare cuts, who can't afford to buy food, and the millions of working poor black men and women, those of the college educated academic black feminists seem trivial." He added that feminists' complaints "must strike the generation of black women, who were mauled by southern cops during the civil rights movement, as a little silly."[75]

This kind of criticism suggests one reason why many women opposed the Million Woman March, which was held two years later in Philadelphia. In short, they did not want to appear to be unsupportive of black men. For example, a Maryland editorialist did not attend the Million Woman March because she thought it the work of "uptight feminists," avenging black women's exclusion from the 1995 Million Man March, women who felt "jealous and left out," when they needed to be "proud, supportive and understanding" of "brothers who had some things they needed to do." Black women, she said, "should not be jealous or competitive when they [black men] finally decide to make a positive effort on behalf of the betterment of us all in the long run." Cleveland resident Paula Brazil thought the march held two years later for black women, a "Me Too" activity for which there was no need. "We need to be supportive of African-American men and their plight in this nation," she said. "We should spend time supporting what African-American men are trying to do instead of stepping out on our own."[76]

Although some women evoked feminism in their opposition to the Million Man March and support of the Million Woman March, most women who took these positions did so on the grounds of family salvation and racial unity. Like

Promise Keeper wives, they thought that women had worked hard to keep the family together, and they wanted black men and women to work *together* to save what they considered an endangered institution. For example, Alexis Nunley, a thirty-six-year-old mechanical engineer from Landover, Maryland, claimed, "To have the family unified, you need all of the elements there. . . . You can't have water without hydrogen and oxygen. If you want the message out, you can't have just guys delivering the message."[77] Ione Biggs, a Cleveland member of Women Speak Out for Peace and Justice, believed the exclusion of women was wrong: "I believe men and women need to work together. I think they could accomplish more."[78] Similarly, many women who supported the Million Woman March did so because they feared the demise of the black family. This was why Pittsburgh resident Linda Austin started organizing her trip to Philadelphia two months in advance, because, she said, the march is "trying to get us together as [a] people, especially the way the family is broken up." And Gloria Graves, a forty-four-year-old Detroit real estate broker traveled to Philadelphia in hopes of bringing "back the family unit that has been lost."[79]

It is impossible to comprehend black women's enormous investment in the family and their support of the Million Man March without examining the fact that black women understood the very real statistics that detailed the status of black men, not just in the context of what these statistics said about the adult men in their lives, but what they said, or might say, about their boys, male teenagers, and young adult sons—their children. Black women internalized the high rates of drug abuse, homicide, incarceration, school dropouts, unemployment, and police harassment and thought not about their sons thriving but whether their boys could survive. "I've got a six-year-old boy and I feel like I'm raising a target," said a black woman contributor to writer Marita Golden's book *Saving Our Sons*. "Every time the telephone rings, my heart skips a beat," said a black woman interviewed by black *Washington Post* reporter Courtland Milloy. Golden poignantly captured the feelings of so many black mothers when she wrote, "As a mother of a black son, I have raised my child with a trembling hand that clutches and leads. . . . I am no slave mother, my sleep plundered by images of the auction block. I dream instead of my son slaying the statistics that threaten to ensnare and cripple him, statistics that I know are a commentary on the odds for my son, who isn't dead or in jail." Golden knew what so many black mothers knew—even those who had the wherewithal to provide a middle-class lifestyle or better—that while they could do everything that was within their power to keep their sons on the straight and narrow, "always there is the fear that he will make a fatal detour, be seduced, or be hijacked by a white or a black cop, or a young black predator, or a Nazi skinhead, or his own bad judgment, or a weakness that I as his mother cannot love or punish or will out of him."[80]

This fear for their sons, the *next* generation of black men, was arguably the most important driving force behind black women's overwhelming support for the Million Man March. Take Professor Smitherman's objection to "feminist" opposition. Before cautioning black women to "beware the feminist trap," she described herself as a "mother of a son" who the school system labeled "hyperactive" and in need of medication and special classes. Had another black woman not intervened, her son, like so many other black males who, she claimed, were "disproportionately placed in special education and other kinds of slow track classes in the educational systems of this nation," would have been someone who was not taught because he had been classified as someone unable to learn. Said Smitherman, "Yeah, we needed that March—and anything else that will highlight what is happening to our boys and men."[81]

This is apparently what led many women seen along the sidelines of the march to not only support the march but to attend it as well. Assistant prosecuting attorney Charlita Anderson, a single mother raising a seven-year-old son, thought it important to go because she wanted her son "to grow into a strong man."[82] She was joined in this sentiment by Sylvia White, a DC resident who had left her thirteen-year-old son home but intended to go back and get him because she wanted him to "see what was going on."[83] Vanessa Davis-Harper, a widow, stood holding each of her young sons by the hand. "I want them to understand what this means this coming together of our black men, finally."[84] Another woman, from Manassas, Virginia, attended with her twenty-one-year-old son, Michael, in mind. 'I want him to understand the importance of being black and liking it," she said.[85]

This kind of thinking from black women who supported the Million Man March was not unusual. They did not separate the family from the race; the strength of one presaged the strength of the other. If the family could be made whole—meaning if men could be brought back in as husbands and fathers— then the race would thrive and black people could survive postindustrialism and anything else. But their support was not just about the race; it was about them. It was self-interested realism. Frustrated with being both mother and father, both provider and nurturer, to the majority of children born black, they reached out, almost desperately, to black men for help. From the numbers of men who showed up at the march, they were not disappointed. Indeed, they were heartened. For them the march translated into hope for the race, because it meant that the next generation of men—their sons—would survive and make life easier for their daughters than it had been for them.

Promise Keeper and Million Man March Women Compared

When we compare these two groups of women, the differences, at first, seem stark. Promise Keeper women clearly did not have the same sense of dread for their sons that black women across socioeconomic classes did. However we interpret the phenomenon of the "endangered black male," few black women did not know, or have, a black boy to be fearful for—hence, the overwhelming support for and lack of organized opposition to the Million Man March. Promise Keeper women also did not consciously attach their well-being, or their family's well-being, to their race. It is likely that, like their husbands, they felt that the fabric of America was only as strong as its families. But their interviews and testimonials do not speak directly to this. This reflects not only the nature of the sources, which mostly query PK wives about their husbands, but also the fact that in America racial minorities are "the other." Because whites represent the normalized presence, they are privileged to not think of themselves as raced. Most African American women, however, clearly linked their well-being to the family and by proxy to their race. This raises another important difference: the fact that these black and white women brought different histories to the family table. Race mattered in the 1990s. Because it had always mattered, it colored the different way that these women experienced familial relationships.

These are important differences, but their significance depends in part on the depth of the similarities between Promise Keeper and Million Man March women. We should not, for example, lose sight of the fact that both these white and black women attached enormous significance to the family. It was their haven in the unfamiliar new America of the 1990s, an America where job security had disappeared, where women composed the majority of poorly paid workers, and where women were increasingly likely to raise children without the help of men. It was not that they felt the family to be free of oppression, an institution whose unequal distribution of familial labor and domestic abuse harmed women; it was that they wanted to transform the family to make it work for them. Neither group targeted the structural makeup of America that had made the family so unstable, nor did these black and white women look to the government for solutions. Instead, in keeping with an ethos that saw the family as part of the private domain, they felt that men and women could, with the help of the Promise Keepers and the Million Man March, work things out on their own. This made PK and MMM women quite similar.

The counternarrative that they offered to their critics was equally similar. Black and white feminists criticized PK and MMM women for allowing men to control their lives, for being unequal marriage partners, and for diminishing their self-worth as wives and mothers. On the other hand, both black and white antifeminist critics painted an unpleasant picture of feminists as socialist, man-hating, lesbians who were antifamily, out of touch with the mainstream, and, in the case of black women, race traitors. As noted earlier, equalitarian Christian women were considered destructive and dangerous. Their actions were thought to be "against no less than the Christian doctrine of God, man, and the Church."[86] Likewise, black women were warned not to sow "disunity" by opposing the march.[87] Caught between feminists who cried patriarchy and antifeminists who decried equalitarianism, both PK and MMM women carved out a precarious middle ground. They supported men without supporting male supremacy, endorsed families without endorsing gender hierarchy. They did not see themselves as conceding to patriarchy or women's stated inferiority. Rather, because they believed in the centrality of the two-parent heterosexual family, they believed their own self-interest was at stake. From their perspective, women who raised children alone, without emotional and financial support, were hardly liberated. In spite of their differences, therefore, Million Man March and Promise Keeper women had a lot in common.

In this they were like nineteenth- and early twentieth-century women in the forefront of the temperance, or antialcohol, movement. Temperance women were just as likely to be ardent supporters of equal rights for women and women's suffrage, as were well-known leaders of the latter movement such as Susan B. Anthony, Elizabeth Cady Stanton, and Sojourner Truth. But temperance women were more likely to couch their politics in the rhetoric of the family than to boldly tout women's right to vote and the equality of men and women. Since custom demanded that proper feminine women refrain from public speaking and participating in politics, temperance women advocated for divorce reform, gender equality, and women's need for power in the context of the injustice of leaving women and children at the mercy of abusive drunkards who bankrupted families. Though they were forceful public speakers, they feigned modesty and shyness while they insisted on a woman's right to legal equality. Their demur manner disarmed critics and enabled female temperance advocates to escape the epithets endured by suffragists and women's rights advocates disparagingly referred to as "unsexed" and "masculine." As historian Carol Mattingly concludes, "by carefully presenting their cause as an unselfish effort on behalf of suffering women and children, and by scrupulously maintaining the cultural expectations that defined their sphere (except for their uncharacteristic public speaking), these women 'more than half convinced' powerful and influential newspaper editors to reconsider the legal position of their sex."[88]

Promise Keeper and Million Man March women functioned like temperance women. They were not the most radical in their personal politics, but neither were they the most conservative. In fact, these terms fall short of describing them. Had they been ardent feminists, they would have provoked even greater ire and malevolence from male supporters of patriarchy and been accused of sowing societal chaos. Fundamentalists were already prepared to excommunicate women who reinterpreted Ephesians 22 to mean mutual cooperation. Black women, particularly academics, who objected to a men-only march were already ridiculed as being out of touch with the masses. Whether it was self-consciously political or not, it was easier to support woman's equality from the protective quarters of the family than to boldly come out as a feminist.

Useful here is the concept of postfeminism. Researchers have found that while most women eschew activism on behalf of feminist precepts, they "have semiconsciously incorporated feminist principles into their gender and kin-ship expectations and practices." They take feminist accomplishments for granted, and yet, like Promise Keeper and Million Man March women, they are searching for a strategy to deal with America's new realities. In the seven-ties and eighties feminists helped women understand themselves as sexually autonomous beings, develop independent work lives, and build self-esteem. But, as argued by Stacey, "neither feminism nor other progressive family reform movements have been useful in addressing the structural inequalities of post-industrial occupational structure or the individualistic, fast-track cul-ture that makes all too difficult the formation of stable intimate relations on a democratic, or any other basis."[89] Feminism has also not been able to redress racial inequalities that subject black people to greater rates of homicide and put black men in prison in disproportionate numbers. Both PK and MMM women looked to the family, to themselves, and to their respective movements for solutions. This made them similar. Perhaps they should have sought help from the state, which has far more resources than they or their movements to redress the racial and gender discrimination that made their lives so precari-ous. But they did not, and this too made them similar.

Postfeminism also allowed both PK and MMM women to distance them-selves from issues that their respective communities opposed. One of them was homosexuality. Although the interviews and testimonials of PK and MMM women do not speak directly to this issue, in the United States there has always been an association between women's rights and gender inversion. Histori-cally, equal rights proponents were opposed because they upset proper gender roles and relations. Throughout the nineteenth and early twentieth century, the home was thought to be a woman's proper sphere, and women who moved beyond it or who advocated for women's rights in the public sphere, the male domain, were criticized and mocked.[90]

Christian fundamentalists, in particular, held fast to the doctrine of sepa-rate spheres. To them, it preserved the integrity of the Christian family. They believed that as mothers and wives, women were the guardians of societal morality, and if they forsook that role by either refusing to have children or straying toward politics or the pulpit, then they, like the devil, damned the world. As one contributor to a Christian journal noted after claiming that the scripture supported the essential difference between men and women, "When this difference is lost and man becomes womanish, or woman becomes man-nish, then the proper balance is lost and harmony gives way to discord."[91] Until the 1930s Christian fundamentalists believed that societal stability was founded on a world organized around families. The family, or divinized home, was ordained by God as a marriage between one man and one woman made to inhabit their separate spheres. "No nation or people can long survive in power, influence or greatness if the home is destroyed," wrote one fundamentalist teacher. One sure way for it to be destroyed was for women to step away from their "natural" roles. "Oh woman, stay a woman," said a popular evangelical minister. "Do not try to cross over."[92]

This thinking remained steadfast with many fundamentalist leaders of the 1990s who associated radical feminism with homosexuality. For example, in his critique of "A Christian Woman's Declaration," S. M. Hutchins, the senior editor of the Christian journal *Touchstone*, praised the signers for their opposition to homosexuality because, he said, "all reasonable citizens should join the attempt to curb the political and social influence of radical feminism and its attendant homosexualism, which are manifestly perverse and genocidal." He also did not care for the equalitarianism endorsed in the declaration. He thought it as detrimental to the church as "sexual radicalism" was to society, "and the church's message to its crumbling society must include its traditional teachings about men and women if it is to be like the Church at all."[93] Those traditional teachings, according to Hutchins, had men and women in their proper roles as husband and wife, father and mother.

The point, however, is that by roundly denouncing radical feminism, signers of the declaration endorsed the fundamentalist condemnation of homosexuality and thus escaped the most damning fundamentalist criticism, something that Promise Keeper wives were most likely doing by proxy when they insisted that they were not feminists. When they supported the complementarity and mutuality of men and women, PK wives, like supporters of the woman's declaration, veered to the left of traditional fundamentalists who believed in gender hierarchy and women's obligation to obey men. They did not, however, place themselves entirely out of the Christian fold. They endorsed families, supported men, and held fast to the belief that a marriage was between a man and a woman. In this way they put a lot of space between themselves and radical feminists who this Christian community defined as "perverse and genocidal."

African American women supporters of the Million Man March also secured their inclusion in black America by steering clear of feminism, which had many negatives attached to it. For example, because many white women had not opposed slavery but had in fact benefited from it and because they had historically used their white privilege to exclude black women from their organizations, in fact from any white female orbit, many African Americans thought it treasonous for black women to align with white women against black men, who were considered the natural allies of black women. Furthermore, since throughout American history women's rights advocates fought for rights that had been denied black men, many African Americans objected to black women fighting with white women for rights that white men had denied black men. The emasculation of the black male by white people was seen by many blacks as tantamount to the emasculation of the race. For these reasons many black women steered clear of organized feminism.[94]

But like the wives of Promise Keepers they also steered clear of feminism, because for many African Americans it was a code word for lesbianism, which when added to the other inhibitors put feminism off limits. Historically, most, though by no means all, African Americans have steered clear of formal movements that associated them with gender inversion and "improper" sexual desire. Underlying this avoidance is the fact that throughout American history black men were lynched for allegedly having abnormal sexual desire for white women, and black women were treated as though they were sexual hybrids.[95] Beginning with the importation of Africans as slaves, black women were worked in the fields and taxed as if they were men. By definition they were considered "mannish" women because they could, unlike native-born white women, be exploited for both their productive and reproductive labor. Like Sojourner Truth, who was made to bear her breast before an antislavery audience because male attendees did not believe that she was a woman, black women carried the burden of proving that they were not perversions of femaleness. One way free black women did this was to create a cult of respectability designed to show that they were just as maternal, sexually pure, and domestically inclined as white women. Necessarily coded heterosexual, the cult of respectability helped shore up the public character of black men as well as women, and it prevailed throughout the nineteenth and twentieth century among the black striving classes. It was utilitarian. Not only did it serve as a defensive mechanism against the lynching of black men and the sexual assault of black women, but the cult of respectability showed America that blacks, having embraced proper gender and sex roles, were worthy of equality with whites. "A race can rise no higher than its women," was a phrase heard among African Americans throughout the nineteenth and twentieth centuries. As long as women maintained proper feminine roles, men would be enabled to be properly masculine, and the race, it was thought by leading men and women alike, would achieve equality.[96] As important as women's rights was to black women, the masses steered clear of formal movements because of the aspersions their participation might cast on black people's sexuality.

Black women who publicly supported feminism risked not only severe ridicule from whites, who throughout history mercilessly lampooned black women as unsexed emasculating behemoths, but also being called race traitors by African Americans.[97] Even though many men supported feminist causes, most African Americans did not believe that they could fight on two fronts at the same time, especially one dominated by white women, whose race and sex implicated them in the historical oppression of black people, including the lynching of black men and women. Moreover, because women's rights and feminist movements upset prevailing understandings of proper gender roles and sexual desire, and these undergirded African American claims to equality, most blacks prioritized race rather than gender in their fight for equality.[98] One need look no further than the comments of Ishmael Reed, Geneva Smitherman, and Abdul Allah Muhammad to get a sense of what Million Man March women were up against. By getting behind men and the family and by

252 DEBORAH GRAY WHITE

linking the heterosexual family to the future of the race, Million Man March women silently proved that they were not race traitors, not in league with white feminists, and not in any way sexually transgressive. In this they were like Promise Keeper women who, while challenging their community from within, kept their insider status intact.

The Paradoxes of Postmodernity

At first glance the differences between the Promise Keepers and Million Man March women seem clearer than the commonalities. Their men gathered in separate arenas at different times. One was mostly white and the other overwhelmingly black. Race mattered, whether from a distant or up-close analysis. Black women did not consider the family apart from their race; for them it was *the* foundational institution, not of America, as Promise Keeper women would have it, but of black people. Their concern for their men, especially their sons, was predicated on the reality of peer and police inhumanity. Promise Keeper women worried about the males in their lives, their emotional well-being, and their status as men, but they did not connect their whiteness to the family. Rather, their families were connected to their Christian faith, and they tried to construct their families according to their interpretations of Christ's teachings.

Despite the difference that race made, however, there were paradoxical similarities in the ways and means used by each group to address the realities that beset them in the 1990s. Faced with high divorce rates, high rates of singleness, new formulations of the family, and the feminization of poverty, these black and white women supported their men's efforts to reconstitute the family as the central institution in their lives. They did not believe that the family would or could destroy them. Rather, it was a place for self-realization, an institution to be used to restore the familiar. In their search for security they were like other postfeminists who did not concede the fundamental feminist principles of women's autonomy and equality but still insisted that they were not feminist. Whether they knew it or not, both groups reached back to well-worn tactics of women, like the members of the Women's Christian Temperance Union, who demurely fought for women's rights without appearing to do so and without alienating the power brokers of their respective communities. Promise Keeper and Million Man March women wanted to stay connected to their communities and did not step outside community boundaries on issues like homosexuality. Neither did either group endorse a public policy that might strengthen the family. Rather, these women, who differed in so many ways, held fast to the family as a private domain.

Generally speaking, black and white women are usually perceived to be, if not on the opposite ends of the political spectrum, far apart on social issues. This comparison of female support for the Promise Keepers and Million Man

March demonstrates otherwise. For better or worse (in sickness and health, and whether rich or poor) these black and white women thought husbands and wives, mothers and fathers, could make the family work and for that end they gave overwhelming support to their men.

Notes

1. Judith Newton, *From Panthers to Promise Keepers: Rethinking the Men's Movement* (Lantham, MD: Rowman and Littlefield, 2005), 31–32.

2. "Public Pulse," *Omaha World-Herald*, August 14, 1998, 24.

3. Alice Lambert, "Much to Fear From Promise Keepers," *Hartford Courant*, September 14, 1999, A12.

4. Julianne Malveaux, "A Woman's Place Is in the March; Why Should I Stand by My Man, When He's Trying to Step over Me?," *Washington Post*, October 8, 1995, C12.

5. Rhonda Williams, "Absent from the March; A Woman Wonders about the Agenda," *Baltimore Sun*, October 22, 1995, E1.

6. A. Leon Higginbotham Jr., "I Couldn't Separate the Message from the Messenger," *Newsday*, October 18, 1995, A34.

7. Newton, *Panthers to Promise Keepers*, 31–32.

8. Although there are many different kinds of feminism, I use the term here the way my subjects did. Sometimes they used the term "radical feminism" to distinguish what they perceived as extreme views, but often they used just the word "feminism" or "feminist." As this chapter proceeds it problematizes the term.

9. Marc Fisher, "Million Man March: Behind the Scenes, the Women Count," *Washington Post*, October 14, 1995, Final Edition, Style, D1.

10. Michael Flethcher and Hamil R. Harris, "Black Men Jam Mall for a 'Day of Atonement'; Fiery Rhetoric, Alliances, Skepticism Mark March," *Washington Post*, October 17, 1995, A1.

11. Haki R. Madhubuti and Maulana Karenga, eds., *Million Man March/Day of Absence* (Chicago: Third World Press, 1996), 140–54.

12. Michael Fletcher and Mario Brossard, "March Has Solid Support of Blacks, Poll Finds," *Washington Post*, October 5, 1995, A1.

13. "How Black Academics Viewed the Million Man March," *Journal of Blacks in Higher Education*, no. 10 (Winter 1995–96): 61.

14. Jeanne Parrott, "Dale Came Home a Different Husband and Father" in *Standing on the Promises: The Promise Keepers and the Revival of Manhood*, ed. Dane S. Claussen (Cleveland: Pilgrim, 1999), 161.

15. "Group Has Promises to Keep: Men's Organization Plans Giant Gathering in Washington," *Arizona Republic*, September 2, 1997, Final Chaser, B1.

16. Suzanne Fields, "The Power of a Promise," *Tampa Tribune*, December 26, 1996, Final Edition, Nation/World, 19.

17. A note about methodology is in order. This chapter draws heavily on participant testimonials published in American newspapers. This very rich source consists of letters, editorials, and articles. I have read thousands of published materials from

newspapers serving large and small cities around the country. They have allowed me to tap into the thoughts and feelings of average Americans who expressed ideas and opinions often ignored by historians, because before the use of the Internet it was not possible to access so many and compare and contrast them. The opinions quoted here represent typical, not atypical responses. They have been used in conjunction with the research of scholars who do American culture and society, especially specialists in women and gender and African American studies.

18. For a lucid discussion of postmodernity, see especially David Harvey, *The Condition of Postmodernity: An Enquiry into the Origins of Cultural Change* (Malden, MA: Blackwell, 1990), 284–306.

19. Stephanie Coontz, *The Way We Really Are: Coming to Terms with America's Changing Families* (New York: Basic Books, 1997), 44–50; Harvey, *Condition of Postmodernity*, 330–31; Judith Stacey, *Brave New Families: Stories of Domestic Upheaval in Late-Twentieth-Century America* (New York: Basic Books, 1990), 256; Stacey, *In the Name of the Family: Rethinking Family Values in the Postmodern Age* (Boston: Beacon, 1996), 13.

20. Coontz, *Way We Really Are*, 44–50; Harvey, *Condition of Postmodernity*, 330–31; Stacey, *Brave New Families*, 256; Stacey, *Name of the Family*, 13.

21. Unless otherwise noted, throughout this chapter the term "family" is used to describe the two-parent heterosexual nuclear family.

22. Cassandra Cantave and Roderick Harrison, *Marriage and African Americans*, Joint Center for Political and Economic Studies, October 2001, http://www.jointcenter.org/DB/factsheet/marital.htm. See also the Associated Press report stating that at the end of the 1990s, 27 percent of those describing themselves as born-again Christians were currently or had previously been divorced, compared to 24 percent among other adults. Baptists had the highest divorce rate of any Christian denomination (34 percent) and were more likely to be divorced than atheists and agnostics. See Associated Press, "Baptists Have Highest Divorce Rate," December 30, 1999, ReligiousTolerance.org, http://www.jointcenter.org/DB/factsheet/marital.htm.

23. News/Letters from Readers, *Star Tribune Minneapolis*, August 24, 1997, 18A; Peter Maller and Meg Jones, "Men Find Mission in Promise Keepers Vows," *Milwaukee Journal Sentinel*, February 15, 1996, News, 1.

24. Larry B. Stammer, "Teaching Patriarchs to Lead," *Los Angeles Times*, June 19, 1994, Metro Desk, 1.

25. "What Promise to Keep: Stadium Faith Events Sexist?," *Kansas City Star*, April 25, 1996, FYI, E1.

26. Martha Sawyer Allen, "Promise Keepers: A Growing Movement Returns to Minnesota," *Star Tribune Minneapolis*, May 9, 1996, Focus, 1A.

27. Richard Vara, "He's Ok, I'm Ok: These Wives Staunchly behind Husbands as Promise Keepers," *Houston Chronicle*, June 22, 1996, Religion, 1.

28. Judy Tarjanyi, "Men Flock to Learn How to Be All They Can Be," *St. Petersburg Times*, September 18, 1993, Religion, 2.

29. Marlene Cimons and Kasper Zeuthen, "Participants, Doubters Ponder Meaning of Promise Keepers Movement," *Los Angeles Times*, September 30, 1997, National Desk, A5.

30. Helen Gray, "What Promises to Keep?" *Kansas City Star*, April 25, 1996, FYI, E1.

31. Allen, "Promise Keepers."

32. Gray, "What Promises to Keep?" See also Marilyn Kenaga, "Fulfilling God's Role for the Woman Is the Most Rewarding Feeling," in Claussen, *Standing on the Promises*, 168.

33. Iris Marion Young, "The Logic of Masculinist Protection: Reflections on the Current Security State," *Signs: Journal of Women in Culture and Society* 29, no. 1 (2003): 2–5.

34. Historian Jacqueline Dowd Hall made this point somewhat differently. Describing the dynamic at work when chivalric white men came to the rescue of white women supposedly violated by black male rapists, Hall described the trade-off implicit in the protection the white woman received. According to Hall, "the right of the southern lady to protection presupposed her obligation to obey." In other words, men rescued only proper women, women who kept their place and behaved according to rules established by patriarchs. The protection, like the pedestal, thus became a prison, one that white southern women escaped at their peril. See "'The Mind That Burns in Each Body': Women, Rape, and Racial Violence" in *Powers of Desire: The Politics of Sexuality*, ed. Ann Snitow, Christine Stansell, and Sharon Thompsons (New York: Monthly Review Press, 1983), 335–36. See also Deniz Kandiyoti, "Bargaining with Patriarchy," *Gender and Society* 2, no. 3 (September 1988): 274–90.

35. Michael Romano, "Keeping the Promise of God," *Denver Rocky Mountain News*, July 17, 1994, News/National, 16A.

36. Ken Hamblin, "The Roles of God and Responsible Fathers," *Denver Post*, August 2, 1994, Denver and the West, B7.

37. Ephesians 5:22–25 in the King James Bible reads, "Wives, submit yourselves unto your own husbands, as unto the Lord. For the husband is the head of the wife, even as Christ is the head of the church; and he is the savior of the body. Therefore as the church is subject unto Christ, so let the wives be to their own husbands in every thing. Husbands, love your wives, even as Christ also loved the church, and gave himself for it." This verse reads differently in different Bibles.

38. Diana Butler, "Keeping Promises for Men Only," *Plain Dealer*, April 30, 1997, Editorials and Forum, B11.

39. Gray, "What Promises to Keep?"

40. Valerie Bridgeman Davis, "A Womanist/Feminist Lives with a Promise Keeper and Likes It," in Claussen, *Standing on the Promises*, 154–60.

41. Jim Stingl, "Journey of Spirit Begins with a Jet to Washington," *Milwaukee Journal Sentinel*, September 28, 1997, News, 1.

42. Kenaga, "Fulfilling God's Role," in Claussen, *Standing on the Promises*, 167–68.

43. Stingl, "Journey of Spirit."

44. Vara, "He's Ok, I'm Ok."

45. Donna Schaper, *New York Newsday*, October 2, 1997, Viewpoints, A49; This idea of complementary roles was not new. For example, in the nineteenth century Sarah Grimké expressed the view that men and women were different but coequal. She resented the fact that men discriminated against women in the antislavery movement. She argued that women's childbearing and mothering made them different from men in the realm of the family and in domestic and social life, but in public and political matters women were coequals. See Alison Parker,

Articulating Rights: Nineteenth-Century American Women on Race, Reform and the State (Dekalb: Northern Illinois University Press, 2010), 84–85.

46. Several scholars have theorized that the nation is imagined and configured like a family. Both are hierarchal and men control both. As hearth keepers women birth children and transmit culture and thus reproduce the family and the nation. When men circumscribe the behavior of women they simultaneously police the boundaries of family and nation and thereby control who is included and excluded in both. See, for example, Nira Yuval Davis, "Gender and Nation," *Ethnic and Racial Studies* 16, no. 4 (October 1993): 621–32; McClintock, "Family Feuds," *Feminist Review* 44 (Summer 1993): 61–80.

47. Lauren F. Winner, "Wives, Daughters, Mothers, and Sisters as Kept Women," in Claussen, *Standing on the Promises*, 143, 150–51.

48. *A Christian Women's Declaration*, Concerned Women for America, accessed September 18, 2009, http://www.cwfa.org/articles/5338/CWA/misc/index.htm.

49. Ibid.

50. It is tempting to see PK women as theological feminists, yet there are several reasons to resist categorizing them as such. For one, theological feminists are a varied group themselves. Some are critical of racism, sexism, classism, and heterosexism, and some are not. Many endorse reproductive freedom and same-sex marriage, and some do not. Another reason to resist categorizing PK women as theological feminists has to do with the source material mined for this study. It allows for an analysis of PK women and the Promise Keepers but does not easily lend itself to an analysis of PK women and the church or religion.

51. S. M. Hutchins, "Papering Over a Rift," in "A Christian Women's Declaration: On Coalitions and Biblical Orthodoxy," in *Touchstone: A Journal of Mere Christianity* 12, no. 3 (May/June 1999), www.touchstonemag.com/archives/article.php?id=12-03-014-o.

52. Stacey, *Brave New Families*, 139–45, 260.

53. R. Marie Griffith, *God's Daughters: Evangelical Women and the Power of Submission* (Berkeley: University of California Press, 1997), 208–9.

54. Fisher, "Million Man March."

55. Elena Battista, "FSU Women Unite, Join Historic March of Millions," *Florida Flambeau* via U-Wire, October, 22, 1997.

56. Hamil Harris, "Despite Paradox, Black Women Support March," *Washington Post*, October 1, 1995, Final Edition, Metro, B1.

57. Cantave and Harrison, *Marriage and African Americans*; "Topics in Minority Health Homicide among Young Black Males: United States, 1978–1987," *Morbidity and Mortality Weekly Report* 39, no. 48 (December, 1990): 869–73; David A. Camp, "Incarceration Rates by Race," *Oklahoma Criminal Justice Research Consortium Journal*, 1994, www.doc.state.ok.us/offenders/ocjrc/94/040650K.htm; Lois A. Fingerhaut, Deborah D. Ingram, and Jacob J. Feldman, "Homicide Rates among US Teenagers and Young Adults: Differences by Mechanism, Level of Urbanization, Race, and Sex, 1987 through 1995," *Journal of the American Medical Association* 280, no. 5 (August 1998): 423–27; Daniel T. Lichter, Diane K. McLaughlin, George Kephart, and David J. Landry, "Race and the Retreat from Marriage: A Shortage of Marriageable Men?," *American Sociological Review* 57, no. 6 (December, 1992): 781–99; Patri-

cia Hill Collins, *Black Sexual Politics: African Americans, Gender, and the New Racism* (New York: Routledge, 2004), 80–81.

58. Fisher, "Million Man March." Between 1950 and 2000 the percentage of never-married black women doubled from 20.7 percent to 42.4 percent. The percentage of African American women who were married declined from 62 percent to 36.1 percent between 1950 and 2000. Among white women the corresponding decline was from 66 percent to 57 percent. Trends in divorce have shown less difference between the races, rising from 3 percent to 11.7 percent among blacks and from 2 percent to 10.2 percent among whites. See Cantave and Harrison, *Marriage and African Americans.*

59. Tamara Kerrill, "Black Women Split on Staying out of March," *Chicago Sun Times,* October 5, 1995, Late Sports Final Edition, News, 14.

60. Nanette Asimov and Lori Olszewski, "Hundreds of Bay Area Students Stay Home, Some Take Time Out to Fast, Reflect," *San Francisco Chronicle,* October 17, 1995, News, 7. See also Andrea L. Mays and Robert Davis, "Women's Reactions Run from Elation to Disdain," *USA Today,* October 17, 1995, News, A3.

61. Geneva Smitherman, "A Womanist Looks at the Million Man March" in Madhubuti and Karenga, *Million Man March,* 105.

62. Kerrill, "Black Women Split."

63. Paul Shepard, "Exclusion Bothers Some Women," *Plain Dealer,* October 1, 1995, Metro, B8.

64. Kimberly Hayes Taylor, "Million Woman March," *Star Tribune Minneapolis,* October 26, 1997, News A1.

65. Dyann Longwood, "One Million Strong: An Insider's Diary of the Million Woman March," *Contemporary Women's Issues* 4, no. 1 (Winter 1998): 15–19.

66. A recent work that takes up the issue of Stewart and Truth and the intersection of race and sex is Martha S. Jones, *All Bound up Together: The Woman Question in African American Public Culture, 1830–1900* (Chapel Hill: University of North Carolina Press, 2007), 23–85. On stereotypes of black women and charges of race traitor, see Deborah Gray White, *Ar'n't I a Woman? Female Slaves in the Plantation South,* 2nd ed. (New York: Norton, 1999), 27–61, 176–77; White, *Too Heavy a Load: Black Women in Defense of Themselves, 1894–1994* (New York: Norton, 1999), 56–68, 216–23. For a discussion of recent charges against black women, see Nikol G. Alexander-Floyd, *Gender, Race, and Nationalism in Contemporary Black Politics* (New York: Palgrave Macmillan, 2007), 109–45. Most of the articles in Toni Morrison's edited book *Race-ing Justice, En-gendering Power: Essays on Anita Hill, Clarence Thomas, and the Construction of Social Reality* (New York: Pantheon Books, 1992) deal with some aspect of the idea of black women as race traitors.

67. Kerrill, "Black Women Split."

68. Shepard, "Exclusion Bothers Some Women."

69. "Many Women Attended March . . . ," *St. Louis Post-Dispatch,* October 17, 1995, News A8.

70. Charshee McIntyre, "Why Focus on the Men," in Madhubuti and Karenga, *Million Man March,* 114.

71. Karen DeWitt, "Themes from the March Resonate," *New York Times,* October 18, 1995, National Desk, B9.

72. Alexander-Floyd, *Gender, Race, and Nationalism*, 3, 75–107.

73. Smitherman, "Womanist," in Madhubuti and Karenga, *Million Man March*, 104.

74. Fisher, "Million Man March."

75. Ishmael Reed, "Buck Passing: The Media, Black Men, O.J. and the Million Man March," in Madhubuti and Karenga, *Million Man March*, 129–33. For a more extensive discussion of the way black feminists have been villainized, see Alexander-Floyd, *Gender, Race, and Nationalism*, 71–74, 109–45.

76. "From the AFRO Website," editorial, *Baltimore Afro-American*, November 8, 1997.

77. Harris, "Despite Paradox."

78. Shepard, "Exclusion Bothers Some Women."

79. Monica Haynes, "Million Woman March Powering Up," *Pittsburg Post-Gazette*, September 23, 1997, Local, B5.

80. Marita Golden, *Saving Our Sons: Raising Black Children in a Turbulent World* (New York: Doubleday, 1995), 7–8; Courtland Milloy, "Stepping In to Stop the Heartbreak," *Washington Post*, September 10, 1995, Metro, B1.

81. Smitherman, "Womanist," in Madhubuti and Karenga, *Million Man March*, 104–5.

82. Marcia Slacum Greene, "A Welcome for Women on the Mall," *Washington Post*, October 17, 1995, A21.

83. "Many Women Attended March."

84. Marilyn McCraven, "Day of Unity, Civility, Kindness," *Baltimore Sun*, October 22, 1995, Perspective, E1.

85. Harris, "Despite Paradox."

86. Hutchins, "Papering Over a Rift."

87. Alexander-Floyd, *Gender, Race, and Nationalism*, 73.

88. Carol Mattingly, *Well-Tempered Women: Nineteenth-Century Temperance Rhetoric* (Carbondale: Southern Illinois University Press, 1998), 13–38, 96–120, 17. For an example of a black women who used this tactic, see Jones, *All Bound Up Together*, 153.

89. Stacey, *Brave New Families*, 263, 260; Pamela Aronson, "Feminist or 'Postfeminist'? Young Women's Attitudes towards Feminism and Gender Relations," *Gender and Society*, 17, no. 6 (December 2003): 903–22; Anne Machung, "Talking Career, Thinking Job: Gender Differences Career and Family Expectations of Berkeley Seniors," *Feminist Studies* 15, no. 1 (Spring 1989): 35–58.

90. See, for example, Estelle B. Freedman, *No Turning Back: The History of Feminism and the Future of Women* (New York: Random House, 2002), 48–54.

91. Betty A. DeBerg, *Ungodly Women: Gender and the First Wave of American Fundamentalism* (Macon, GA: Mercer University Press, 2000), 45. This opinion was also expressed by some black ministers. See Jones, *All Bound Up Together*, 190–99.

92. DeBerg, *Ungodly Women*, 66, 43–74. See also Mattingly, *Well-Tempered Women*, 97.

93. Hutchins, "Papering Over a Rift."

94. See Alexander-Floyd, *Gender, Race, and Nationalism*, esp. 51–74; Paula Giddings, *When and Where I Enter: The Impact of Black Women on Race and Sex in America* (New York: Morrow, 1984), 314–24; White, *Too Heavy a Load*, 216–20; and Jones, *All*

Bound Up Together. For a comprehensive understanding of these issues, see James Oliver Horton, *Free People of Color: Inside the African American Community* (Washington, DC: Smithsonian Institution Press, 1993), especially "Violence, Protest, and Identity: Black Manhood in Antebellum America," written with Lois E. Horton, and "Freedom's Yoke: Gender Conventions among Free Blacks." Other aspects of these issues can be found in Calvin C. Hernton, *Sex and Racism in America* (New York: Doubleday, 1965), 128–55; William H. Grier and Price M. Cobbs, *Black Rage* (New York: Basic Books, 1968), 41, 47; and Eldridge Cleaver, *Soul on Ice* (New York: Random House, 1968), especially part 4, "White Woman, Black Man."

95. For a discussion of these ideas, see Carol A. Stabile, *White Victims, Black Villains: Gender, Race, and Crime News in US Culture* (New York: Routledge, 2006), 85–104; George Fredrickson, *The Black Image in the White Mind: The Debate on Afro-American Character and Destiny, 1817–1914* (New York: Harper and Row, 1971), 256–82; White, *Ar'n't I a Woman?*, 176–77; and Giddings, *When and Where*, 85–94.

96. For a discussion of these issues, see Hazel Carby, *Reconstructing Womanhood: The Emergence of the Afro-American Women Novelist* (New York: Oxford University Press, 1987), 89–94; Carby, *Race Men* (Cambridge, MA: Harvard University Press, 1998), 9–41; Kevin Gaines, *Uplifting the Race: Black Leadership, Politics and Culture in the Twentieth Century* (Chapel Hill: University of North Carolina Press, 1996), 67–99; Willard B. Gatewood, *Aristocrats of Color: The Black Elite, 1880–1920* (Bloomington: Indiana University Press, 1990), 332–48; Evelyn Brooks Higginbotham, *Righteous Discontent: The Woman's Movement in the Black Baptist Church, 1880–1920* (Cambridge, MA: Harvard University Press, 1993), esp. 185–230; and White, *Too Heavy a Load*, 56–109.

97. See, for example, the illustrations in Jones, *All Bound Up Together*, 127–28. See also Wahneema Lubiano's discussion of Anita Hill and the representations of black women in "Black Ladies, Welfare Queens, and State Minstrels: Ideological War by Narrative Means," in Morrison, *Race-ing Justice*, 323–61.

98. This issue is taken up at length by recent works on tension between black and white women in the feminist movement and black women in the civil rights and feminist movements. See, for example, Winifred Breines, *The Trouble between Us: An Uneasy History of White and Black Women in the Feminist Movement* (New York: Oxford University Press, 2006). See also Benita Roth, *Separate Roads to Feminism: Black, Chicana, and White Feminist Movements in America's Second Wave* (New York: Cambridge University Press, 2004).

Epilogue

Gender and Race as Cultural Barriers to Black Women in Politics

Carol Moseley Braun

In 2003 I stood for nomination by the Democratic Party for the presidency of the United States. That this is a little-known fact doesn't bother me much: it was a very personal exercise that I hoped then and believe now helped shape attitudes about the proper place to be occupied by women and people of color in American society. From that experience, and many others in my personal odyssey, I can say without reservation that in America, gender is more of a cultural barrier than is race.

It is a curiosity to me that I have throughout my life been an accidental pioneer; my journey has broken ground and opened doors only because, in my humble opinion, that ground and those doors illogically excluded me in the first place. The script of our lives is always written in relationship to the other dramas being played out by the people who share our world. This is an inescapable fact of life. It all depends on timing and context. But I think that my life, more pointedly than most, is comprehensible only in the context of the times in which I live and that my decisions over time, whether rational or not, have come about out of an ever-changing milieu.

The 2003 campaign was inspired by the same motivations that had always inspired my choosing the "road less taken." I had returned to the United States from New Zealand, where I had served as ambassador, with the full intention of restoring the family farm. My great grandfather had bought a farm in Alabama during that little window after the Civil War when blacks could buy property in the South. Most of that land is still in my family. I had an abiding interest in issues pertaining to health and health care and determined to restore the land with ancient agricultural methods to create an organic farm. In spite of the derision from family and friends (my brother thought the idea of me living in a double-wide trailer especially comical), I set about to plan my new life on my ancestors' farm.

I didn't get very far. On September 11, 2001, the world changed for Americans. The deliberate bombing of the World Trade Center evoked a response that transcended every division Americans had ever acknowledged. We were united as one people in grief, in patriotism, in purpose. It also made me leave the farm and return to Illinois, where all of my family resides. After a few months of a tortured commute, I finally concluded that I needed to be with the people I love, and that required the shelving of my pastoral vision. I returned to Chicago and set about taking a slightly different path. I would become an organic food entrepreneur.

This new vision was sidetracked by my ten-year-old niece, Claire. In the aftermath of September 11, our president, George Bush, began almost immediately to rattle sabers with promises of revenge. Nobody called it bloodlust, but that was what it actually was. The bombing had so shattered Americans' sense of security that retribution was simply assumed. The clouds of war began to gather. Those clouds were deeply troubling to me, and heated family discussions ensued during that time. In the middle of one such discussion, Claire called out to me from her room. I can still vividly remember seeing her sitting at her desk, her feet barely touching the floor, looking genuinely perplexed. She called my attention to the center page of her social studies book, where pictures of all of the presidents of the United States were displayed. "But Auntie Carol," she said, "all the presidents are boys!" I think it was her innocence and confusion that touched my heart the most, and so to mollify her, I responded, "Oh sweetheart, girls can be president too."

My reaction surprised even me. I was shaken to the bone that I had told this dear girl such a lie. It must have shown on my face, because when I rejoined the kitchen table conversation, my brother, her father, asked me what was wrong. I told him, and his remarkable response was "Well, what are you going to do about it?"

My campaign for president was the response. Many in the political class snickered that I was delusional to even imagine that I could be nominated, much less elected. Many of the country's leading females made the point that they would like to see "a woman, but not just ANY woman" in the race. Some of the black political leadership reacted violently, as though my effort was an affront to black men. In short, I encountered once again my traditional nemesis, the triple whammy of class, race, and gender. As a friend once told me, "You are just not supposed to be there."

Never mind that I had been elected to the United States Senate with more votes than any of the male candidates in the race, outstripping even the presidential candidate, Bill Clinton, in my home state of Illinois in the 1992 election. Never mind that I had two elections in that campaign season, the primary and then the general election, and had prevailed in both. Or that I had, at that point, served in elective office at all three levels of government, state, local, and national. Or that I had a record of successful campaigns, save the one in which I (narrowly) lost reelection. (Close, but no cigar!) Or that I was the only candidate in the field of nine who had experience as a diplomat. Or that I had law enforcement credentials and had raised a wonderful, successful (and to my mind, extraordinary) son in the process. My political resume and history were dismissed, disregarded, or diminished in every imaginable way, all to make the point that I was not a legitimate candidate for the highest office in the land.

Some of the derision stemmed from the drubbing I had received, particularly from the media, during my single term in the US Senate. I had been accused of just about every imaginable wrongdoing and excoriated for failings that I hadn't even known existed. The most serious of the allegations had been aired and affirmatively disproved by the time of my ambassadorial confirmation, but that did not inspire anyone's apology. The people in my personal life who had been surrogates for the assaults on my reputation had either died or left the country, but that didn't change attitudes. Never mind that even taken at their worst, the claims of my perfidy paled in comparison to the actual proven missteps and misdeeds of some of the other candidates: as a woman it was simply not acceptable for me to have a platform for my views without permission.

Culture precedes politics. If there was a single lesson that I took away from my Senate years (which, by the way, will ever loom in my memory as the worst six years of my life, the honor of the election notwithstanding), it was that all politics in this country emerges out of a climate of public opinion about the world, and that climate of opinion starts with cultural assumptions. Or, as I like to say, a climate of opinion is just like any other weather system: it depends on the hot air rising from the ground. And so, just as cultural conservatives will point to the biblical admonition by Saint Paul to "let your women keep silence in the churches, for it is not permitted unto them to speak" (1 Cor. 14:34), even the more "liberated" differentiate acceptable public conduct for women. And so it goes, still.

This distinction does not, necessarily, apply to race. To begin, race is seen through different lenses in different places in the world. Gender is universal, and it is a universal fact that women occupy the subordinate rung in public society. This is true whether in Europe or sub-Saharan Africa. I have a Nigerian friend whose brilliant, Oxford-educated wife runs the family business. At an intimate dinner party she started to pass around after-dinner nuts, and he joked with her that in the "old days" she would have been required to present them to him from a kneeling position. Even though she dropped to her knees and bowed her head in mock humility and humor, the exercise was tinged with no small indignity.

By contrast, when I arrived in New Zealand as ambassador, I was prepared for the fact that this was a country that epitomized progressiveness, that had selected two female prime ministers, a female chief justice, and various female heads of major organizations. Nonetheless, the prime minister had not been permitted to speak at an important ceremony involving the indigenous people, and I had not been allowed to touch a symbolic icon during my installation ceremony because of gender. (My son accepted the "challenge" on my behalf, and today I am actually glad that he did, because it gave him "mana" or status in the community—and I have a great picture of him doing it!) In any event, gender remained an issue even there, while race, or my color, was a nonissue. It took me about a month to figure out that there wasn't even the language in that community to discuss issues of race.

By the time of the presidential campaign, I had learned to be careful of gender-specific stereotypes. Women candidates do have a more difficult threshold in regard to what has been called the "Three *H*s: Husbands, Hemlines, and Hair." During my 1992 campaign for the Senate, my campaign manager (later to become fiancé) chose the very moment I was about to go on stage for what was then the most important debate of the campaign to tell me that my nail polish had a chip. He, of course, became the target or reason for a lot of the press enmity, but even he couldn't be blamed for the Women's Wear Daily picture of my backside mounting the Capitol Steps titled "this is what a Chanel sweater set should NOT look like!"

During the 2004 campaign I discovered that more people than even I imagined were prepared to consider a nontraditional candidate for president. In places where no black people live, citizens were cordial, welcoming, and genuinely nice. I was well received at every stop on the campaign trail and found it especially heartwarming that many brought their little girls to meet me. On more than one occasion, a parent would tell me they had come so their daughters could meet a woman running for president. Claire had psychic friends all over America.

I tried to share this good news from the heartland with the media, but they were so busy marginalizing my candidacy that no one bothered to report it. In fact, my experiences in the 2004 campaign made me one of the least surprised Americans when Barack Obama won the nomination, and then the election in 2008. He had something to say, and his color did not keep the American people from hearing it.

But then, the 2008 campaign also underscored impressions I took from the 2004 effort. Gender remains a more elusive touchstone in the march to liberate the human spirit than race. This perspective is bitterly disputed by all the people—black and white—who point to America's shameful legacy of slavery and the segregation and exploitation of people of color. But that is my perspective and belief, and it doesn't mean that I am any less committed or clear about the significance of race in this country. Indeed, I challenge anyone to dispute my credentials as a civil rights advocate who has consistently, even at great personal cost, fought for equality and opportunity for black people. Black males, particularly, have had a tough go of it, and even a modicum of knowledge of history will suffice to make the point of their suffering—as a group—from the peculiar institution of slavery and its legacy. Black women have been there with them every step of the way, often to the point of forgoing opportunity so that their men could prosper. As a former friend told me when I asked for her support in the 2004 campaign, black women aren't feminists.

I am an African American feminist. I love men, but my humanity tells me that the physical form should not be an impediment to a person's participation in this society. God's gifts to us do not come wrapped in a black body, or a female one, or a hetero or homosexual one, or a short or tall one; God's gifts are to who we are as people, as human beings, and are expressed in how we live our lives and treat one another. The liberation of the human spirit, so all people can share in the talents and gifts of everyone else, is at the heart of all the movements for human rights, or civil rights, or gay rights, or disability rights, or indigenous peoples' rights. I come to these debates secure in the knowledge that we all have a stake in the freedom of everyone to contribute to the best of their ability to the whole of human society.

I left the 2004 campaign feeling much better about the future of America. What I saw was progress in the effort to break down barriers that do not serve our country's interests, as well as movement in the direction of inclusion and integration of Americans of every stripe and description. When we can tap the talents of 100 percent of the people, as opposed to just half, or less, we will have a wider talent pool from which to choose, and the peoples' interests will have a better chance of being understood, heard, and served by those in government. I saw that the American people were way ahead of the political class at that moment in time, and they proved it in 2008.

Having both a black male and a white woman in the 2008 campaign brought home the issue in remarkable ways. I was provoked to walk into and protest an item hanging in the window of a gift and novelty shop on Michigan Avenue in Chicago that had a picture of both Barack Obama and Hillary Clinton with the legend "Bros before Hoes." The shopkeeper did take the T-shirt down from the window, but in fact it expressed (in a disgustingly crude way) a notion that remains a cultural trip wire: some (including a popular "liberal" talk show host) maintained that the "debt" of the larger society to blacks was greater than it was to women, ergo, the greater good was to strike a blow against racism first. Perhaps. History will tell. But the history buff in me tells me we have been here before, when women ran smack into cultural norms that diminish their acceptability in the public realm. (This is not something only men experience; many times it is women who are the most challenged, and put off, by other women in the public sphere).

The electoral franchise was extended to women more than half a century after black men were (at least theoretically) granted the right to vote. I have on many occasions recounted the story of Harry Burn, the Tennessee legislator who switched his vote to support suffrage for women after receiving a letter from his mother telling him, "Vote for Suffrage, and don't keep them in doubt. . . . Don't forget to be a good boy and help Mrs. Catt with her rats. Is she the one that put rat in ratification, Ha!"[1] This bit of political history and humor goes a long way toward making the point that an individual voice, a single vote, makes a difference, as Burn's vote ratified the Nineteenth Amendment in Tennessee, and that state's approval confirmed the inclusion in the US Constitution of the right of women to vote. But it is the backstory of Mrs. Burn's letter that is, for purposes of this discussion, the most telling. She had written to her son, the state representative, to ask him to change his position out of her own sense of indignity about her second-class citizenship. A college graduate, it was not acceptable to her that a less educated black man could vote while she could not. The irony here, of course, is that at the time of the suffrage amendment, black men were being lynched in the South, while white women were being patronized as flowers of society in need of protection from themselves.

Adopting Kimberlé Crenshaw's construct about the "intersectionality of race and gender" makes such ironies clearer, I think.[2] The real intersection is that of our humanity and of the press of history on the liberation of the human spirit. In this "city on a hill" individuals have a greater chance than almost anywhere else on the planet to challenge and even contradict traditional limitations, whether of class or race or gender or sexuality or disability or religion. That is the genius of America, and that is why we continue to press the issue of equality of opportunity for women in public life.

When I told Claire, "Girls can be president too," I was doing no more than restating my faith in the promise of our Constitution and the intent of its framers. It has been a long time coming, but as Dr. King put it, "The arc of the moral universe is long, but it bends toward justice."[3] Justice for Claire and for all those little girls who came out to listen during the 2004 campaign will arise out of their expectation that they have every right and no limitation on their ability to participate in public life. They will create the cultural expectation that women have every right to equality of opportunity and power in the public arena. Agitating for justice for them was my motivation to run for president in 2003.

Clearly, I had no choice but to run, and it turned out to be an experience like none other. My faith in this country and optimism for the American people were restored by that campaign, and I was able to turn the page on a political career secure in the knowledge that America is great because we are still trying to get it right and be the best people we can be.

Carol Moseley Braun
Chicago, Illinois

Notes

1. Febb E. Burn to Harry T. Burn, August 17, 1920, Harry T. Burn Papers, C. M. McClung Historical Collection, "'Don't Forget to Be a Good Boy': Harry T. Burn's Letter from Mom and the Ratification of the 19th Amendment in Tennessee," accessed

February 14, 2012, http://www.teachamericanhistory.org/index.cfm/m/56/The_
Emergence_of_Modern_America_(1890-1930).

2. Kimberlé Crenshaw, "Demarginalizing the Intersection of Race and Sex: A
Black Feminist Critique of Antidiscrimination Doctrine, Feminist Theory, and Antiracist Politics," *University of Chicago Legal Forum*, 1989, 139–67.

3. Martin Luther King Jr., "Where Do We Go from Here?," Address to the Eleventh
Annual Southern Christian Leadership Conference, August 16, 1967, accessed February 14, 2012, mlk-kpp01.stanford.edu/index.php/encyclopedia/documentsentry/
where_do_we_go_from_here_delivered_at_the_11th_annual_sclc_convention.

Selected Bibliography

Each chapter contains relevant citations on the author's specific topic. This selected bibliography lists books and articles that take on larger theoretical and historical issues that more than one of the contributors discussed.

Alexander-Floyd, Nikol G. *Gender, Race, and Nationalism in Contemporary Black Politics.* New York: Palgrave Macmillan, 2007.

Boydston, Jeanne. "Gender as a Question of Historical Analysis." *Gender and History* 20, no. 3 (2008): 558–83.

Breines, Winifred. *The Trouble between Us: An Uneasy History of White and Black Women in the Feminist Movement.* New York: Oxford University Press, 2006.

Brown, Kathleen M. *Good Wives, Nasty Wenches and Anxious Patriarchs: Gender, Race, and Power in Colonial Virginia.* Chapel Hill: University of North Carolina Press, 1996.

Carby, Hazel V. *Reconstructing Womanhood: The Emergence of the Afro-American Woman Novelist.* New York: Oxford University Press, 1987.

Collins, Patricia Hill. *Black Feminist Thought: Knowledge, Consciousness, and the Politics of Empowerment.* New York: Routledge, 1991.

———. *Black Sexual Politics: African Americans, Gender, and the New Racism.* New York: Routledge, 2004.

———. *Fighting Words: Black Women and the Search for Justice.* Minneapolis: University of Minnesota Press, 1998.

———. "Toward a New Vision: Race, Class, and Gender as Categories of Analysis and Connection." In *Oppression, Privilege, and Resistance: Theoretical Perspectives on Racism, Sexism, and Heterosexism,* edited by Lisa Heldke and Peg O'Connor, 529–43. Boston: McGraw Hill, 2004.

Coontz, Stephanie. *The Way We Really Are: Coming to Terms with America's Changing Families.* New York: Basic Books, 1997.

Cott, Nancy. *Public Vows: A History of Marriage and the Nation.* Cambridge, MA: Harvard University Press, 2000.

Crenshaw, Kimberlé. "Demarginalizing the Intersection of Race and Sex: A Black Feminist Critique of Antidiscrimination Doctrine, Feminist Theory, and Antiracist Politics." *University of Chicago Legal Forum,* 1989, 139–67.

———."Mapping the Margins: Intersectionality, Identity Politics, and Violence against Women of Color." *Stanford Law Review* 43, no. 6 (July 1991): 1241–99.

Davis, Angela Y. *Women, Race, and Class.* New York: Vintage, 1981.

DeBerg, Betty A. *Ungodly Women: Gender and the First Wave of American Fundamentalism.* Macon, GA: Mercer University Press, 2000.

D'Emilio, John, and Estelle B. Freedman. *Intimate Matters: A History of Sexuality in America.* New York: Harper and Row, 1988.

Deutsch, Sarah. "Being American in Boley, Oklahoma." In *Beyond Black and White: Race, Ethnicity, and Gender in the U.S. South and Southwest*, edited by Stephanie Cole and Alison M. Parker, 97–122. College Station: Texas A&M University Press, 2004.

Dorr, Lisa Lindquist. *White Women, Rape, and the Power of Race in Virginia, 1900–1960*. Chapel Hill: University of North Carolina Press, 2004.

Dray, Philip. *At the Hands of Persons Unknown: The Lynching of Black America*. New York: Random House, 2002.

DuBois, Ellen Carol. *Feminism and Suffrage: The Emergence of an Independent Women's Movement in America, 1848–1869*. Ithaca, NY: Cornell University Press, 1978.

DuBois, Ellen Carol, and Richard Càndida Smith, eds. *Elizabeth Cady Stanton Feminist as Thinker: A Reader in Documents and Essays*. New York: New York University Press, 2007.

Faulkner, Carol. *Women's Radical Reconstruction: The Freedmen's Aid Movement*. Philadelphia: University of Pennsylvania Press, 2004.

Feimster, Crystal. *Southern Horrors: Women and the Politics of Race and Lynching*. Cambridge, MA: Harvard University Press, 2009.

Fields, Barbara. "Slavery, Race, and Ideology in the United States of America." *New Left Review* 181 (1990): 95–118.

Freedman, Estelle B. *No Turning Back: The History of Feminism and the Future of Women*. New York: Random House, 2002.

Gaines, Kevin. *Uplifting the Race: Black Leadership, Politics and Culture in the Twentieth Century*. Chapel Hill: University of North Carolina Press, 1996.

Garber, Marjorie. *Vested Interests: Cross-Dressing and Cultural Anxiety*. New York: Routledge, 1997.

Gatewood, Willard B. *Aristocrats of Color: The Black Elite, 1880–1920*. Bloomington: Indiana University Press, 1990.

Giddings, Paula. *When and Where I Enter: The Impact of Black Women on Race and Sex in America*. New York: Morrow, 1984.

Gilmore, Glenda. *Defying Dixie: The Radical Roots of Civil Rights, 1919–1950*. New York: Norton, 2008.

———. *Gender and Jim Crow: Women and the Politics of White Supremacy in North Carolina, 1896–1920*. Chapel Hill: University of North Carolina Press, 1996.

Griffith, R. Marie. *God's Daughters: Evangelical Women and the Power of Submission*. Berkeley: University of California Press, 1997.

Gross, Ariela J. *What Blood Won't Tell: A History of Race on Trial in America*. Cambridge, MA: Harvard University Press, 2008.

Hale, Grace Elizabeth. *Making Whiteness: The Culture of Segregation in the South, 1890–1940*. New York: Pantheon Books, 1998.

Hall, Jacquelyn Dowd. "'The Mind That Burns in Each Body': Women, Rape, and Racial Violence." In *Powers of Desire: The Politics of Sexuality*, edited by Ann Snitow, Christine Stansell, and Sharon Thompson, 335–36. New York: Monthly Review, 1983.

———. *Revolt against Chivalry: Jessie Daniel Ames and the Women's Campaign against Lynching*. Rev. ed. New York: Columbia University Press, 1993.

Harding, Sandra. *The Feminist Standpoint Theory Reader: Intellectual and Political Controversies*. London: Routledge, 2004.

Hicks, Cheryl D. *Talk with You Like a Woman: African American, Justice, and Reform in New York, 1890–1935*. Chapel Hill: University of North Carolina Press, 2010.

Higginbotham, Evelyn Brooks. "African-American Women's History and the Metalanguage of Race." *Signs* 17, no. 2 (1992): 251–74.

———. *Righteous Discontent: The Woman's Movement in the Black Baptist Church, 1880–1920*. Cambridge, MA: Harvard University Press, 1993.

Hine, Darlene Clark. *A Shining Thread of Hope: The History of Black Women in America*. New York: Broadway Books, 1998.

Hine, Darlene Clark, Wilma King, and Linda Reed, eds. *We Specialize in the Wholly Impossible: A Reader in Black Women's History*. Brooklyn, NY: Carlson, 1995.

Hodes, Martha. *Sex, Love, Race: Crossing Boundaries in North American History*. New York: New York University Press, 1999.

———. *White Women, Black Men: Illicit Sex in the Nineteenth-Century South*. New Haven, CT: Yale University Press, 1997.

Holloway, Pippa. *Sexuality, Politics, and Social Control in Virginia, 1920–1945*. Chapel Hill: University of North Carolina Press, 2006.

hooks, bell. *Feminist Theory from Margin to Center*. Cambridge, MA: South End, 1984.

Hull, Gloria, Patricia Bell Scott, and Barbara Smith, eds. *All the Women Are White, All the Blacks Are Men, but Some of Us Are Brave: Black Women's Studies*. Old Westbury, NY: Feminist Press, 1982.

James, Joy, and T. Denean Sharpley-Whiting, eds. *The Black Feminist Reader*. Malden, MA: Blackwell, 2000.

Jones, Jacqueline. *Labor of Love, Labor of Sorrow: Black Women, Work, and the Family from Slavery to the Present*. New York: Basic Books, 1985.

Jones, Martha S. *All Bound Up Together: The Woman Question in African American Public Culture, 1830–1900*. Chapel Hill: University of North Carolina Press, 2007.

Kandiyoti, Deniz. "Bargaining with Patriarchy." *Gender and Society* 2, no. 3 (September 1988): 274–90.

Kennedy, Elizabeth Lapovsky, and Madeline D. Davis. *Boots of Leather, Slippers of Gold: The History of a Lesbian Community*. New York: Penguin Books, 1994.

Kerber, Linda K. *No Constitutional Right to Be Ladies: Women and the Obligations of Citizenship*. New York: Hill and Wang, 1998.

Klarman, Michael J. *From Jim Crow to Civil Rights: The Supreme Court and the Struggle for Racial Equality*. New York: Oxford University Press, 2004.

Lorde, Audre. *Sister Outsider: Essays and Speeches*. Trumansburg, NY: Crossing, 1984.

May, Vivian M. *Anna Julia Cooper, Visionary Black Feminist: A Critical Introduction*. New York: Routledge, 2007.

McCall, Leslie. "The Complexity of Intersectionality." *Signs* 30, no. 3 (2005): 1771–800.

McGuire, Danielle L. *At the Dark End of the Street: Black Women, Rape, and Resistance; A New History of the Civil Rights Movement from Rosa Parks to the Rise of Black Power*. New York: Knopf, 2010.

McKivigan, John R., ed. *Abolitionism and Issues of Race and Gender*. New York: Garland, 1999.

Meyerowitz, Joanne. "A History of 'Gender.'" *American Historical Review* 113, no. 5 (December 2008): 1346–56.

Mitchell, Michele. *Righteous Propagation: African Americans and the Politics of Racial Destiny after Reconstruction.* Chapel Hill: University of North Carolina Press, 2004.

Moraga, Cherrie, and Gloria Anzaldúa, eds. *This Bridge Called My Back: Writings by Radical Women of Color.* New York: Kitchen Table, 1983.

Morgan, Jennifer L. *Laboring Women: Reproduction and Gender in New World Slavery.* Philadelphia: University of Pennsylvania Press, 2004.

Morrison, Toni, ed. *Race-ing Justice, En-gendering Power: Essays on Anita Hill, Clarence Thomas, and the Construction of Social Reality.* New York: Pantheon Books, 1992.

Mumford, Kevin J. *Interzones: Black/White Sex Districts in Chicago and New York in the Early Twentieth Century.* New York: Columbia University Press, 1997.

Nash, Jennifer. "Re-Thinking Intersectionality." *Feminist Review* 89, no. 1 (2008): 1–15.

Newman, Michelle Louise. *White Women's Rights: The Racial Origins of Feminism in the United States.* New York: Oxford University Press, 1999.

Newton, Judith. *From Panthers to Promise Keepers: Rethinking the Men's Movement.* Lantham, MD: Rowman and Littlefield, 2005.

Painter, Nell Irvin. *The History of White People.* New York: Norton, 2010.

Parker, Alison M. *Articulating Rights: Nineteenth-Century American Women on Race, Reform and the State.* Dekalb: Northern Illinois University Press, 2010.

Pascoe, Peggy. *What Comes Naturally: Miscegenation Law and the Making of Race in America.* New York: Oxford University Press, 2009.

Penningroth, Dylan C. *The Claims of Kinfolk: African American Property and Community in the Nineteenth-Century South.* Chapel Hill: University of North Carolina Press, 2003.

Perdue, Theda. *Mixed Blood Indians: Racial Construction in the Early South.* Athens: University of Georgia Press, 2003.

Ritter, Gretchen. *The Constitution as Social Design: Gender and Civic Membership in the American Constitutional Order.* Stanford, CA: Stanford University Press, 2006.

Rose, Tricia. *Longing to Tell: Black Women Talk about Sexuality and Intimacy.* New York: Farrar, Straus, and Giroux, 2003.

Roth, Benita. *Separate Roads to Feminism: Black, Chicana, and White Feminist Movements in America's Second Wave.* New York: Cambridge University Press, 2004.

Ruiz, Vicki L., and Virginia Sánchez Korrol, eds. *Latina Legacies: Identity, Biography, and Community.* New York: Oxford University Press, 2005.

Saunt, Claudio. *Black, White, and Indian: Race and the Unmaking of an American Family.* New York: Oxford University Press, 2005.

Schwalm, Leslie A. *A Hard Fight for We: Women's Transition from Slavery to Freedom in South Carolina.* Urbana: University of Illinois Press, 1997.

Shah, Nayan. "Between 'Oriental Depravity' and 'Natural Degenerates': Spatial Borderlands and the Making of Ordinary Americans." *American Quarterly* 57, no. 3 (September 2005): 703–25.

———. *Stranger Intimacy: Contesting Race, Sexuality, and the Law in the North American West.* Berkeley: University of California Press, 2012.

Sommerville, Diane Miller. *Rape and Race in the Nineteenth-Century South.* Chapel Hill: University of North Carolina Press, 2004.

Stacey, Judith. *Brave New Families: Stories of Domestic Upheaval in Late-Twentieth Century America.* New York: Basic Books, 1990.

Stoler, Ann Laura, ed. *Haunted by Empire: Geographies of Intimacy in North American History.* Durham, NC: Duke University Press, 2006.

Sweet, Frank W. *Legal History of the Color Line: The Rise and Triumph of the One-Drop Rule.* Palm Coast, FL: Backintyme, 2005.

Welke, Barbara Young. *Recasting American Liberty: Gender, Race, Law, and the Railroad Revolution, 1865–1920.* New York: Cambridge University Press, 2001.

White, Deborah Gray. *Ar'n't I a Woman: Female Slaves in the Plantation South,* 1985. Rev. ed. New York: Norton, 1999.

———. *Too Heavy a Load: Black Women in Defense of Themselves, 1894–1994.* New York: Norton, 1999.

Wolcott, Victoria W. *Remaking Respectability: African American Women in Interwar Detroit.* Chapel Hill: University of North Carolina Press, 2001.

Wood, Amy Louise. *Lynching and Spectacle: Witnessing Racial Violence in America, 1890–1940.* Chapel Hill: University of North Carolina Press, 2009.

Yellin, Jean Fagan. *Women and Sisters: The Antislavery Feminists in American Culture.* New Haven, CT: Yale University Press, 1989.

Yuval-Davis, Nira. "Gender and Nation." *Ethnic and Racial Studies* 16, no. 4 (October 1993): 621–32.

———. "Intersectionality and Feminist Politics." *European Journal of Women's Studies* 13, no. 3 (August 2006): 193–209.

Contributors

CAROL MOSELEY BRAUN was a United States senator for the state of Illinois from 1993 to 1999. She served as US ambassador to New Zealand from 1999 to 2001. A candidate for the Democratic nomination during the US presidential election of 2004, she is now a lawyer in Chicago and has a line of organic food products.

MEREDITH CLARK-WILTZ is an assistant professor of history at Franklin College. She received her BA from the University of Louisiana, Lafayette; her MA from Bowling Green State University; and her PhD from Ohio State University, where she worked with Paula Baker. She is currently preparing a book manuscript titled "Revising Constitutions: Race and Sex Discrimination in Jury Service, 1868–1979."

CAROL FAULKNER is an associate professor of history at Syracuse University. She is the author of *Women's Radical Reconstruction: The Freedmen's Aid Movement* (University of Pennsylvania Press, 2004), *Lucretia Mott's Heresy: Abolition and Women's Rights in Nineteenth-Century America* (University of Pennsylvania Press, 2011), and *Women in American History to 1880: A Documentary Reader* (Wiley-Blackwell, 2011). With Alison M. Parker, she coedits the Gender and Race in American History series at the University of Rochester Press.

KENDRA TAIRA FIELD is an assistant professor of history at the University of California at Riverside. She received her PhD in American history from New York University and is currently completing her first book, *Growing Up with the Country: A Family History of Race and American Expansion* (under contract with Yale University Press). Field served as assistant editor to David Levering Lewis in the abridgment of his *W. E. B. Du Bois: A Biography* (Henry Holt, 2009). She has received the Huggins-Quarles Award of the Organization of American Historians and has been awarded fellowships from the Ford Foundation, the Andrew W. Mellon Foundation, and Dartmouth College. Field also holds a master's degree in public policy from Harvard University's Kennedy School of Government and a BA from Williams College.

RASHAUNA JOHNSON is an assistant professor of history at Dartmouth College. She received her BA from Howard University and her PhD from New York University. Her dissertation, "Antebellum New Orleans: Hub of the Enslaved Atlantic, 1791–1825," received the 2011 Dean's Outstanding Dissertation Award in the Humanities. She is the recipient of the Andrew Mellon Predoctoral Fellowship in Humanistic Studies, the Henry M. MacCracken Fellowship, and the Morse Academic Plan Postdoctoral Fellowship.

MICHELLE KUHL is an associate professor of history at the University of Wisconsin, Oshkosh. She received her PhD from Binghamton University, State University of New York. She is currently writing a book on the antilynching movement titled *Manly Martyrs: African Americans and the Anti-Lynching Battle*. An essay of hers appears in *The Souls of W. E. B. Du Bois*, edited by Edward J. Blum and Jason R. Young (Mercer University Press, 2009), a collection of works on the religious side of the American activist and author. She is also the author of "We Have Seen the Fate of the Indian: Western Influences on African American Leadership in the Gilded Age," in *American Nineteenth Century History* 12, no. 1 (March 2011): 25–48.

VIVIAN M. MAY is an associate professor of women's and gender studies at Syracuse University. She is the author of *Anna Julia Cooper, Visionary Black Feminist* (Routledge, 2007). She is currently working on a book, *Intersectionality: Theories, Histories, Practices*, forthcoming from Routlege. Her work has also been published in several journals, including *African American Review, Callaloo, Hypatia, NWSA Journal, Prose Studies*, and *Women's Studies Quarterly*.

MICHELE MITCHELL is an associate professor of history at New York University and former North American editor of *Gender and History*. She is the author of *Righteous Propagation: African Americans and the Politics of Racial Destiny after Reconstruction* (University of North Carolina Press, 2004), among other works. She is now writing a book tentatively titled "Idle Anxieties: Race and Sexuality during the Great Depression."

ALISON M. PARKER is a professor and chair of the History Department at the College at Brockport, State University of New York. She is the author of *Articulating Rights: Nineteenth-Century American Women on Race, Reform, and the State* (Northern Illinois Press, 2010) and *Purifying America: Women, Cultural Reform, and Pro-Censorship Activism, 1873–1933* (University of Illinois Press, 1997). With Carol Faulkner, she coedits the Gender and Race in American History series at the University of Rochester Press.

HÉLÈNE QUANQUIN is an associate professor of American civilization at Université Paris 3-Sorbonne Nouvelle. She is writing a book on male feminists in nineteenth-century America. Her recent articles include "Wendell [Phillips], Don't Make a Fool of Yourself": Feminist Consciousness as Dialogue and Process in the American Antebellum Society," in *The Construction of Feminism: Exchanges and Correspondences*, edited by Françoise Orazi and Claudette Fillard

(Cambridge Scholars, 2010). She has received fellowships from the American Antiquarian Society, the Sophia Smith Collection at Smith College, the Massachusetts Historical Society, and the Schlesinger Library.

DEBORAH GRAY WHITE is the Board of Governors Professor of History at Rutgers University. She is the author of several books, including the classic *Ar'n't I a Woman? Female Slaves in the Plantation South*, 2nd ed. (Norton, 1999) and *Too Heavy a Load: Black Women in Defense of Themselves, 1894–1994* (Norton, 1999). She is currently working on a book titled "'Can't We All Just Get Along?': The Cultural Awakenings of the 1990s."

Index

An italicized page number indicates a figure or table.

Columbia University, 20–21, 211n1

Colver, Nathaniel, 88

Commercial Appeal (Memphis newspaper), 147

Congregationalist (religious journal), 148

Constitution, US. *See* Supreme Court (US) cases; *specific amendments*

Cooke, Marvel, 192

Coontz, Stephanie, 232–33

Cooper, Anna Julia, 3–5; biographical information, 19–21, 22, 27, 30; intersectional approach, 18, 21–23, 28, 28–29, 32, 34–35, 37–38, 39, 43n22; Sorbonne dissertation, 4, 21, 22, 23, 30–38; *A Voice from the South by a Black Woman of the South*, 4, 20, 22, 24–27, 28–29, 30, 42n18, 47n73

Cott, Nancy, 79, 86, 101n61

Councill, William Hooper, 137

courts/justice system: black male roles in, 169–70; and black women, 2, 40n1, 178–79; and slavery, 55, 57, 60, 62–63, 101n61; white women as passive victims, 9, 162–63, 169, 170, 173–74, 177–78, 255n34; women's jury service, 176, 181n20. *See also* lawyers, black; NAACP jury service campaign; Supreme Court cases; *specific cases*

Cox, Annette, 234

Crawford, George, 170

Crawford v. Commonwealth of Virginia (1933), 163, 166–70, 182n31, 182nn37–38

Crazy Snake Rebellion (1909), 114, 128n23

Creek nation: citizenship, 6, 106–7, 111, 112–16, 119–21, 122, 123, 130n47; matrilineal practices, 6, 110, 115, 128n28; and noncitizens, 108; non-national status of Brown, 105–6; organization of, 112, 114; population data, 128n23; slavery within, 110–11, 119, 122. *See also* African Creeks *(Estelvste);* Indian identity

Crenshaw, Kimberlé, 265; on both/and logic, 17, 40n1; descriptions of inter-

sectionality, 2, 40n1, 227n121; long history of intersectionality, 3, 18; on "single-axis" logic, 28, 41n1, 44n30

Cresswell, Tim, 197

Crisis (NAACP magazine): antilynching material, 147, 148, 149, 150–51; on black female cult of secrecy, 153; on sex work in Great Depression, 192

cross-dressing, 9, 199–200, 208–9, 219n43

Crummell, Alexander, 28–29

Cunard, Nancy, 194

Cunningham, Sam, 173

Currell, Susan, 190

Curtis, Edwin U., 146

Curtis Act (1898), 112

Dancy, John C., 146

Davies, Carole Boyce, 38

Davis, Valerie Bridgeman, 236

Davis-Harper, Vanessa, 246

Dawes General Allotment Act (1887), 7, 112–16, 119–21; Dawes Commission, 106, *113, 121,* 122, 125, 129n38; Dawes rolls, 105, 128n22

Dayan, Joan, 34

DeBaptiste, R., 145

DeBerg, Betty A., 249–50

Debo, Angie, 113, 119

Delancy, Martin R., 28

Delery v. Mornet (1822), 62–63

Delille, Henriette, 70n16

DePastino, Todd: on promiscuity of transient women, 220n56; race/gender and transiency, 198, 213n15, 220n58; transient terminology, 212n9, 220n51

Detroit, Michigan, unemployment rates during Great Depression, 191

Diallo, Nafissatou, 160n96

divorce, 75, 232, 233, 248, 252, 257n58

Douglass, Frederick: biographical information, 97n3, 99n27; black male suffrage support, 75; failure of Reconstruction, 135; on racism and sexism, 93–94

Douglass, Sarah Mapps, 84, 101n47

intersectional understandings of race and gende—*(cont'd)* 210; in jury service/citizenship, 22, 161–63, 178; in political career of Braun, 11–12, 260–65; and slavery metaphor, 92–97

intersectionality, 2–5; definitions, 2, 14n8, 40n1, 227n121; history of, 3–5, 18–19, 38–40, 104n100; and identity, 1, 2–3; reductive understandings, 17

"interzones," 5, 52

invisibility. *See* silences/invisibility

Jackson, Andrew, 59
Jackson, Nelson C., 198
Jacobs, Harriet, 53, 93, 102n79
James, C. L. R., 4, 31, 42n20
James, Jamilla, 243
Jefferson, Silas, 113
Jefferson, Thomas, 81
Jelinski, Allyson, 234
Jensen, Karen, 231
Jim Crow laws: criticism of, 35; and internalized oppression, 27; negative impact on black activism, 135, 156n10; in Oklahoma, 7, 114, 122–23, 124, 125. *See also* lynching
Johnson, Rashauna, 5, 274
Johnson, W. Bishop, 137
Johnson, Walter, 74n49
Jones, Anna H., 40n10
Jones, Grace, 242
Jones, Martha, 77, 86
Jones, Peggy, 234
The Journal of Charlotte Forten: A Free Negro in the Slave Era (C. F. Grimké), 21
jury service. *See* courts/justice system; NAACP jury service campaign
justice system. *See* courts/justice system; NAACP jury service campaign; Supreme Court (US) cases

Kandiyoti, Deniz, 235
Keller, Frances Richardson, 31, 44n35
Kelley, Abby, 6, 87–88, 95
Kellow, Margaret M. R., 77, 100n29

Kenaga, Marilyn, 236
Kentucky: *Hale v. Commonwealth of Kentucky* (1938), 161, 162, 163, 175–77, 181n3; lynching in, 152
King, Martin Luther, Jr., 265
Klein, Abbé Félix, 21, 40n11
knowledge production, 24–25, 26–27, 43n22
Kornbluh, Joyce L., 203
Kuhl, Michelle, 7–8, 273–74

Lafitte, Jean, 59, 71n25
Lafitte's Blacksmith Shop (New Orleans), 59, 64
Lambert, Alice, 229
Laronde, Pierre Denis de, 73n42
lawyers, black: black women as lawyers, 181n22; and courtroom status/power, 169; NAACP reliance on, 8, 166, 181n21; numbers of, 181n21, 183n46; and Southern violence, 182n35; and white witnesses, 182n24
Lenox, John, 172
Lerner, Gerda, 77, 84
lesbianism/homosexuality: and feminism, 11, 238, 239, 249, 250, 250–51, 252; in New Deal camps, 202, 205–6; same-sex marriage, 238, 256n50; and transient women, 9–10, 199–200, 205–6, 206–8
L'esperanza, Victoire, 56–57
Letters on the Equality of the Sexes and the Condition of Woman (Sarah Grimké), 82–83, 86–87
Letters to Catharine E Beecher, in Reply to an Essay on Slavery and Abolitionism, Addressed to A. E. Grimké (Angelina Grimké), 83
Liberator (abolitionist paper), 89–90
The Life and Writings of the Grimké Family (Cooper), 21
Lindley, Betty and Ernest K., 213n15
Linebaugh, Peter, 64
Literary Digest (magazine), 194
Litwack, Leon, 156n10
Livermore, Mary A., 28
location, 24, 26–27